The American Mortgage System

THE CITY IN THE TWENTY-FIRST CENTURY

Eugenie L. Birch and Susan M. Wachter, Series Editors

A complete list of books in the series is available from the publisher.

The American Mortgage System
Crisis and Reform

Edited by

Susan M. Wachter and Marvin M. Smith

PENN

UNIVERSITY OF PENNSYLVANIA PRESS

PHILADELPHIA

Copyright © 2011 University of Pennsylvania Press

Published by
University of Pennsylvania Press
Philadelphia, Pennsylvania 19104-4112
www.upenn.edu/pennpress

Printed in the United States of America
on acid-free paper

10 9 8 7 6 5 4 3 2 1

A Cataloging-in-Publication record is available from the Library of Congress.
ISBN 978-0-8122-4351-2

Contents

Introduction 1
Marvin M. Smith and Susan M. Wachter

PART I CRISIS: ORIGINS AND SOLUTIONS

1 The Secondary Market for Housing Finance in the United States: A Brief Overview 7
Ingrid Gould Ellen, John Napier Tye, and Mark A. Willis

2 Reasonable People Did Disagree: Optimism and Pessimism
About the U.S. Housing Market Before the Crash 26
Kristopher S. Gerardi, Christopher L. Foote, and Paul S. Willen

3 Exploring the Determinants of High-Cost Mortgages to Homeowners
in Low- and Moderate-Income Neighborhoods 60
Michael S. Barr, Jane K. Dokko, and Benjamin J. Keys

4 Implications of the Housing Market Bubble for Sustainable Homeownership 87
Paul S. Calem, Leonard Nakamura, and Susan M. Wachter

5 A Framework for Consumer Protection in Home Mortgage Lending 112
Kathleen Engel and Thomas J. Fitzpatrick, IV

PART II COMMUNITY IMPACT

6 A Profile of the Mortgage Crisis in a Low- and Moderate-Income Community 137
Lynn Fisher, Lauren Lambie-Hanson, and Paul S. Willen

7 Constructive Credit: Revisiting the Performance of Community Reinvestment Act Lending During the Subprime Crisis   159
      Carolina Reid and Elizabeth Laderman

8 Navigating the Housing Downturn and Financial Crisis: Home Appreciation and Equity Accumulation Among Community Reinvestment Homeowners   187
      Sarah F. Riley and Roberto G. Quercia

9 The Community Reinvestment Act: Evaluating Past Performance and Reviewing Options for Reform   209
      Mark A. Willis

   PART III REFORMING THE FINANCIAL ARCHITECTURE

10 Information Failure and the U.S. Mortgage Crisis   243
      Adam J. Levitin and Susan M. Wachter

11 The Expanding Financial Safety Net: The Dodd-Frank Act as an Exercise in Denial and Cover-Up   271
      Edward J. Kane

12 A Private Lender Cooperative Model for Residential Mortgage Finance   286
      Toni Dechario, Patricia C. Mosser, Joseph Tracy, James Vickery, and Joshua Wright

13 Improving U.S. Housing Finance Through Reform of Fannie Mae and Freddie Mac: A Framework for Evaluating Alternatives   305
      Ingrid Gould Ellen and Mark A. Willis

14 Some Thoughts on What to Do with Fannie Mae and Freddie Mac   339
      Robert Van Order

15 The Road Not Taken: Our Failure in Redoing the Financial Architecture   358
      Vincent Reinhart

   List of Contributors   369

   Index   377

   Acknowledgments   391

Introduction

Marvin M. Smith and Susan M. Wachter

Erica and James are the best of friends. They went to the same schools, grew up in the same neighborhood, and got jobs at the same company. Their spouses work together, their children play together, and their families celebrate Fourth of July together. On paper, a mortgage lender would have trouble differentiating them. They have the same household income, the same credit score, and are the same age.

But that is where their similarities end. Imagine we are in 2005: Erica pays 6.9 percent in mortgage interest each year. She can pay off the principal as early and as often as she likes, and she has no balance payable when the loan is due. James pays 8 percent interest annually.[1] If he tries to "prepay" his mortgage principal, he gets hit with a significant prepayment penalty, and he will face a "balloon" balance at the end of his contract. Erica has a prime mortgage and James' mortgage is subprime.[2]

How did these nearly identical homeowners receive such divergent treatment? The answer to that question is one of the most pressing reasons that we must reinvent the American mortgage system.

Successful homeownership requires the availability of appropriate mortgage products. In the years leading up to the housing bubble, homebuyers frequently accepted mortgages that were not only wrong for them but catastrophic for the economy as a whole. When the housing market crumbled, so did a cornerstone of the American dream for many families. Restoring the promise of this dream requires an unflinching inspection of lending institutions and the right tools to repair the structures that support solid home purchases in the future.

The aftermath of the bubble has been devastating: house prices fell 30 percent; nearly 14 percent of mortgages are either delinquent or in foreclosure; housing starts fell by 68 percent; and house values declined by $9 trillion.[3] In September 2008, the U.S. government put Fannie Mae and Freddie Mac—the traditional pivots of the nation's housing finance structure—into conservatorship to avoid bankruptcy and systemic collapse. In the three decades prior to the collapse, American homeownership benefited from falling interest rates, low macroeconomic volatility, and large capital flows from foreign investors. The coming years are not likely to be so generous.

Erica and James, and millions like them, lived through a revolution in housing finance but "recent events suggest that, just as in 1789, a revolution has produced a terror."[4] From the moment that Salomon Brothers traded the first mortgage-backed security almost three decades ago, the forces constraining mortgage originators have loosened at an exponential rate.[5] From 1997 to 2006, that unraveling fueled a 71 percent increase in real home prices, an asset sector that hadn't appreciated in real terms since the end of World War II.[6]

The federal government pushed Fannie, Freddie, and commercial banks to issue more mortgages to low-income and minority households.[7] Investment banks devoted increasing resources to securitizing mortgages. The new "private-label securitization" barely resembled the market once dominated by Fannie and Freddie. In the pursuit of greater market share, Wall Street traders engaged in a "race to the bottom," securitizing ever riskier mortgages. Nonstandard mortgages, such as teaser rates and no creditworthiness requirements, began to overtake the long-term, fixed-rate mortgage that had dominated America's unique system for six decades.[8]

For a sustainable mortgage system, redesign is necessary. This volume offers hope that such a redesign is possible. Perhaps the best place to start is to separate innovations that increased—and *sustained*—homeownership from those that merely increased profits and risk. It may seem wise to abandon a system that has cost taxpayers billions of dollars, but we must not allow the memory of this crisis to blind us to the difficult decisions that lie ahead. The American mortgage system is broken, but some proposed alternatives would only leave consumers with a higher-risk burden. With interest rates preparing to rise and sovereign debt at nosebleed levels, consumers need the long-term, fixed-rate mortgage now more than ever.

How to create such a system and safeguard it from recurrences of the recent catastrophe is the focus of this volume. The questions it proposes and attempts to answer will form the discussion we will have as Americans building a better mortgage system in the coming decades:

- Can asset price bubbles be identified in real-time? If so, are there safe ways to defuse speculative excess before it reaches dangerous heights?
- Does the mortgage system discriminate among borrowers of different race, gender, and socioeconomic status by the products offered?
- How did the housing bubble adversely affect households, even those that did not take on risky mortgages, and what can we do to protect them from future house price volatility?
- What obligation does the government have to protect consumers from predatory lending practices? What practices qualify as "predatory," and how does that definition apply to different households?
- What role did the Community Reinvestment Act play in the subprime crisis? Can the government encourage low-income homeownership without abandoning prudent lending standards? Should it?
- What misaligned incentives led investment banks to misprice risk? How well suited are private securitizers to assess the default probability of diverse mortgage pools?
- Is recent legislation strong enough to survive regulatory arbitrage? How did regulators miss the avalanche of warning signs that the system was in distress? What information channels do they need to anticipate future cracks in the edifice?
- How can we deliver long-term, fixed-rate mortgages to consumers without putting taxpayers on the line for an endless boom-and-bailout cycle? Who should bear credit and interest-rate risks, and what insurance should support the liable parties?

These are the questions of a reborn economy. We can rethink, recover, and rebuild. The promise of this nation depends upon it.

Notes

The authors wish to thank Gregory Scruggs for assistance in preparation of this introduction.

1. Erica and James do not exist, but they represent the average experience of low- and moderate-income households, minority and majority, in the Detroit area from July 2005 to March 2006. See Barr, Dokko, and Keys, this volume.

2. See Riley and Quercia, this volume.

3. For house prices, see Standard and Poor's Case-Shiller 20 City Composite Index, http://www.standardandpoors.com/indices/sp-case-shiller-home-price-indices/en/us/?indexId=spusa-cashpidff--p-us----; for mortgage delinquency and foreclosure rates, see LPS Mortgage Monitor, December 2010, http://www.lpsvcs.com/NewsRoom/IndustryData/Documents/2010%2012%20Mortgage%20Monitor.pdf; for housing starts, see the U.S. Census Bureau's New Residential Construction Index, http://www.census.gov/const/www/quarterly_starts_completions.pdf; for home value changes, see Zillow.com, http://www.zillow.com/blog/early-2010-housing-stabilization-fizzles-u-s-homes-set-to-lose-1-7-trillion-this-year/2010/12/09. All changes are from 2006 through 2010.

4. Green, Richard, and Susan Wachter. 2007. "The Housing Finance Revolution." Prepared for the 31st Economic Policy Symposium: Housing, Housing Finance & Monetary Policy, Jackson Hole, Wyoming, Federal Reserve Bank of Kansas City.

5. The story of Salomon Brothers' pioneering work in "collateralized mortgage obligations" is documented most vividly in Michael Lewis's infamous firsthand account, *Liar's Poker: Rising Through the Wreckage on Wall Street*. 1989, New York: Penguin.

6. Standard & Poor's. 2010.

7. Part II of this volume discusses this "push" and its consequences in depth.

8. Levitin and Wachter, this volume.

PART I

Crisis: Origins and Solutions

Chapter 1

The Secondary Market for Housing Finance in the United States: A Brief Overview

Ingrid Gould Ellen, John Napier Tye, and Mark A. Willis

Understanding both the current problems in the secondary market and the proposed solutions requires an understanding of the role of the secondary market in U.S. housing finance.[1] In this chapter, we focus in particular on the government-sponsored enterprises (GSEs), Fannie Mae and Freddie Mac, which for decades were the largest players in the U.S. system.[2] We first review the history of the secondary market and summarize the basic operations of the GSEs before they were placed into conservatorship by the U.S. Treasury in September 2008. We then outline the key arguments that are made about the strengths and weaknesses of the GSEs' structures, for both the single-family and multi-family housing finance markets.

A Brief History of the GSEs and the Secondary Market

Fannie Mae and Freddie Mac are only two of many entities that bring capital to the housing market to help borrowers finance the purchase of single-family and multi-family homes. Until the 1930s, most loans for the purchase of residential property came from banks, which held the resulting mortgages in their portfolios and financed these holdings through deposits. To supplement deposits as a source of funds to loan out, the Federal Home Loan Banks provided additional funding to their members through "advances," which are loans secured by mortgages themselves.[3]

The problem with this system is that funds for mortgages were limited by the volume of local deposits, creating significant shortfalls and bottlenecks in some regions. This problem has only been compounded in recent years, as people have shifted their savings from banks into money markets, mutual funds, and other investments. Indeed, given the high demand for mortgages today and the level of bank deposits, it would be impossible for banks alone to provide the necessary funding for all U.S. mortgages. Consider that as of the end of 2009, total mortgage debt outstanding in the United States stood at $14.2 trillion (Federal Reserve Board 2010), whereas total bank deposits within the United States totaled $7.5 trillion (Federal Deposit Insurance Corporation 2009).[4]

During the Depression, the Federal National Mortgage Association—Fannie Mae—was created to allow banks to originate a greater number of mortgages, effectively launching a secondary market for housing finance.[5] Fannie Mae would purchase loans insured by the Federal Housing Administration (FHA), another Depression-era agency, from banks so that the banks could fund additional mortgages. Until 1968, Fannie Mae was a government agency and so could borrow money in private capital markets based on the financial strength of the federal government. The Federal Home Loan Mortgage Corporation—Freddie Mac—was established in 1970 as part of the Federal Home Loan Bank system (a set of regional cooperatives owned by the banks) and so was able to raise capital based on the implicit backing of the federal government enjoyed by that system. Both GSEs used the money they raised to buy mortgages from banks and others who had originated them, thus allowing those originators to provide even more mortgages. As major buyers of mortgages, Fannie Mae and Freddie Mac helped to standardize the documents used to originate mortgages and, perhaps more important, the mortgage products that were offered and the underwriting standards that the property and the borrower had to meet.

In 1968, Fannie Mae was privatized (thus removing its liabilities from the federal budget), but a portion of its activity was maintained as part of the government and was folded into a new agency called the Government National Mortgage Association (GNMA), or Ginnie Mae (Jaffee and Quigley 2010: 171). As a government entity, Ginnie Mae remained explicitly backed by the full faith and credit of the federal government; therefore its securities traded with pricing close to that of the federal debt.[6] Ginnie Mae carried on the role of helping to ensure liquidity for mortgages made under such federal programs as the FHA, the VA (Veterans Administration), and the RHS (Rural Housing Services), which already provided loan-level guarantees on the loans originated under their programs. These programs set their own underwriting standards for the loans they backed and so did not require additional underwriting or oversight by Ginnie Mae. The new, private Fannie Mae, by contrast, provided liquidity for mortgages that did not have direct government backing.[7]

Starting in the 1970s, Fannie Mae and Freddie Mac moved from a buy-and-hold model to one in which they would buy mortgages, package them into mortgage-backed securities (MBSs), and sell them. Fannie Mae and Freddie Mac gave these MBSs their corporate guarantee of timely payment of principal and interest. By selling these types of securities, the GSEs were able to pass on the interest-rate risk (the risk that interest rates on liabilities will increase above the rates on assets as well as the risk that falling interest rates will cause significant prepayments) to the investors, although they kept the credit risk.[8] The GSEs also provided structuring services to allow investors to manage interest-rate risk to allocate the streams of interest and principal payments into different tranches, each with its own expected payment and maturity schedules.

Although the U.S. government has refrained from explicitly guaranteeing GSE corporate obligations, investors have generally assumed that GSE obligations are backed by the federal government.[9] A combination of the firms' congressional charters, large size, and special regulatory treatment (such as exemption from both state and local taxes and some securities laws) has, over the years, signaled to investors that the government would not allow the firms to default on their obligations—hence the implicit guarantee.[10] The GSEs did not have to pay any fee for this implicit guarantee, although, presumably, the government expected the savings generated by their lower borrowing costs to be put toward public purposes.[11] With the implicit backing of the federal government, the two agencies were able to sell these securities to investors, including banks, that were willing to take the interest-rate risk but not the credit risk of the underlying mortgages.

In fact, with the implicit federal guarantee, the GSEs were able to market the securities even before the mortgages that backed them were created. This forward market, or "to be announced" (TBA) market, in which the

GSE MBSs are traded before the underlying mortgage loans are specifically identified, helped borrowers to lock in rates in advance of closing their loans (see Davidson and Sanders 2009). The existence of the guarantee has been crucial to the TBA market, because investors are unlikely to be willing to buy securities with credit risk when the underlying loans are not specified.[12] The standardization of documents and procedures that lie behind the GSE MBSs has also helped to increase investor confidence in the TBA market. This confidence, together with the overall scale of the TBA markets, has helped to make these MBSs attractive investments.

Despite the implicit federal guarantee, a competing, private secondary market for mortgages arose that dates back to 1977. Several financial firms started buying up mortgages, packaging them into securities, and selling the resulting securities to investors. The securities were typically collateralized by prime jumbo mortgages that were ineligible for purchase by Freddie Mac or Fannie Mae because they were above the conforming loan limit allowed by the GSEs.[13] This market came to be known as the private-label securities (PLS) market.

In the early years of the twenty-first century, the PLS market ballooned, attracting even more funds and investors to the housing market. The growth came mainly from securities backed by subprime and Alt-A mortgages (i.e., loans to borrowers with lower credit scores and/or requiring lower documentation of income and assets) (Chomsisengphet and Pennington-Cross 2006). PLSs had no government backing, so they were structured to deal with credit risk. Typically, a PLS is divided into tranches, each with different priorities for the pass-through of the interest and principal payments from borrowers/mortgagors. Those tranches that were first in the "waterfall" to receive payment were the highest-rated (often AAA); those that were last in the waterfall were often rated below investment grade and often had to be retained by the issuer in the absence of investor interest.

Demand from investors was quite high, in part because they underestimated the riskiness of the securities (and their underlying mortgages), as did the ratings agencies upon which they relied.[14] Because the securities were issued by non-banks (i.e., investment banks, some of which were part of the same holding companies as banks) and many of the underlying mortgages were originated by non-bank mortgage companies, the PLS market was only lightly regulated (U.S. GAO 2007). Thus, the originators of these non-agency mortgages were able to offer borrowers products with little scrutiny of their ability or willingness to pay. Many of these products had low introductory rates (or even options to allow borrowers to choose how much they wished to pay each month, with the remaining interest costs added to the principal—called negative amortization) and adjustable rates that rose sharply after the first two or three years.

As a result of this new and aggressive competition from the PLS market, the GSEs saw their market share erode, jeopardizing the continued growth of their revenues and profits.[15] In response, the GSEs loosened their underwriting guidelines to buy Alt-A mortgages. After the issuance of new private-label MBSs collapsed in the third quarter of 2007, the share of the market held by the GSEs more than rebounded, reaching roughly 70 percent by 2009.

In addition to the guarantee business, Fannie Mae and Freddie Mac generated profits over the years by holding mortgages and other direct investments in their portfolios.[16] Expanding these portfolios was thus another way for the GSEs to grow their bottom lines. Specifically, by issuing more corporate debt, Fannie and Freddie were able to purchase and hold whole loans, along with their own MBSs and the AAA tranches of PLSs. Until recently, the GSEs were even permitted to invest in non-housing investments such as tobacco company bonds.[17] Because the implied government backing allowed them to borrow at artificially low interest rates, the GSEs were able to earn especially high margins on their portfolio investments, encouraging them to maintain and grow their portfolios. Low capital requirements (2.5 percent) allowed the GSEs to leverage their capital at 40:1 and thereby transform these high profit margins into high rates of return on capital (Frame and White 2005: 170).[18]

The standard critique of GSE portfolios is that they exposed the firms (and, implicitly, taxpayers) to interest-rate risk (unlike their MBS business, which passed on the interest-rate risk to investors). In terms of credit risk, the firms' charters set the same underwriting standards for both MBS and portfolio investments: "[they] shall be confined, so far as practicable, to mortgages which are deemed by the corporation to be of such quality, type, and class as to meet, generally, the purchase standards imposed by private institutional mortgage investors" (see Fannie Mae Charter 1992; Freddie Mac Charter 2009). However, while the written standard was the same for MBS and portfolio operations, they did not contain the same mix of underlying products (i.e., only their portfolios were vulnerable to PLS subprime risk).[19]

Before 2003, GSE portfolios performed quite well.[20] Until that year, their portfolios were composed largely of conforming prime loans that met "high"

underwriting standards. Between 2003 and 2007, the GSEs started buying AAA-rated private-label tranches of subprime MBSs and whole Alt-A
loans for their portfolios.[21] (The firms also guaranteed and securitized some
Alt-A debt to investors as MBSs.) While it appears that the primary impetus for their movement into risky, non-prime investments was the higher
interest rates that these investments paid, there is considerable debate about
whether the GSEs were also partially motivated by their need to meet the
affordability goals mandated by Congress (see Jaffee 2010; Stein 2008; Wallison and Calomiris 2009). Established by the Federal Housing Enterprise
Financial Safety and Soundness Act of 1992 and defined and enforced by
the U.S. Department of Housing and Urban Development (HUD), the goals
set targets for the share of loans purchased by the GSEs that should be made
to low-income individuals and in low-income neighborhoods. Clearly, the
goals made it easier to justify investments in securities backed by subprime
loans that had been targeted to low-income borrowers and neighborhoods.

Although the bulk of their operations have involved single-family mortgages, the GSEs have been key investors in the multi-family mortgage market
as well. Before entering conservatorship, the firms were the largest players
in the market for purchasing and securitizing multi-family loans, responsible for almost one third of all outstanding multi-family debt (Joint Center for Housing Studies 2009: 7). Their involvement dates back to the 1970s,
when Freddie Mac pioneered securitization of multi-family loans. GSE participation in the market started to grow fairly steadily in the mid-1990s, perhaps in part as a result of the establishment of the affordable housing goals,
which rewarded the GSEs for expanding their investments in multi-family
housing. The expansion in the past decade has been particularly notable.
Between 1999 and 2008, the GSEs' direct holdings and guarantees increased
from 16.9 percent of the total outstanding multi-family debt to almost one
third (Abt Associates 2001: viii; Joint Center for Housing Studies 2009: 7).

While the GSEs are recognized for their work in creating and standardizing common multi-family loan documents (Abt Associates 2001), they
retain a majority of their multi-family loans in their portfolios. In mid-2008,
just prior to conservatorship, 62 percent of the GSEs' multi-family loans
were retained in their portfolios. By contrast, only 7 percent of their single-family loans were held in their portfolios (National Multifamily Housing Council 2009). It is not clear whether the GSEs held a majority of their
multi-family loans in portfolio because of the difficulty of securitizing the
loans and/or finding investors or because it was simply more profitable

for them to retain these loans because of their higher yields and the common inclusion of prepayment penalties or "yield maintenance agreements," which mitigated the interest-rate risk of prepayment.

Notably, the GSEs have resisted funding or purchasing multi-family loans of less than $5 million and have done little to help stimulate this market. The economics of this part of the market is difficult because of the fixed costs of underwriting, which cannot easily be made up in fees. Without a nationally competitive primary or secondary market product to enable these projects to access fixed-rate financing, these small loans often have had to be structured as adjustable-rate balloon mortgages.

The Strengths and Weaknesses of the Pre-Conservatorship GSE Model

The pre-conservatorship structure of Fannie Mae and Freddie Mac provided significant benefits to both the single-family and multi-family housing markets, but it also had important weaknesses. Perhaps the most notable strength of the model was that the firms improved liquidity by creating a national secondary market for single-family mortgage credit that significantly reduced regional differences in credit access.[22] Several factors contributed to the liquidity of the GSEs' MBSs, including the standardization of the MBS structure and documents, effective mortgage pooling procedures, the large size of GSE MBS issuances, decades of marketing and brand building, the structure of the TBA MBS market, and the perception by investors that the firms' obligations were backed by the U.S. government.[23]

Second, the implied government backing of GSEs is often credited with preserving the wide availability of the 30-year fixed-rate, self-amortizing, no-prepayment-penalty mortgage as an affordable standard within the United States.[24] With credit risk eliminated, investors have needed to worry only about interest-rate and prepayment risk, both of which can now be hedged in myriad ways and which have been structured into tranches to appeal to a large range of investor appetites for risk. The result has been that borrowers have available a product that is safer than others because of its constant payments, thus eliminating one of the causes of default, and that also allows the borrower to refinance if interest rates should fall.

Third, the GSEs helped to develop useful standards in the mortgage market. They created standard underwriting criteria and mortgage products, which allowed both large and small originators to sell loans to them and for borrowers across the country to have access to basic products, such as the 30-year, fixed-rate, self-amortizing mortgage. While this aspect has been talked about less, the GSEs have also helped to set standards for servicing agreements. Early in the subprime crisis, when clarity was needed on how servicers should interpret pooling and servicing agreements, the GSEs established the requisite standard industry practice. In addition, the GSEs set standards for capital market products that have become key instruments in the secondary market.

Fourth, at least until 2007, the firms helped to provide countercyclical stability to the secondary market as a result of their federal backing, preserving wide access to mortgage credit during the recessions in the early 1980s and the early 1990s, the Asian financial crisis and the Long Term Capital Management collapse in the late 1990s, and the recession in 2001 (Peek and Wilcox 2006; Quigley 2006).[25]

Fifth, the firms have played an important role in providing capital to the multi-family mortgage market through portfolio investments and in developing new forms of commercial mortgage-backed securities (CMBSs) that were more appealing to investors, who have traditionally seen multi-family mortgages as non-standardized and risky (DiPasquale and Cummings 1992; Segal and Szymanoski 1997). The multi-family rental units financed by the GSEs have been an important source of affordable housing for households in the United States; one estimate suggests that 90 percent of the multi-family units financed by Fannie Mae and Freddie Mac over the past 15 years have been affordable to families earning incomes below the median in their metropolitan area (Dewitt 2010).

The GSEs also appear to have played an important countercyclical role in the multi-family market, providing some backstop for the multi-family market during economic downturns. For example, between 2007 and 2008, the GSEs increased their purchases of multi-family mortgages as private investors withdrew (Joint Center for Housing Studies 2009; National Multifamily Housing Council 2009). In the current market, the GSEs hold 35 percent of total outstanding multi-family mortgage debt and are providing nearly 90 percent of all mortgage capital to the market. Significantly, the GSEs have managed to provide this capital while still ensuring high loan performance. Over the past two decades, defaults in their multi-family portfolio have been fairly minimal. Even at the end of 2009, the delinquency rate on GSE multi-family loans was roughly .5 percent, fourteen times lower than defaults in the CMBS market (Dewitt 2010). That said, their involvement has not always been consistent. Most notably, Freddie withdrew completely from the multifamily business for a period in the early 1990s (National Multifamily Housing Council 2009).

Sixth, the GSEs have provided capital to underserved markets. (The degree to which the congressionally mandated affordability goals have encouraged this lending is debated.[26]) The GSEs have clearly played an important role in providing equity capital for the Low Income Housing Tax Credit (LIHTC) program around the country. As of 2007, the GSEs accounted for almost 40 percent of the LIHTC investment market. These investments allowed the GSEs to invest in multi-family housing while reducing their tax exposure. Of course, now that the GSEs are no longer profitable, they do not need such a tax shelter. Indeed, they are unlikely to need the level of tax shelter being provided by these investments for some time, even if they become profitable again (Timiraos 2009).

Finally, the GSEs have been important partners in state and local housing efforts. They have provided credit enhancement for state housing finance bonds, which typically target first-time homebuyers.[27] They have also partnered with nonprofits such as Self-Help and foundations such as the Ford Foundation to develop specialized loan products and to expand the secondary market for loans to low- and moderate-income borrowers. The GSEs have also been involved in philanthropic activities. In 2007, the GSEs contributed $47 million to nonprofits in Washington, D.C., while the Fannie Mae Foundation (before it was dismantled and moved back into the corporation) supported financial education, housing research, and nonprofits across the country.[28]

While these accomplishments are considerable, the GSEs' pre-conservatorship structure also had disadvantages. First, the existence of the implicit federal guarantee made the GSEs susceptible to moral hazard by tempting their executives and shareholders to take on excessive risk and expand their portfolios beyond what was needed to provide a reliable secondary market and meet mission requirements. Besides contributing to their insolvency, the high-risk investments made by the two firms might have worsened the unsustainable rise in housing prices that occurred between 2003 and 2006. That said, while the implicit government guarantee likely encouraged the growth of the GSE portfolios beyond what was required for a healthy secondary market and pushed the GSEs to buy a greater share of subprime MBS than they would have otherwise, the contribution of the GSEs to the housing bubble is still open to debate.[29] Subprime lending increased between 2003 and 2006, a period during which the GSEs lost almost half of their market share to private-label firms. Moreover, while the volume of private-label subprime MBSs purchased by the GSEs between 2005 and 2007 was significant, it still amounted to only a small share of the total subprime securities purchased by the market. According to FHFA Director James Lockhart (2007: 13), Fannie Mae and Freddie Mac owned $170 billion of subprime mortgages in AAA tranches of PLSs, representing about 11 percent of the total outstanding subprime debt.

A second weakness was that their favored regulatory status (their higher leverage, lower capital requirements, and lower cost of funds) allowed the GSEs to attract investment dollars away from other sectors of the economy, resulting in the creation of a net bias toward investing in housing in the economy overall.

Third, the firms' political power and questionable congressional lobbying activities allowed them to exert some control over both Congress and their regulator and evade proper oversight (McKinley 1997; Wallison and Calomiris 2009). One key example is the firms' low capital requirements. Although the regulators had raised the requirements by 30 percent following the discovery of accounting and other deficiencies in the GSEs, the regulators were in the process of lowering them back toward the statutory minimums just before the GSEs were taken into conservatorship. The firms' lack of sufficient capital forced the Treasury to inject capital to allow them to continue to function.

Fourth, Fannie and Freddie may have suppressed competition by exerting duopoly power and dominating the prime MBS market.[30] Lower price competition may have allowed the GSEs to retain more of the implicit subsidy resulting from lower borrowing costs and to pass less of the benefits on in the form of lower interest rates for borrowers. Estimates vary, but it appears that only about half of the savings due were passed on to borrowers, a similar share being retained by the GSEs themselves (Jaffee and Quigley 2007). Less competition may have also dampened the incentive to innovate.

Fifth, their for-profit status pushed them to respond to the inroads being made by the PLS market. The result was a race to the bottom as the firms tried to preserve their market share by lowering underwriting standards. (In the face of the same competitive pressure, FHA saw its market share fall from 19 percent to 6 percent from 1996 to 2005 and was unable to respond [GAO 2007].)

Finally, the GSEs' large size served to concentrate systemic risks and arguably made them too big to be allowed to fail, because their failure could threaten the entire economy.[31]

In short, the pre-conservatorship structure of the GSEs had significant strengths but also considerable weaknesses. Still, while these weaknesses are important and the structure of the GSEs should surely be improved (some potential reforms are discussed in Chapter 13), it would be a mistake to assume that simply reforming the GSEs, without making significant reforms to the private-label market, would prevent another crisis.

References

Abt Associates, Inc. 2001. *Study of the Multifamily Underwriting and the GSE's Role in the Multifamily Market: Expanded Version*. Prepared for U.S. Department of Housing and Urban Development. www.abtassociates.com/reports/ES-2001871779298_81131.pdf.

Ambrose, Brent W., and Tao-Hsien Dolly King. 2002. "GSE Debt and the Decline in the Treasury Debt Market." *Journal of Money, Credit, and Banking* 34, 3: 821–39.

Ambrose, Brent W., Michael LaCour-Little, and Anthony B. Sanders. 2005. "Does Regulatory Capital Arbitrage, Reputation, or Asymmetric Information Drive Securitization?" *Journal of Financial Services Research* 28, 1/2/3: 113–33.

An, X., with R.W. Bostic, Y. Deng, and S. Gabriel. 2007. "GSE Loan Purchases, the FHA, and Housing Outcomes in Targeted, Low-Income Neighborhoods." In *Brookings-Wharton Papers on Urban Affairs: 2007*, ed. Gary Burtless and Janet Rothenberg Pack. Washington, D.C.: Brookings Institution Press.

Andrews, Edmund L. 2009. "Federal Reserve to Lower Safety Net, But Gingerly." *New York Times*, September 23, B1.

Associated Press 2007. "Freddie Mac Settles Accounting Fraud Charges." MSNBC.com, September 28, 2007. http://www.msnbc.msn.com/id/21027918/#.

Bhutta, Neil. 2009. "GSE Activity and Mortgage Supply in Lower-Income and Minority Neighborhoods: The Effect of the Affordable Housing Goals." Working Paper 2009-03. Federal Reserve Board, http://www.federalreserve.gov/pubs/feds/2009/200903/revision/200903pap.pdf.

Blasko, Matej, and Joseph F. Sinkey, Jr. 2006. "Bank Asset Structure, Real Estate Lending, and Risk-Taking." *Quarterly Review of Economics and Finance* 46: 53–81.

Bostic, Raphael W., and Stuart A. Gabriel. 2006. "Do the GSEs Matter to Low-Income Housing Markets? An Assessment of the Effects of the GSE Loan Purchase Goals on California Housing Outcomes." *Journal of Urban Economics* 59, 3: 458–75.

Bradford, Calvin. 1979. "Financing Home Ownership: The Federal Role in Neighborhood Decline." *Urban Affairs Quarterly* 14, 3: 313–35.

Chomsisengphet, Souphala, and Anthony Pennington-Cross. 2006. "The Evolution of the Subprime Mortgage Market." *Federal Reserve Bank of St. Louis Review* 88, 1: 31–56.

Congressional Budget Office.. 1996. "Assessing the Public Costs and Benefits of Fannie Mae and Freddie Mac." http://www.cbo.gov/ftpdocs/0xx/doc13/Fanfred.pdf.

———. 2010. "CBO's Budgetary Treatment of Fannie Mae and Freddie Mac." http://www.cbo.gov/ftpdocs/108xx/doc10878/01-13-FannieFreddie.pdf.

Coval, Joshua, Jakub Jurek, and Erik Stafford. 2008. "The Economics of Structured Finance." *Journal of Economic Perspectives* 23, 1: 3–25.

Davidson, Andrew, and Anthony B. Sanders. 2009. "Securitization After the Fall." Prepared for Second Annual Mid-Winter Symposium on Urban Research.

Day, Kathleen. 2006. "Study Finds Extensive Fraud at Fannie Mae." *Washington Post*, May 24, 2.

Dewitt, Robert E. 2010. Testimony Before House Committee on Financial Services, March 23, www.house.gov/apps/list/hearing/financialsvcs_dem/dewitt_testimony.pdf.

DiPasquale, Denise, and Jean L. Cummings. 1992. "Financing Multifamily Rental Housing: The Changing Role of Lenders and Investors." *Housing Policy Debate* 3, 1: 77–115.

Fannie Mae. 2007. "Fannie Mae 2007 Q1-Q3 10-Q Investment Summary. Credit Supplement." November 9, https://mail.nyu.edu/attach/FannieMae_10K_20080227.pdf.

Fannie Mae Charter. 1992. 12 U.S.C. 1716 et seq., as amended through October 28, 1992. http://www.fanniemae.com/global/pdf/aboutfm/understanding/charter.pdf.

Federal Deposit Insurance Corporation. 2009. "Summary of Deposits: Deposits of FDIC-Insured Commercial Banks and Savings Institutions." http://www2.fdic.gov/sod/createStat.asp?System=SOD&Item=ddep.

Federal Reserve Board. 2009. Press Release, September 23. http://www.federalreserve.gov/newsevents/press/monetary/20090923a.htm.

———. 2010. "Mortgage Debt Outstanding." http://www.federalreserve.gov/econresdata/releases/mortoutstand/current.htm.

Fishback, Price V., William C. Horrace, and Shawn Kantor. 2001. "The Origins of Modern Housing Finance: The Impact of Federal Housing Programs During the Great Depression." Working Paper. Tucson: University of Arizona.

Frame, W. Scott, and Lawrence J. White. 2004. "Regulating Housing GSEs: Thoughts on Institutional Structure and Authorities." *Federal Reserve Bank of Atlanta Economic Review* 89, 2: 87–102.

———. 2005. "Fussing and Fuming over Fannie and Freddie: How Much Smoke, How Much Fire?" *Journal of Economic Perspectives* 19, 2: 159–84.

———. 2010. "The Industrial Organization of the U.S. Single-Family Residential Mortgage Industry." Draft for the *International Encyclopedia of Housing and Home.*

http://w4.stern.nyu.edu/economics/docs/workingpapers/2010/Frame,%20White_
The%20Industrial%20Organization%20of%20the%20U.S.%20Single-Family%20
Residential%20Mortgage%20Industry.pdf.

Frankel, Allen. 2006. "Prime or Not So Prime? An Exploration of U.S. Housing Finance in the New Century." *BIS Quarterly Review* (March): 67–78.

Freddie Mac Charter. 2009. P.L. No. 91-351, as amended through February 17, 2009. http://www.freddiemac.com/governance/pdf/charter.pdf.

Furlong, Frederick T. 1992. "Capital Regulation and Bank Lending." *Federal Reserve Bank of San Francisco Economic Review* 3: 23–33.

Geithner, Timothy F., Treasury Secretary. 2010. Written testimony to the House Committee on Financial Services, March 23. http://www.house.gov/apps/list/hearing/financialsvcs_dem/testimony_-_geithner.pdf.

Green, Richard K., and Ann B. Schnare. 2009. "The Rise and Fall of Fannie Mae and Freddie Mac: Lessons Learned and Options for Reform." Washington, D.C.: Empiris LLC.

Green, Richard K., and Susan M. Wachter. 2005. "The American Mortgage in Historical and International Context." *Journal of Economic Perspectives* 19, 4: 93–114.

Hancock, Diana, Andreas Lehnert, Wayne Passmore, and Shane M. Sherlund. 2006. "The Competitive Effects of Risk-Based Bank Capital Regulation: An Example from U.S. Mortgage Markets." *Federal Reserve Board Finance and Economics Discussion Series* 46.

Jaffee, Dwight M. 2000. "The Effect on the Mortgage Markets of Privatizing Fannie Mae and Freddie Mac." Prepared for the conference Thinking About the Future of Fannie Mae and Freddie Mac, American Enterprise Institute, May 23. http://faculty.haas.berkeley.edu/jaffee/papers/aeimay00.pdf.

———. 2003. "The Interest Rate Risk of Fannie Mae and Freddie Mac." *Journal of Financial Services Research* 24, 1: 5–29.

———. 2010. "The Role of the GSEs and Housing Policy in the Financial Crisis." Paper prepared for presentation to the Financial Crisis Inquiry Commission, Washington D.C., February 27. http://www.fcic.gov/hearings/pdfs/2010-0227-Jaffee.pdf.

Jaffee, Dwight M., Anthony Lynch, Matthew Richardson, and Stijn Van Nieuwerburgh. 2009. "What to Do About the Government Sponsored Enterprises?" In *Restoring Financial Stability: How to Repair a Failed System*, ed. Viral V. Acharya and Matthew Richardson. Hoboken, N.J.: Wiley.

Jaffee, Dwight M., and John M. Quigley. 2007. "Housing Subsidies and Homeowners: What Role for Government-Sponsored Enterprises?" In *Brookings-Wharton Papers on Urban Affairs: 2007*, ed. Gary Burtless and Janet Rothenberg Pack. Washington, D.C.: Brookings Institution Press. 103–49.

———. 2010. "Housing Policy, Mortgage Policy, and the Federal Housing Administration." In *Measuring and Managing Federal Financial Risk,* ed. Deborah Lucas. Cambridge, Mass.: NBER Books. 163–213.

Joint Center for Housing Studies. 2009. *Meeting Multifamily Housing Finance Needs During and After the Credit Crisis.* Cambridge, Mass.: Joint Center for Housing Studies, Harvard University.

Kopecki, Dawn. 2007. "Philanthropy, Fannie Mae Style." *Business Week*, April 2, http://www.businessweek.com/magazine/content/07_14/b4028049.htm.

Lea, Michael. 2006. "Securitization: A Primer on Structures and Credit Enhancement." Philadelphia: Wharton School, University of Pennsylvania, http://housingfinance. wharton.upenn.edu/2009Readings/Lea%20-%20Securitization%20Primer.pdf.

Listokin, David, Elvin K. Wyly, Brian Schmitt, and Ioan Voicu. 2001. "The Potential and Limitations of Mortgage Innovations in Fostering Homeownership in the United States." *Housing Policy Debate* 12, 3: 465–513.

Lockhart, James B., III. 2007. "GSE Challenges: Reform and Regulatory Oversight." Speech at MBA's National Secondary Market Conference and Expo, May 21, http://www.mortgagebankers.org/files/CREF/docs/2007/RegulatoryandLegislativeRoundup-JamesB.LockhartIII.pdf.

———. 2009. Speech at the American Securitization Forum. Las Vegas, February 9, http://www.fhfa.gov/webfiles/823/ASFSpeech2909.pdf.

McKinley, Vern. 1997. "The Mounting Case for Privatizing Fannie Mae and Freddie Mac." Cato Institute Policy Analysis 293. http://www.cato.org/pubs/pas/pa-293. html.

National Council of State Housing Agencies. 2010. "Housing Government-Sponsored Enterprises (GSEs)." http://www.ncsha.org/advocacy-issues/housing-government-sponsored-enterprises-gses.

National Multifamily Housing Council. 2009. "The GSEs' Role in Multifamily Housing Finance." NMHC Research Notes. http://www.nmhc.org/Content/ServeContent. cfm?ContentItemID=5039.

New York State Housing Finance Agency. 2008. Minutes of the 401st Members' Meeting July 23.

Office of Federal Housing Enterprise Oversight. 2003. "OFHEO Issues Capital Classifications for Fannie Mae and Freddie Mac." Press release, June 30, http://www. mortgagebankers.org/files/Industry/reports/03/ofheo_0630.pdf.

Peek, Joe, and James A. Wilcox. 2006. "Housing, Credit Constraints, and Macro Stability: The Secondary Mortgage Market and Reduced Cyclicality of Residential Investment." Working Paper 298. Berkeley: Fisher Center for Real Estate and Urban Economics, University of California.

Pennington-Cross, Anthony. 2002. "Subprime Lending in the Primary and Secondary Markets." *Journal of Housing Research* 13, 1: 31–50.

Quigley, John M. 2006. "Federal Credit and Insurance Programs: Housing." *Federal Reserve Bank of St. Louis Review* 88, 4: 1–29.

Reiss, David. 2008. "The Federal Government's Implied Guarantee of Fannie Mae and Freddie Mac's Obligations: Uncle Sam Will Pick up the Tab." *Georgia Law Review* 42: 1019–81.

Segal, William, and Edward J. Szymanoski. 1997. "The Multifamily Secondary Mortgage Market: The Role of Government Sponsored Enterprises." Working Paper HF-002. Washington, D.C.: U.S. Department of Housing and Urban Development, Office of Policy Development and Research.

Stein, Eric. 2008. "Turmoil in the U.S. Credit Markets: The Genesis of the Current Economic Crisis." Testimony Before Senate Committee on Banking, Housing, and Urban Affairs, October 16.

Tatom, John A. 2008. "New Actions on the Housing and Financial Crisis: Do No Harm?" *Research Buzz* 4, 6: 1–5.

Taylor, John B. 2007. "Housing and Monetary Policy." Working Paper W13682. Cambridge, Mass.: NBER.

Timiraos, Nick. 2009. "Treasury Blocks the Sale of Tax Credits by Fannie." *Wall Street Journal*, November 7, B1.

U.S. Government Accountability Office. 2007. "Decline in the Agency's Market Share was Associated with Product and Process Developments of Other Mortgage Market Participants." Report to Congressional Requesters, http://www.gao.gov/new.items/d07645.pdf.

Van Order, Robert. 2007. "Government-Sponsored Enterprises and Resource Allocation: Some Implications for Urban Economies." In *Brookings-Wharton Papers on Urban Affairs: 2007*, ed. Gary Burtless and Janet Rothenberg Pack. Washington, D.C.: Brookings Institution Press. 151–90.

Wallison, Peter J., and Charles W. Calomiris. 2009. "The Last Trillion-Dollar Commitment: The Destruction of Fannie Mae and Freddie Mac." *Journal of Structured Finance* 15, 1: 71–80.

Notes

1. For readers who wish to explore these issues further, an extensive literature already exists. Thorough overviews of the federal government housing agencies and the role of the GSEs are provided by Bradford 1979 (on federal involvement in housing through this date), Frame and White 2004 (on the specific role of the GSEs in the mortgage market), Green and Schnare 2009, Jaffee and Quigley 2007 (on the role of federal guarantees in the housing market), Pennington-Cross 2002 (a comparison of FHA and subprime lending market shares), and Quigley 2006 (on the federal role in the mortgage market and homeownership).

Coverage of the history of the mortgage market as well as discussions about the causes of the current housing crisis can be found in Chomsisengphet and Pennington-Cross 2006 (on subprime lending), Fishback, Horrace and Kantor 2001 (on the origins of the modern mortgage market), Green and Wachter 2005 (for a history and comparison of U.S. to international mortgage markets), Listokin et al. 2001 (on mortgage innovations and homeownership), and Taylor 2007 (on the influence of interest rates on housing cycles). For a review of the history and evolution of bank portfolio lending, see Ambrose, LaCour-Little, and Sanders 2005 (for an analysis of the choice to retain a loan portfolio), Blasko and Sinkey 2006 (on the restructuring of bank portfolios and real estate lending during the 1990s), Furlong 1992 (for an overview of bank regulatory changes), and Hancock et al. 2006 (examining the impact of Basel II capital regulations on the mortgage market).

Finally, for an outline of the role of the private sector in mortgage securitization, see Frankel 2006 (on housing market appreciation and mortgage-backed securities valuations), Van Order 2007 (for a review of securitization, including agency [GSE] and non-agency [non-GSE] MBS), and Lea 2006.

2. The Federal Home Loan Banks are also GSEs, but here we use the term "GSEs" to refer only to the Federal National Mortgage Association (Fannie Mae) and the Federal Home Loan Mortgage Corporation (Freddie Mac).

3. In more recent years, some banks, as well as other mortgage companies, have been able to raise additional funds by issuing equity and debt obligations. One proposal, discussed in a subsequent chapter, would make it easier for banks to borrow money through the use of covered bonds, which are backed by mortgages or other debt instruments as well as by the credit of the issuing bank.

4. For the growth of mortgage debt relative to GDP, see http://money.cnn.com/2009/05/27/news/mortgage.overhang.fortune/index.htm.

5. Before the late 1930s, the typical mortgage had a term of five years (or less) and no amortization, requiring a balloon payment at the end of the term (see Frame and White 2010).

6. Also, GNMA has limited its backing to three types of investment vehicles, thus helping to ensure that the markets for these three types of securities will be both broad and deep.

7. Fannie Mae and then Freddie Mac were still able to buy FHA and VA loans but did not generally do so.

8. The interest-rate risk is discussed in Jaffee (2003). Rising interest rates made Fannie's net worth in the early 1980s negative (11), as the value of its portfolios fell below the values of its outstanding debt obligations (Frame and White 2005).

9. The banks also receive a form of guarantee through the Federal Deposit Insurance Corporation (FDIC) but are charged a fee for that insurance. FDIC insurance protects deposits below a certain level, which facilitates bank portfolio lending.

10. See, for example, Fannie Mae Charter 1992, especially §304(e) (regarding exemptions from SEC requirements) and §309(c)2 (regarding exemption from state and local taxation). Five of the eighteen board members were appointed annually by the President of the United States (see §308[b] for the case of Fannie Mae).

11. For more information on their regulatory advantages and implicit guarantee, see Ambrose and King 2002; Frame and White 2005; Jaffee and Quigley 2007; Quigley 2006; and Reiss 2008, among others.

12. A TBA market is not possible in most debt markets, because debt investors typically are not willing to pay for debt when the credit risk is unknown. A TBA market is possible for GSE MBSs because investors are confident that the issuing agencies will eliminate credit risk for the as-yet-unspecified underlying loans, as a result of the implicit government guarantees and perhaps the quality of their underwriting of the individual loans. By removing credit risk in this way, the TBA market allows investors to focus only on interest-rate risk. Some observers think that the TBA market will collapse without government guarantees (implicit or explicit), because investors will not buy MBSs that require them to bear unknown credit risk. And without the TBA market, originators would face the risk that interest rates will rise in the window between when they write a loan and when they can resell it to the GSEs. Although there are other ways to hedge most of this risk, they would probably result in a higher cost to the borrower.

13. Fannie Mae and Freddie Mac are authorized by the government to buy conforming loans, the dollar loan limits of which are set by the GSEs' regulator. Loans above the conforming loan limit in their area are called jumbo loans.

14. Experience since 2007 has shown that even the highest-rated securities were much riskier than expected, and many of those that were issued in years 2005–2007 have been significantly downgraded (see Coval, Jurek, and Stafford 2008).

15. Fannie's and Freddie's combined market share in the mortgage market was 55 percent in 2003; this sank dramatically to under 35 percent by 2006, as the PLSs came to dominate the market (Lockhart 2009: 2).

16. The GSEs also provided a limited number of wraps for MBSs backed by subprime mortgages that were not eligible for their standard guarantee programs (Fannie Mae 2007).

17. Freddie Mac briefly invested in tobacco company bonds in the late 1990s. The rationale for allowing non-housing portfolio investments was that it permitted the firms to diversify, which arguably improved their stability.

18. For their guarantee business, the GSEs needed a capital ratio of only 0.45, allowing even greater leverage (Office of Federal Housing Enterprise Oversight 2003).

19. It is important to note that banks and investment banks also held these tranches in their portfolios, the latter often ending up holding the higher-risk tranches that they created but were unable to sell.

20. However, in the early years of the first decade of the twenty-first century, the two firms were caught up in significant accounting scandals. Their regulator charged that they were manipulating their books to show steady earnings growth, which appealed to investors and helped to maximize bonuses for their senior executives. Both have paid fines as part of settlements with the SEC and with their regulator (Associated Press 2007; Day 2006).

21. According to Geithner (2010), while in 2000 the GSEs held a negligible amount of private-label securities backed by subprime or Alt A loans, by 2007, 23 per-

cent of the GSE's portfolios was made up by PLSs backed by subprime or Alt-A loans. See also, from Wallison and Calomiris (2009: 77):

> There are few data available publicly on the dollar amount of junk loans held by the GSEs in 2004, but according to their own reports, GSE purchases of these mortgages and MBS increased substantially between 2005 and 2007. Subprime and Alt-A purchases during this period were a higher share of total purchases than in previous years. For example, Fannie reported that mortgages and MBS of all types originated in 2005–2007 comprised 49.8 percent of its overall book of single-family mortgages, which includes both mortgages and MBS retained in their portfolio as well as mortgages they securitized and guaranteed.

22. It should be noted that for mortgages requiring private mortgage insurance (i.e., generally those with a loan to value of greater than 80 percent), the underwriting of the private mortgage insurance companies determined where these products were available.

23. Liquidity of an asset is the ease with which it can be converted into cash without a price discount. While this definition sounds simple, the concept is deceptively subtle, and the many factors that can affect liquidity are not intuitive. In choosing between two assets with identical risk profiles but different liquidity, investors are willing to pay a significant premium to buy the more liquid assets. One of the major factors in creating liquidity for debt products is simply the size of the market: Larger markets are more liquid because there are more buyers and sellers.

24. The rationale for this claim is that originators may refuse to write long-term, fixed-rate mortgages without the assurance of guarantees against potential losses. International comparisons suggest that while most other national governments do not provide guarantees in their mortgage finance systems, they also lack long-term, fixed-rate no-prepayment-penalty mortgages.

25. The GSEs are currently providing substantial liquidity to the mortgage market, but only because of the injection of hundreds of billions of dollars in government capital, and because the Federal Reserve was, until April 1, 2010, buying over 80 percent of the agencies' MBSs in a $1.25 trillion buying plan (Andrews 2009; see also Federal Reserve Board 2009).

26. See, for example, Bostic and Gabriel (2006) (examining the impacts of GSE loan purchasing activities in targeted communities). See also An et al. (2007) (examining the impact of GSE as well as FHA activities in these communities). Some critics have pointed to the affordable housing goals as a main culprit in the GSEs' insolvency, particularly after 2004, when the GSEs were allowed to count risky private-label subprime MBSs held in their portfolios toward their affordable housing goals. But the evidence is not strong. A recent Federal Reserve paper found that while the affordable housing goals did little for the intended low-income beneficiaries, there was also no evidence that the goals led the GSEs to take greater risks (Bhutta 2009).

27. The GSEs play a major role in enhancing the credit of state Housing Finance Agency (HFA) bonds. For instance, in 2008 in New York, the GSEs enhanced the credit of $4 billion in HFA bonds, out of $10 billion issued (see National Council of State Housing Agencies 2010; New York State Housing Finance Agency 2008).

28. Some observers have charged that Fannie Mae used its foundation dollars to curry favor with members of Congress (Kopecki 2007).

29. The actual extent of the GSE contribution through non-prime investments to housing bubble inflation is unclear. For example, Tatom (2008) notes: "As recently as 2007, Freddie and Fannie restricted their purchases of mortgages to about 15 percent of the market, as noted by Poole 2008, with no obvious effect on housing, mortgage or financial markets." Nevertheless, others note that their sheer size quite possibly contributed to some part of the current crisis. According to Jaffee et al. (2009), "By 2007, over 15 percent of their own outstanding mortgage portfolio was invested in non-prime assets, an amount representing 10 percent of the entire market for these assets. While not the only institutional culprit here, it is reasonable to assume that the mere size of the GSEs created 'froth' and 'excess' liquidity in the market."

30. However, there may be economies of scale that make concentration in the MBS market desirable. In particular, the presence of a few dominant players in the secondary market makes it easier to set standards that provide clear information to investors (and lenders and borrowers). The presence of a few large players and a limited set of products may also encourage a high trading volume, which aids liquidity. For further discussion, see Jaffee (2000).

31. Of course, many of the other private financial institutions, such as JPMorgan, Chase, and Bank of America, which would likely step in to play a more active role in the secondary market if the GSEs were dismantled, have arguably also become "too big to fail." In fact, even if the GSEs continue to operate with an implicit (or even explicit) government guarantee, they arguably do not have a unique competitive advantage, because private institutions are seen as having an implicit guarantee as well.

Chapter 2

Reasonable People Did Disagree: Optimism and Pessimism About the U.S. Housing Market Before the Crash

Kristopher S. Gerardi, Christopher L. Foote, and Paul S. Willen

> The home-price bubble feels like the stock-market mania in the fall of 1999, just before the stock bubble burst in early 2000, with all the hype, herd investing and absolute confidence in the inevitability of continuing price appreciation.
> —Robert Shiller, quoted in Laing (2005)

Optimism about future house price growth shoulders much of the blame for the mortgage crisis that swamped the U.S. and world economies starting in 2007. Had borrowers and investors in 2006 known that the nearly decade-long expansion of the U.S. housing sector had ended and that house prices would decline 30 percent over the next three years, few would have made the decisions they did.

To many people, the fact that investors and borrowers were optimistic about house prices in 2006 seems inexplicable or even inexcusable. The experience up to that point showed all the hallmarks of an asset-pricing bubble. From the first quarter of 1997 to the first quarter of 2005, real home prices went up 72 percent according to the Case-Shiller repeat-sales index and by 41 percent according to the Office of Federal Housing Enterprise

Oversight (OFHEO) (now FHFA) repeat-sales index.[1] To put these numbers in perspective, according to Shiller (2006), real house prices in the United States were basically flat between the late 1940s and the mid-1990s. Even more striking is the fact that average real house prices in the mid-1990s were at essentially the same level as they were in the late 1890s.[2] The divergence of house price appreciation from long-run trends appears not only when one looks at the level of house prices, but also if one considers the ratio of house prices to income or rents.

The view that optimism was unjustified in 2005 is not just hindsight. Some observers argued at the time that housing was overvalued and likely to crash. Among the pessimists were economists such as Robert Shiller, quoted at the beginning of the chapter. Some journalists, most notably at the *Economist*, also argued for the inevitable collapse of the U.S. residential real estate market.[3]

Why were market participants so optimistic? In other words, why did they largely ignore the pessimists? Our answer is somewhat surprising: The pessimistic case was a distinctly minority view, especially among professional economists. We review the academic literature that was written during the housing boom, focusing closely on the period 2004–2006, which turned out to be the peak of the boom. This review indicates that there were widely dispersed opinions on whether the market accurately valued housing. As was noted previously, some economists were truly pessimistic and warned of an impending collapse in real estate markets with severe consequences. But other economists were truly optimistic and dismissed such warnings. Granted, some of these optimists were real estate industry boosters such as David Lereah, an economist with the National Association of Realtors, who in 2006 published *Why the Real Estate Boom Will Not Bust— And How You Can Profit from It*. But many in the optimistic camp were serious researchers with established reputations who made convincing arguments in respected academic forums. These optimists cannot be dismissed as purveyors of self-serving industry propaganda, nor as scholars who would dismiss counterarguments without giving such opposing viewpoints due consideration.

The most prevalent opinion among economists who studied house pricing during the bubble was essentially no judgment at all. We call it an agnostic view. Agnostics were unwilling to make anything more than guarded, highly qualified statements on the future path of U.S. housing prices. The discussion by Gallin (2008: 19) is typical of this genre.

Because a low rent-price ratio has been a harbinger of sluggish price growth since 1970, it seems reasonable to treat the rent-price ratio as a measure of valuation in the housing market. Indeed, one might be tempted to cite the currently low level of the rent-price ratio as a sign that we are in a house price "bubble." However, several important caveats argue against such a strong conclusion and in favor of future research.

In a sense, this reluctance to commit should not surprise anyone familiar with modern asset-pricing theory. The Fundamental Theorem of Asset Pricing implies that the evolution of asset prices is, to a first approximation, unpredictable. If housing was so obviously overvalued, as the pessimists suggested, then investors stood to make huge profits by betting against housing. By doing so, investors would have ensured that house prices would have fallen immediately. Regardless of whether the theory of the unpredictability of asset prices is correct, the theory is part of the basic training of almost every economist. Consequently, any economist who suggests to his or her peers that an asset is overvalued or undervalued faces a heavy burden of proof.[4] This hurdle may explain why the arguments of some of the pessimists early in the boom were largely dismissed at the time.

It is instructive to read the logic of non-economists who looked at house price data in the same period. Paolo Pellegrini and John Paulson, whose wildly successful 2006 bet against subprime mortgages is now the stuff of Wall Street legend, made the following argument, as chronicled in Zuckerman (2009). First, they noted that house prices had deviated from trend:

> Housing prices had climbed a puny 1.4 percent annually between 1975 and 2000, after inflation was taken into consideration. But they had soared over 7 percent in the following five years, until 2005. The upshot: U.S. home prices would have to drop by almost 40 percent to return to their historic trend line. (Zuckerman 2009: 107)

Those facts are indisputable, but the logic that followed would have earned the two investors a zero on an undergraduate finance exam: "to Paulson and Pellegrini, their discovery meant that housing prices were bound to fall, at least at some point, no matter what the moves in unemployment, interest rates, or the economy" (Zuckerman 2009: 108).

The Fundamental Theorem of Asset Pricing, in its pure form, largely rejects the idea that prices mean-revert, which is what Paulson and Pellegrini assumed. Researchers have found evidence of mean reversion, but Lo and MacKinlay (2001) argue that it operates on a relatively small scale and that research has not "uncovered tremendous untapped profit opportunities" (Lo and MacKinlay 2001: xxii). In other words, academic finance provided little support for mean reversion on the scale that Paulson and Pellegrini expected.

Economists who argued that house prices were going to fall made two closely related arguments. The first was that key relationships in the data had deviated from long-run averages. The second was that there was a bubble in house prices, so buyers were willing to pay high prices today because of their expectations of even higher prices tomorrow. Proving either claim was a challenge.

Regarding the first argument, the key data relationships that were most often analyzed were the ratios of house prices to either incomes or rents. Making a convincing argument that these relationships had deviated from long-run or equilibrium values was far harder than it sounds. Simply measuring these ratios, for example, was an enormous challenge, because different repeat-sales indices of house prices often yielded different results. Moreover, results based on repeat-sales measures of prices differed sharply from results generated by hedonic pricing models. An additional practical complication with using the rent-price ratio to evaluate housing markets is that for residential housing, renters' and buyers' markets are qualitatively distinct, so finding comparable properties proved challenging. Theoretical challenges also confronted work with price-income or price-rent ratios. Economic theory predicts that the level of interest rates should affect price-income and price-rent ratios, but researchers faced questions over the proper interest rates to use in their calculations. Finally, researchers using price-income or price-rent ratios were forced to take a stand on whether a deviation from a long-term trend reflected disequilibrium behavior or simply a change in the equilibrium ratio itself. All these issues made it difficult to mount a convincing counterargument at the time.

What about asset-price bubbles? While there is great interest in bubbles among research economists, the science of analyzing them remains primitive. The starting point for a formal analysis of bubbles is the standard idea taken from partial equilibrium analysis of individual choice: that the amount someone should pay for something depends only on the market price and not on any link between that price and the notion of its fundamental underlying value. If the something is a financial asset, then the expected return is the key determinant for the investor, and the investor correctly ignores the question of why that return is as high or low as it is when making decisions. In most contexts in economics, equilibrium—the invisible hand—ensures that the value of the asset is tied to its fundamentals, typically because a deviation from fundamentals would allow someone to make infinite profits. But in recent years, economists have constructed theoretical examples in which investors cannot, for one reason or another, bring prices into line with fundamentals and therefore bubbles can persist. Matching such models with the real world, however, has proved problematic.

Later in this chapter, we review the arguments of a prominent pessimist: Paul Krugman. Although his arguments were made in his widely read *New York Times* column (Krugman 2005) rather than in a formal academic paper, Krugman, now a Nobel Prize-winning economist, has substantial credibility. He argued that because it is difficult to build in coastal areas of the United States, those areas are more "bubble-prone." Consequently, the rapid price increases on the coasts but not elsewhere were prima facie evidence that there was a bubble and that prices would eventually collapse.

It is tempting to call Krugman prescient because beginning in late 2006, prices did indeed crash. But his arguments were problematic both ex ante and ex post. Ex ante, it is unclear why Krugman thinks the coasts are more "bubble-prone." The models we have of asset-price bubbles do a reasonable job of explaining why they can persist but have little to say about where we might expect them to start. As one prominent researcher in the field writes, "we do not have many convincing models that explain when and why bubbles start" (Brunnermeier 2008). Krugman's thesis seems to hinge on the idea that scarce coastal land is valuable and bubbles can happen only when assets are in short supply. The whole point about bubbles, however, is that the fundamentals of supply and demand do not matter. Therefore there is no reason why land in places where it is easy to build could not experience bubbles. Ex post, as we will explore at length, the places in the United States where the housing market most resembled a bubble were Phoenix and Las Vegas. According to recent research, both locations are characterized by relatively high housing-supply elasticities; unlike certain coastal areas, the two cities have an abundance of surrounding land on which to accommodate new construction.

Ultimately, we argue that the academic research that was available in 2006 was basically inconclusive and could not convincingly support or refute any hypothesis about the future path of asset prices. Investors who believed that house prices were going to fall could find evidence to support their position, while those who wanted to believe that house prices would continue to rise could not be dissuaded either. There were reasonable arguments on both sides.

We view a retrospective understanding of the real-time evolution of beliefs about the path of house prices as central to understanding the financial crisis of 2007–2009. Many lending decisions that were made during the housing boom seem daft in light of what happened. Why would lenders extend credit to borrowers with troubled credit histories, low (or no) down payments, or poorly documented incomes? Loans to these borrowers make sense for investors who are optimistic about the future trajectory of house prices, because even small amounts of positive appreciation protect mortgage investors from large losses. If house prices fall, however, then borrowers are likely to have negative equity, leaving them vulnerable to adverse life events, such as job loss, that reduce their ability to make regular mortgage payments. In particular, owners with negative equity are unable to pay off their mortgages by selling their homes, so foreclosures often follow adverse life events.[5] Gerardi et al. (2008) show that the negative relationship between house price appreciation and mortgage losses was well understood by market participants in 2006. Specifically, the paper shows that investors could and did understand that subprime loans in particular carried a high degree of risk if house prices fell. Other work, such as Foote et al. (2009), shows that prime loans, while generally less risky than subprime loans, were also adversely affected by the unexpected decline in housing prices. It is clear that understanding the sources of optimism about house prices in 2006 in light of the catastrophe that followed is more than an exercise in the history of economic thought. Rather, it is a starting point toward an understanding of the role that economic theory and the pronouncements of economists might have played in the biggest financial crisis since the Great Depression.

The Housing Pessimists

In this section, we focus on economists who took a strong position on the unsustainability of future house price growth. We start with some research that pointed to the existence of a housing bubble as early as 2002 and 2003, several years before housing markets peaked in the United States. We then review arguments advanced by Krugman and others that geographical differences in residential building restrictions were important in getting a bubble started.

Early Warnings on the U.S. Housing Market

One of the first prominent housing pessimists was Dean Baker of the Center for Economic and Policy Research in Washington, who in 2002 wrote:

> In the absence of any other credible theory, the only plausible explanation for the sudden surge in home prices is the existence of a housing bubble. This means that a major factor driving housing sales is the expectation that housing prices will be higher in the future. While this process can sustain rising prices for a period of time, it must eventually come to an end.

Baker (2002) focused on the price-rent ratio, the housing equivalent of the price-dividend ratio used to assess valuation in equity markets.[6] According to standard theory, the price of an asset should be equal to the present value of the sum of expected future dividends. A housing asset's dividend is essentially the service flow that it provides (i.e., the flow value of shelter), which is in turn roughly equal to the house's rental value. By this reasoning, the price-rent ratio (or its inverse) can be used as a measure of how close housing prices are to fundamentals.

Baker showed that from 1995 to 2002, U.S. housing prices, as measured by the OFHEO index, rose by almost 50 percent in nominal terms, an increase that was substantially greater than the increase in overall prices (i.e., inflation) during the same period. Akin to Shiller's findings, Baker found that before 1995, changes in nominal house prices moved in tandem with overall prices, so real house prices displayed no upward trend. The rise in the price index in the seven-year period analyzed by Baker was also significantly greater than the rise in rents; the Bureau of Labor Statistics (BLS) rental index rose by roughly 10 percent in real terms during this seven-year period, while the house price index rose by almost 30 percent.

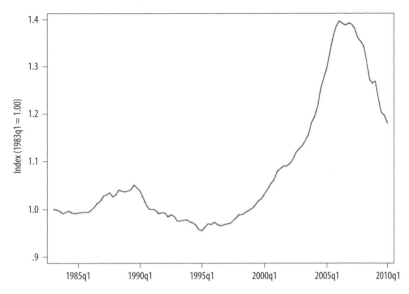

Figure 2.1. Housing price-rent ratio in the United States: 1983Q1–2010Q1. National house price series from the Office of Housing Enterprise Oversight; owner's equivalent rent series from the Bureau of Labor Statistics.

This difference is consistent with the time-series pattern of the price-rent ratio we present in Figure 2.1. Baker noted that the rental and house price indexes had diverged in the late 1970s and again in the late 1980s, when growth in housing prices outpaced growth in rents, but that both episodes were followed by periods in which housing prices declined relative to rents. In addition, he noted that the rental vacancy rate in 2002 was 9 1 percent—the highest rate on record since the Census Bureau had begun collecting the data. The large number of vacancies suggested some downward pressure on rents going forward.

In addition to the divergence between rents and prices in the U.S. housing market, Baker called attention to changes in demographic trends that could put additional downward pressure on house prices. He noted that during the 1970s and early 1980s, housing grew from about 17 percent of consumption to more than 25 percent, in large part owing to increased demand for housing from the first baby boom cohorts, who were then entering adulthood. From the early 1980s to the mid-1990s, the housing share of consumption remained relatively constant, consistent with the modest demographic changes that were taking place in the United States at that time. In the future, Baker argued, as the baby boomers entered retirement, housing demand—and hence prices—would likely fall. (See also Mankiw and Weil 1989 on this point.)

Finally, Baker discussed the role of interest rates in moving prices higher. As we will discuss in more detail later, many economists pointed to low interest rates as justifying higher housing prices, but Baker was skeptical of this claim. Nominal interest rates were indeed low in the early 2000s, because the Federal Reserve had adopted a loose monetary policy to combat the effects of the 2001 recession. However, Baker pointed out that nominal rates could not explain the divergence of housing prices from fundamentals, as it is the *real* interest rate (the difference between the nominal rate and expected inflation) that should influence prices. During the boom period, real mortgage interest rates did not seem to be significantly lower than their levels in the mid-1990s before the run-up in house prices began. To further illustrate the point, Baker noted that from the early 1980s to the late 1980s, there was a large drop in nominal rates (from almost 15 percent in 1981 to approximately 9 percent in 1988) without a large divergence between the rental and price indexes.

Another important early study in the pessimist camp was a 2003 Brookings paper by Karl Case and Robert Shiller. Its analysis can be separated into two parts. The first part consists of a state panel-data analysis of the fundamentals that should have driven the trajectory of U.S. housing prices from 1985 through 2002. The main focus is on the relationship between prices and income per capita, although population, employment, unemployment rates, housing starts, interest rates, and debt-to-income ratios (DTIs) also enter into the regression models. The empirical findings did not provide conclusive evidence one way or the other regarding the stability of housing prices relative to what the authors perceived to be housing-market fundamentals. In particular, the results were sensitive to the particular geographic regions considered. For example, ratios of house prices to income per capita were stable in the vast majority of states over the 18-year period, but in eight states, the price-income ratios displayed pronounced cyclical patterns.[7] In those eight states, the other variables that proxy for housing-market fundamentals (besides income) added significant explanatory power to the house-price panel regressions. However, in an out-of-sample forecasting exercise for those states, Case and Shiller found that the fundamentals significantly underpredicted the actual movements in housing prices. Therefore while there was some evidence of a potential bubble in these eight coastal states, the authors concluded from their empirical analysis that, overall, U.S. housing prices tracked market fundamentals fairly well.

The authors came to a different conclusion in the second part of their paper, which consisted of a survey of recent homebuyers in Orange County (Los Angeles), Alameda County (San Francisco), Middlesex County (Boston), and Milwaukee County (Milwaukee) in 2003. The survey was virtually identical to a 1988 survey that Case and Shiller had conducted in the same areas, in which they found what they believed to be fairly strong evidence of a housing bubble at that time. After the 1988 survey, housing prices in many coastal areas fell dramatically, partially reversing the price gains of the mid- to late 1980s. Relative to the 1988 survey, the results of the 2003 survey were somewhat mixed. The majority of homebuyers surveyed in 2003 reported that investment was a "major consideration" in their purchase or that they at least "in part" thought of their housing purchase as an investment. Far fewer said that they were buying a house "strictly for investment purposes," compared to 1988. In addition, while only a small fraction of borrowers believed that purchasing a house involved a great deal of risk in the 2003 survey, the perception of risk in 1988 was even smaller in three out of the four areas (Milwaukee being the one exception). The most striking difference involved the respondents' expectations of future price appreciation. In both the 1988 and 2003 surveys, more than 90 percent of respondents expected an increase in prices over several years, the average expected increase over the next year being extremely high (between 7.2 and 10.5 percent in 2003 and between 6.1 and 15.3 percent in 1988). Expectations over a longer-term horizon (10 years) were even higher in all four cities, varying from 11.7 percent per year in Milwaukee to 15.7 percent in San Francisco in 2003.[8] Given these survey findings, Case and Shiller concluded that while the indicators of a bubble were perhaps not as strong in 2003 as they were in 1988 (except in Milwaukee), they were still present. In their concluding remarks, Case and Shiller acknowledged that in the majority of states, home prices seemed to track well with housing-market fundamentals, yet they took the position that a bubble had likely formed:

> Nonetheless, our analysis indicates that elements of a speculative bubble in single-family home prices—the strong investment motive, the high expectations of future price increases, and the strong influence of word-of-mouth discussion—exist in some cities. For the three glamour cities we studied, the indicators of bubble sentiment that we docu-

mented . . . remain, in general, nearly as strong in 2003 as they were in 1988. (Case and Shiller 2003: 341)

The Role of Building Restrictions in Housing Pessimism

Paul Krugman, among others, claimed that the geographic distribution of price increases in the boom years proved the existence of a bubble and the inevitability of a crash. In an August 8, 2005, column for the *New York Times*, Krugman wrote that with respect to housing supply, the United States was really two countries: "Flatland" and the "Zoned Zone":

> In Flatland, which occupies the middle of the country, it's easy to build houses. When the demand for houses rises, Flatland metropolitan areas, which don't really have traditional downtowns, just sprawl some more. As a result, housing prices are basically determined by the cost of construction. In Flatland, a housing bubble can't even get started. But in the Zoned Zone, which lies along the coasts, a combination of high population density and land-use restrictions—hence "zoned"—makes it hard to build new houses. So when people become willing to spend more on houses, say because of a fall in mortgage rates, some houses get built, but the prices of existing houses also go up. And if people think that prices will continue to rise, they become willing to spend even more, driving prices still higher, and so on. In other words, the Zoned Zone is prone to housing bubbles. And Zoned Zone housing prices, which have risen much faster than the national average, clearly point to a bubble. (Krugman 2005)

As the Krugman excerpt illustrates, it is easy to find individual cities (e.g., New York and San Diego) that support a Flatland/Zoned Zone dichotomy. But a more systematic look at the data reveals a more complicated story. Many cities with highly elastic supply curves for housing also experienced rapid increases in prices, especially in the last few years of the housing boom (2002–2005). Moreover, there does not seem to be a negative correlation between the price increase of new homes and the number of new homes built during the boom, as a simple dichotomy would predict.

A recent paper by Saiz (2010) allows a precise look at the correlations between housing-supply elasticities and price increases during the recent U.S.

housing boom. Saiz uses the unique geographic features of different metropolitan areas to construct exogenous housing-supply elasticities. Topographical features that limit new building projects include coastlines, large bodies of water near city centers, and land that is steeply sloped. By calculating the prevalence of these features for each large city in the United States, Saiz constructs housing-supply elasticities that do not rely on the (potentially endogenous) use of legal restrictions that limit the construction of new homes.

Saiz finds that his elasticity measure correlates strongly with changes in housing prices at the level of the metropolitan statistical area (MSA), a finding that we replicate in Figure 2.2. On the vertical axes of each of the three panels in the figure is the percentage change in OFHEO-measured prices from a given time period (1995–2005, 1999–2002, and 2002–2005).[9] The horizontal axes feature the Saiz elasticities for ninety-two U.S. cities that had populations greater than 500,000 as of 2000.[10] As we might expect, cities with very high supply elasticities saw only small increases in housing prices during the three time periods. The two cities on the far right of each panel, with supply elasticities above 5, are Fort Wayne, Indiana (elasticity = 5.36), and Wichita, Kansas (elasticity = 5.45). With elasticities so high, whatever demand increase these cities might have experienced resulted in more supply via new construction, not higher prices.

As we move to the left from these two points, price increases become more common. However, we do not have to move all of the way to the left to find large price increases; many cities with relatively high elasticities (above 1.5) also experienced substantial price increases during the housing boom. Figure 2.3 presents the same data as the previous figure but restricts the sample to cities with elasticities of 3 or less.[11] The fitted regressions lines in these panels also illustrate a negative correlation between supply elasticities and price increases. But these lines also leave a lot of variation unexplained. For example, in panel A of Figure 2.3, which uses data from 1995:Q4 through 2005:Q4, the R^2 of the regression line is only 0.42. The corresponding R^2 for panel B (1999:Q4–2002:Q4) is 0.29, while that for panel C (2002:Q4–2005:Q4) is 0.30.[12]

The takeaway point from Figure 2.3 is that house price increases occurred in many cities where new construction could have occurred with relative ease. We can press this point further by noting that new construction did in fact occur in areas that also had large price increases. For this analysis, we switch to annual state-level data, owing to inconsistencies in the

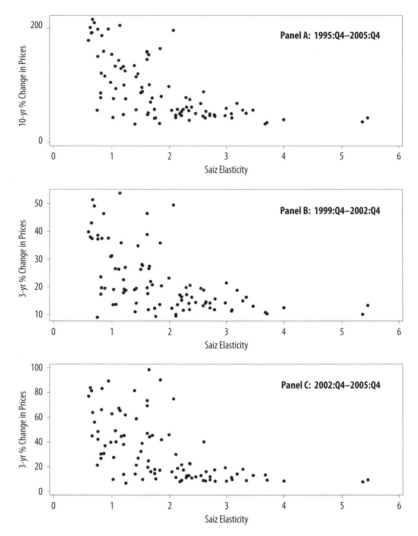

Figure 2.2. House-price growth and supply elasticities in 92 metropolitan areas: 1995–2005. Supply elasticities from Saiz (2010); house prices from the Office of Federal Housing Enterprise Oversight.

reporting of building permits at the city level.[13] Figure 2.4 presents a scatterplot of state-level increases in OFHEO house prices from the three periods against increases in new building permits.[14]

Krugman's Flatland/Zoned Zone theory, combined with a uniform increase in demand across the different states, would predict a negative relation-

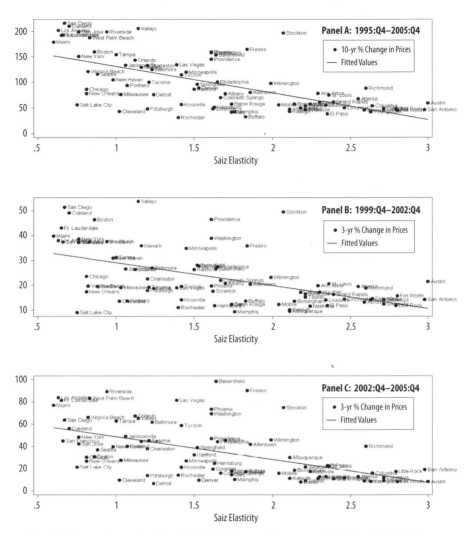

Figure 2.3. House-price growth and supply elasticities in metropolitan areas with Saiz elasticities below 3: 1995–2005. Supply elasticities from Saiz (2010); house prices from the Office of Federal Housing Enterprise Oversight.

ship between price increases and construction. Yet there is little evidence of a negative correlation in this graph. In unreported regressions, we found that the raw correlations between price increases and new construction were actually often positive, though these correlations often declined to insignificance in regressions in which state-level unemployment rates were also included.

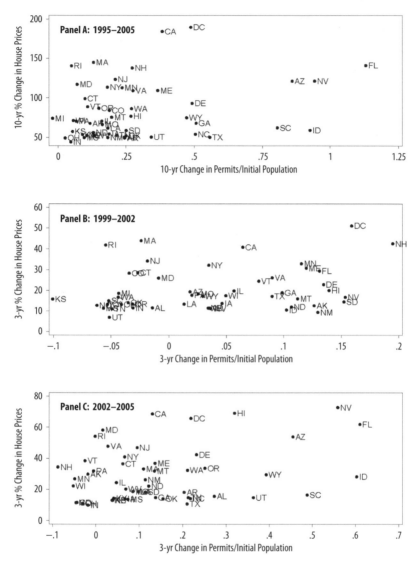

Figure 2.4. House-price appreciation and new construction on the state level: 1995–2005. House prices from the Office of Federal Housing Enterprise Oversight; state-level building permits and initial population levels from the Bureau of the Census.

Of course, raw correlations between highly endogenous variables such as house prices and new construction do not provide airtight evidence for any particular theory of the housing market. But such correlations can provide evidence against theories that predict different correlations. Simply put, it is hard to tell a story that during the housing boom, the main driver of differential price increases across states was varying supply elasticities combined with a uniform increase in demand. It appears that some states with abundant land, such as Arizona, Nevada, and Florida, experienced much larger increases in demand than other states did, including states located on the coasts.[15]

Do our findings suggest that Krugman was mistaken to point to differential price increases in support of the bubble story? Not at all. For one thing, it is true that as a general matter, price-inelastic cities such as New York and Boston saw higher house price increases than did price-elastic cities such as Fort Wayne and Wichita. More to the point, however, one could argue that big price increases in elastic cities such as Las Vegas and Phoenix provided even stronger evidence that bubble psychology had gripped the market. Because there was abundant surrounding land, Las Vegas and Phoenix had been long able to accommodate large numbers of new migrants without big increases in house prices. The fact that some people became willing to buy houses in these cities at prices far above construction costs, especially after 2002, is perhaps a signal that price expectations had become irrational. Unfortunately, the uneven pattern of price increases that we find across U.S. cities was interpreted differently by the anti-bubble camp. This group sometimes conceded that prices in some cities had gotten out of line but argued that a few overheated markets do not necessarily reflect a national housing bubble. Indeed, as a general matter, geographic differences in house price appreciation played a large role in the writings of many anti-bubble economists. (For more on this, see Gyourko 2010.) We turn to a detailed analysis of these arguments in the next section.

The Housing Optimists

Some economists expressed deep skepticism about the possibility of a bubble and went on the record in stating that they did not expect house prices to fall:

> As of the end of 2004, our analysis reveals little evidence of a housing bubble. In high-appreciation markets like San Francisco, Boston and

New York, current housing prices are not cheap, but our calculations do not reveal large price increases in excess of fundamentals. For such cities, expectations of outsized capital gains appear to play, at best, a very small role in single-family house prices. Rather, recent price growth is supported by basic economic factors such as low real long-term interest rates, high income growth and housing price levels that had fallen to unusually low levels during the mid-1990s. (Himmelberg, Mayer, and Sinai 2005)

This quotation comes from the introduction of Himmelberg, Mayer, and Sinai (2005), which became perhaps the most widely cited evidence against a housing bubble upon its publication. The authors offered a persuasive critique of the usual measures marshalled by pro-bubble advocates, including the price-rent ratio and the price-income ratio. Himmelberg, Mayer, and Sinai based their analysis on the more formal "user cost of housing" concept, which recognizes that the cost of owning a house reflects more than the purchase price of the property. For example, other variables that affect the cost of ownership include tax benefits (e.g., the mortgage interest deduction), property taxes, maintenance costs, anticipated capital gains, opportunity costs, and the risk of large capital losses. Therefore studying the ratio of rental costs to *ownership costs* is a more theoretically sound way to investigate whether a bubble may exist than by investigating the ratio of rents to *house prices*. We can write such a relationship as follows:

$$R_t = P_t \cdot \mu_t, \tag{1}$$

where t, the user cost of housing, is defined as

$$\mu_t = r_t^{rf} + \omega_t - \tau_t(r_t^m + \omega_t) + \delta_t - g_{t+1} + \gamma_t. \tag{2}$$

In this expression, r_t^{rf} is the one-year, risk-free interest rate, ω_t is the one-year cost of property taxes, the term $\tau_t(r_t^m + \omega_t)$ represents the tax deductibility of mortgage interest and property taxes (for those that itemize their returns), δ_t reflects maintenance costs, and g_{t+1} is the expected capital gain over a one-year horizon.[16] Finally, γ_t is a risk premium, reflecting the higher risk of owning versus renting.

Equation 1 tells us that the price-rent ratio equals the inverse of the user cost $(1/\mu_t)$, so variation in the price-rent ratio should reflect variation in the user cost of housing. Himmelberg, Mayer, and Sinai (2005) made the correct point that simply looking at time-series variation in price-rent ratios or cross-sectional differences in these ratios without considering possible variation in user costs is misleading and could not shed light on the bubble question.

The right thing to do is to work with careful estimates of user costs in various cities, so the authors constructed measures of user costs for forty-six metropolitan areas from 1980 through 2004. Himmelberg, Mayer, and Sinai compared differences in user costs across cities as well as changes in user costs over time within a city. Their first observation was that user costs can vary greatly across U.S. cities. The highest user-cost market (Pittsburgh) had user costs that were more than double those of the lowest user-cost market (San Jose). In addition, user costs were falling over time and by 2004 were below their long-run averages in most cities. According to equation 1, declining user costs imply rising price-rent ratios. Consequently, the increasing price-rent ratios that were used as evidence to support a bubble actually reflected, in large part, changes in user costs and thus in fundamentals.[17]

To make their analysis more precise, the authors then compared the ratio of imputed rent (calculated by multiplying their user cost estimates by the OFHEO house price index) to actual rent (the BLS index) in 2004 to its 25-year average in each city (figure 2 in their paper). In the vast majority of cities, they found the ratio in 2004 to be very close to or below its 25-year average. Moreover, the cities in which the ratio in 2004 was substantially above its average were not places that had experienced rapid price appreciation (e.g., Detroit, Milwaukee, Minneapolis). The authors also constructed the ratio of imputed rent to per capita income as an alternative measure of housing valuations and came to a similar set of conclusions: The ratio in 2004 was below its 25-year average in most cities in their sample.

Another study that took a skeptical view of the housing bubble was McCarthy and Peach (2004). The paper analyzed the arguments in support of a housing bubble and concluded that there was very little credible evidence:

> Our main conclusion is that the most widely cited evidence of a bubble is not persuasive because it fails to account for developments in the housing market over the past decade. In particular, significant declines in nominal mortgage interest rates and demographic forces have sup-

ported housing demand, home construction, and home values during this period. Taking these factors into account, we argue that market fundamentals are sufficiently strong to explain the recent path of home prices and support our view that a bubble does not exist. (McCarthy and Peach 2004: 2)

The authors' first argument was that the most popular types of house price indices that were used at the time—repeat-sales indices and median price indices—were not very accurate in measuring the value of the U.S. housing stock. Median price indices had the most severe problems. According to McCarthy and Peach, median price indices are too volatile in the short run because the composition of sales fluctuates substantially from month to month. Moreover, the pricing data that are used to construct the indices reflect only recent sales transactions, so they are likely not very representative of the nation's entire housing stock. The repeat-sales indices largely solve these issues, but even these measures cannot control for changes in the quality of the housing stock over time due to depreciation or renovations.

As an alternative price index, the authors advocated the constant-quality new-home price index that is published by the U.S. Bureau of the Census. This is a hedonic index that accounts for changes in the quality of homes over time.[18] Compared to the other price indices, the Census Bureau series showed significantly less home price appreciation over the authors' sample period (1977–2003). The implication was that a significant portion of the house price appreciation that was measured by using the median price and repeat-sales indices was attributable to quality increases. When the authors used the hedonic constant-quality index instead of the repeat-sales index to calculate a time series of the aggregate price-rent ratio, they found much less support for a housing price bubble (see chart 7 in McCarthy and Peach 2004).

The paper then pointed out a list of shortcomings with respect to the most common statistics used by proponents of the housing bubble perspective: the price-income ratio and the price-rent ratio. According to McCarthy and Peach, the first significant drawback of the two statistical series is that they ignore the effect of nominal interest rates. As we discuss below, decreases in nominal interest rates make homeownership more affordable for borrowing-constrained households. Lower nominal rates also lower the opportunity cost of homeownership, as these rates imply lower yields on competing assets.[19] To support their argument, the authors pointed out that from 1990 to 2003, the decline in nominal interest rates resulted in a 130 percent increase in the maximum mortgage debt for which a family earning the median U.S. household income could qualify, using a then-standard maximum debt-income ratio of 27 percent (the debt-income ratio is simply the ratio of the monthly mortgage payment to monthly income).[20]

Finally, McCarthy and Peach used a stylized structural model of the housing market to compare predicted equilibrium prices from the model with actual prices in the data. They then decomposed price changes into contributions from growth factors such as income and consumption as well as from user-cost declines that were largely due to interest-rate movements. According to the model, housing prices were expected to appreciate in the late 1990s and early 2000s, in large part because of a substantial decline in user costs induced by declining interest rates over the period. But more significant is their finding that the model's predicted prices were *greater* than actual prices at the end of the sample period, leading the authors to conclude that U.S. house prices during this period were actually lower than what the fundamentals would justify.

John Quigley is another well-respected real estate economist who was highly skeptical that a housing bubble was present. Along with Christopher Mayer, he was tasked with providing formal comments to the Brookings paper written by Case and Shiller (2003). In those comments (Quigley 2003), he discussed numerous reasons for skepticism about how they interpreted their survey results. In addition, Quigley listed eight specific reasons for questioning the existence of a housing bubble in 2003. First, he pointed to Case and Shiller's finding of a stable co-movement of income and house prices for the large majority of U.S. states. Second, in an argument similar to that of Himmelberg, Mayer, and Sinai (2005), Quigley pointed out that the user cost of housing in the United States had been trending downward since the early 1980s. Third, Quigley noted that demographic trends would probably increase the demand for housing in the United States, a claim that stood in contrast to the discussion in Baker (2002).[21] Fourth, Quigley wrote that the continued desirability of the amenities available in many coastal cities, along with the inelasticity of housing supply in those areas, would put continued upward pressure on prices in many cities.[22] Fifth, Quigley noted the severe downward rigidity in nominal housing prices, which would make large nominal price declines unlikely. Sixth, Quigley claimed that high transactions costs in housing markets would tend to decrease the amount of speculation and trading volume. Seventh, like McCarthy and Peach (2004),

Quigley noted the inability of popular house price indices to capture the increasing quality of U.S. homes. Finally, Quigley emphasized the point that U.S. housing markets are local, so the imperfect correlation across local housing markets would make a large national price decline unlikely.

Of all the pre-crisis papers that were skeptical of the housing bubble, perhaps Smith and Smith (2006) was the most adamant. The paper used a net present value (NPV) framework to calculate the fundamental value of housing in various areas across the United States. The valuation framework that was used was based on the ideas that underpin much of the price-rent analysis discussed above. The starting point is that a house, like any other traded asset, can be valued by calculating the projected stream of future service flows, discounted by an appropriate rate of return. However, unlike a stock, which has only future cash dividends, the future service flows associated with homeownership come from many sources. Some of these flows are largely observable financial variables. Examples include the imputed rent net of mortgage payments as well as expenses such as maintenance costs and property taxes. Yet the service flows to homeownership also include unobservable nonfinancial benefits, such as privacy and the discretion to modify the property. According to this framework, a homebuyer should be able to use projected cash flows and an assumed required rate of return to determine whether the NPV of homeownership is positive or negative. If it is positive, then purchasing the house is a worthwhile investment; if it is negative, renting is the more attractive option. Smith and Smith focus most of their analysis on calculating internal rates of return (IRRs), which are defined as the rates of return that would make NPVs zero. Equivalently, these IRRs are the rates of return that would make potential buyers indifferent between owning and renting.

Smith and Smith's innovation was to obtain estimates of the imputed rent of owner-occupied properties, which are by definition unobservable. This calculation was made possible by using matched data on rental properties in areas with owner-occupied houses of similar quality. Thus the authors could obtain relatively precise estimates of the rental income that the owner-occupied houses would command if they were placed on the rental market. Their data included ten U.S. markets that were representative of both the Flatland and the Zoned Zone: Atlanta, Boston, Chicago, Dallas, Indianapolis, Los Angeles County, New Orleans, Orange County, San Bernardino County, and San Mateo County. The results of their IRR calculations were striking. Only one of the markets (San Mateo County) appeared to be significantly overpriced at the time the paper was written. Moreover, even some widely perceived bubble areas—such as Boston, Chicago, and San Bernardino County—were significantly *underpriced* relative to the estimated fundamental values.

The Housing Agnostics

As we explained in the introduction to this chapter, the most prevalent view among economists in the pre-crisis period was an unwillingness to make strong predictions about the future path of U.S. housing prices. We turn first to Mayer (2003), who investigated the role of real and nominal interest rates in the determination of housing prices. Two important empirical findings in this paper are (1) that real mortgage rates were actually higher in the early 2000s than in the 1970s and not significantly lower in comparison to their levels in the 1990s (figure 3 in Mayer 2003) and (2) that estimates from historical data do not show large correlations between real interest rates and housing prices. Given these results, Mayer pointed toward low nominal rates as perhaps the only rational explanation for the increase in housing prices during the 2001 recession, though he recognized that standard theory predicts that real and not nominal rates should influence housing demand. One way in which nominal prices could matter, Mayer wrote, would be if target payment-income ratios were important in the housing market. If there were some maximum payment-income ratio that lenders refused to exceed for a significant fraction of potential borrowers, then this constraint would essentially be relaxed if the nominal mortgage rate fell. The demand for housing would therefore increase, and prices would rise. However, Mayer was skeptical about this channel, stating:

> There are many reasons to be skeptical of a model in which demand
> for housing is generated by a fixed payment-to-income ratio. For
> example, this model clearly does not hold when one examines
> cross-sectional data for U.S. metropolitan areas, which show that
> consumers do not have a fixed ratio of housing costs to income. Evi-
> dence suggests that homeowners and renters spend a higher per-
> centage of income in high-priced areas like San Francisco than
> in low-priced ones like Milwaukee. So, at least cross-sectionally,
> this theory does not hold. Whether it is true within metropoli-

tan areas, one could make some arguments. Although it is hard
to believe in a target payment-to-income ratio completely, it is the
only model that I can come up with that predicts that lower nominal interest rates will lead to higher home prices. (Mayer 2003: 352)

Haines and Rosen (2007) found evidence that a measure of housing
affordability, driven in large part by changes in nominal mortgage interest rates, was in fact an important determinant of U.S. housing prices in
the period from 1980 to 2006. The paper estimated a reduced-form regression of housing prices on a number of housing supply and demand determinants, including an "affordability index," defined as the ratio of median
household income to the annual payment on a fixed-rate, 30-year, $100,000
mortgage with a 20 percent down payment. The affordability index rises
with either an increase in household income or a decrease in the nominal
mortgage rate, as these movements make it easier for a household to buy a
home at any given price. The authors pooled data across the largest forty-
three MSAs and found that the affordability index was a significant determinant of movements in housing prices over time and price differences
across markets.[23]

In addition to their focus on the relationship between affordability and
house prices, Haines and Rosen (2007) attempted to shed light on whether a
bubble existed in the national housing market. On the one hand, they noted
that most of the academic literature had taken a skeptical view of bubble
claims, writing: "The general consensus of the academic literature is that
home prices are largely in line with fundamentals. Overpriced markets, if
any, are limited in number and in the scope of overpricing" (Haines and
Rosen 2007: 18). However, the authors also pointed out that many non-
academic studies had firmly concluded that a bubble existed; a key example
is a study by Global Insight and National City Corporation (2006). Haines
and Rosen (2007) hypothesized that the difference was due to the use of
more recent data in non-academic research. The publication lag in scholarly journals meant that many recent academic papers had not made use
of data from 2005 and 2006, a period that was beginning to show a soften-
ing in the national housing market. For their part, Haines and Rosen (2007)
ran house-price regressions on data through 2006, using the predicted values from these regressions as proxies for fundamental housing prices. They
then compared these predictions to actual prices at the end of the sample
period. Results were mixed. In many markets, actual 2006 prices were below

predicted prices, while in some other markets, actual prices were 10 to 20 percent above their predicted values. The authors noted that the MSAs that seemed to be the most overvalued according to the model (e.g., New York and San Francisco) had generally been more volatile than the majority of U.S. markets, so the authors downplayed the significance of these findings somewhat. At the end of the day, the authors did not interpret their empirical work as strong evidence for either side of the bubble debate.

Krainer and Wei (2004) was one of the pre-crisis studies that focused on the price-rent ratio. A key contribution of this paper was to study the price-rent ratio for housing using statistical techniques that had been developed to model the *price-dividend* ratio for stocks (see, for example, Campbell and Shiller 1988; Cochrane 1992). Previous stock market research had pointed out that the price-dividend ratio could be decomposed into two terms: one that reflected expected growth in dividends and another that reflected expected future discount rates (or, equivalently, the rates of return that future investors would require). If dividends were expected to rise sharply in the future or if we expected future discount rates to be low, then we would predict that the today's price-dividend ratio would be high. Conversely, if dividends were expected to fall or if we thought that future investors would discount income highly, then investors today would be unwilling to pay high prices for stocks. The current price-dividend ratio would therefore be low. One crucial issue in this line of research is that discount rates are unobservable. Consequently, researchers often proxied for required rates of return with the *actual* rates of return observed in the stock market. In particular, the required rate of return from period t to $t + 1$ was set equal to the sum of the dividend yield in period t and the capital gain in the stock price between periods t and $t + 1$.

To apply this methodology to the housing market, Krainer and Wei constructed a time series of the price-rent ratio at the national level going back to the early 1980s. The numerator of this ratio was the repeat-sales existing house price series from OFHEO. The owner's equivalent rent series from BLS was used for the denominator.[24] The authors then decomposed their price-rent series into movements in future returns (i.e., movements in the proxy for future discount rates) and movements in rent growth. Because this exercise used *actual* future values of dividend growth and rates of return to proxy for *expected* future values of these two variables, the authors could not decompose movements in the price-rent ratio at the end of the sample, as not enough future values of rents and returns were available.

Krainer and Wei reported two main findings. First, they found that future rents and returns did a reasonable job of explaining the total variation in the price-rent ratio. In other words, the price-dividend decomposition that was originally developed to explain the stock market did a good job of explaining patterns in the housing market as well. Second, the authors found that most of the movements in the price-rent ratio could be explained by movements in required rates of return rather than movements in rents.[25]

What did these results imply about the possibility of a bubble in the housing market? On one level, the authors were comforted by the fact that a rational model based on fundamental factors such as future rents and discount factors explained much of the historical variation in the price-rent ratio. "Put another way," Krainer and Wei (2004: 3) wrote, "other factors, such as bubbles, do not appear to be empirically important for explaining the behavior of the aggregate price-rent ratio." Yet the authors had mixed feelings about whether a bubble existed in the current market. Like other researchers, Krainer and Wei used actual returns to proxy for the unobserved discount rates. These returns included capital gains, which are simply changes in prices. Thus the statement that future *discount rates* were likely to explain the high price-rent ratio during the housing boom was really a statement that future *prices* should be expected to move in ways that were unrelated to rents. Specifically, house-price appreciation should slow down, reflecting the lower discount rates required by future investors. These lower discount rates, in turn, could justify the high level of the price-rent ratio at the time the article was written. Of course, there would be no way to know for sure whether movements in future prices had anything to do with future discount rates, because the discount rates are unobservable. All in all, while the model could conceivably explain movements in housing's price-rent ratio in the past, there were no observable factors that conclusively proved that the *current* price-rent ratio did not reflect a bubble. The model could only point out how future prices would be expected to move if a bubble did not exist.

Gallin (2008) also provided a technical analysis of house prices and rents, focusing on the rent-price ratio (which, of course, is simply the inverse of the price-rent ratio discussed above). To construct this ratio, Gallin used a repeat-sales index developed by the Federal Home Loan Mortgage Corporation (Freddie Mac) and a price index for tenants' rent from the BLS.[26] The sample period was 1970 through 2003; although Gallin's paper was published in 2008, the first draft of the paper was completed in 2004, and the data were not updated in the intervening time period. The paper focused on determining how well the rent-price ratio predicts future changes in real rents and house prices. Gallin's first finding was that there is a stable long-run relationship between house prices and rents (or, more formally, that rents and prices are co-integrated over the sample period). Given this finding, he estimated an error-correction model (ECM) to determine how rents and prices fluctuate in the short run around their stable long-run relationship. The ECM model estimates suggested that rents and prices both correct back toward each other, but the findings were inconclusive because the estimates were imprecise. Gallin then turned to an analysis of long-horizon regressions (in contrast to the higher frequency ECM). Specifically, he tested the hypothesis that the rent-price ratio predicts future movements of rents and house prices over a three-year horizon. The data showed that periods of low rent-price ratios were followed by periods in which real rent growth was faster than usual and real house price growth was slower than usual.[27] This observation is consistent with the finding of mean reversion from the ECM estimates. In addition, the response of house prices to the rent-price ratio in returning to the long-run relationship was found to dominate the response of rents.

Gallin concluded that it was reasonable to use the rent-price ratio as a measure of valuation and a gauge for housing price fundamentals. But he was disinclined to interpret the rapid decline in the ratio at the end of his sample period as conclusive evidence of a bubble:

> Because a low rent-price ratio has been a harbinger of sluggish price growth since 1970, it seems reasonable to treat the rent-price ratio as a measure of valuation in the housing market. Indeed, one might be tempted to cite the currently low level of the rent-price ratio as a sign that we are in a house price "bubble." However, several important caveats argue against such a strong conclusion and in favor of future research. (Gallin 2008: 19)

The caveats included potential measurement error in rents and house prices, concerns that the theory motivating the empirical work was too simplistic and ignored important issues such as risk and transactions costs, and misgivings over relying too much on any particular statistic to provide out-of-sample forecasts of a volatile and notoriously unpredictable asset price.

Davis, Lehnert, and Martin (2008) constructed the longest time series of rent-price ratios (to our knowledge), using the Decennial Census of Housing (DCH) to obtain data going all the way back to 1960. The authors used the DCH to construct five benchmark estimates of the average rent-price ratio for the stock of owner-occupied housing.[28] They then used quarterly rent and price indexes (BLS tenants rent index and the Freddie Mac repeat-sales index) to interpolate rent and price data between the DCH years and to extrapolate the data beyond 2000. They found that between 1960 and 1995, the rent-price ratio fluctuated in a relatively narrow range of between 5.0 and 5.5 percent (except for a brief period in the early 1970s when it rose to approximately 6.0 percent). In the period 1995–2006, however, the ratio declined sharply, to a historical low of 3.5 percent. The authors speculated that this dramatic decline could have occurred because of a drop in the discount rate on housing dividends (rents), because of an increase in expected future capital gains, or both. They concluded that a return of the rent-price ratio to its historical average would likely require a modest decline in housing prices: "If the rent-price ratio were to rise from its level at the end of 2006 up to about its historical average value of 5 percent by mid-2012, house prices might fall by 3 percent per year, depending on rent growth over the period" (Davis, Lehnert, and Martin 2008: 280).

This summarizes the views of the agnostics quite nicely. Despite finding fairly convincing evidence that the U.S. housing market was overvalued in 2004–2006, they were unwilling to take a strong position on the existence of a housing bubble for various reasons, including a lack of confidence in the data and ambiguity regarding the predictions of economic theory.

House Price Forecasts and Public Policy

From our review of the pre-crisis housing literature from the early to mid-2000s, it is apparent that well-trained and well-respected economists with the best of motives could and did look at the same data and come to vastly different conclusions about the future trajectory of U.S. housing prices. This is not such a surprising observation once one realizes that the state-of-the-art tools of economic science were not capable of predicting with any degree of certainty the collapse of U.S. housing prices that started in 2006. The asset-pricing literature does not yet have a firm grasp on when and why prices can deviate from market fundamentals for long periods of time. Even the best models have a difficult time explaining many of the extremely large movements in asset prices that have characterized our financial markets in the past, including the stock market crashes of 1929, 1987, and 2000–2002. One wonders how market participants might have responded to a consensus position in the economics profession that housing prices were unsustainable, meaning that highly leveraged bets on housing would be likely to end disastrously. But as this chapter shows, market participants were never forced to respond to such a consensus because consensus did not exist.

While the assumption that asset markets are efficient in an informational sense has undoubtedly improved our understanding of financial markets in many ways, it appears that large and systematic departures from efficiency can and do take place. Concerns that real-world asset markets can be subject to irrational exuberance has been heightened by the results of laboratory experiments, in which bubbles often form in artificial trading environments. Smith, Suchanek, and Williams (1988), a seminal paper in this field, documented that bubbles arose in controlled experiments in which participants had full knowledge of the environment, including the intrinsic dividend value of the asset. In a more recent study, Haruvy, Lahav, and Noussair (2007) followed the same methodology and not only verified the existence of bubbles in controlled settings, but also found substantial evidence of adaptive expectations:

> We find that individuals' beliefs about prices are adaptive, and primarily based on past trends in the current and previous markets in which they have participated. Most traders do not anticipate market downturns the first time they participate in a market, and, when experienced, they typically overestimate the time remaining before market peaks and downturns occur. (Haruvy, Lahav, and Noussair 2007: 1901)

One of the more positive aspects of Haruvy, Lahav, and Noussair's study was the finding that bubbles are much less likely to occur as traders become more experienced. However, in a follow-up study, Hussam, Porter, and Smith (2008) showed that this experience effect is not robust to changes in the underlying environment:

> in order for price bubbles to be extinguished, the environment in which the participants engage in exchange must be stationary and bounded by a range of parameters. Experience, including possible "error" elimination, is not robust to major new environment changes in determin-

ing the characteristics of a price bubble. (Hussam, Porter, and Smith 2008: 924)

These findings seem especially relevant to the experience of housing markets both in the United States and around the world over the past decade. The expansion of housing credit to previously underserved segments of the U.S. population (i.e., to subprime borrowers) meant an influx of new and potentially less financially sophisticated housing-market participants. In addition, the introduction and widespread use of more complicated structured finance products, such as the many types of collateralized debt obligations, implied a rapidly changing menu of financial products.

The evolving landscape of mortgage lending is also relevant to an ongoing debate in the literature about the direction of causality between reduced underwriting standards and higher house prices. Did lax lending standards shift out the demand curve for new homes and raise house prices, or did higher house prices reduce the chance of future loan losses, thereby encouraging lenders to relax their standards? Economists will debate this issue for some time. For our part, we simply point out that an in-depth study of lending standards would have been of little help to an economist trying to learn whether the early to mid-2000s increase in house prices was sustainable. If one economist argued that lax standards were fueling an unsustainable surge in house prices, another could have responded that reducing credit constraints generally brings asset prices closer to fundamental values, not farther away.[29]

In our view, understanding the ways in which economists try to evaluate asset prices in real time is critically important with regard to the direction of future policy. First, it should give substantial pause to those who believe that we can eliminate the formation of bubbles by simply curbing corruption and by imposing more regulation on markets. Because bubbles arise even in the most controlled environments, we may need to acknowledge that we do not currently have the ability to prevent a bubble from forming or the ability to identify a bubble in real time. Instead, we could focus on ensuring that potential homeowners and investors understand the risks associated with their investments and take necessary precautions against such declines. If we have learned anything from this crisis, it is that large declines in house prices are always a possibility, so regulators and policymakers must take them into account when making decisions. A 30 percent fall in house prices over three years may be very difficult, if not impossible, to generate in any plausible econometric model, but a truly robust financial institution must be able to withstand one. The fact that so many professional investors as well as individual households ignored this possibility, even in 2006, suggests that we cannot allow investors to try to time market collapses.

Finally, individual homeownerships should also be robust to significant declines in housing prices. A standard way to do this is by requiring a substantial down payment, which reduces the probability of negative equity when prices fall. In the future, robustness might also be enhanced by requiring the purchase of insurance against house price declines, a financial product that is made at least theoretically possible by the development of new markets in house price risk. At the very least, any policy that encourages buyers to take on loans with low down payments deserves to be evaluated carefully, given the sharp decline in house prices we have recently experienced.

References

Baker, Dean. 2002. "The Run-Up in Home Prices: A Bubble." *Challenge* 45, 6: 93–119.

Brunnermeier, Markus K. 2008. "Bubbles." In *The New Palgrave Dictionary of Economics*, ed. Steven N. Durlauf and Lawrence E. Blume. 2nd ed. Basingstoke: Palgrave Macmillan. http://www.dictionaryofeconomics.com/article?id=pde2008_S000278.

Campbell, John Y., and Robert J. Shiller. 1988. "The Dividend-Price Ratio and Expectations of Future Dividends and Discount Factors." *Review of Financial Studies* 1, 3: 195–228.

Case, Karl E., and Robert J. Shiller. 2003. "Is There a Bubble in the Housing Market?" *Brookings Papers on Economic Activity* (Fall): 299–342.

Cassidy, John. 2002. "The Next Crash." *New Yorker*, November 11, 123–28.

Cochrane, John H. 1992. "Explaining the Variance of Price-Dividend Ratios." *Review of Financial Studies* 5, 2: 243–80.

Davidoff, Thomas. 2010. "Supply Elasticity and the Housing Cycle of the 2000s." Working Paper. Vancouver: Sauder School of Business, University of British Columbia. http://strategy.sauder.ubc.ca/davidoff/shark.pdf.

Davis, Morris, Andreas Lehnert, and Robert Martin. 2008. "The Rent-Price Ratio for the Aggregate Stock of Owner-Occupied Housing." *Review of Income and Wealth* 54, 2: 279–84.

Foote, Christopher L., Kristopher Gerardi, Lorenz Goette, and Paul S. Willen. 2009. "Reducing Foreclosures: No Easy Answers." *NBER Macroeconomics Annual* 22: 89–138.

Gallin, Joshua. 2008. "The Long-Run Relationship Between House Prices and Rents." *Real Estate Economics* 36, 4: 635–58.

Gerardi, Kristopher, Andreas Lehnert, Shane M. Sherlund, and Paul Willen. 2008. "Making Sense of the Subprime Crisis." *Brookings Papers on Economic Activity* (Fall): 69–145.

Global Insight and National City Corporation. 2006. "House Prices in America: Valuation Update for the 2nd Quarter of 2006." http://www.globalinsight.com/gcpath/Q22006report.pdf.

Gyourko, Joseph. 2010. "The Supply Side of Housing Markets." http://www.nber.org/reporter/2009number2/gyourko.html.

Haines, Cabray L., and Richard J. Rosen. 2007. "Bubble, Bubble, Toil, and Trouble?" *FRB Chicago Economic Perspectives.* http://www.chicagofed.org/digital_assets/publications/economic_perspectives/2007/ep_1qtr2007_part2_haines_rosen.pdf.

Haruvy, Ernan, Yaron Lahav, and Charles N. Noussair. 2007. "Traders' Expectations in Asset Markets: Experimental Evidence." *American Economic Review* 97, 5: 1901–20.

Himmelberg, Charles, Christopher Mayer, and Todd Sinai. 2005. "Assessing High House Prices: Bubbles, Fundamentals, and Misperceptions." *Journal of Economic Perspectives* 19, 4: 67–92.

Hussam, Reshmaan N., David Porter, and Vernon L. Smith. 2008. "Thar She Blows: Can Bubbles Be Rekindled with Experienced Subjects?" *American Economic Review* 98, 3: 924–37.

Krainer, John, and Chischen Wei. 2004. "House Prices and Fundamental Value." *FRBSF Economic Letter* (2004–27). San Francisco: Federal Reserve Bank of San Francisco. http://www.frbsf.org/publications/economics/letter/2004/el2004-27.pdf.

Krugman, Paul. 2005. "That Hissing Sound." *New York Times*, August 8, A15.

Laing, Jonathan R. 2005. "The Bubble's New Home." *Barron's Online*, June 20, http://4sarasotahomes.com/images/6-20-05Barrons-Bubble.pdf.

Leamer, Edward E. 2002. "Bubble Trouble? Your Home Has a P/E Ratio Too." *UCLA Anderson Forecast*, June, http://www.anderson.ucla.edu/faculty/edward.leamer/pdf_files/Leamer Forecasts/2002 2006 Bubble Trouble.pdf.

Lo, Andrew W., and A. Craig MacKinlay. 2001. *A Non-Random Walk down Wall Street*. Princeton, N.J.: Princeton University Press.

Mankiw, N. Gregory, and David N. Weil. 1989. "The Baby Boom, the Baby Bust, and the Housing Market." *Regional Science and Urban Economics* 19, 2: 235–58.

Mayer, Christopher. 2003. "[Is There a Bubble in the Housing Market?]. Comments and Discussion." *Brookings Papers on Economic Activity* (Fall): 343–54.

McCarthy, Jonathan, and Richard W. Peach. 2004. "Are Home Prices the 'Next Bubble'?" *Economic Policy Review.* New York: Federal Reserve Bank of New York. http://www.newyorkfed.org/research/epr/04v10n3/0412mcca.pdf.

Pavlov, Andrey D., and Susan M. Wachter. 2006. "Subprime Lending and Real Estate Prices." Zell-Lurie Working Paper. http://papers.ssrn.com/sol3/papers.cfm?abstract_id=1489435.

Quigley, John. 2003. "[Is There a Bubble in the Housing Market?]. Comments and Discussion." *Brookings Papers on Economic Activity* (Fall): 354–58.

Saiz, Albert. 2010. "The Geographic Determinants of Housing Supply." Working Paper. Philadelphia: Wharton School of Business, University of Pennsylvania. http://real.wharton.upenn.edu/~saiz/GEOGRAPHIC%20DETERMINANTS.pdf.

Shiller, Robert J. 2006. "Long-Term Perspectives on the Current Boom in Home Prices." *Economists' Voice* 3, 4: 1–4.

Smith, Margaret Hwang, and Gary Smith. 2006. "Bubble, Bubble, Where's the Housing Bubble?" *Brookings Papers on Economic Activity* (Spring): 1–50.

Smith, Vernon L., Gerry L. Suchanek, and Arlington W. Williams. 1988. "Bubbles, Crashes, and Endogenous Expectations in Experimental Spot Asset Markets." *Econometrica* 56, 5: 1119–51.

Zuckerman, Gregory. 2009. *The Greatest Trade Ever: The Behind-the-Scenes Story of How John Paulson Defied Wall Street and Made Financial History.* New York: Broadway Books.

Notes

We thank Susan Wachter, Jeff Fuhrer, Elizabeth Murry and two anonymous reviewers for helpful comments. The views expressed in this paper are those of the authors and not necessarily those of the Federal Reserve System or the Federal Reserve Banks of Atlanta or Boston.

1. OFHEO regulated the large government-sponsored housing enterprises (Fannie Mae and Freddie Mac) before they were placed into conservatorship in September 2008. OFHEO's regulatory role has been taken over by the Federal Housing Finance Agency (FHFA), which has also continued to produce OFHEO's repeat-sales house price index.

2. According to Shiller (2006), there was a large decline in real prices after World War I that was completely offset by a large increase in prices from 1942 to 1947.

3. In addition, John Cassidy (2002), a journalist at the *New Yorker*, wrote "The Next Crash," a prescient discussion of housing-market valuations relatively early in the boom. Many blogs also followed housing-market developments in real time. "Calculated Risk" was one of the notable blogs that took a pessimistic view of the market.

4. We argue that the fundamental theory of asset pricing is one reason why the agnostic economists were reluctant to predict falling housing prices, but it might not

have been the only reason. Economists at policy institutions might have shied away from making pessimistic predictions for fear of spooking the markets, and economists both inside and outside academia might have been reticent to make any sort of predictions for fear of damaging their reputations if they were wrong.

5. Falling house prices can also cause foreclosures if negative-equity borrowers believe that house prices will not recover in any reasonable length of time—the so-called "ruthless" or "strategic" default.

6. Leamer (2002) conducted a price-rent ratio analysis for a few markets in California and came to mixed conclusions. He found the San Francisco Bay Area to be overvalued in the early 2000s but concluded that prices in the Los Angeles market were more consistent with fundamentals.

7. The volatile states, ordered alphabetically by region, were Connecticut, Massachusetts, New Hampshire, Rhode Island, New Jersey, New York, California, and Hawaii.

8. In an accompanying comment to the Case and Shiller paper, Quigley raises the possibility that the respondents did not understand the concept of compounding interest and might have answered differently if the question had been framed in a slightly different manner.

9. The periods are measured from the fourth quarters of the given years, so the 1995–2005 span covers 1995:Q4–2005:Q4, and so forth.

10. There are actually ninety-five U.S. cities that meet this population criterion. However, there are no OFHEO price indexes for Ventura, California; Sarasota, Florida; and Jersey City, New Jersey. Therefore the panels of Figure 2.3 have only ninety-two data points each.

11. This restriction generates a legible graph that includes the names of the remaining cities. Eleven cities are eliminated by this restriction, so each panel of Figure 2.3 has eighty-one cities.

12. Including the square of the Saiz elasticity raises the R^2 by less than .04 in all cases. Linear regressions that include all ninety-two cities in Figure 2.3 have R^2s of .39 (1995–2005), .30 (1999–2002), and .32 (2002–2005).

13. We found that tabulations of city-level building permits were less consistent than the price data from OFHEO, owing to definitional changes for metropolitan areas that occurred in the mid-2000s (which is our main period of interest). Nevertheless, we investigated the relationship between new construction and price increases for about seventy cities that we could match. Our results were consistent with the state-level evidence presented here.

14. The absolute changes in building permits are divided by the state's initial population.

15. Davidoff (2010) makes a similar point but does not use the Saiz elasticities. He shows that coastal markets saw greater average price growth during the boom but did not experience greater crashes or greater volatility than non-coastal areas, where supply elasticities are assumed to be larger.

16. The g_{t+1} term is negative if capital losses are expected. The authors use the average one-year growth rate of housing prices from the period 1940–2000 in each MSA to proxy for g_{t+1}.

17. In this exercise, the authors were not comparing user costs across cities but were looking only at trends within cities over a 25-year period. In this exercise, variation in user costs does not come from assumptions about cross-city variation in expected capital gains (the g_{t+1} term), as the authors set expected capital gains in each city to the one-year average realized return calculated over the entire 25-year period. Thus by assumption, there was no variation in expected capital gains across cities.

18. A hedonic index is constructed by regressing sale prices on various housing and neighborhood characteristics.

19. In standard versions of asset-pricing theory, which do not include borrowing constraints, the real interest rate, not the nominal rate, should matter for housing valuations. Whether the real or the nominal interest rate matters more in practice is a topic we return to below.

20. This is the same argument that Mayer (2003) discussed in his effort to rationalize a role for nominal rates in house price increases (although he was skeptical of this channel). We discuss this argument in more detail later.

21. Unlike Baker, who argued that the baby boomers would likely downsize their homes as they crossed the retirement threshold, Quigley (2003: 357) argued that they would "continue to resist downsizing."

22. Note the contrast with Krugman on this point. Quigley saw higher prices in coastal areas as evidence that prices were in line with fundamentals, while Krugman argued that coastal areas were more bubble-prone.

23. The R^2 of a univariate regression was .76.

24. Krainer and Wei found that this ratio had substantially increased in the early 2000s after having been roughly flat over the previous 15 years. As we saw in Figure 2.1, there was a dramatic rise in the price-rent ratio from around 1.0 in the late 1990s to nearly 1.4 by 2006.

25. This result is similar to what Cochrane (1992) found in a decomposition of the price-earnings ratio in equity markets.

26. Gallin used the tenant's rent index rather than the owner's equivalent rent index because of the former's superior time series coverage.

27. In these regressions, Gallin controlled for the user cost of housing.

28. They estimated imputed rents using data on rental properties and a hedonic regression technique to map the rental property data to owner-occupied houses.

29. For an early discussion of credit's impact on pricing, see Pavlov and Wachter (2006).

Chapter 3

Exploring the Determinants of High-Cost Mortgages to Homeowners in Low- and Moderate-Income Neighborhoods

Michael S. Barr, Jane K. Dokko, and Benjamin J. Keys

In spite of the recent impetus to reform home mortgage markets, particularly as they affect low- and moderate-income (LMI) households, little systematic evidence is available about how potential abuses in mortgage lending manifest in the mortgages held by those households. While racial discrimination in mortgage markets has a long history in the United States, the role of mortgage brokers in lending has only recently increased and become controversial.[1] In this chapter, we uncover two mechanisms through which differential mortgage pricing occurs among LMI homeowners: black borrowers and borrowers who use mortgage brokers pay more for mortgage loans than other borrowers, after controlling for a wide variety of factors.

To the best of our knowledge, this is the first robust household-level survey to report data on different dimensions of high-cost mortgage pricing, such as balloon payments, up-front points and fees, "teaser" rates, and prepayment penalties, along with whether a household uses a mortgage broker.[2] We exploit a new micro-dataset, the Detroit Area Household Financial Services study, which we designed and implemented with the Survey Research Center of the University of Michigan. The dataset links household and mortgage characteristics to describe mortgage pricing among LMI households, their creditworthiness and attitudes about borrowing, and their use of mortgage brokers. Especially noteworthy is that the survey was conducted at the height of the subprime lending boom in 2005 and 2006 and in a state— Michigan—where anti-predatory lending statutes were relatively weak.

We establish a profile of the demographic characteristics of homeowners in LMI neighborhoods in the Detroit metropolitan area.[3] We then estimate differences in mortgage pricing arising between these homeowners and include as much available information about the borrower as possible to account for the demand-driven explanations that are correlated with race or using a mortgage broker for the high costs some homeowners pay. We focus on the intensive margin of differences in pricing rather than on how lenders may limit access to credit, ration credit, or require prohibitively high down payments. The characteristics of mortgages may differ across borrowers because of their incomes, the size of their down payments, their taste for risk, their creditworthiness, and their willingness to shop around for the best terms. While our approach cannot completely rule out these demand-driven explanations, our descriptive results are most consistent with supply-driven origins for differences in loan terms.

We find that within similar low-income neighborhoods, black homeowners pay higher interest rates—110 basis points, on average—than similar non-black homeowners, and are more than twice as likely to have prepayment penalties or balloon payments attached to their mortgages than non-black homeowners, even after we control for age, income, gender, creditworthiness, and a proxy for default risk. In addition, we observe that borrowers who used a mortgage broker are over 60 percent more likely to pay points or fees than those who did not use a broker.

The heterogeneity in pricing that we observe across racial groups and across transaction types (broker versus non-broker) is unexplained after accounting for many demand-driven explanations that we present in greater detail later in the chapter. However, there may be other potentially important sources of heterogeneity that are unobservable to us but may be observed by the lender, such as more precise measures of income volatility or earlier documentation of income and assets (see Edelberg 2007 for a discussion of these issues). Our approach cannot distinguish between racial differences in pricing and the presence of omitted financial characteristics that are correlated with race but are not included in our data. Nonetheless, a well-functioning mortgage market should eliminate the disparate treatment of minority borrowers and of borrowers who use mortgage brokers.

Our analysis sheds light on the average homeowner's experience in Detroit's LMI neighborhoods, which are similar to many rust belt communities such as Cleveland, Ohio, or Gary, Indiana.[4] The differences in loan terms by race, particularly in the up-front costs, which are not formally collected by fair lending enforcement mechanisms such as the Home Mortgage Disclosure Act (HMDA), suggest that collecting and scrutinizing a broader set of loan terms might be a way to extend our analysis to other types of communities.[5] The prevalence of brokers in this market and the finding that so many borrowers are presented with just a single mortgage option (and therefore know little about alternatives) potentially provide empirical support for models of predatory lending in which lenders use an informational advantage to their benefit (e.g., Bond, Musto, and Yilmaz 2009). These results provide new insights into the ways in which brokers operated in LMI communities and help researchers to understand the full costs of homeownership to LMI borrowers.

Data and Summary Statistics

The Detroit Area Household Financial Services Study

We use a unique dataset to analyze homeownership in LMI neighborhoods. We created the Detroit Area Household Financial Services (DAHFS) study to gain a richer understanding of low- and moderate-income households' finances and housing costs and their financial services behavior and attitudes. The DAHFS study is the first survey to use a random, stratified sample to explore the full range of financial services used by low- and moderate-income households, along with systematic measures of household preference parameters and financial services supply. The survey data also contain a detailed set of demographic and socioeconomic variables, including employment, sources of income, household savings behavior and asset levels, and a wide range of financial services behaviors and attitudes.

No other randomized survey contains such a rich set of information pertaining to LMI household experiences regarding financial services and homeownership, including measures of creditworthiness and mortgage default risk (see Barr, Dokko, and Keys 2009 for a more detailed description of the data and sample). Unlike other datasets that do not directly observe up-front costs such as points and fees (e.g., Haughwout, Mayer, and Tracy

2009), the DAHFS study has the unique advantage of providing information to obtain a more detailed picture of the total costs of a mortgage. The survey questions about housing, homeownership, and mortgage finance make up a portion of the overall survey. All information from the survey is based on respondents' self-reports of their mortgages and experiences and therefore is not validated by administrative data; however, interviewers encouraged respondents to consult their mortgage and tax documents when answering more financially detailed questions. Consistent with Bucks and Pence (2008), not all homeowners knew all aspects of their mortgage contracts. These responses are treated as "missing" and were excluded from the analysis.[6]

The Survey Research Center (SRC) at the University of Michigan interviewed households from July 2005 through March 2006. All interviews were computer-assisted and conducted in person, usually at the respondent's home. The average interview length was 76 minutes. SRC completed 1,003 interviews and achieved a response rate of 65 percent. The sample members were selected to form a stratified random sample of the Detroit metropolitan area (Wayne, Oakland, and Macomb Counties).[7] We drew sample members from census tracts with median incomes that are 0 to 60 percent ("low"), 61 to 80 percent ("moderate"), and 81 to 120 percent ("middle") of the Detroit area's median income of $49,057 (U.S. Census Bureau 2000). This chapter uses only those households in the low- and moderate-income strata, with a final sample size of 938 respondents.

Reflecting the demographics of the Detroit area, 69 percent of those surveyed in the LMI subsample of the DAHFS study are African American, 20 percent are white, and 2 percent identify themselves as Arab American (Table 3.1). The remaining 9 percent are Asian, Hispanic, or respondents in other racial categories. Because of this nearly bimodal distribution of race, we focus on black and non-black comparisons of mortgage pricing terms later in the chapter. The respondents, like many Detroit residents, are long-term residents; over 90 percent have lived in the Detroit area for more than 10 years. The Detroit area has a sizable low-income population. Over one third of respondents live on an income that is considered to be below the federal poverty line, and 30 percent of the sample never completed high school. The demographics of the DAHFS study reflect the national demographics of LMI households: largely African American female-headed households, living close to the federal poverty line. Also, the DAHFS sample looks similar to households in LMI census tracts in the Detroit area (see Barr, Dokko, and Keys 2009 for a table with this comparison).

Table 3.1. Demographic Characteristics of DAHFS Study Sample

	All	Rent	Own	Own Outright	Own Mortgage
Age					
18–24	11.9	66.9	33.2	29.0	71.0
25–60	71.8	57.3	42.7	26.1	73.9
61 and up	16.3	31.4	68.7	66.2	33.8
Race					
African American	68.6	58.3	41.7	38.7	61.3
White	20.3	41.0	59.0	33.7	66.3
Asian	2.1	69.2	30.8	34.7	65.3
Hispanic	3.5	56.7	43.3	41.7	58.3
Arab	1.9	32.0	68.0	0.0	100.0
Other	3.6	60.1	39.9	28.8	71.2
Educational Attainment					
Less than high school diploma	29.6	61.5	38.5	47.9	52.1
High school diploma or equivalent	23.0	58.9	41.2	37.9	62.1
More than high school diploma	47.4	48.1	51.9	30.4	69.7
Gender					
Male	35.8	48.1	51.9	36.8	63.2
Female	64.2	58.1	41.9	35.8	64.2
Time in Detroit					
<2 years	1.8	80.3	19.7	0.0	100.0
2–5 years	3.3	71.1	28.9	0.0	100.0
5–10 years	4.1	59.9	40.1	16.7	83.3
10+ years	31.3	49.0	51.0	42.1	57.9
Whole life	59.5	55.5	44.5	35.7	64.3
Marital Status					
Married	19.7	27.7	72.3	24.6	75.4
Cohabiting	4.1	61.0	39.0	19.8	80.2
Divorced/separated	21.6	57.8	42.2	34.1	65.9
Widowed	9.0	36.2	63.8	67.3	32.7
Never Married	45.6	68.1	31.9	39.7	60.3
Homeownership Status					
Rent	54.6				
Own	45.4				

Table 3.1 (Continued)

				Own	
	All	*Rent*	*Own*	*Outright*	*Mortgage*
Homeowners:					
Mortgage Status					
Own outright	35.2				
Have mortgage	62.1				
Have land contract	2.7				
Annual Household Income					
Mean	$28,163	$19,399	$39,530	$33,006	$45,506
Median	$20,000	$12,500	$30,000	$23,000	$38,000
Average Monthly Mortgage/Rent Payment					
Mean		$497	$660		
Median		$500	$650		
Annual Home Payment *(calculated based on above)*					
Mean		$5,958	$7,920		
Median		$6,000	$7,800		
Annual Payment to Annual Income Ratio					
Mean		0.80	0.29		
Median		0.36	0.19		
Sample Size	938	503	419	237	135

Note: This paper uses only the low- and moderate-income households interviewed by the DAHFS. Sample weights are used throughout to make the sample representative of the Detroit area LMI population. Payment-to-income ratio calculated by using annual household income and annual rent/mortgage payment. 922 respondents answered the own/rent question.

Characteristics of Homeowners

In the DAHFS study, 922 out of 938 respondents answered questions about their housing situation. Nearly half of the sample, 45 percent, owned their homes. This proportion is well below the national average of 69 percent and the Midwest average of 73 percent (Joint Center for Housing Studies 2006) but is roughly consistent with the nationwide homeownership rate for blacks (49 percent) as well as for LMI households (see Bucks, Kennick-ell, Mach, and Moore 2009). The relatively low rates of homeownership in the sample reflect the difficulty LMI households in general, and minorities in particular, have in accumulating assets.

As shown in Table 3.1, older households were much more likely to own their homes. Respondents who were over age sixty were twice as likely to own their homes than eighteen- to twenty-four-year-olds, with an owner-ship rate of 69 percent compared to just 33 percent for the younger cohort. White respondents in the DAHFS were 20 percent more likely to own their homes than blacks. The degree of homeownership among whites in LMI areas, 59 percent, is still well below nationwide homeownership rates. More educated and married households were also much more likely to own their homes relative to their less educated and unmarried counterparts. Female-headed households owned their homes only 42 percent of the time in the sample. Importantly, homeowners also had significantly larger annual incomes than renters; owners' average income was nearly double that of renter households.

On the basis of the DAHFS survey data, we calculate a measure of home equity, which is defined by the self-reported "hypothetical selling price" minus any outstanding amount remaining on all mortgages, including second liens.[8] The median level of home equity is $45,000, a substantial amount of money for families with moderate income and few or no alter-native sources of wealth. The median purchase price of housing is $38,000, while the median stated selling price is $88,900, significantly below the Mid-west average but consistent with actual sales prices in Detroit.[9] The median amount remaining on a mortgage is $54,000.

By one measure, annual housing costs are much less burdensome for homeowners than for renters. While the median mortgage payment is higher than median rent in our sample ($650/month versus $500/month), this comparison does not capture the fact that homeowners earn signifi-cantly more income each year. Defining housing outlays as the annual payments toward housing (either mortgage payments or rent) divided by annual income, median housing outlays for homeowners are only 20 per-cent of annual income, and this figure does not include homeowners who own their homes outright and so have only maintenance, insurance, and property tax costs. In contrast, median housing outlays for renters are dou-ble this amount; renters in the DAHFS pay on average 35 percent of their annual income toward housing. This juxtaposition actually may understate the value of homeownership for some households, since the mortgage payments are reported without considering the increase to after-tax income from the mortgage interest deduction or the fact that the payments include the payment of principal, which increases the homeowner's net worth.

An alternative way to view the relationship between payments and income is to compute annual payment to income ratios. Homeowners earn twice as much as renters, yet mortgage payments are roughly 1.3 times greater than monthly rent. Consequently, the annual payment to annual income ratio is much lower for homeowners than for renters, whose housing payments make up a larger portion of their household income. In this respect, homeownership seems advantageous in the sense that a higher percentage of income can be distributed towards non-housing expenses.

Reasons for Delaying Payment and Measuring the Risk of Default

In addition to household demographics, the DAHFS survey collected information on the creditworthiness of homeowners. Specifically, measures of creditworthiness include whether the household has a bank account, whether the household has ever been denied a loan during the three years before the survey interview, whether the household typically pays less than the minimum amount on a credit card bill, whether the household has ever filed for bankruptcy, whether the household has ever had a bank account closed because of poor credit, and whether the household is behind on any vehicle loans.[10] These are some of the measures that credit bureaus use to create summary indices of creditworthiness, such as the FICO score.[11] However, our measures are taken at the time of the survey rather than when the mortgage was approved, so it is possible that the survey measures do not fully capture the borrower's creditworthiness observed by the lender when the mortgage was originated.

In our sample of homeowners, 84 percent of households had a bank account. Non-black households were 5.5 percent more likely to have an account. Six percent of the sample had been denied a loan in the past three years. Fewer than 1 percent reported that they paid less than the minimum on their credit cards, and only 1 percent said that they had had a bank account closed because of poor credit. Of homeowners in the DAHFS report, 15 percent reported that they had filed for bankruptcy at some point; 3 percent were behind on their vehicle loans.

We use borrowers' self-reports of whether they have had problems paying their mortgage as a measure of (ex post) default risk. In the survey, we ask whether households have delayed their mortgage payment for one month or longer, or are past due on their mortgage at the time of the survey interview. We combine these two reasons into one indicator variable that is intended to capture the likelihood of delinquency and default, in addition to our measures of creditworthiness. Ex post default risk serves as a proxy for a more complete model of ex ante risk used in lenders' risk-based pricing models and matrices. If lenders possessed all information about the determinants of default, this variable would be, on average, little different from one measuring ex ante default risk, such as a credit score.

There are two caveats to using self-reports of problems paying the mortgage as a measure of ex ante default risk. First, if lenders charge higher prices to blacks based on race, and this leads more black homeowners to default, then ex post default risk would be positively correlated with the likelihood of being black (Apgar, Duda, and Gorey 2005). In this case, controlling for ex post default would lead us to understate the differences in pricing between blacks and non-blacks. Second, most missed payments do not lead to foreclosure, as borrowers cure. While the self-reported measures might overstate the level of default risk, we do not expect the degree of overstatement to be systematically different for blacks and whites, leaving the difference in self-reported default risk little different from the true difference. All told, the inclusion of this variable is a conservative approach to control for unobservable risk characteristics of the household, which may be available to the lender at the time of mortgage origination.

It is fairly common for homeowners in the DAHFS to have problems paying their mortgages between the time of loan origination and the survey interview. Roughly one third of homeowners who were still paying their mortgages said that they had delayed payment for a month or more (Table 3.2). Forty percent of those who had ever delayed paying their mortgage cited a job loss or unemployment as the reason for falling behind, while 24 percent said that they had too many other bills to pay, 8 percent cited unexpected medical expenses, and 12 percent cited emergencies. Those who had delayed payment also were more likely to be black; 34 percent of black homeowners had fallen behind at some point compared to 25 percent of non-black homeowners.

Table 3.2. Mortgage Characteristics in the DAHFS

	All Owners	Black	Non-Black	Difference	Adjusted Difference
Number of mortgages currently outstanding					
0	2.2	1.6	3.1	−1.5	
1	89.5	88.4	91.1	−2.7	
2	8.3	10.0	5.8	4.2	
Loan obtained through a mortgage broker	58.4	57.4	60.0	−2.7	−2.9
Broker offered loans from more than one lender	32.6	34.6	29.9	4.7	−5.5
Points or fees paid up front	28.5	29.5	27.0	2.5	0.0
Amount paid	$2,255	$2,829	$1,488	$1,341*	$1,112
Amount currently owed	$56,024	$54,964	$57,575	−$2,611	−$1,394
Current annual rate of interest (APR) on mortgage	7.4	7.8	6.7	1.1†	1.1†
Adjustable-rate mortgage (ARM)	29.3	32.1	25.1	7.0	3.8
Amount of most recent payment	$660	$654	$668	−$14	−$14
Payment includes property taxes and insurance	59.8	56.4	64.7	−8.3	−6.6
Payment record					
Ahead of schedule	13.1	11.2	15.9	−4.7	
Behind schedule	5.4	5.8	5.0	0.8	
On schedule	81.5	83.1	79.1	4.0	
Mortgage has prepayment penalty	23.3	28.6	15.3	13.3†	15.8†
Mortgage has balloon payment	11.1	14.8	5.7	9.1†	9.3†
Ever delayed paying the mortgage for a month or more	30.4	33.8	25.4	8.4	6.5
Refinanced the original mortgage	49.2	47.3	51.9	−4.6	−7.2

(continued on next page)

Table 3.2 (Continued)

	All Owners	Black	Non-Black	Difference	Adjusted Difference
Reasons for refinancing					
Get better terms	36.4	37.7	34.7	3.0	
Borrow additional money on your home equity	17.5	17.2	17.9	−0.7	
Both	46.2	45.2	47.5	−2.3	
Refinance because a broker or lender recommended it	20.2	18.9	21.9	−3.0	0.0
Number of observations	419	263	156		

Source: DAHFS.

*Significant at the 10 percent level; †significant at the 5 percent level. Significance is noted if, controlling for age, gender, income, creditworthiness, and loan performance, the difference between black and non-black owners is significant at the 10 percent level. Creditworthiness is measured by indicators for whether the homeowner has a bank account, has been denied a loan, has filed for bankruptcy, has had a bank account closed due to poor credit, pays less than the minimum due on a credit card, or is behind on a vehicle loan. Loan performance measures are whether the owner has ever delayed a mortgage payment and whether the owner is currently behind on the mortgage payment. Significance is qualitatively unchanged if the difference between black and non-black owners is estimated.

Mortgage Pricing

In the DAHFS, many homeowners held mortgages that had the characteristics of a subprime loan. Over 10 percent of the homeowners in our sample had interest rates above 10 percent, which is the HUD-Treasury definition of "D" class subprime lending (4 percentage points above prime) (U.S. Department of Housing and Urban Development and U.S. Department of the Treasury 2000).[12] In contrast, on July 1, 2005, when we began collecting survey responses, the prime offer rate was 5.5 percent, according to the Federal Home Loan Mortgage Corporation. More than half the sample paid above prime interest rates; the median reported annual percentage rate (APR) was 6.9 percent.[13] On average, the current annual interest being charged on a mortgage for all respondents was 7.4 percent.

Sixty percent of homeowners with a mortgage used a mortgage broker. Although one of the financial functions of a mortgage broker is to provide buyers and sellers with opportunities to find the best fit in mortgage product and price, only one third of those who used a mortgage broker were offered a loan from more than one lender. Put another way, two thirds of those who used a mortgage broker likely received little benefit from the shopping services brokers provide, despite their high costs. However, it might be that had these households not used a broker, they would not have been able to obtain any loan. We explore this possibility in more detail later in this chapter.

The costs of obtaining a mortgage are seemingly high. Approximately 29 percent of mortgage-holding respondents paid points or fees to acquire the loan; it does not appear that these points resulted in a reduction in interest rate. Median amounts are 2 points or $2,000 in fees, significant costs for access to the credit market. Over one fourth of the homeowners in our sample had adjustable-rate mortgages (ARMs). At the time of the survey, the median APR was 6.9 percent, with a mean of 7.4 percent. In the region, one-year ARMs were 4.8 percent in July 2005, while five-year ARMs were at 5.5 percent. Our finding of rates well above those posted suggests that homeowners, on average, are paying more than average market rates for mortgage borrowing.

Nearly one fourth (23 percent) of the LMI homeowner sample had prepayment penalties written into their mortgages, which results in an additional fee if these borrowers decide to repay their mortgage (by either paying off the balance or refinancing) within, typically, the first two to three years after origination of the loan. In comparison, at the national level, only 2 percent of prime loans include a prepayment penalty, whereas an estimated 80 percent of subprime loans include this surcharge (Farris and Richardson 2004; Goldstein and Son 2003). In our study, 11 percent of homeowners have a balance payable, or balloon payment, when their loans are due. While the inclusion of balloon payments in mortgage contracts is controversial, one benefit is that they allow borrowers to pay less each month at the expense of a large future payment. However, balloon payments may mask the true costs of homeownership to the extent that borrowers take out larger loan balances or pay higher rates or fees for the same monthly payment as a mortgage without a balloon payment. Balloon payments may prove difficult to make or refinance at the time they are due.

Among those who reported being behind on their payments at the time of the survey interview, 31 percent had a prepayment penalty, and 20 percent faced a balloon balance at the end of their mortgage contract. Consistent with these correlations, Quercia, Stegman, and Davis (2005) report that mortgages with prepayment penalties attached are 20 percent more likely to be foreclosed than those mortgages without, and the effect for balloon payments is even larger; such loans are 50 percent more likely to foreclose. The relationship between these high-cost mortgage features and the likelihood of default is an equilibrium outcome when lenders tailor mortgages to borrowers based on their risk characteristics.

Heterogeneity in Mortgage Pricing

Differences in race and the use of a mortgage broker are two channels by which differences in mortgage pricing arise among LMI homeowners. Our approach compares observably similar borrowers who differ along one of these characteristics. We compare differences in prices paid by black and non-black borrowers as well as those paid by borrowers using and not using a mortgage broker, and we assess whether these differences are attributable to differences in demographic characteristics, employment, income, creditworthiness, and default risk. These comparisons provide unbiased estimates of the differences in mortgage pricing if these groups are also, on average, unobservably similar (such as in terms of their default risk or the moral stigma they associate with not repaying their debt).[14] But if, for example, blacks are more (or less) likely to default on their mortgages, a simple comparison of interest rates between blacks and non-blacks would overstate (or understate) the true difference in pricing. However, in the DAHFS study's cross-sectional sample of borrowers, as in any cross section, we do not observe all information about the borrower, particularly the information that lenders use to price loans. Instead, in the discussion below, we describe the variables available in the DAHFS study and discuss how including these variables addresses the biases that are likely to arise.

Racial Dispersion

Overall, our results support the view that observably similar blacks and whites receive different loan terms along most, though not all, dimensions of their mortgage contracts. First, we find that black homeowners have interest rates that are 1.1 percentage points greater than those of whites (see Table 3.2). Because blacks and whites differ in many observable dimensions, in Tables 3.3a and 3.3b we present regression-adjusted differences in mortgage pricing between these two groups of homeowners.[15] Since we are simply interested in characterizing the average differences in pricing between blacks and non-blacks, we use ordinary least squares to estimate these differences. In Table 3.3a, we show how the interest rate difference seen in Table 3.2 is unaffected by adjusting for income, loan size, home value, origination date, creditworthiness, and default risk.[16] In other words, this point estimate of 110 basis points does not vary with the inclusion of the borrower characteristics that a lender would observe to gauge default risk. The magnitude of this result upon controlling for default risk is particularly striking, since blacks are more likely to delay their mortgage payment or be behind on their mortgage, and the point estimate does not decrease once we include this variable. This result suggests that blacks obtain loans with higher interest rates, on average, and the disparity is not explained by the observable creditworthiness or default risk of the borrower.[17]

This sizable black-white difference in interest rates is larger than previous estimates that control for default risk (Courchane 2007), or those found in studies of HMDA data, which contain data on both high-priced mortgages and race. The APRs for high-priced originations in the 2005 and 2006 HMDA data differ between blacks and whites by 49 to 56 basis points (see table 12 of Avery, Brevoort, and Canner 2007). However, this disparity accounts only for the intensive margin of the difference in high-cost loans, as loans with APRs below the high-price threshold need not report their APR. The black-white difference of the likelihood of appearing in the high-cost sample (i.e., the extensive margin) is 29.8 percent, since 47 percent of blacks receive loans classified as higher-priced, as opposed to only 17.2 percent of whites (see table 11 of Avery et al. 2007). Our sample is of all mortgages, not just high-priced mortgages, so it is plausible that the combination of both the intensive margin and the extensive margin would lead to estimated black-white differences in interest rates that are much larger than the difference that was observed on the intensive margin alone.

Next, we examine points and fees, balloon payments, and prepayment penalties, since, in principle, the inclusion of these mortgage terms may result in lower interest rates. Overall, we do not find this to be the case. Inclusion of these terms does not lower interest rates and black households

Table 3.3a. Regression Version of Mortgage Characteristics Table: Amount of Fees and APR

	Amount of Fees			APR		
	(4)	(5)	(6)	(7)	(8)	(9)
Black	1001	781.8	736.1	1.165‡	1.126‡	1.009‡
	(750.4)	(879.5)	(1007)	(0.399)	(0.353)	(0.352)
Female	195.9	53.87	1942	−0.350	−0.124	−0.127
	(968.3)	(894.4)	(1423)	(0.396)	(0.454)	(0.471)
Age 25–60	−1472	−1658	−2877	0.450	0.600	0.315
	(1099)	(1543)	(2398)	(0.569)	(0.557)	(0.572)
Age 61+				−0.347	−0.145	−0.369
				(0.930)	(1.062)	(1.054)
Married	−772.2	−1505	−2103	−0.213	−0.288	−0.323
	(910.3)	(1054)	(1286)	(0.414)	(0.452)	(0.438)
Income		−0.0762	0.0527		−8.64e-05	−9.63e-05*
		(0.104)	(0.0908)		(5.22e-05)	(5.09e-05)
Income^2		1.52e-06	−1.56e-07		1.38e-09	1.58e-09*
		(1.72e-06)	(1.39e-06)		(8.62e-10)	(8.55e-10)
Income^3		−0	0		−0	−0*
		(0)	(0)		(0)	(0)
Delayed paying mortgage			49.79			0.915†
			(739.3)			(0.417)
Banked			−2692			−0.0645
			(3610)			(0.787)
Denied a loan			5755			0.691
			(4148)			(0.672)
Pay less than minimum on credit card						1.727
						(2.841)
Ever bankrupt			756.1			0.567
			(2101)			(0.412)
Ever account closed because of poor credit			−1592			−1.787‡
			(2423)			(0.679)
Behind on vehicle loan			−567.1			0.689
			(2245)			(1.006)
Purchase price	0.0428	0.0371	0.0491	−6.18e-06	−7.01e-06	−8.70e-06
	(0.0375)	(0.0291)	(0.0345)	(5.50e-06)	(5.61e-06)	(5.69e-06)

Table 3.3a (Continued)

	Amount of Fees			APR		
	(4)	*(5)*	*(6)*	*(7)*	*(8)*	*(9)*
Value if sold today	−0.0137 (0.0136)	−0.0152 (0.0154)	−0.00529 (0.0166)	2.99e-06 (4.37e-06)	1.31e-06 (4.94e-06)	4.84e-06 (5.31e-06)
Loan remaining	−0.0167 (0.0240)	−0.0184 (0.0246)	−0.0492 (0.0302)	−9.03e-06 (6.82e-06)	−5.61e-06 (7.06e-06)	−8.01e-06 (7.28e-06)
Refinance	961.8 (639.9)	1014 (729.2)	2774* (1385)	−0.687† (0.344)	−0.761† (0.357)	−0.660* (0.365)
Date of purchase controls?	Yes	Yes	Yes	Yes	Yes	Yes
Observations	39	37	37	173	163	163
R^2	0.295	0.406	0.573	0.174	0.217	0.264

Robust standard errors in parentheses. DAHFS sample weights used in all regressions.
*Significant at the 10 percent level; †significant at the 5 percent level. ‡significant at the 1 percent level.

pay higher fees and are more likely to have balloon payments and prepayment penalties than non-black borrowers.

Blacks pay roughly twice the amount in fees or points that whites pay (see Table 3.2). Black respondents paid roughly $2,829 up front in fees, whereas non-black respondents paid roughly $1,488. Owing to very small sample sizes, this difference is not statistically significant after controlling for demographics, income, and creditworthiness. However, the magnitude of the adjusted difference is very similar to the unadjusted difference and remains economically large at over $1,100.

The presence of prepayment penalties also varies considerably by race. Nearly 29 percent of blacks have prepayment penalties compared to roughly 13 percent of white respondents, a statistically significant difference (see Table 3.2). This difference remains statistically meaningful even after controlling for income, age, gender, and various measures of creditworthiness (regression results are reported in Table 3.3b). Also, as shown in Table 3.2, a higher fraction of black homeowners (15 percent) have balloon payments written into their mortgage contracts, compared to white homeowners (6 percent). This difference is also statistically significant after controlling for

Table 3.3b. Regression Version of Mortgage Characteristics Table: Prepayment Penalty and Balloon Payment

	Prepayment Penalty			Balloon Payment		
	(13)	(14)	(15)	(16)	(17)	(18)
Black	0.112*	0.151†	0.133*	0.0821*	0.0920*	0.0951*
	(0.0666)	(0.0742)	(0.0732)	(0.0458)	(0.0514)	(0.0493)
Female	−0.0443	−0.0813	−0.0828	0.0586	0.00679	0.00670
	(0.0704)	(0.0751)	(0.0776)	(0.0482)	(0.0525)	(0.0521)
Age 25–60	−0.149	−0.107	−0.158	−0.111	−0.0855	−0.0890
	(0.131)	(0.137)	(0.144)	(0.123)	(0.122)	(0.114)
Age 61+	−0.372†	−0.386†	−0.440‡	−0.0442	−0.0347	−0.0699
	(0.152)	(0.161)	(0.165)	(0.145)	(0.155)	(0.139)
Married	0.0701	0.101	0.0994	0.0331	0.0711	0.0737
	(0.0696)	(0.0781)	(0.0801)	(0.0484)	(0.0552)	(0.0547)
Income		−1.91e-06	−.16e-06		−2.26e-06	−4.25e-06
		(5.66e-06)	(5.80e-06)		(4.92e-06)	(4.68e-06)
Income^2		−0	0		−0	−0
		(9.34e-11)	(9.28e-11)		(7.15e-11)	(6.75e-11)
Income^3		0	0		0	0
		(0)	(0)		(0)	(0)
Delayed paying mortgage			0.0469			0.166‡
			(0.0804)			(0.0636)
Banked			0.0351			0.0343
			(0.119)			(0.103)
Denied a loan			−0.203*			−0.0904
			(0.103)			(0.0592)
Pay less than minimum on credit card			0.417			0.737‡
			(0.496)			(0.113)
Ever bankrupt			0.151			−0.0777
			(2101)			(0.412)
Ever account closed because of poor credit			0.000386			−0.126
			(0.444)			(0.127)
Behind on vehicle loan			0.0827			−0.173†
			(0.186)			(0.0669)

Table 3.3b (Continued)

	Prepayment Penalty			Balloon Payment		
	(13)	(14)	(15)	(16)	(17)	(18)
Purchase price	−1.55e-06†	−1.40e-06	−1.61e-06*	5.59e-07	6.89e-07	5.06e-07
	(7.64e-07)	(8.76e-07)	(8.96e-07)	(5.45e-07)	(5.64e-07)	(5.36e-07)
Value if sold today	−1.39e-06*	−1.31e-06	−1.20e-06	−1.01e-06†	−7.95e-07	−5.63e-07
	(7.73e-07)	(7.98e-07)	(8.24e-07)	(4.97e-07)	(4.99e-07)	(4.94e-07)
Loan remaining	2.70e-06‡	2.47e-06†	2.25e-06†	3.14e-07	2.55e-07	2.98e-07
	(9.28e-07)	(1.00e-06)	(1.04e-06)	(7.07e-07)	(7.90e-07)	(8.43e-07)
Refinance	0.0617	0.0473	0.0481	−0.118†	−0.0990*	−0.0900*
	(0.0705)	(0.0764)	(0.0782)	(0.0510)	(0.0519)	(0.0526)
Date of purchase controls?	Yes	Yes	Yes	Yes	Yes	Yes
Observations	188	174	174	197	183	183
R^2	0.136	0.149	0.187	0.100	0.115	0.224

Robust standard errors in parentheses. DAHFS sample weights used in all regressions.
*Significant at the 10 percent level; †significant at the 5 percent level. ‡significant at the 1 percent level.

other demographic characteristics, loan size, house value, income, and creditworthiness (full regression results are reported in Table 3.3b).

Overall, these high-cost loan practices differ substantially along racial lines. These disparities are consistent with the findings of Avery, Brevoort, and Canner (2006), who analyze HMDA data on mortgages originated in 2005 and find that African Americans disproportionately obtained high-cost mortgages relative to their share of mortgages received. Our results also support the finding of race-based disparities in audit-based studies, which focus on a different dimension of the mortgage process: the loan approval stage (e.g., Ross and Yinger 2002 or Bocian, Ernst, and Li 2006). Charles and Hurst (2002) find that black households are less likely to apply for mortgages and, conditional on applying, are less likely to be approved. That we find racial differences in loan terms in a cross section of homeowners who have successfully received a mortgage loan suggests that race-based disparities persist even after differential treatment during the approval process. Also note that in a cross section of homeowners, such as this one, riskier borrowers are not as likely to be observed as in samples drawn from loan originations, since, conditional on having taken a mortgage at some point, they might have already defaulted, are no longer homeowners, and therefore are not observed in the data. As a result, if blacks have, on average, greater default risk than whites, then a comparison by race of those remaining in the sample will understate the differences in pricing arising at origination.[18]

Mortgage Broker Use

We next explore differences in loan pricing based on the usage of mortgage brokers. While brokers are criticized for aggressively selling high-cost mortgages with potentially predatory loan terms (see Jackson and Burlingame 2006), in theory, one function of a broker is to match borrowers with competitively priced mortgage offers from lenders. Indeed, El Anshasy, Elliehausen, and Shimazaki (2006) estimate that subprime borrowers using a broker obtain APRs that are 15 to 190 basis points *lower* than those that were obtained by using a retail lender. However, in our data, we observe that borrowers who use a mortgage broker are 60 percent more likely to pay points or fees than are those who do not use a broker. As Table 3.4 shows, 36 percent of homeowners who purchased through a broker paid points and fees, whereas only 21 percent of homeowners who did not use a broker did so. The average difference in the size of these fees is over $800. We also observe interest rates that are 40 basis points higher as well as a greater prevalence of balloon payments among those who used a mortgage broker; owing to sample size limitations, the differences in interest rate and balloon payment are not statistically different from zero. That is, despite being more likely to pay points and fees, borrowers using a mortgage broker do not seem to obtain lower interest rates.

Our findings are consistent with the work of Jackson and Burlingame (2007), who find that average yield spread premiums were on the order of $1,500 to $1,800 in additional costs to the borrower and that these costs were not offset by lower upfront fees. In addition, over two thirds of homeowners who used a broker were offered only one mortgage product (see Table 3.2), which undermines the view that brokers provide borrowers with a diverse range of loan options.

Table 3.4. Mortgage Characteristics: The Role of Brokers

	Broker	Non-Broker	Difference	Adjusted Difference
Fraction of homeowners	58.4	41.6	16.8	
Paid points/fees	35.5	21.3	14.2†	13.6†
Mean fee amount	$2,356	$2,032	$324	$827
Adjustable rate	31.7	25.7	6.0	8.4
Mean interest rate	7.6	7	0.7†	0.4
Mean purchase price	$68,613	$55,264	$13,348	$11,492†
Mean year of purchase	1993.3	1993.3	0.0	0.8
Prepayment penalty	24.4	22.5	1.9	0.1
Balloon payment	14.6	6.7	7.9†	5.1
Ever delayed payment	33.3	27.4	5.9	4.7

Sample consists of DAHFS respondents who have a mortgage.
†Significant at the 5 percent level. Significance is noted if the difference between broker and non-broker loans is significant at the 10 percent level. Controls: age, race, gender, income, marital status, creditworthiness indicators. Creditworthiness is measured by indicators for whether the homeowner has a bank account, has been denied a loan, has filed for bankruptcy, has had a bank account closed due to poor credit, pays less than the minimum due on a credit card, or is behind on a vehicle loan. Loan performance measures are whether the owner has ever delayed a mortgage payment and whether the owner is currently behind on the mortgage payment

Furthermore, we find that there is no difference in the likelihood of using a broker based on age, race, or income in our sample of homeowners, which suggests that there is no support for differential demand-driven use of brokers across demographic groups.[19] Indeed, the estimated coefficients on the demographic variables are small in magnitude (as well as statistically insignificant). The borrowers who used a broker do not differ statistically in terms of creditworthiness measures. Thus it seems unlikely that brokers helped marginal borrowers to obtain access to credit they otherwise would have been unable to acquire. Because blacks and whites are equally likely to use brokers, it is unlikely that the racial differences in pricing arise in our sample through the broker channel. Specifically, the coefficient on being black remains significant in regressions, including the interaction of race and broker usage, while the coefficient on the interaction term is statistically insignificant (result not shown). These results present new puzzles about how LMI borrowers use mortgage brokers and about the mechanisms by which LMI borrowers incur the costs of a mortgage.

Conclusion

This chapter has made use of a unique survey dataset of LMI households to identify two mechanisms through which high-cost mortgages can arise: racial differences in pricing and the role of mortgage brokers. We find that within similar low-income neighborhoods, black homeowners pay higher interest rates than similar non-blacks do—110 basis points on average—and are more than twice as likely to have prepayment penalties or balloon payments attached to their mortgages as non-black homeowners are, even after controlling for age, income, gender, creditworthiness, and a proxy for default risk. In addition, we observe that borrowers who used a mortgage broker are over 60 percent more likely to pay points or fees than those who did not use a broker. Overall, the results suggest that across some dimensions of pricing, similar borrowers are treated differently by mortgage lenders and brokers.

Observing differential treatment in the mortgage market is puzzling for at least three reasons. First, advances in mortgage underwriting technology have standardized the mortgage origination process for many lenders (Collins, Belsky, and Case 2004). The underwriting software does not include race as an input in either mortgage approval rates or pricing. Second, information on pricing has become less costly to obtain since the supply of mortgage brokers has increased dramatically over the last 15 years. Furthermore, the Internet has made interest rate comparisons and price quotes readily available. Together, these developments ought to have enhanced competition and standardized contracts across borrowers with similar risk profiles. Finally, fair lending laws prohibit discriminatory practices and have been in place for decades (see, for example, Ross and Yinger 2002 or Barr 2005). However, while differences in pricing may have decreased over time, they nonetheless persist among LMI households (Apgar and Calder 2005), including those we surveyed in Detroit in 2005 and 2006.

Our descriptive findings are most consistent with supply-driven origins for differences in loan terms. Our rich dataset can account for differences in the demand for mortgages across borrowers because of their incomes, desired mortgage size, creditworthiness, and default risk. By including as much available information about the borrower as possible, we have attempted to address demand-driven explanations that are correlated with race or using a mortgage broker for the high costs some homeowners pay.

Our results suggest that enhanced fair lending enforcement and improved mortgage market regulation may be in order. One direction in which fair lending laws could be bolstered is through enhanced disclosure policies, coupled with financial education. Differences in pricing between blacks and non-blacks could potentially arise through different disclosure practices and conventions. In the DAHFS study, black borrowers were less informed on their APR and on whether their mortgage had an adjustable rate, prepayment penalty, or balloon payment. Further research is needed to understand the relationship between race and disclosure practices and whether certain types of disclosure practices lead to higher-priced loans. Improved disclosures may reduce these disparities.

Another direction is to improve the interaction between brokers and lenders with customers (see Barr, Mullainathan, and Shafir 2008). For example, a ban on yield spread premiums that vary by the terms of the loan, as recently contained in the Federal Reserve's proposed mortgage rules and in the Dodd-Frank Act, should help to reduce disparities that are produced through the broker channel. To the extent that differences in pricing arise because of decisions made by borrowers who do not understand loan terms or fee structures because of excessively opaque financial products or practices, the more that consumers are exposed to straightforward mortgages with sound underwriting, the easier it may be for them to make borrowing decisions that better meet their needs.

References

Aaronson, Daniel. 2000. "A Note on the Benefits of Homeownership." *Journal of Urban Economics* 47: 356–69.

Apgar, William C., and Allegra Calder. 2005. "The Dual Mortgage Market: The Persistence of Discrimination in Mortgage Lending." In *The Geography of Opportunity: Race and Housing Choice in Metropolitan America*, ed. de Souza Briggs. Washington, D.C.: Brookings Institution Press, 2005. 101–26.

Apgar, William C., Mark Duda, and Rochelle Nawrocki Gorey. 2005. "The Municipal Cost of Foreclosures: A Chicago Case Study." Housing Finance Policy Research Paper 2005-1. Minneapolis: Homeownership Preservation Foundation.

Avery, Robert B., Kenneth P. Brevoort, and Glenn B. Canner. 2006. "Higher-Priced Home Lending and the 2005 HMDA Data." *Federal Reserve Bulletin* (September): A123–66.

———. 2007. "The 2006 HMDA Data." *Federal Reserve Bulletin* (December): A73–A109.

Barr, Michael S. 2005. "Credit Where It Counts: The Community Reinvestment Act and Its Critics." *New York University Law Review* 80, 2: 513–652.

Barr, Michael S., Jane K. Dokko, and Benjamin J. Keys. 2009. "And Banking for All?" Finance and Economics Discussion Series 2009-34. Washington, D.C.: Federal Reserve Board.

Barr, Michael S., Sendhil Mullainathan, and Eldar Shafir. 2008. "Behaviorally In-formed Home Mortgage Regulation." Cambridge, Mass.: Joint Center on Housing Studies, Harvard University.

Bocian, Debbie Gruenstein, Keith S. Ernst, and Wei Li. 2006. "Unfair Lending: The Effect of Race and Ethnicity on the Price of Subprime Mortgages." Durham, N.C.: Center for Responsible Lending.

Bond, Philip, David K. Musto, and Bilge Yilmaz. 2009. "Predatory Mortgage Lend-ing." *Journal of Financial Economics*, 94, 3: 412–427.

Bucks, Brian K., Arthur B. Kennickell, Traci L. Mach, and Kevin B. Moore. 2009. "Changes in U.S. Family Finances from 2004 to 2007: Evidence from the Survey of Consumer Finances." *Federal Reserve Bulletin*, 95 (February): A1–A55.

Bucks, Brian and Karen Pence. 2008. "Do Borrowers Know Their Mortgage Terms?" *Journal of Urban Economics* 64, 2: 218–33.

Charles, Kerwin Kofi, and Erik Hurst. 2002. "The Transition to Home Ownership and the Black-White Wealth Gap." *Review of Economics and Statistics* 84, 2 (May): 281–97.

Collins, Michael, Eric Belsky, and Karl E. Case. 2004. "Exploring the Welfare Effects of Risk-based Pricing in the Subprime Mortgage Market." Working Paper BABC 04-8. Cambridge: Mass.: Joint Center for Housing Studies, Harvard University.

Courchane, Marsha. 2007. "The Pricing of Home Mortgage Loans to Minority Bor-rowers: How Much of the APR Differential Can We Explain?" *Journal of Real Estate Research* 29, 4: 399–439.

Daily Real Estate News. 2006. "Home Sales Dip in June as Market Stabilizes." July 25, http://www.realtor.org/rmodaily.nsf/pages/News2006072502 [No author infor-mation provided.]

Edelberg, Wendy. 2007. "Racial Dispersion in Consumer Credit Interest Rates." FEDS Working Paper 2007-28. Washington, D.C.: Federal Reserve Board.

El Anshasy, Amany, Gregory Elliehausen, and Yoshiaki Shimazaki. 2006. "The Pric-ing of Subprime Mortgages by Mortgage Brokers and Lenders." Working Paper. Washington, D.C.: George Washington University.

Farris, John, and Christopher A. Richardson. 2004. "The Geography of Subprime Mortgage Prepayment Penalty Patterns." *Housing Policy Debate* 15, 3: 687–714.

Goldstein, Debbie, and Stacy Strohauer Son. 2003. "Why Prepayment Penalties are Abusive in Subprime Home Loans." Policy Paper 4. Durham, N.C.: Center for Responsible Lending.

Harkness, Joseph, and Sandra J. Newman. 2002. "Homeownership for the Poor in Distressed Neighborhoods: Does This Make Sense?" *Housing Policy Debate* 13, 3: 597–630.

Haughwout, Andrew, Christopher Mayer, and Joseph Tracy. 2009. "Subprime Mortgage Pricing: The Impact of Race, Ethnicity, and Gender on the Cost of Borrowing." In *Brookings-Wharton Papers on Urban Affairs: 2009*, ed. Gary Burtless and Janet Rothenberg Pack. Washington, D.C.: Brookings Institution Press. 33–63.

Jackson, Howell E., and Laurie Burlingame. 2007. "Kickbacks or Compensation: The Case of Yield Spread Premiums." *Stanford Journal of Law, Business, and Finance* 12, 2: 289–361.

Joint Center for Housing Studies of Harvard University. 2007. "The State of the Nation's Housing 2006." Cambridge, Mass.: Joint Center for Housing Studies, Harvard University.

LaCour-Little, Michael, and Gregory Chun. 1999. "Third-Party Originators and Mortgage Prepayment Risk: An Agency Problem?" *Journal of Real Estate Research*, 17, 1–2: 55–70.

Kling, Jeffrey R., Jeffrey B. Liebman, and Lawrence F. Katz. 2007. "Experimental Analysis of Neighborhood Effects." *Econometrica* 75, 1: 83–119.

Michigan Association of Realtors. 2005. "Residential Sales Statistics, December 2005 YTD." http://www.mirealtors.com/Content/Upload/AssetMgmt/Site/HOUSING/Dec05stats.pdf

National Community Reinvestment Coalition. 2006. "The 2005 Fair Lending Disparities: Stubborn and Persistent II." Washington, D.C.: National Community Reinvestment Coalition.

Quercia, Roberto G., Michael A. Stegman, and Walter R. Davis. 2005. "The Impact of Predatory Loan Terms on Subprime Foreclosures: The Special Case of Prepayment Penalties and Balloon Payments." UNC-Chapel Hill Center for Community Capitalism Paper. Chapel Hill: University of North Carolina.

Quigley, John. 2008. "Compensation and Incentives in the Mortgage Business." *Economists' Voice* 5, 6: Article 2.

Rohe, William M., and Michael A. Stegman. 1994. "The Effects of Homeownership on the Self-Esteem, Perceived Control and Life Satisfaction of Low-Income People." *Journal of the American Planning Association* 60, 2: 173–84.

Ross, Stephen L., and John Yinger. 2002. *The Color of Credit*. Cambridge, Mass.: MIT Press.

Rossi, Peter H., and Eleanor Weber. 1996. "The Social Benefits of Homeownership: Empirical Evidence from National Surveys." *Housing Policy Debate* 7, 1: 1–35.

Schloemer, Ellen, Wei Li, Keith Ernst, and Kathleen Keest. 2006. "Losing Ground: Foreclosures in the Subprime Market and their Cost to Homeowners." Durham, N.C.: Center for Responsible Lending Report.

Scholz, John Karl, Ananth Seshadri, and Surachai Khitatrakun. 2006. "Are Americans Saving "Optimally" for Retirement?" *Journal of Political Economy* 114, 4: 607–43.

Shan, Hui. 2009. "Reversing the Trend: The Recent Expansion of the Reverse Mortgage Market." Finance and Economics Discussion Series Working Paper 2009-42. Washington, D.C.: Board of Governors of the Federal Reserve.

Sullivan, Teresa A., Elizabeth Warren, and Jay Lawrence Westbrook. 1999. *The Fragile Middle Class: Americans in Debt.* New Haven, Conn.: Yale University Press.

U.S. Census Bureau. 2000. State and County QuickFacts. www.census.gov.

U.S. Department of Housing and Urban Development and U.S. Department of the Treasury. 2000. "Joint Report on Predatory Lending." Washington, D.C.: U.S. Department of Housing and Urban Development.

Woodward, Susan E., and Robert E. Hall. 2010. "Diagnosing Consumer Confusion and Sub-Optimal Shopping Effort: Theory and Mortgage-Market Evidence." NBER Working Paper w16007.

Notes

We thank Neil Bhutta, Glenn Canner, and Andreas Lehnert for helpful comments and discussions. Dario Borghesan, Maria Dooner, and Robyn Konkel provided excellent research assistance. The study received generous support from the Ford Foundation; Fannie Mae Foundation; Mott Foundation; MacArthur Foundation; Annie E. Casey Foundation; and the Community Foundation of Southeastern Michigan; as well as the National Poverty Center; Center on Local, State, and Urban Policy; and the Provost, Vice President for Research, and Law School of the University of Michigan. The views in this paper solely represent those of the authors and do not necessarily reflect those of the Federal Reserve Board or its staff.

1. Until recently, 60 to 70 percent of loans were originated through the broker channel. Some economists have argued that mortgage brokers contributed to the subprime boom and bust by aggressively marketing high-cost and potentially confusing mortgages to low-income borrowers (Quigley 2008).

2. Woodward and Hall (2010) use loan-level data with mortgage pricing variables but not many household-level characteristics while Haughwout, Mayer, and Tracy (2009) merge data from LoanPerformance (LP) and HMDA to examine racial differences in subprime mortgage pricing.

3. This includes Wayne, Oakland, and Macomb Counties.

4. LMI communities in coastal cities, such as New York and Los Angeles, are quite different from Detroit in having Hispanic and immigrant populations as well as different housing markets.

5. Specifically, the reported annual percentage rate (APR) in HMDA includes up-front costs such as points and fees, but lenders are not required to disclose these separately. In addition, the APR is disclosed only for high-cost originations.

6. Specifically, 25 percent of black homeowners reported that they did not know their APR, in contrast to 18 percent of non-blacks. Nine percent of black homeowners did not know whether they had an adjustable-rate mortgage compared to 4 percent of non-blacks. For prepayment penalties, just under 20 percent of blacks and non-blacks did not know whether they had one, while just over one in ten households did not know whether they had a balloon payment. None of these differences are statistically significant.

7. Because of privacy concerns, we are not permitted to disclose the specific randomly selected census tracts from which the sample members were drawn.

8. The hypothetical selling price is a response to the question "If you were to sell your house today, how much would it be worth?," which was provided by the owner and thus is likely measured with some error (Bucks and Pence 2008). Home equity lines of credit are not included in this calculation of home equity.

9. The median sales price in July 2005 in the Midwest was $178,000, according to the *Daily Real Estate News* (2006) at Realtor.org. According to the Michigan Association of Realtors, average sales prices in Oakland and Macomb Counties were $234,000 and $175,000, respectively, in January to July 2005. The Detroit Board of Realtors reported an average sale price of $73,307 for the sales made in 2005, more in line with our reported estimates (Michigan Association of Realtors 2005).

10. Using a common factor of these creditworthiness measures derived from factor analysis as a control variable (rather than each variable individually) yields qualitatively similar results (available upon request).

11. We recognize that these variables do not fully cover all of the information used by credit bureaus, such as credit card or student loan delinquencies. However, these variables are highly correlated with the information that a credit bureau would use. We also surveyed homeowners about borrowing behaviors and attitudes that are typically unobserved by credit bureaus to gauge profligate spending habits, tendencies toward financial irresponsibility, and perceived stigma of indebtedness. Including these variables in the analysis does not qualitatively change our conclusions.

12. Among those with interest rates above 10 percent, 35 percent purchased their home after 2000 during a period with low interest rates. In our data, we are not able to discern why those with high interest rates who bought their homes before 2000 did not refinance amid widespread availability of lower interest rates.

13. We refer to the annual rate of interest reported by the borrower as the APR. However, borrowers could be reporting the note rate rather than the APR. The APR combines the note rate with other fees charged by the lender and expresses them as a yearly percentage. Our estimated "APR" differences across demographic groups are biased only if groups differentially report their note rate instead of their APR.

14. Borrowers using brokers would be unobservably similar to those not using brokers if mortgage broker usage were randomly assigned.

15. The number of observations in each column varies owing to individuals opting to report that they "don't know" certain terms of their mortgage.

16. We do not have information on the loan-to-value ratio of the loan at origination, so we use measures of the current amount outstanding and the value of the loan if sold today as comparable (albeit imperfect) controls.

17. We also included a variable measuring how much borrowers generally shopped around for financial services. The inclusion of this variable led to effectively identical results.

18. In contrast, samples drawn from loan originations, such as HMDA data, are not susceptible to this bias.

19. In contrast, El Anshasy, Elliehausen, and Shimazaki (2006) find that race, education, and income are highly predictive of broker use. Their results are based on a sample of subprime borrowers rather than both prime and subprime borrowers living in LMI neighborhoods. Still, it may be that black and white borrowers use different types of mortgage brokers. However, given the limitations of the survey questions about broker use, we are unable to investigate this issue further.

Chapter 4

Implications of the Housing Market Bubble for Sustainable Homeownership

Paul S. Calem, Leonard Nakamura, and Susan M. Wachter

The recent housing market bubble and subsequent meltdown dealt a triple blow to sustainable homeownership in the United States. First, the rapid rise in housing prices that characterized the period from 2004 to 2006 reduced housing affordability as traditionally measured. Second, an expansion of high-risk mortgage lending helped to fuel, or at a minimum helped to sustain, the rise in house prices, facilitated the drawing out by households of accumulated home equity, and left homeowners at greater risk of default. The subsequent meltdown generated the ongoing wave of foreclosures that has further eroded homeownership. Third, although affordability has recovered, the episode has reduced household creditworthiness and prompted a procyclical response—increased capital assessments and tightened credit standards in mortgage credit markets—making entrance or return to homeownership more difficult for many families.

This chapter presents preliminary evidence on the impact of the housing bubble, the flood of high-risk mortgage lending, and the subsequent meltdown on homeownership. We then review the developing literature on the factors behind the expansion of the high-risk lending that played such an important role in the bubble and meltdown. We end by discussing how policymakers, by being conscious of these factors, may be able to mitigate potential recurrence of this episode and more successfully promote sustainable homeownership.

In our discussion of the factors driving the expansion of high-risk lending, we emphasize agency or information problems in the mortgage origination and securitization market, incomplete risk transfer, and underassessment of systemic risk. We argue that policymakers must take into account these factors and their relationship to exaggerated house price dynamics or housing bubbles, which are clearly harmful to the objective of sustainable homeownership. We highlight several matters that require increased attention from policymakers, including consumer protection and education, potentially misaligned incentives of mortgage originators and other market participants, capital requirements for mortgages, and improved financial and regulatory data.

The Impact of the Bubble and Meltdown on Homeownership

The housing market bubble, the accompanying surge in high-risk lending, and the subsequent meltdown in the mortgage market have coincided with a substantial decline in the homeownership rate for U.S. households. As Figure 4.1 shows, the U.S. homeownership rate peaked in 2004 at an annual average rate of 69 percent, following a steady increase over the previous decade. It fell back a bit in 2005 and 2006 and then began a steady decline to its current level of 67.1 percent (as of the first quarter of 2010). The peaking of the homeownership rate in 2004 may in part reflect demographic factors, such as rates of household formation. Still, it is somewhat puzzling, given the greatly expanded availability of mortgage credit during the housing market boom of 2004 through 2006.[1]

It is also worth noting that while homeownership rates fell from 2004 to 2008, the size of the U.S. housing stock increased by six million new home completions (including five million single-family units), representing an estimated 5 percent of the housing stock. This additional housing stock was not primarily absorbed by new homeownership (owner occupation increased by 2.5 percentage points), but by rentals, vacancies, and vacation or second homes. Thus much of the run-up in the housing stock and in house prices during the height of the housing boom reflected investment motives.

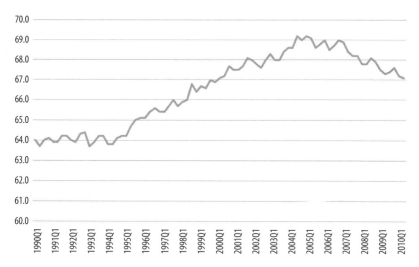

Figure 4.1. U.S. homeownership rate: 1999–2010. Housing Vacancy Survey.

Further evidence of growth in demand for investment and vacation properties as a driver of the housing boom is provided in Figure 4.2, derived from Home Mortgage Disclosure Act (HMDA) data.[2] As the figure illustrates, the percentage of mortgages for the purchase of one to four family properties in metropolitan areas that were associated with a non-primary residence increased steadily from 2003 through 2006. Moreover, cities with larger increases in the share of home purchase loans associated with non-primary residences tended to have steeper declines in affordability. Figure 4.3 displays this relationship in a scatterplot for the seventy-five largest U.S. metropolitan areas, relating the change in affordability between the first quarter of 2005 and the first quarter of 2007 to the change in the non-primary residence share of home purchase loans between the first quarter of 2004 and the first quarter of 2006.[3]

Categories of High-Risk Lending

Although demand for investment properties is one explanation, the fact that the homeownership rate stopped rising after 2004 is still somewhat surprising, given the expanded availability of mortgage credit during the housing boom. Indeed, the run-up in housing prices was accompanied by

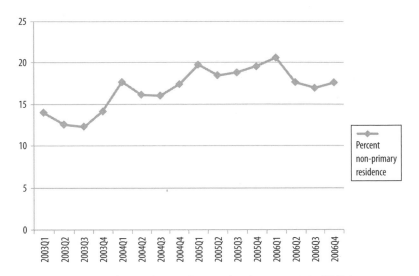

Figure 4.2. Occupancy status of metropolitan area home purchase loans: 2003–2006. HDMA data.

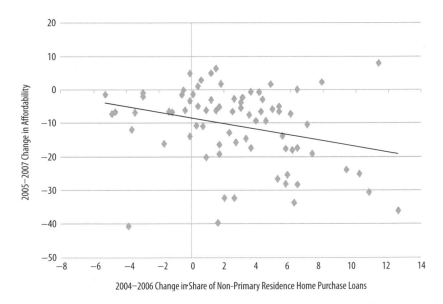

Figure 4.3. Change in affordability versus change in share of home purchase mortgage: 2004–2007.

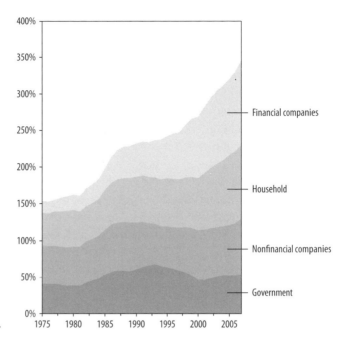

Figure 4.4. Sectoral contributions to U.S. gross debt: 1975–2005.

a credit expansion of historically unprecedented dimensions. Mortgage debt expanded as a share of gross national product, as shown in Figure 4.4, largely as a result of the expansion of high-risk and nontraditional credit.

For understanding the role of this surge in lending, it is helpful to distinguish among three categories of higher-risk lending associated with the credit expansion during 2004–2006: subprime, Alt-A, and second-lien. Although the distinction among these categories was sometimes blurry, they generally represented different sectors and served different purposes in the mortgage and housing markets.

The first category, subprime lending, primarily served borrowers with impaired credit histories or is associated with combinations or layering of risk factors. A relatively large proportion of subprime loans during this period were associated with high debt payment-to-income ratios for the borrower combined with vulnerability to future payment shocks tied to adjustable-rate mortgage (ARM) or interest-only products with scheduled resets of the interest rate or monthly payment.[4] Subprime mortgages that were originated with piggyback second liens and combined loan-to-value ratios of 100 percent also were common.[5]

A substantial portion of the growth of subprime lending during the housing boom was associated with borrowers cashing out home equity that accumulated as house prices rose. It is likely that an additional, substantial component consisted of borrowers who could no longer qualify for prime or near-prime rates because of the impact of rising house prices on their loan-to-value or debt payment-to-income ratios.

The second category, so-called Alt-A lending, consisted largely of nontraditional credit products originated to prime or near-prime borrowers. These products, including interest-only and option adjustable-rate mortgages and low-documentation, stated-income loans, enabled borrowers to purchase a larger home (or to cash-out a larger amount of equity in connection with a refinancing) than they could have under traditional underwriting standards. These products likely fueled demand for higher-priced homes and accelerated the decline in housing affordability. Conceivably, by spurring demand for higher-priced homes, they may have contributed in some localities to net declines in homeownership during the housing boom.

Many mortgages in this category were jumbo loans (larger than the conforming loan size limits established for the Federal National Mortgage Association, or Fannie Mae, and the Federal Home Loan Mortgage Corporation, or Freddie Mac), and a relatively large proportion were securitized. The elevated credit risk associated with the Alt-A category was a reflection of several factors, including the potential for large payment shocks, loose underwriting (in the case of low-documentation loans), and adverse selection or cohort effects (which occur when borrowers are willing to risk payment shocks or exaggerate their incomes).

The third category, second-lien loans, consisted of closed-end home equity loans and home equity lines of credit (HELOCs). Some of these loans were issued as "piggyback" second liens in association with first-lien home purchase or refinance loans, often resulting in a combined loan-to-value ratio of 100 percent. Most of these loans or credit lines, however, were originated to prime borrowers with existing first-lien mortgages for the purpose of drawing out accumulated home equity.

The market share of each of these mortgage categories rose significantly during the period of the housing boom. Their combined share grew from under 15 percent in 2002 to almost half of originations by 2006 (the sum of the market share of HELOCs, Alt-A, and subprime, as shown in Table 4.1).

Table 4.1. Mortgage Originations by Product

	FHA/VA ↓ (%)	Conv/Conf ↓ (%)	Jumbo ↓ (%)	Subprime ↑ (%)	Alt-A ↑ (%)	HEL ↑ (%)
2001	8	57	20	7	2	5
2002	7	63	21	1	2	6
2003	6	62	16	8	2	0
2004	4	41	17	18	6	12
2005	3	35	18	20	12	12
2006	3	33	16	20	13	14
2007	4	48	14	8	11	15

Inside Mortgage Finance. *2008 Mortgage Market Statistical Annual.*

These mortgages also, as shown in Figure 4.5, had an increasing and relatively high rate of securitization, compared to traditional, nonconforming mortgages such as prime jumbo.

The credit expansion during 2004–2006 was characterized by loosened underwriting standards across all mortgage categories (Table 4.2). In particular, borrowers' equity share of financing declined, largely a consequence of piggyback second liens often involving combined loan-to-value ratios at

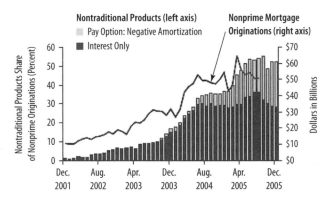

Figure 4.5. Growth in nontraditional mortgages: 2002–2005. Nonprime mortgage originations data are securitized originations of Alt-A and subprime product. Data on nonprime mortgage originations are not fully available after August 2005 and are not displayed. Loan Performance Corporation (Alt-A and B&C mortgage securities database). From "FDIC Outlook: Breaking New Ground in U.S. Mortgage Lending," Summer 2006. http://fdic.gov/bank/analytical/regional/ro20062q/na/2006_summer04.html.

Table 4.2. Deterioration in Underwriting

Orig Yr	CLTV	CLTV %>80	Seconds	Full Doc	%IO	DTI	FICO <700	Investor	WAC	Spd to WAC
Prime										
2002	66.5	4.1	1.9	56	46	31	20.7	0.7	5.5	—
2003	68.2	10.1	10.9	48.6	53	31.8	21.8	1.6	4.6	—
2004	73.5	20.7	23.1	51.2	71	33.5	22	2.1	4.5	—
2005	74.1	21.7	26.8	47.3	81	33.6	18.9	1.9	5.4	—
2006	75.3	26.2	35.3	33.6	91	37.2	19.5	2.3	6.2	—
Alt-A										
2002	74.3	20.8	2.7	29.3	26	35.4	46.4	9.9	6.3	0.8
2003	78	33.3	23.4	28.1	56	35.3	44.7	12.9	5.6	1
2004	82.6	46.9	39.1	32.6	75	36.2	44.3	15.3	5.5	1
2005	83.5	49.6	46.9	28.3	83	37	40.5	16.5	6	0.6
2006	85	55.4	55.4	19	87	38.3	44.2	13.5	6.8	0.6
Subprime										
2002	81.2	46.8	3.7	66.9	1	40	93.4	4.7	8.5	3
2003	83.5	55.6	9.9	63.5	5	40.2	91.6	4.9	7.5	2.9
2004	85.3	61.1	19.1	59.9	20	40.6	90.6	5.3	7.1	2.6
2005	86.6	64.4	28.1	55.9	32	41.2	89.7	5.4	7.3	1.9
2006	86.7	64	31	54.6	20	42.1	91.8	5.7	8.2	2

CLTV, CLTV %>80, and use of seconds increased	% Full doc declined	Not much change in FICO or DTI	Spreads declined

Loan performance data as of November 2006 from Thomas Zimmerman, "How Did We Get Here and What Lies Ahead." UBS, April 16, 2007.

origination of 100 percent. Borrower debt payment-to-income ratios also rose during this period, and documentation and verification standards were eased.

High-Risk Lending and Homeownership

The preceding discussion suggests that removal of traditional constraints on access to mortgage credit during this period created only an illusion of making homeownership more accessible while helping to sustain rising house prices. Indeed, new research supports the view that the flood of high-risk mortgage credit had a feedback effect on house price growth by helping to sustain demand as house prices rose (Coleman, LaCour-Little, and Vandell 2008; Pavlov and Wachter 2011). While enabling entry into home-ownership for some households despite rising prices and declining afford-ability, these credit products may have encouraged purchase of larger homes by some households and kept others out by sustaining the bubble.

That these credit products provided an illusory or at best temporary antidote to stressed affordability can be gleaned from examining the relationship between affordability and the rate of homeownership across cities. Panels 1 and 2 of Figure 4.6 display this relationship in a scatterplot for the seventy-five largest U.S. metropolitan areas as of the first quarters of 2005 and 2007, respectively, and panel 3 provides the corresponding scatterplot as of the last quarter of 2009.[6] In each year, lower affordability is associated with a lower homeownership rate across large U.S. metropolitan areas (in the appendix to this chapter, we establish that these relationships are statistically significant). The relationship is observably flatter in 2007 (although not to a statistically significant degree). This analysis suggests that any solution these products provided was at best short lived. Neither the lending itself nor the homeownership it supported has been sustainable, so post-crisis affordability remains a major barrier to homeownership.

Indirect evidence on the potential role of nontraditional mortgage products is provided by a cross-city analysis of the drop in homeownership rates since 2005 in relation to the percentage of jumbo mortgage originations in 2005 and 2006 that were securitized. Securitized jumbo mortgages are a proxy for nontraditional products, including interest-only, option-ARM, and low-documentation loans. Figure 4.7 displays this relationship in a scatterplot, again for the seventy-five largest U.S. metropolitan areas.[7] Clearly, a larger share of securitized jumbo loans originated in 2005–2006 is associated with a larger drop in homeownership between 2005 and 2009, consistent with the view that these products fueled demand for higher-priced homes, thereby contributing to a net decline in homeownership in some localities. In the appendix to this chapter, we establish that this relationship is statistically significant, and it remains significant when controlling for housing market affordability.[8]

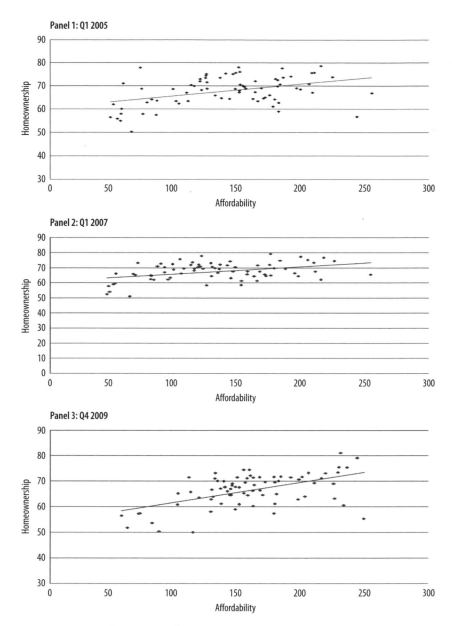

Figure 4.6. Homeownership rate versus affordability in the 75 largest U.S. metropolitan areas: 2005–2009.

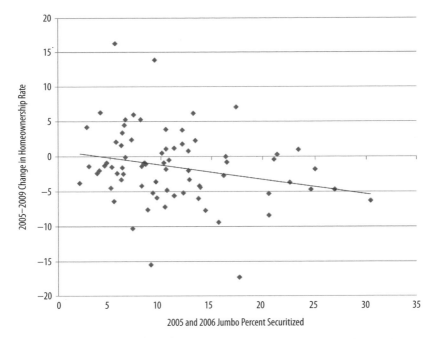

Figure 4.7. Securitized share of jumbo loans versus change in homeownership rate in the 75 largest U.S. metropolitan areas: 2005–2009.

Impact of the Mortgage Meltdown on Homeownership

Cyclical fluctuations—periods of rising house prices, increased sales of new homes, and increased credit availability, followed by periods of contraction—commonly occur in mortgage and housing markets, both in the United States and internationally. However, the recent cycle was unique, at least in the United States, with respect to the rate and geographic scope of house price appreciation, the accompanying surge in high-risk lending during the peak years of the boom in 2004 through 2006, and the severity of the subsequent contraction (Abraham, Pavlov, and Wachter 2008).

As we now know, the mortgage meltdown that ensued when the housing boom subsided and prices receded was closely linked to the expansion of high-risk lending. There are several aspects to this linkage. First, as was previously noted, the high-risk mortgage products helped to sustain the rise in house prices, causing the market to be less stable and more dependent on the continued supply of such credit. Second, the risk factors associated with these products—which included little or no borrower equity for home purchase or drawing out of existing equity through cash-out refinance and second liens, high debt payment-to -income ratios, low documentation, and general lax underwriting as well as adverse selection effects—led directly to extremely high default rates when house values declined. Third, the risks (and, subsequently, the credit losses) associated with these loan products were spread throughout the financial system through securitization and related structured finance activities such as credit default swaps. Moreover, with hindsight, it is now clear that the system held far too little capital against these risks. The consequences have been severe, not only for the mortgage market, which suffered a loss of liquidity and greatly reduced credit availability (particularly in the jumbo market), but also for the economy as a whole.

Therefore it is not surprising that the homeownership rate has been declining during the recent contraction in the housing market, and it likely will continue to decline into the near future. The drop in the homeownership rate likely reflects the combined impact of tighter mortgage credit markets; hesitancy on the part of potential new homeowners due to concerns about the stability of house values, the general economic recession, and loss of ownership through foreclosure. Quantifying the impact of each of these potential factors on the recent decline in homeownership is beyond the scope of this chapter. Moreover, it is too early to assess the impact of the spike in delinquencies and foreclosures, many of which have not yet been resolved. These can take many months to resolve, all the more so given the widespread efforts that are now under way (through various loan modification initiatives) to "rescue" distressed homeowners.

Factors Driving the Expansion of High-Risk Lending

The collapse of subprime lending and private-label securitization and the beginning of the foreclosure crisis in 2007, along with the subsequent turmoil in mortgage and housing markets, have spurred a variety of research on problems in the nonprime market or the broader mortgage market that were at the root of the crisis. Much of this research has focused on the deterioration of underwriting standards and the house-price run-up and subsequent decline as primary factors (Demyanyk and van Hemert 2009; Gerardi, Shapiro, and Willen 2007; Hahn and Passell 2008; Sherlund 2008;

Smith 2007). Haughwout, Peach, and Tracy (2008) focus on early payment default and emphasize that only part of the increase in default during 2007 is attributable to these factors. Demyanyk and van Hemert (2009) argue that the decline in underwriting standards prior to the crisis could have been detected but was masked by rapid house-price appreciation. Coleman, LaCour-Little, and Vandell (2008) and Pavlov and Wachter (2011) present evidence that the expansion of credit resulting from looser underwriting standards contributed to the rise in house prices.

The role of securitization and associated moral hazard problems has also garnered attention, with several researchers pointing to securitization as the principal culprit in the crisis. Ashcraft and Schuermann (2008) identify a number of market frictions affecting the subprime mortgage origination and securitization process and argue that the associated misaligned incentives and adverse selection were largely responsible for the market's collapse. A partial list includes agency problems associated with mortgage brokers, such as incentives to misrepresent borrower credit quality; cream-skimming by portfolio lenders; and rating agency conflicts of interest.[9] Golding, Green, and McManus (2008) and Hull (2009) also focus on misaligned incentives of market participants, while Wray (2007) adds lax regulation to the mix. Specific problems discussed include compensation of loan originators and security traders disassociated from subsequent credit performance of the loans and ratings agencies being paid by the issuers of the securities being rated. These authors put forth recommendations aimed at increasing transparency and reducing moral hazard in both the primary and secondary mortgage markets.

Calem, Henderson, and Liles (2010) find evidence that sale of nonprime loans by depository institutions during 2005 and 2006 was associated with "cherry picking," that is, transfer of risk along dimensions that investors were likely to disregard or where risks were likely to be undervalued. They argue that such inattention to or misperception of risk by the securitization market was a primary cause of the subprime lending boom and subsequent market collapse.

Rajan, Seru, and Vig (2009) draw a distinction between the "hard information" that investors rely on to value securitized loans and "soft information" that is accessible to originators but not verifiable by a third party. They argue that securitization of subprime mortgages reduced the incentive to collect soft information, resulting in less effective credit screening. Keys et al. (2009, 2010) provide an important contribution to this line of argument by finding that lenders apply less effort to screening soft information in the low-documentation subprime loan market when originating loans that can more easily be sold to investors. They identify a key point of discontinuity around the FICO score threshold of 620, such that lenders securitized more low-documentation loans with scores above this threshold and screened them less aggressively.

However, hard information was often less informative than it appeared to be. Appraisals were typically upwardly biased as a matter of industry practice, as was first pointed out in Cho and Megbolugbe (1996) and discussed in Nakamura (2010a). These biases were apparently exacerbated by the willingness of lenders to tolerate misrepresentation of transaction prices. Ben-David (2007) focuses on the propensity to overstate collateral values by borrowers, intermediaries, and originators when it is advantageous to do so in the presence of asymmetric information. In particular, originators are able to expand their business by securitizing more loans as house prices rise.

Moreover, as Lang and Nakamura (1993) have shown, appraisals have an inherent procyclical bias; during housing booms, large numbers of housing transactions occur, resulting in relatively high precision of measured housing price estimates. As a result, appraisals are more likely to be relied upon in booms, whereas in the subsequent downturns, appraisers may find it difficult to find relevant recently completed home transactions upon which to base their home price estimates, causing mortgage applications to be declined. Indeed, Blackburn and Vermilyea (2007) found relatively strong evidence that these informational factors were important in thin housing markets.

White (2009) emphasizes the role of overly optimistic evaluations of the credit risk of mortgage-backed securities, in part owing to agency problems and in part to inadequate information and "carelessness." Coval, Jurek, and Stafford (2009a, b) point to the amplification of errors in evaluating the risk of the underlying securities of structured finance products and in the mispricing of these products. They emphasize the concentration of systemic risk that occurred through these structured products and the mispricing of this risk. While these instruments appeared to be paying a high rate of return, they were, in fact, earning a negative return because of the failure to price "tail" risk.

Four culprits can be identified from this research: incomplete risk transfer, moral hazard and incentive problems, regulatory limitations, and the undervaluation of systemic risk in structured finance. The growth of private-label securitization and the increasing complexity of structured finance products underlie many of these potential market failures. As Belsky and Wachter (2010) explain, the "housing finance revolution" exacerbated the asymmetric information problems that affect mortgage credit markets, and regulatory responses have been inadequate.

While securitization of mortgages by the government-sponsored enterprises Fannie Mae and Freddie Mac has long played a major role in housing finance in the United States, investors in mortgage-backed securities backed by the credit guarantees of Fannie Mae or Freddie Mac generally were exposed only to interest-rate risk. With the growth of the private-label securitization market, investors were additionally exposed to mortgage default risk, which was neither contained by underwriting nor adequately priced. Default rates were initially low because inflated asset prices shrouded the growing risk. The short-run incentives to securitize these loans continued even though systemic risk was not priced.

Investors could hedge their risk also. With the purchase of newly available credit default swaps, their positions could be insured against possible loss. There was counterparty risk to be considered, but if this was evaluated, investors might have concluded that these instruments had to be backed up or the entire system would fail. The providers of the credit default swaps perhaps likely had been viewed as—and certainly in this event were—too big to fail. The difficult issue of "too big to fail" is one in which regulators come to realize that the failure of a financial firm will lead to further contagion and risk of failure for a large part of the financial sector. If a firm is perceived as being too big to fail, then other counterparties may treat it as if it were riskless and thus will financially reward it by being more willing to trade with it at lower prices.

The increasingly complex process of housing finance introduced new principal-agent problems, or exacerbated existing ones, that regulators did not address. Banks' capital requirements depended on the grade their mortgage-backed securities received from rating agencies, but the agencies were paid by the very banks they were judging. Traders set the price of their new securities and derivatives, but they were paid for quantity, not quality. Internal risk managers oversaw the traders' decisions, but they were discouraged from disrupting the profit flow by executives who had an eye toward stock options. Executives had the final say over their mortgage department's strategy, but their bonuses came in the form of cash and options that could be sold before the housing market deflated (Bebchuk, Cohen, and Spamann

2010). Originators lowered lending standards and expanded their product offerings in response to an increasing demand for mortgage-backed securities, but consumers often had little understanding of the new, complicated products and loan terms.

As Pavlov and Wachter (2004, 2006, 2009) have documented, these institutional failures guaranteed an undervaluation of risk. Because mortgages are non-recourse loans, they can be priced like put options. If the homeowner defaults, the homeowner simply "puts" the house back to the bank. The bank's gain or loss is equivalent to the difference between the exercise price of the option and the market price of the underlying security. Using the Black-Scholes formula, these studies demonstrate that the increase in the price of mortgage-backed securities corresponded with a decrease in their yield rates, which proxy as a price of risk. Although the riskiness of mortgage pools was increasing, Wall Street was not appropriately pricing the higher risk. Regression analyses in these studies shed light on the crisis by revealing that such misjudgment and mispricing of risk in financial markets are associated with economies that experienced the worst market crashes in the preceding decades.

Policy Discussion

The run-up in housing prices and their subsequent decline were clearly exacerbated by powerful procyclical drivers that exaggerated underlying housing demand during the boom and whose absence will tend to drive house prices below equilibrium in the boom's aftermath. Ex post, asset-price cycles are more likely to have ex ante bubble-like properties and ex post harsh economic consequences to the extent to which procyclical factors are allowed to multiply.

Gallin (2008) has argued that in the United States, house prices, measured on a regional basis, typically overshoot in booms. It may prove very difficult to end this cyclical behavior entirely. Nevertheless, if policymakers and regulators can moderate the influence of procyclical factors, this could lead to moderated asset booms and busts.

Our discussion has highlighted a series of private behaviors that have had procyclical effects. A fundamental problem is that backward-looking risk parameterizations (such as those embedded in empirical value-at-risk models) will tend to be excessively lenient in upswings and excessively tight in the subsequent downturns. However, to the extent to which forward-looking macroeconomic factors can be included in these risk rules, these procyclical effects will be minimized.

As Nakamura (2010a) has emphasized, appraisals that were biased during the upturn are now facing stronger scrutiny and regulation and are likely exacerbating the difficulty of making home purchases and refinancing. To take action to avoid property market bubbles induced by procyclical erosion in credit standards, it is necessary to observe that this is occurring. Without market indicators, regulators will not be prompted to take appropriate prudential action. There is now an emerging consensus that balance sheets of banks and large non-bank entities must be kept well capitalized. But how is it to be known that capital that includes value deriving from property is sufficient?

The recent housing market bubble highlights the issue of procyclicality of economic capital as it concerns the mortgage market. Appreciating house values were reflected in overly optimistic assessments of exposure to credit risk from mortgages held on the book as well as from securitizations, which would imply reduced economic (and, under the current Basel II rule, regulatory) capital. The subsequent collapse of the market brought a dramatic reversal of credit risk assessments, implying large increases in economic (and Basel II regulatory) capital. Recent research on the sources of the housing bubble highlights an additional concern: that assessments of credit risk (and of economic capital based on credit value at risk) helped to perpetuate the rise in house prices. Thus these assessments became endogenous.

Procyclical effects are to some extent an unavoidable trade-off to maintaining a risk-sensitive approach to bank capital. However, consideration of ways to mitigate procyclicality of economic and Basel II regulatory capital assessments may be warranted. Moreover, there is a natural inclination to draw on the recent collapse in house prices for applying stress tests to mortgage portfolios and as a source of data for recalibrating economic capital models or, at some point, the Basel II regulatory capital formula for mortgages. In light of the potential endogeneity of credit value-at-risk assessments, such inclinations could lead to excessive tightening of mortgage credit. From this perspective, capital regulation might be usefully required to have a countercyclical component, rising above normal requirements during housing booms.

As was noted previously, the proliferation of risk, masked by a cloak of opacity, began at the ground level: mortgage origination. As early as 2002, observers noticed a decline in lending standards and an increase in non-standard mortgages, especially to unsophisticated consumers. Only in retrospect have researchers documented the connection between this trend and the decline in homeownership, increase in foreclosures, and magnification of systemic risk.

From originator to securitizer, the lack of transparency only increased. Banks had an incentive to transform loans into securities to minimize capital requirements (and thus maximize profits). The measurement of capital requirements itself required sophisticated risk analysis, a duty that regulators often delegated to the banks' internal risk managers. For other banks, rating agencies used models to grade the default probability of different tranches within the securities. Both methods represented an agency problem, as the arbiters were compensated by the very entities they supposedly judged. The models they used, moreover, often assumed an incorrect probability distribution and failed to account for correlation among tranches (Coval et al. 2009a). When the new securities did not benefit their balance sheets, banks shifted the securities to structured-investment vehicles or conduits.

Thus the financial crisis of 2007–2009 also revealed regulatory weakness. Multiple market failures proliferated to a degree that surprised most observers upon discovery. Had regulators known the extent of risky behavior, they would have been better positioned to protect, and later to rescue, the system. That such a proliferation of risk could go unnoticed should alert us to a dangerous information asymmetry in the regulation of financial markets. Regulators had difficulty monitoring the degeneration of lending standards, growing complexity of securitization, mispricing of risk, manipulation of balance sheets, increasing use of "shadow banking," and accelerating speculation of real estate.[10] When prices finally collapsed, both market participants and regulators suffered from this lack of transparency, as high counterparty risk spiraled into a liquidity crisis.

As any financial historian can testify, there is no sure way to predict or prevent an asset price bubble. Yet many of the weak spots in regulatory law had been clear in the economic literature for decades before this particular bubble occurred. Pending legislation will likely rectify some of those gaps, but a law is only as good as its enforcement. It would be an abuse of experience to repeat the same mistakes because we did not give our enforcers the proper tools to do their job. Regulators need real-time information on financial innovation and how it affects individual firms and the financial system. They need the knowledge to monitor risk, including its holder and originator and the pricing, modeling, accounting, and covariance relationships of that risk. If a systemic regulator is to fortify the system, it will need to underpin flow-of-funds financial aggregates with microdata that can pinpoint growing dangers and, if necessary, shield the market from their collateral damage.

Nakamura (2010b) proposes one possible way to mitigate some of these problems in the form of a financial monitoring database that can be built upon the Federal Reserve Flow of Funds, the U.S. Treasury Survey of Cross-Border Derivatives, the U.S. Survey of Terms of Bank Lending, and many sources within the private and academic spheres. The database would need to be versatile and compatible with many different inputs. Data would be cross-referenced for quick access and easy recognition of related risks. For example, if mortgage datasets can be cross-referenced with credit bureau data, the financial dataset might readily indicate the extent to which speculative investors are buying multiple homes for investment purposes when they appear to be buying them as owner-occupiers.

The database would of necessity have to encompass all financial instruments that are claims against nonfinancial institutions and would need to use a variety of data-gathering options, including frequent surveys of financial institutions and aggregation of third-party registries. This system would provide regulators with information that might be used to detect the buildup of systemic risks, including the ability to relatively quickly analyze procyclical moral hazard problems such as those that arose during the recent crisis. It should also provide an ability to detect the buildup of risks within specific financial entities; risks that are removed from the balance sheet of highly regulated financial intermediaries onto the balance sheets of less closely regulated entities could be more readily detected, for example. And the system could assist regulators in providing alternative pricing benchmarks, which would aid in the detection of systematic mispricing of risk. Regulators also could compile reports and analyses that the public could read (without confidential identifying information).

Consider the difficult issue of "too big to fail." Part of what makes it difficult is that policymakers may protect a firm—as they did with AIG—on an ad hoc basis because it has come to play a systemically important role and not be aware of this until the firm actually is about to fail. As a consequence, they protect the firm because they are not prepared to shield other financial firms from the fallout of the bankruptcy. A financial database that captures the full range of risks held by financial firms could conceivably help policymakers to be more alert to the firms that occupy such systemically important roles and either force the firms to divest the crucial securities in question or subject the firms to greater capital requirements.

Such a data system has been included in the recently passed Dodd-Frank Wall Street Reform and Consumer Protection Act as the responsibility of the novel Office of Financial Research.[11] If a systemic regulator is to fortify the system, it will need microdata that can pinpoint growing dangers and, if necessary, shield the market from their collateral damage. To quote Federal Reserve Board Chairman Ben Bernanke: "The events of the past year or two have highlighted regulatory gaps and deficiencies that we must address. . . . As we recover from the current crisis, it will be important to address these issues as soon as possible, to develop a regulatory structure that will better respond to future economic challenges" (Bernanke 2008). There is much work yet to be done.

In addition to improved financial and regulatory data, there must be a greater focus on strengthening regulatory oversight in general and consumer protection in particular. Recent policy responses include the establishment of a Consumer Protection Bureau by the Dodd-Frank Act, which attempts to thwart deception and unfair business practices within financial markets. However, consumers also need to be better informed throughout the homeownership process. Increased consumer education through pre-purchase counseling, especially for borrowers who have lower credit scores and post-purchase counseling for those with declining credit scores, could help to ensure that consumers understand their mortgages. Rules-based lending standards could be part of the discussion as well, such as verification of income and employment or maximum loan-to-value ratios. Finally, agency conflicts and misaligned incentives such as those involving mortgage brokers should be specifically addressed in the public policy discussion.

All these steps are important tools to correct the lack of safeguards that led to the Great Recession and had such a negative impact on U.S. homeownership. The goal now is not simply to recoup the losses in homeownership, but to ensure sustainable homeownership, in which the mortgage product and economic conditions of the homebuyer are conducive to long-term financial stability. Such a condition will enable homeowners to weather the inevitable future economic storms. The regulatory steps outlined above are designed to moderate procyclicality, one of the results of the financial crisis that had the most deleterious effect on sustainable homeownership.

With procyclicality in check, homeownership is poised to become a lasting feature of U.S. life in the twenty-first century.

Appendix: Regression Analysis

First, we examine the relationship between affordability (denoted AFFORD) and homeownership rate (OWN_RATE) across the seventy-five largest U.S. metropolitan statistical areas (MSAs), controlling for the percentage of housing units in the MSA that are classified as single-family units on the basis of the 2000 Census (%SF2000). This control variable is included to broadly represent long-term demographic or housing-market-related conditions other than affordability that might affect the homeownership rate.

Separate equations are estimated for the average homeownership rate during the first two quarters of 2005, the first two quarters of 2007, and the last two quarters of 2009. The two-quarter average was used to reduce noise in the data; similar results are obtained when only a single quarter's observation was used (the first quarter of 2005 or 2007 or the last quarter of 2009), but the model fit (R^2) is lower. Affordability is measured as of the first quarter of 2005 and 2007 and as of the last quarter of 2009, respectively. The regression results are summarized in Table 4.3.

Next, we examine the relationship between the drop in homeownership rates since 2005 and the percentage of jumbo mortgage originations in 2005 and 2006 that were securitized, again across the seventy-five largest MSAs. Specifically, we regress the average homeownership rate during the last two quarters of 2009 (OWN_RATE09) on affordability as of the fourth quarter of 2009 (AFFORD), average homeownership rate during the first two quar-

Table 4.3. Dependent Variable: OWN_RATE

	2005Q1	2007Q1	2009Q1
Intercept	45.9 (9.0)*	44.9 (9.0)*	41.4 (8.7)*
AFFORD	0.039 (2.9)*	0.027 (2.1)†	0.045 (3.5)*
%SF2000	0.249 (2.9)*	0.289 (3.5)*	0.259 (3.1)*
R^2	0.306	0.287	0.386

T-statistics in parentheses.
*$p < .01$; †$p < .05$.

Table 4.4. Dependent Variable: OWN_RATE09

	(1)	(2)
Intercept	27.8 (4.7)*	27.9 (4.8)*
AFFORD	0.022 (2.0)†	0.026 (2.2)†
OWN_RATE05	0.546(6.3)*	0.558 (6.3)*
JUMBO_PCT_SECURITIZED	−0.203 (2.4)†	−0.196 (2.3)†
PCT_HIGH_COST		−0. 087 (0.9)
R^2	0.596	0.601

T-statistics in parentheses.
*$p < .01$; †$p < .05$.

ters of 2005 (OWN_RATE05), and percentage of jumbo mortgages in 2005 and 2006 that were securitized (JUMBO_PCT_SECURITIZED). The latter is measured by using HMDA data, where the proxy for securitized is sold to investment banks. We also estimate a second specification that includes the percentage of HMDA-reported 2005 and 2006 mortgage originations that were high cost (PCT_HIGH_COST). The regression results are summarized in Table 4.4.

References

Abraham, Jesse M., Andrey D. Pavlov, and Susan M. Wachter. 2008. "Explaining the United States' Uniquely Bad Housing Market." *Wharton Real Estate Review* (Fall).

Adrian, Tobias, Adam Ashcraft, Hayley Boesky, and Zoltan Pozsar. 2010. "Shadow Banking." Staff Report 458. New York: Federal Reserve Bank of New York.

Ashcraft, Adam, and Til Schuermann. 2008. "Understanding the Securitization of Subprime Mortgage Credit." Staff Report 318. New York: Federal Reserve Bank of New York.

Bebchuk, Lucian, Alma Cohen, and Holger Spamann. 2010. "The Wages of Failure: Executive Compensation at Bear Stearns and Lehman 2000–2008." *Yale Journal on Regulation* 27: 257–82.

Belsky, Eric, and Susan Wachter. 2010. "The Public Interest and Mortgage Credit Markets." University of Pennsylvania Institute for Law and Economics Research Paper 10-15. http://papers.ssrn.com/sol3/papers.cfm?abstract_id=1582947.

Ben-David, Itzhak. 2007. "Financial Constraints, Inflated Home Prices, and Borrower Default during the Real-Estate Boom." Working Paper 2009-03-001. Columbus, Ohio: Fisher College of Business, Ohio State University.

Bernanke, Ben. 2008. *Wall Street Journal*, October 14.

Blackburn, McKinley, and Todd Vermilyea. 2007. "The Role of Information Externalities and Scale Economies in Home Mortgage Lending Decisions." *Journal of Urban Economics* 61: 71–85.

Calem, Paul, Christopher Henderson, and Jonathan Liles. 2010. "Cherry Picking in Subprime Mortgage Securitization: Which Subprime Mortgages Were Sold by Depository Institutions Prior to the Crisis of 2007?" Draft. Washington, D.C.: Federal Reserve Board.

Cho, Man, and Isaac Megbolugbe. 1996. "An Empirical Analysis of Property Appraisal and Mortgage Redlining." *Journal of Real Estate Finance and Economics* 13: 45–55.

Coleman, Major, Michael LaCour-Little, and Kerry Vandell. 2008. "Subprime Lending and the Housing Bubble: Tail Wags Dog?" *Journal of Housing Economics* 17, 4: 272–90.

Coval, Joshua, Jakub Jurek, and Erik Stafford. 2009a. "The Economics of Structured Finance." *Journal of Economic Perspectives* 23, 1: 3–25.

———. 2009b. "Economic Catastrophe Bonds." *American Economic Review* 99 (June): 628–66.

Demyanyk, Yuliya, and Otto Van Hemert. 2009. "Understanding the Subprime Mortgage Crisis." *Review of Financial Studies Mini Issues*, May 4, published online, http://papers.ssrn.com/sol3/papers.cfm?abstract_id=1020396.

Ernst, Keith, Debbie Bocian, and Wei Li. 2008. "Steered Wrong: Brokers, Borrowers, and Subprime Loans." Durham, N.C.: Center for Responsible Lending.

Gallin, Joshua. 2008. "The Long-Run Relationship Between House Prices and Rents." *Real Estate Economics* 36, 4: 635–58.

Gerardi, Kristopher, Adam Hale Shapiro, and Paul Willen. 2007. "Subprime Outcomes: Risky Mortgages, Homeownership Experiences, and Foreclosures." Working Paper 0715. Boston: Federal Reserve Bank of Boston.

Golding, Edward, Richard K. Green and Douglas A. McManus. 2008. "Imperfect Information and the Housing Finance Crisis." Report UCC08-6. Cambridge, Mass.: Joint Center for Housing Studies, Harvard University.

Hahn, Robert, and Peter Passell. 2008. "Better That the Fed Regulates Subprime Mortgages." *Economists' Voice* 5, 1 (February): Article 4.

Haughwout, Andrew, Richard Peach, and Joseph Tracy. 2008. "Juvenile Delinquent Mortgages: Bad Credit or Bad Economy." Staff Report No. 341, August. New York: Federal Reserve Bank of New York.

Hull, John C. 2009. "The Credit Crunch of 2007: What Went Wrong? Why? What Lessons Can Be Learned?" Toronto: Joseph L. Rotman School of Management, University of Toronto. http://www.rotman.utoronto.ca/~hull/downloadablepublications/CreditCrunch.pdf.

Keys, Benjamin J., Tanmoy Mukherjee, Amit Seru, and Vikrant Vig. 2009. "Financial Regulation and Securitization: Evidence from Subprime Loans." *Journal of Monetary Economics* (July): 700–20.

———. "Did Securitization Lead to Lax Screening? Evidence from Subprime Loans." *Quarterly Journal of Economics*, 125: 307–62.

Lang, William, and Leonard Nakamura. 1993. "A Model of Redlining." *Journal of Urban Economics* 33: 223–34.

Nakamura, Leonard. 2010a. "How Much Is That Home Really Worth: Appraisal Bias and House Price Uncertainty." *Federal Reserve Bank of Philadelphia Business Review* Q1: 11–22.

———. 2010b. "Durable Financial Regulation: Monitoring Instruments as a Counterpart to Regulating Financial Institutions." Working Paper 10-22. Philadelphia: Federal Reserve Bank of Philadelphia.

Pavlov, Andrey, and Susan Wachter. 2004. "Robbing the Bank: Non-Recourse Lending and Asset Prices." *Journal of Real Estate Finance and Economics* 28, 2–3: 147–60.

———. 2006. "The Inevitability of Market-Wide Underpriced Risk." *Real Estate Economics*, 34, 4: 479–96.

———. 2009. "Systemic Risk and Market Institutions." *Yale Journal on Regulation* 26, 2: 445–55.

———. 2011. "Subprime Lending and Real Estate Prices," *Real Estate Economics* 39, 1: xx.

Rajan, Uday, Amit Seru, and Vikrant Vig. 2009. "The Failure of Models That Predict Failure: Distance, Incentives and Defaults." Research Paper 08-19. Chicago: University of Chicago Graduate School of Business.

Reeves, Katie, and Karen Weaver. 2007. "The Impact of Underwriting Subprime ARMs at the Fully Indexed Rate: An Analysis of Debt-to-Income Ratios." *Market Pulse* (March): 2–3.

Sherlund, Shane. 2008. "The Past, Present, and the Future of Subprime Mortgages." Finance and Economics Discussion Series 2008-63. Washington, D.C.: Federal Reserve Board.

Smith, Brent C. 2007. "The Subprime Mortgage Market: A Review and Compilation of Research and Commentary." North Palm Beach, Fla.: Homer Hoyt Institute.

White, Lawrence J. 2009. "The Credit Rating Agencies and the Subprime Debacle." *Critical Review* 21, 2–3: 389–99.

Wray, L. Randall. December 2007. "Lessons from the Subprime Meltdown." Working Paper 522, December. Annandale-on-Hudson, N.Y.: Levy Economics Institute, Bard College.

Notes

The views expressed are those of the authors and do not represent those of the Federal Reserve Board of Governors, the Federal Reserve System, or Federal Reserve Bank of Philadelphia.

1. In this discussion, we restrict attention to a limited number of housing and mortgage market factors because of sample size and data limitation. Consideration of demographic trends is outside the scope of this study.

2. Attention is restricted to metropolitan areas because reporting of occupancy status is voluntary for loans originated outside of metropolitan areas. Comparison between 2003 and later years may be slightly affected by changes in metropolitan area definitions after 2003 and by exclusion of second-lien mortgages after 2003 (which were not distinguished in HMDA data until 2004).

3. The correlation is 28 percent.

4. Reeves and Weaver (2007) find that if the index rate is held constant, the bulk of securitized subprime ARM mortgages that were originated in 2005 and 2006 would migrate to higher debt payment-to-income ratios following the reset date, reflecting the presence of an initial teaser rate and/or interest-only period. For example, more than 90 percent of mortgages with initial debt payment-to-income ratios in the 40–45 percent range would migrate to a higher debt payment-to-income bucket.

5. Calem, Henderson, and Liles (2010) infer, on the basis of HMDA data, that about half of first-lien high-cost loans that were originated in 2005 and 2006 had a piggyback second lien, representing a considerable increase compared with 2004 and even more so compared with previous years.

6. The local area affordability index is from Moody's Analytics Housing Affordability Index, while the local area homeownership rates are from the housing vacancy survey of the U.S. Census. http://www.census.gov/hhes/www/housing/hvs/hvs.html.

7. Share of securitized jumbo mortgages is obtained from HMDA data.

8. An alternative interpretation is that a larger share of nontraditional mortgages (as represented by securitized jumbo share) reflects reduced affordability that is not captured by the housing affordability measure owing to measurement error.

9. Ernst, Bocian, and Li (2008) argue that mortgage brokers also often exploit an information advantage relative to the borrower to engage in predatory lending.

10. Adrian et al. (2010) provide a concise overview of the shadow banking system.

11. The intent of the Office of Financial Research is to enable regulators and the Treasury to better understand complex financial products, to uncover fraud more effectively, and to better monitor risks from large financial institutions.

Chapter 5

A Framework for Consumer Protection in Home Mortgage Lending

Kathleen Engel and Thomas J. Fitzpatrick, IV

In this chapter, we catalog and describe the various dimensions to regulating home mortgages. We do not discuss specific lending practices, loan terms, or legal prohibitions; rather, we discuss the major issues that policymakers should consider when framing a system to protect consumers who take out loans secured by their homes. The chapter's discussion has been broadened and deepened with the passage by Congress of a sweeping financial reform bill, the Dodd-Frank Wall Street Reform and Consumer Protection Act of 2010 (Dodd-Frank Act), which includes provisions governing mortgage loans.

The task of regulating mortgages is not finished. In the Dodd-Frank Act, Congress created a new Consumer Financial Protection Bureau (CFPB) and vested the agency with authority to address many of the thorny issues we identify in this chapter. States are also expanding some of their consumer protection laws in an effort to avert abuses in mortgage lending. As lawmakers continue the process of reforming mortgage regulation, they will have to choose among the paths we describe.

Invariably, laws governing mortgages fall along a spectrum from more to less onerous or protective, depending on the viewer's perspective. At one end are laws that impose extensive prohibitions on loan terms and lending practices and subject everyone involved in the financial food chain to the potential for unlimited liability. On the other end there is "regulation lite," which requires only that borrowers receive disclosures specifying the terms of their loans. The ideal regulatory approach finds the right balance between protecting consumers from abusive lending and avoiding regulations that impose unnecessary burdens on the financial services industry. To the extent to which we favor particular approaches in this chapter, it is with the goal of finding this balance.

Market Structure and Evolution

Capital markets have transformed home mortgage lending. Until the last few decades, obtaining a home loan was a simple process: A borrower applied for a loan from a traditional depository institution such as a bank or credit union. The lender underwrote the loan and held it to maturity. Revolutions in financial markets have supplanted this model of home mortgage lending and necessitated a reframing of consumer protection.

One relatively recent revolution was the rise of structured finance, a process by which loans are originated and sold into a trust that issues securities for sale on the secondary market. This process, also called securitization, was made possible through improvements in information technology and processing power that enabled computers to calculate borrowers' credit risk, which in turn facilitated the conversion of income streams from mortgage loans into securities. Structured finance changed the way in which loans are funded, altered the incentives for loan originators, and led to the emergence of a host of new players in the mortgage market. Funding for loans no longer depends on customer deposits at banks and ongoing relationships with depositors and borrowers. Instead, investors in mortgage-backed securities provide money for home mortgages, and non-depository "mortgage banks" can originate loans for the sole purpose of selling them on the secondary market. This ability to link borrowers and investors through capital markets is important to housing markets, as it can lower the cost and increase the availability of home mortgage credit. Securitization has not, however, come without costs.

The incentives among the many actors involved with home financing vary considerably and are not necessarily aligned with consumers' interests.

The upfront fees that originators receive, coupled with their ability to sell the loans they make, incentivizes originators to generate high volumes of loans without regard to the risk of borrower defaults. Similarly, mortgage brokers, who began playing a more significant role in mortgage markets over the past few decades, serve as intermediaries between borrowers and originators and earn fees at loan origination without retaining credit risk. Investment banks and other arrangers that put together securitization deals engage in due diligence that is not designed to protect consumers. Investors in bonds backed by mortgages have, at least until the subprime crisis, relied primarily on credit ratings in deciding whether to buy mortgage-backed securities and have not conducted any material due diligence of their own.[1] This is not to say that these players were motivated by ill will toward consumers. Rather, the point is that the mortgage market that emerged through securitization changed the incentives of the players and eliminated the structures that had previously helped protect borrowers from wrongdoing.[2]

The law lagged behind the changes in the home mortgage market. Many of the types of loan originators that emerged were subject to, at most, scant regulation. Even the biggest depository institutions had subsidiaries or affiliates that were able to fly under much of the regulatory radar. Markets don't guarantee against bad actors employing deceptive and abusive practices. Effective consumer protections minimize the space in which these bad actors have to operate by preventing bad acts where possible and otherwise ensuring that borrowers are informed enough to avoid them. Had there been effective regulation of home mortgage lending, these bad actors would have steered fewer consumers into loans they couldn't afford, fewer borrowers would have entered loans on terms they did not understand, and the bad actors would not have reaped huge profits by confusing and, in some cases, defrauding borrowers.

During the subprime heyday, the mantra was that self-discipline and disclosing loan terms to borrowers were sufficient consumer protection (Braunstein 2010). Currently, the most pressing issue is not whether to regulate mortgage lending, but how to craft reforms to ensure that the market will facilitate borrowers' obtaining loans with terms that are reasonable given their credit risk, that are not the result of deceptive practices, and that are affordable.

The Dodd-Frank Act fills some of the regulatory gaps, and more regulation is in the works. As the regulatory landscape changes, markets will adapt and innovate as part of what is referred to as the "regulatory dialectic" (Kane 1981). Just as markets respond to reform, reforms should be able to adjust to market changes. This dialectic should be a guiding principle of all future consumer protection and is the framework that we bring to this article. By properly aligning incentives, whatever innovations lie ahead will be consistent with consumer protection.

Who Should Be Subject to Mortgage Regulation?

Mortgage regulation has been uneven. Some institutions have been subject to more stringent regulation than others based not on their activities, but on their structural attributes. For example, banks that take deposits have had to comply with more onerous standards than have non-depository mortgage banks, even though both provide home loans. As a result of this regulatory approach, form has trumped function. Forward-looking consumer protections should focus on function, not on entity types. The three primary functions in mortgage markets are loan origination, securitization of loans, and investment in loans.

Origination Channel

Loan originators are the entities that actually extend credit to borrowers. Any mortgage regulation should cover all originators: depository institutions and their subsidiaries, mortgage banks, and any other types of loan originators that may evolve in the future. Regardless of what they are called, the defining feature of loan originators is that they extend credit to borrowers.

The origination channel also includes intermediaries between borrowers and loan originators. These intermediaries typically are mortgage brokers who help borrowers shop for credit and give the appearance of acting on behalf of borrowers, whether or not they actually do. Lenders can benefit from using mortgage brokers as intermediaries in numerous ways. Brokers may have a comparative advantage in lead generation and customer service. Importantly for the issue of consumer protection, the use of brokers can insulate lenders from consumer litigation. Under many consumer protection laws, defendants have to actively participate in wrongdoing to be liable. By using intermediaries, lenders avoid direct involvement with borrowers. This can make it hard for consumers to succeed in claims against the entities that finance their loans, even if those entities are somehow complicit in the intermediaries' wrongdoing. Borrowers can, of course, bring claims against intermediaries. The possibility of recovery is low, however, because intermediaries need little in the way of capital to function in the market and thus often do not have the resources to pay monetary judgments. In legal parlance, we refer to insolvent defendants as "judgment-proof."

Brokers can play an important role in matching borrowers with beneficial loans. Mortgage products and markets are complex and are generally understood much better by lenders than by borrowers. It stands to reason that many consumers would benefit from a trusted advisor who acts in borrowers' interests and helps them to navigate home mortgage credit markets. The fact is, however, that not all brokers act in borrowers' interests. This is in part because intermediaries can maximize their own compensation at the expense of the borrowers they claim to represent, and there are few incentives for them to do otherwise.[3] Borrowers who are working with intermediaries typically do not have enough information to distinguish between self-serving brokers and those that are representing their clients' interests.

As the law stands now, incentives are misaligned in that intermediaries do not owe any duties to act in ways that benefit borrowers. It is our position that policymakers should align borrowers' and intermediaries' interests to eliminate the potential for abuse. This can be accomplished by imposing a duty of care on intermediaries. Duties of care—be they duties to offer borrowers only products that are "suitable" for them or more stringent duties to hold the borrower's interests above the intermediary's—are common in other markets. Intermediaries that offer consumers investment advice owe those consumers a duty to hold the consumers' interests above their own, and securities brokers owe their customers a duty only to sell securities that are suitable for those customers. In nonfinancial markets, lawyers and doctors owe a duty to put clients' and patients' interests ahead of their own as they help them to navigate the complexities of law and medicine. Implied warranties attach to sales of goods by merchants; if a product is defective, consumers have recourse under warranty law.

The law should also require that intermediaries have adequate capitalization or insurance, or post bonds to prevent them from being judgment-proof. These requirements will ensure that consumers who have been hurt by legal violations will be able to recover and be made whole.

Assignee Liability

"Assignee liability" is a legal term of art that refers to the liability of owners of loans for any unlawful origination practices of an originator or intermediary who helps a borrower to obtain a mortgage. Assignees can be arrangers who own loans that are in the pipeline for securitization, but most often assignees are the trusts that own notes that back the securities issued to investors. Assignee liability is a critical ingredient of any consumer protection regime because it aligns the incentives of the owners of loans with borrowers.[4] If owners of loans are concerned about liability arising from illegal origination practices, they will cut off capital flows to originators or intermediaries who repeatedly commit unlawful acts.

Currently, there is limited assignee liability in home mortgage markets. Where it exists, borrowers are allowed to assert claims against assignees either affirmatively by filing suit or defensively in response to collection actions. An antiquated aspect of commercial law—the holder in due course (HDC) rule—shields the vast majority of holders of notes from assignee liability for claims under contract law (Greenlee and Fitzpatrick 2009).

In practice, the HDC rule creates an incentive for arrangers to *not* investigate originators' practices when purchasing loans for securitization. This is because knowledge that a loan was tainted by illegal activities can destroy arrangers' status as holders in due course. If arrangers are not HDCs, then there is also a risk that securitization trusts will not have HDC status, which in turn can make it difficult to collect on loans. If, on the other hand, arrangers "warrant their ignorance" of wrongdoing by conducting little or no due diligence, whoever owns the notes will be able to enforce them even if they were unlawfully obtained or contain illegal terms. The effect of such a rule is to diminish the incentive for the marketplace to police itself. If arrangers have no incentive to investigate the practices of loan originators, they will be less likely to cut off funding to originators that routinely engage in unlawful acts.

There are laws that have abolished the HDC rule, but their scope is limited. The federal Home Ownership and Equity Protection Act of 1994 (HOEPA) amended the Truth in Lending Act to, among other things, provide assignee liability for "high-cost" loans.[5] HOEPA was an effort to ensure that the "high-cost mortgage market policed itself."[6] High-cost loans are closed-end home mortgage loans,[7] other than purchase money loans or reverse mortgages, that secure a principal residence and have interest rates that exceed the rate of comparable Treasury securities by 8 percent for first-lien loans and 10 percent for second-lien loans.[8] Alternatively, if the points and fees associated with the loan exceed the *greater* of either 8 percent of the loan amount or $400, the loan is high cost.[9] If a loan is subject to HOEPA and the loan violates any HOEPA provisions, borrowers can pursue claims against assignees and raise HOEPA as a defense to claims for non-payment. HOEPA does contain a safe harbor, providing that loan purchasers can escape liability if "a reasonable person exercising ordinary due diligence" would be unable to determine that a loan met the requirements that would trigger HOEPA coverage.[10] There are also state laws that impose liability on assignees in specific limited situations and the federal Truth in Lending Act, which primarily governs the adequacy of disclosures, permits borrowers to exercise rescission rights against assignees.[11]

Laws that contemplate assignee liability explicitly recognize that those who purchase loans or securities backed by loans are in a better position than borrowers to monitor the origination practices of lenders. Arrangers, in particular, can monitor originators' practices and determine legal compliance by investigating randomly sampled loan files. To a lesser extent, investors, depending on their size and resources, can also conduct due diligence, on both originators and arrangers. The bottom line is that the secondary market, which has direct access to loan-level information, is in a better position than borrowers to assume these burdens and can spread the costs over all loans purchased (Engel and McCoy 2007).

Those who oppose assignee liability claim that it will make credit unaffordable and reduce its availability. Empirical evidence supporting or disproving this position is scant. In the 1970s, the Federal Trade Commission (FTC) became concerned about the impact of the holder in due course rule on the sale and financing of consumer goods. Some merchants were selling and financing defective goods and then selling the consumers' loans. Owners of loans could enforce the loans using the shield of the HDC to protect them against fraud claims or defenses by consumers. The FTC responded by abolishing the HDC rule in consumer credit sales.[12] The financial and consumer goods industries predicted a decline in the sales of items such as furniture and appliances and anticipated increases in the cost of consumer credit. Neither happened. There is also evidence that in states that do impose some form of assignee liability, lenders have not curtailed their mortgage lending. A study compared state laws with and without assignee provisions and found no material decline in lending levels in states that had laws that, under certain conditions, abrogated the HDC rule (Bostic et al. 2008). This evidence is inconsistent with the position that imposition of assignee liability would significantly increase the cost of credit or reduce the availability of credit.

Arranger Liability

The job of arrangers is to package loans into pools for sale as asset-backed securities. During the time between the purchase of loans and the issuance of the securities, arrangers actually own the loans. In this situation, they are like any other assignee. If they are not holders in due course[13] or the loans are subject to laws such as HOEPA, they may be liable for any illegality at origination.

Arrangers also have some exposure to liability in their capacity as arrangers if a court finds that they were actively involved in unlawful activities related to the loan origination. It is also possible for consumers to bring claims against arrangers under theories of joint venture or civil conspiracy or if arrangers aided and abetted originators' unlawful conduct. These theories of liability do not require that the arrangers own the notes or have actively engaged in the illegal acts. There are few cases in which plaintiffs have asserted consumer protection claims against arrangers and even fewer cases in which arrangers have been held responsible. The paucity of cases means that theories of arranger liability are essentially untested. Whether consumers can harness evidence to implicate arrangers in abusive lending cases will be a question for the courts.

One question that policymakers need to answer is whether arrangers should bear responsibility for keeping abuses out of the home mortgage market because of their role as dealmakers, even if they are not tied to any wrongdoing themselves. The rationales for imposing a policing function on arrangers are that arrangers can enable bad actors by funding them through loan purchases, and they can influence what happens at loan origination. Arrangers exert this influence by directly informing originators of the types of loans they are willing to buy and indirectly through the loans they actually purchase (Engel and Fitzpatrick 2010).

Our position is that policymakers should consider imposing liability on arrangers that are not assignees or participants in unlawful activities only if the originators or intermediaries who were directly involved in the illegal acts are insolvent and the arrangers have constructive knowledge of the illegal acts.[14] This approach incentivizes arrangers to carefully review underwriting and loan terms in loan pools and to scrutinize the financial soundness and practices of lenders and brokers with whom they do business. With "skin in the game," arrangers will have good reason to shut off the spigot to lenders that engage in wrongdoing, making it difficult for bad actors to remain in the market. In addition, borrowers will have recourse against arrangers if they enabled judgment-proof lenders and brokers that they knew or should have known were unscrupulous.

The goal of legal liability in the mortgage context should be to align incentives and reserve the harshest sanctions for the entities that engage in the most egregious behavior. Consistent with these goals, we suggest caps on arrangers' and assignees' liability and unlimited relief against lenders and intermediaries that directly engage in patterns of wrongdoing. The scheme that we propose is not all bad news for industry. While responsible actors would have to shoulder new burdens, they would also benefit from measured consumer protections. Increasing scrutiny of the origination channel could help to reduce fraud from bad actors on both the borrowing and lending sides of the market, which would benefit the ultimate owners of loans and help to restore investor confidence in mortgage-backed securities, which in turn could help originators and arrangers.

Preemption

Federal preemption is a particularly divisive topic in consumer protection; no consumer advocates argue for preemption, and no industry advocates argue against it. Preemption comes in two different forms. The first is when a federal law trumps a state law, in which case a stronger state law must yield to a weaker federal law. There is also regulatory preemption, in which a regulator asserts that state laws do not apply to the entities that are subject to the regulator's supervision.

Regulatory Preemption

Regulatory preemption was at issue in a recent Supreme Court decision, *Cuomo v. Clearing House Association*. A collection of banks sought to enjoin the Attorney General of New York's attempt to enforce federal and state fair lending laws against nationally chartered banks and ultimately lost.[15] The case revolved around a regulation issued by the Office of the Comptroller of the Currency (OCC), in which the OCC interpreted its exclusive grant of visitorial powers as preempting any state efforts to prosecute nationally chartered banks under state or federal law in the absence of an explicit grant of power to the states to prosecute. Although the banks lost in this particular round, in an earlier case involving a different factual setting, the Supreme Court upheld the application of the OCC's preemption rule.[16]

The Dodd-Frank Act altered the landscape of regulatory preemption by prohibiting bank regulators from preempting state consumer financial protection laws unless the laws interfere with banks' exercise of their powers. The law leaves open many preemption questions, including the scope of the laws that qualify as consumer financial protection laws. For example, state licensing laws and unfair and deceptive practices laws may fall outside the Dodd-Frank restriction on preemption. This is an area that requires further attention. If bank regulators can circumvent state enforcement of specific consumer laws, there will be an uneven playing field and some consumers will be unable to obtain relief.

Federal Preemption of State Laws

Federal preemption of state laws has obvious value to mortgage lenders operating in several states: They need only adhere to a federal standard and not worry about multiple sets of rules for loans made in different states, which reduces their compliance costs. Similarly, federal preemption makes deploying enterprise-wide data recordation or compliance software a much simpler task. In an era of Internet marketing and lending, it also simplifies the problems that lenders encounter when they advertise credit and borrowers apply for loans through Internet portals that are available to people across the country. Another argument on the side of federal preemption is more theoretical: State borders are arbitrarily drawn political boundaries that do not necessarily denote real differences in population that justify different laws. This justification is essentially an appeal to efficiency.

There are persuasive counterarguments. First, not every state has laws that require more than the federal standard, especially given the breadth of the lending provisions in the new financial reform law, so lenders do not have to navigate different standards in all fifty states in addition to federal regulations. Second, even where there is variation among state laws, it is often minimal, such as lowering HOEPA triggers in a state-law analog. Third, where variations exist across states, they allow for economic analysis to determine the impact of different regimes on the cost, availability, and sustainability of credit. In that sense, variations between states can help in crafting more effective and less costly federal regulations in the long run. Last, electronic compliance programs have greatly reduced compliance costs.

Preemption imposes burdens on states by treating all consumers and markets throughout the country as if they were in need of the same protections. A federal law that functions as a ceiling impedes states' capacity to respond to the unique needs of their citizens. Populations vary in important ways across states, particularly in terms of concentrations of wealth and poverty, which can lead to surprising differences in consumer behavior, credit availability, and borrower outcomes.[17] For this reason, states need the power to customize their regulatory environments. This can be particularly important if federal protections are weak, as many have argued was the case with HOEPA.

The Dodd-Frank Act does not preempt state laws except to the extent to which it permits regulatory preemption by depository institutions in limited circumstances. This means that the new law and the rules written under the law by the CFPB will set a floor, not a ceiling, on consumer protection. This does not signal the end of the preemption debate, however, and policymakers should continue to consider the costs and benefits of preemption.

Who Should Make the Rules Governing Mortgage Lending?

In determining who should regulate mortgages, a problem that cuts across rule-making in general arises: Should a single agency or multiple agencies jointly write the rules? If legislators vest the authority to regulate mortgages in a single agency, the agency can efficiently and carefully analyze the shape of any needed rules. On the other hand, the agency can decide to take no regulatory action at all, even in the face of pressing problems such as those that preceded the subprime meltdown. In addition, there is the risk that the mortgage regulator will be "captured" by those it regulates and will shift its focus away from the agency's public mission and toward furthering the interests of the entities it regulates or those of a specific group of stakeholders.

The alternative is to have a system in which multiple agencies write mortgage regulations together. Under this model, there is a possibility that new rules can emerge even if one or more of the regulators is "captured" or if an agency otherwise opposes regulation. Joint rule-making offers another advantage: The agencies can bring together a wealth of knowledge and resources, which should result in better-informed rules governing mortgages. The obvious downside to joint rule-making is a significant collective action problem: Organizing multiple regulators is cumbersome, and getting them to agree to identical regulations can be impossible.

Under the Dodd-Frank Act, the CFPB has extensive rule-making authority. The law checks this authority by allowing bank regulators to block rules that they believe could threaten the safety of the financial system. This approach is something of a hybrid between a system that vests all rule-making authority in one agency and a system that requires joint rule-making across multiple agencies.

Types of Regulation

Consumer protection laws can take numerous forms. Here, we address two form issues as they relate to mortgage regulation: hard versus soft laws and rules versus standards

Hard Versus Soft Laws

Over the last few decades, federal action in the mortgage arena has involved soft laws issued by bank regulators in the form of policy pronouncements and guidances condemning risky lending practices. Although soft laws are essentially non-binding codes of conduct, they have the same advantages as progressive discipline policies. They enable regulators to address changing conditions with initial steps that are not heavy-handed, which can be especially useful when regulators are unsure about the scope and seriousness of a problem. Another advantage is that when rule-making is across agencies, it can be easier for agencies to reach a consensus on a guidance than on a hard law. Last, when an agency has limited jurisdiction and the consumer protection concerns extend to entities outside its jurisdiction, soft law can be a powerful tool to signal problems to lawmakers who do have the authority to act, as well as to market participants that are directly or indirectly engaging in the suspect activity.

Soft laws are poor instruments for addressing consumer protection when practices are clearly unfair, deceptive, or abusive. In such cases, a generalized warning from regulators sends a weak message unless it is followed by a hard law. Furthermore, because soft law does not contain enforcement mechanisms, regulators' only power is their ability to persuade. Experience with the ineffectiveness of regulatory guidances during the subprime lending boom reveals that hard law is the better route to directly curtail unfair, deceptive or abusive lending.

Rules Versus Standards

Mortgage lending rules, whether regulatory or legislated, can be framed as broad standards or specific prohibitions and requirements. An example of a broad standard is a rule prohibiting unfair lending. A specific rule might say that no loan can contain a prepayment penalty that extends beyond two years.

By providing legal certainty, specific rules make it possible for loan originators and other entities that are subject to mortgage laws to determine their potential liability. From an enforcement and compliance perspective, the objectivity of clear rules also makes it easier to verify compliance. There still can be high compliance costs depending on the number of rules. Hundreds of specific prohibitions may be more burdensome than a broad standard, even with its ambiguity.

Specific rules also make it possible for bad actors to engage in practices that adhere to the letter of the law but are inconsistent with the goals that animated the rules. An innovative, unscrupulous lender could comply with a set of specific rules aimed at preventing unfair lending practices and still engage in unfair lending.

Broad standards, in contrast, are flexible tools that provide potentially broad swaths of protection from an array of practices and loan terms. Lenders who are concerned about liability will have an incentive to comply with the spirit of the law. Another benefit is that the standard can apply to new products and problematic practices without the need for new legislation.

The argument against broad standards is that vague injunctions do not make clear what activities the law prohibits. Instead, borrowers and financial institutions have to wait for courts to decide cases before they know the contours of the standard, and even then, what constitutes a violation of the standard can change over time as courts render new decisions with new interpretations. Conflicting opinions can emerge among courts that hear cases, which only adds to the lack of clarity. Ultimately, fears of liability can cause originators to shy away from innovating, to charge more for credit, or to exit the market completely. In other words, broad standards can discourage good behavior as well as bad.

There is a way to balance this tension. A law can impose a broad standard and then require that a regulatory body write rules implementing the standard. The rules would satisfy the need for specificity, and the broad standard would give the agency the flexibility to adopt new rules as needed (Engel and McCoy 2002). Such a system would still encounter short-run problems with innovative bad actors finding ways to engage in behavior that violates the standard but not any specific rules. Regulation can adapt much faster than legislation, however, and allowing regulators to write specific rules can minimize the amount of time such behavior remains legal. Allowing regulators, rather than courts, to interpret the standard also eliminates the uncertainty that arises from waiting for case law to develop or when case law is inconsistent.

Enforcing the Rules

The effectiveness of any rules depends on enforcement. The strongest of regulations is meaningless unless the subjects of the rules have incentives to comply. Like other aspects of mortgage regulation, the goal is to sanction violations without curtailing good businesses through excessive compliance costs or the risk of frivolous litigation.

The critical questions along this dimension of consumer protection are: Who can enforce the law and what are the sanctions that can be employed when entities do not comply with the law? A conservative scheme vests enforcement solely in a federal agency or agencies. A more expansive law would also allow state agencies, such as attorneys general, to bring actions against transgressors. A third option is to expand the pool of potential enforcers to allow private litigation by aggrieved individuals or entities, including municipalities that suffer injuries from unlawful lending. A related issue that has repeatedly come up in debates about lending reform is whether to permit class-action lawsuits.

The broader the category of possible claimants, the stronger is the deterrent effect of the law. The problem is that a law with a very powerful deterrent effect may drive out risk-averse actors who do comply with the law as well as the bad eggs that the law intends to deter. Just the same, there are benefits to allowing non-governmental entities to bring actions. The most important of these benefits are that it eliminates the risk that politics will determine whether a law is enforced and that it permits injured parties to recover without needing to enlist the aid of a governmental office.[18] On the other hand, litigation imposes significant costs on lenders, and those costs will likely be passed on to consumers in the form of either increasing the cost or reducing the availability of credit.

Similar concerns arise in considering the scope of possible sanctions. The extent to which the threat of litigation informs behavior is based in large part on the consequences for violating the law. Potential sanctions can range from injunctive relief, such as orders to cease the unlawful activity, to compensatory damages, fines, and even unlimited punitive damages.

Given the extraordinary social costs that the United States has experienced as a result of unfair and risky lending, a strong stick is needed. It might be worth the increased cost or reduced availability of credit if that would reduce the likelihood or severity of another housing market disruption of this magnitude. A regime that permits a broad range of plaintiffs to bring claims and that provides substantial remedies should be designed to offset whatever excessive profits the unscrupulous parts of the mortgage industry generate by marketing complex, risky products to consumers.

We recognize that unlimited damages could destroy the market for loans, especially if assignees could be liable for punitive damages. For this reason, we support punitive damages only against entities that engaged in wrongdoing. All others—for example, innocent assignees—would have their liability capped. The size of the cap should relate to the broadness of the categories of plaintiffs who can bring suits; the broader the categories of potential plaintiffs, the more restrictive the damages cap should be.

Forum for Resolution

Another issue to resolve is determining the best forum for resolving consumer claims. In some areas of the law, aggrieved plaintiffs must exhaust administrative avenues before going to court. In other areas, people are allowed to choose whether to pursue their claims through an administrative process or in the courts. For many claims, courts are the only vehicle for relief.

There are good reasons to establish an administrative process for consumer complaints. For starters, administrative enforcement can be less expensive and time consuming because the procedures are typically less formal and complainants can usually secure relief without retaining lawyers. Whenever the costs of enforcement are reduced, plaintiffs, defendants, and society benefit. There are also economies of scale that arise from concentrating claims in one agency rather than having thousands of judges each hearing just a few claims. Consolidation of expertise can increase efficiency and reduce the risk of incorrect and inconsistent rulings. On the other hand, when adjudicators are consolidated in a single agency, there can be a tendency to lose diversity of ideas, which can lead to entrenched views that do not change in response to new market developments.

Administrative processes are not without other problems. One is that agency decisions are rarely published. This means that there is no mechanism for developing a body of law through reported decisions. In addition, class actions are usually disallowed in administrative actions, and the remedies that are available tend to be smaller than court judgments. Together, these factors lessen the incentive to comply with regulations. From a consumer perspective, reducing the incentives to comply with the law might not be an acceptable trade-off for the efficiency gains from administrative procedures, though it is worth noting that many of the problems we identified could be addressed by reworking of the features of administrative resolution, such as publishing decisions and allowing larger damage awards.

Judicial enforcement of consumer laws allows for larger potential awards and class actions. In addition, judges may feel less constrained than administrative adjudicators when it comes to interpreting the law, which can mean greater protection for consumers. At the same time, the high costs of litigation may deter consumers from filing claims and may create incentives for defendants to run up the cost of litigation to dissuade borrowers from pursuing claims. There is also the risk that large potential awards, particularly from class actions, as well as the uncertainty created by varying judicial interpretations of the law, will lead lenders to err on the side of reducing credit and avoiding product innovations. Depending on the magnitude of these costs, smaller lenders may be forced to exit the market.

Beyond the Regulatory Framework

Thus far, our focus has been on the framework for mortgage regulation. In this part of the chapter, we extend the discussion to three more topics: the possibilities for developing systems to review loan products, loan disclosures, and the types of data that could lead to more informed policymaking.

Product Review

There are mechanisms for reviewing loans to identify defects and latent dangers, as well as ways that originators can misuse a product. For example, disclosures can be tested before being released, borrower behavior and decision making can be studied in experimental labs, and loan performance can be tracked over time. Whatever the route, the goals of product review and testing are to identify products that present excessive risks, to identify uses that make products excessively risky, and to find ways to improve the products and their use to make both safer. Importantly, product review requirements should not chill sensible and sustainable adoption of innovative products, but rather should encourage it.

Many consumer protection advocates point out that producers cannot sell toasters if one in five of those toasters explodes. Such producers would face scrutiny from state and federal authorities and would be prohibited from selling defective products. Yet, the analogy goes, consumers can buy loans that "explode"—a borrower default followed by a foreclosure—one in five times. This analogy, despite its power as a simple-to-understand and vivid example, is a poor one. Testing a toaster is much easier than assessing the risks associated with a home mortgage loan. It does not take long to make a slice of toast—maybe a few minutes—and toasters are used daily. Thus if a toaster is faulty, the fault should reveal itself fairly quickly in a laboratory setting. Mortgage loans, especially loan products that are designed to help borrowers build credit and refinance into better products, cannot be thoroughly lab-tested in any reasonable amount of time. It takes adjustable-rate loans between two and five years to experience a rate reset, and the full term can be as long as 40 years. Additionally, home loans can be used in different ways, for example, to acquire a home or invest in property or for speculative purchases.

Requiring laboratory testing akin to product safety testing could impose huge costs on lenders. They would need to use human subjects from a variety of social and economic backgrounds to test new credit products, which would invite the type of extensive regulation that is seen in pharmaceutical testing. But unlike the case for pharmaceuticals, each of which requires years and an average of a billion dollars to develop and approve, lenders cannot be granted patents or other temporary monopolies on credit products that they can use to recoup their costs. Therefore there is little incentive to invest time and money in developing a loan product that can be copied by competitors for free once it has been approved.

An alternative to product testing in a lab is observation of loan products in the market. There is good reason to believe that observation is a weak instrument without adjunctive data collection. For example, adjustable-rate mortgages (ARMs) have been around for decades, and we know that they can be valuable to borrowers. When subprime was peaking, there was observational evidence that people were refinancing ARMs, but that alone did not demonstrate that ARMs were dangerous products. Borrowers could have been refinancing into less expensive products. Where the observation broke down was when those who were looking at the data could not tell what types of loans subprime borrowers were refinancing into. If this can be remedied through more robust data collection, observation could help to identify unfair, deceptive, or abusive products.

Disclosures

The major form of consumer protection over the last 30 years has been laws requiring that lenders disclose loan terms to borrowers. Although disclosures alone are inadequate to protect consumers, they can enhance consumers' ability to comparison shop and understand features of their loans. It is therefore critical that disclosures take into account how consumers process information. Framing effects, pre-decisional bias, and priming all alter the ways in which consumers understand information that is presented to them. Experiments with disclosure prototypes can help policymakers to determine the best method for conveying complex information to borrowers. It is also important that disclosures keep pace with advances in home mortgage lending. As loan terms and the way in which borrowers process information change over time, disclosures should adapt and change to remain relevant.

Data

Policymakers have been missing an important ingredient when regulating lending practices, loan terms, and loan performance: data. The main source of data on mortgage lending is the Federal Reserve Board, which collects information under the Home Mortgage Disclosure Act (HMDA). Congress passed HMDA in 1975 in response to evidence that lenders were refusing to lend in neighborhoods with high concentrations of people of color. The mortgage market has changed dramatically since 1975, and HMDA has not kept abreast of these changes. As a result, regulators have not had rich, quantitative information on many unfair, deceptive, and abusive lending practices. Instead, they have had to rely on anecdotes from consumer activists, which can be useful but often paint an incomplete picture.

The financial sector has massive amounts of information that it collects on loan terms, borrowers' creditworthiness, and defaults and foreclosures. Governmental units that want this information have to spend hundreds of thousands of dollars to purchase the data from private companies. Even after this huge expense, the licensing agreements often restrict how the data can be used.

Effective policy cannot be made in a data-free zone. Without information, enforcers cannot identify bad actors, such as rogue brokers and lenders. Without a sophisticated understanding of loan products on the market, regulators cannot detect risky practices; and without loan performance metrics to complement anecdotal information, no one can detect brewing problems and identify loans that have high probabilities of default.

Data are not free. It is expensive for institutions to collect and submit data to regulators, and it is costly for regulators to collate and analyze data. Any expansion in required data reporting should be sensitive to these costs and try to consolidate data gathering to reduce the burden on providers of information and on regulators.

As a result of the Dodd-Frank Act, more information will be available to policymakers. The act created the Office of Financial Research (OFR), which operates as a support agency for a newly created Financial Stability Oversight Council (FSOC). Headed by an independent director, the OFR collects and standardizes data from the agencies that are members of the FSOC, for use by FSOC or its member agencies in fulfilling the FSOC's duties. The data collection by the OFR focuses on identifying threats to the stability of the financial system. One concern is that, because of the nature of its mandate, the OFR will not assemble the detailed borrower and loan-level information that is necessary to understand the home mortgage market.

There is, however, another mechanism for data collection under the Dodd-Frank Act. The Act amends HMDA to require more detailed reporting of loan terms and the performance of loans. These provisions are not set in stone. Many of the fields are left to the discretion of the CFPB in terms of either defining the fields or deciding whether to collect the information in the first place. Thus the quality of any new data will depend on the CFPB.

Conclusion

From the early days of home mortgage securitization until the subprime crisis, the debate in policy circles was whether the government should regulate home loans beyond simply requiring disclosures. With the crisis, the focus shifted to *how*, not *whether*, to regulate. Congress's creation of the CFPB and passage of new laws governing loans secured by borrowers' homes are the first steps in shaping the future of mortgage regulation on the federal level. More laws and more rules are sure to emerge both in the states and federally. At each step, policymakers will have to sort through the conundrums we have identified.

References

American Securitization Forum. 2009. *ASF RMBS Disclosure and Reporting Packages*.
Bostic, Raphael W., Kathleen C. Engel, Patricia A. McCoy, Anthony Pennington-Cross, and Susan M. Wachter. 2008. "State and Local Anti-Predatory Lending Laws: The Effects of Assignee Liability and Legal Remedies." *Journal of Economics and Business* 60: 47–66.

Braunstein, Sandra. 2010. "Outlook: Where We've Been, Where We're Going." Paper presented at the Federal Reserve Bank of Philadelphia's Reinventing Older Communities Conference, May 12. http://www.philadelphiafed.org/community-development/events/reinventing-2010/agenda.cfm.

Eggert, Kurt. 2002. "Held Up in Due Course." *Creighton Law Review* 35: 503–640.

Engel, Kathleen C., and Patricia A. McCoy. 2002. "A Tale of Three Markets: The Law and Economics of Predatory Lending." *Texas Law Review* 80: 1255–1382.

———. 2007. "Turning a Blind Eye: Wall Street Finance of Predatory Lending." *Fordham Law Review* 75: 2039–2104.

Engel, Kathleen C., and Thomas J. Fitzpatrick, IV. 2010. "False Security: How Securitization Failed to Protect Arrangers and Investors from Borrower Claims." Working Paper (on file with authors).

Greenlee, Mark B., and Thomas J. Fitzpatrick, IV. 2009. "Reconsidering the Application of the Holder in Due Course Rule to Home Mortgage Notes." *UCC Law Journal* 41, 2: 225–289.

Kane, Edward J. 1981. "Accelerating Inflation, Technological Innovation, and the Decreasing Effectiveness of Banking Regulation." *Journal of Finance* 36, 2: 355–67.

Richter, Francisca. 2008. "An Analysis of Foreclosure Rate Differentials in Soft Markets." Working Paper 08-11. Cleveland: Federal Reserve Bank of Cleveland.

———. 2010. "Lending Patterns in Poor Neighborhoods." Working Paper 10-06. Cleveland: Federal Reserve Bank of Cleveland.

Notes

The views and opinions expressed in this chapter are those of the authors alone. They should not be attributed to the Federal Reserve Bank of Cleveland, Board of Governors, or other Banks within the System. Kathleen Engel thanks Suffolk University Law School for its generous support for her work on this chapter.

1. Up until the time that holders of securities backed by subprime mortgages suffered losses, the mantra was that investors could not conduct meaningful due diligence of loan files. That view has changed now that investors are insisting on having full information before investing in RMBS. The market has responded by developing loan-level due diligence products (see American Securitization Forum).

2. As the subprime crisis demonstrated, originators, arrangers, and investors do hold some risk. For example, securitization deals may require that originators hold the riskiest securities, which puts them in the first-loss position relative to holders of more senior securities. Likewise, if borrowers default because their loans are unaffordable, the owners of their loans—arrangers or investors—can suffer losses.

3. The Dodd-Frank Act and recent regulations limit compensation to intermediaries, but there are still mechanisms through which unscrupulous intermediaries can exploit borrowers.

4. When we refer to owners of notes, the owners could be arrangers or trusts. Although the trusts are the ultimate legal owners of the notes, investors are the beneficiaries who receive principal and interest payments on the bonds backed by the notes.

5. Home Ownership and Equity Protection Act of 1994, P.L. 103-325, 108 Stat. 2190 (1994), codified as amended at 15 U.S.C.A. §1637 et seq. (2007), 12 C.F.R. §226.32 (2007).

6. Hearings before the Senate Committee on HOEPA, Senate Report No. 103-169, 28 (1994), reprinted in 1994 U.S.C.C.A.N. 188, 1912 (1994).

7. The closed-end requirement excludes home equity loans.

8. 12 C.F.R. 226.32(a)(1)(i) (2007).

9. 12 C.F.R. 226.32(a)(1)(ii) (2007).

10. 15 U.S.C.A. §1641(d)(1) (2007).

11. During the subprime boom, owners of loans experienced minimal litigation threat from consumers. This was because of the HDC rule and also because borrowers who were on the brink of foreclosure—where they might have raised consumer protection claims in defense—typically ended up refinancing their loans.

12. For an extensive discussion of the FTC rule see Greenlee and Fitzpatrick (2009). See also Eggert (2002).

13. There are many practices common in the industry that can prevent arrangers from becoming holders in due course when they purchase notes.

14. Currently, many jurisdictions require that parties have actual knowledge of illegal acts to be liable as a co-conspirator, aider and abettor, or participant in a joint venture. Because the atomization of the industry has made it relatively easy to avoid what is legally deemed to be "actual" knowledge of wrongdoing, a constructive knowledge requirement, in combination with the lender and intermediary's insolvency, is appropriate. Essentially, a constructive knowledge requirement would impute knowledge to an arranger if the arranger should have known about the illegal activity through the exercise of reasonable care. For instance, if an originator has numerous cases resolved or pending against it for violations of consumer protection statutes and that information is available to the public, an arranger would be considered to have constructive knowledge of the originator's illegal acts.

15. *Cuomo v. Clearing House Ass'n, L.L.C.*, 129 S.Ct. 2710 (2009).

16. *Watters v. Wachovia Bank, N.A.*, 127 S.Ct. 1559 (2007).

17. Richter (2008) illustrates that the differences in foreclosure filing rates in neighborhoods with above-median economic characteristics can be explained through neighborhood characteristics; Richter (2010) suggests that social interaction effects in poor neighborhoods led to increased subprime lending relative to less-poor neighborhoods.

18. To be clear, several different entities cannot recover for the injury experienced by only one of them; for example, a state cannot recover damages that will be passed on to a consumer who has already recovered in his or her own lawsuit.

PART II

Community Impact

Chapter 6

A Profile of the Mortgage Crisis
in a Low- and Moderate-Income Community

Lynn Fisher, Lauren Lambie-Hanson, and Paul S. Willen

It is an accepted fact in the current policy debate that the U.S. housing crisis has damaged communities. A search for newspaper articles with the words "foreclosure" and "community" coupled with such words as "ravaged," "destroyed," and "damaged" turns up thousands of entries. In this chapter, we attempt to measure the effects of the crisis in a systematic way.

We focus on Chelsea, Massachusetts, a city adjacent to and just north of Boston. We chose Chelsea partly because we have an exceptionally good dataset but also because Chelsea was particularly hard hit in the housing crisis. As we will show, from the market's peak in 2005 to 2009, house prices fell by almost half and lenders foreclosed on or agreed to "short sales" on almost 8 percent of the condominiums and one- to three-family properties in the city.

Chelsea is typical of poorer communities in New England: 90 percent of its 34,356 residents live in census tracts identified by the Federal Financial Institutions Examination Council (FFIEC) as low- to moderate-income. Over 56 percent of its residents are Hispanic or Latino. As Calem, Gillen, and Wachter (2004) explain, communities such as Chelsea, with high concentrations of low-income and minority residents as well as borrowers with limited credit records, such as immigrants, became magnets for high-cost lending in the recent housing boom. Chelsea's land mass is small, about two square miles, making it one of the fifty most densely populated municipalities in the country.

According to 2008 census data, there are 12,798 housing units in Chelsea. Its housing stock is old, almost two thirds (8,158 units) having been built before 1940. Only 4,609 of those units are occupied by their owners. Chelsea's typical housing structure is the small multi-family building; more than half, or 6,579, of the units are in two- to four-unit buildings.

What do we find in our study? There is good news and bad news to report.

As was mentioned previously, the bad news surrounds house prices and foreclosures. According to our repeat-sales indices, by 2009, house prices had fallen by nearly 48 percent from their peak in 2005. These price estimates are not driven by foreclosures, as we exclude both foreclosure auctions and the sales of bank-owned properties from our sample. Excluding so-called short sales, in which a lender agrees to take less than the outstanding balance, reduces the city's estimated price decline to about 40 percent from the 2005 peak. Such dramatic price falls, remarkably, are not unprecedented in Chelsea; in fact, through 2009, the descent in this current housing cycle has been significantly short of the drop that occurred during the last cycle: Between 1987 and 1993, Chelsea house prices fell by 57 percent.

Collapsing house prices in the current cycle have led to an explosion in foreclosure activity. Between 1998 and 2005, annual foreclosure numbers in Chelsea were in the single digits every year, and two years—2003 and 2004—registered no foreclosures at all. In 2005, foreclosures started to rise, and in 2008, there were 125 foreclosures—more than five times more than the twenty-four total foreclosures that occurred in the 8-year period between 1998 and 2005. If we include short sales, the numbers are much higher. By our count, between 2006 and 2009, 357 homeowners left their homes through either a foreclosure or a short sale. According to the tax records, there are about 4,500 condominiums and one- to three-family properties in Chelsea, meaning that roughly 8 percent of the city's homeowners have lost their homes since the mortgage crisis began.[1] Maps of the city show that foreclosures were widespread, with at least one foreclosure on virtually every residential block in the city.

Even for homeowners who are not directly affected by foreclosure, falling prices have a deleterious effect. Depending on which price index we use, anyone who bought after 2000 owns a home today that is worth less than they paid. Taking inflation into account makes the situation even worse. Measured by the core PCE deflator, the overall price level has increased by more than 20 percent since 2000. Since the typical homeowner is highly leveraged, falling prices have completely wiped out any down payment investment for most homeowners who purchased after the beginning of the decade.

Of course, buyers benefit from lower prices. In the case of homes, repeat buyers are also sellers, so the reduction in purchase prices is potentially off-set by the reduction in the value of their current property. But for first-time homebuyers, falling prices represent an opportunity to get into the housing market that was not present in 2005.

How has Chelsea dealt with falling house prices and foreclosures? Here, the news is better: The picture is of a fundamentally viable community that is coping imperfectly with a bad situation. What would be worrisome would be if the foreclosure crisis pushed Chelsea over the proverbial tipping point and transformed it into a dying community in which no one wanted to buy, stay, or invest. Yet there seems to be little evidence that any such dynamic is under way. We back up this claim with three points.

First, the stock of bank-owned property, known in the industry as "real estate owned" (REO), appears to be under control. One of the main avenues by which foreclosures purportedly damage communities is by generating vacancies as lenders evict homeowners but then have trouble selling the properties. In his study of REO inventories in metropolitan areas across the United States, Immergluck (2008) argues that there is a vicious cycle of increased REO stocks and declining property values, since lower prices diminish homeowners' equity, leading to more foreclosures, which further depress house prices. Vacancies may also directly affect the value of REO properties themselves. Coulton, Schramm, and Hirsch (2008) document the relationship between longer periods spent in REO status and lower resale prices. They argue that one force behind this relationship is the often prolonged time REOs spend vacant, when they are vulnerable to vandalism and theft of appliances, wiring, pipes, and even siding. During 2008, there was some initial evidence of growing REO stocks, when the ability of lenders to sell distressed properties did not keep pace with the rise in new foreclosures. But starting in 2009, two things happened. First, lenders rapidly increased their sales of distressed properties. More important, lenders made increasing use of short sales, meaning that properties were transferred from one bona fide homeowner to another and never entered the bank-owned portfolio.

Second, homeowners appear to be investing in their properties, despite the collapse in house price appreciation. One fear, as expressed by Haughwout, Peach, and Tracy (2009), among others, is that the collapse in house prices and the resulting number of homeowners with little or no equity would result in homeowners having little or no long-term interest in their properties. But Chelsea's building permit data tell a different story. After a dramatic fall in 2008, which might have been exacerbated by wider credit market problems, the city's permit activity had, by the beginning of 2009, returned to its 2005 level. In particular, among recent buyers, there has been little fall-off in property investment, as those who bought after the local housing market peaked in 2005 are among the most likely to have negative equity. Thus contrary to some predictions, Chelsea's homeowners have lost equity but not an ongoing interest in their homes.

Third, long-term homeowners appear to remain committed to Chelsea. An exodus of homeowners would be one potential piece of evidence that residents consider Chelsea fatally wounded. In particular, we would expect such a trend to be concentrated among the homeowners who could most easily leave: the ones who still had positive equity in their homes despite recent price falls. In fact, we see the opposite effect. Owners with more than five years of tenure typically account for 75 percent of all sales in Chelsea, but in 2008, their share dropped to less than half. The exodus was of those owners who had purchased at the market peak, not the city's long-term owners.

Our study is unapologetically narrow. We are not comparing Chelsea with the rest of the country or elsewhere in Massachusetts, nor are we suggesting that Chelsea is in any way unique. Our goal merely is to come up with some quantitative, absolute measures of what is happening in a hard-hit community during the current mortgage crisis. In the conclusion, we briefly discuss how to apply the lessons from Chelsea more broadly.

Data

Our data come from three sources: public records, mortgage servicers, and building permits. Using the public records data enable us to track transactions of specific properties and the mortgages secured by these properties over time. This dataset includes both foreclosure petitions and foreclosure deeds. However, many mortgages that become delinquent never enter the foreclosure process, so the public records dataset gives us information on only a subset of distressed property owners. Loan-level data from mortgage servicers can give us a clear picture of a given loan's delinquency status over time, which remedies this problem. Finally, building permits serve as a useful indicator of investment activity and owners' confidence in the future health of the community.

Public Records

We use a dataset of property-level transactions assembled by the Warren Group, a Massachusetts-based company that specializes in collecting residential property records in New England.[2] The dataset includes information on all one- to three-family and condo transactions carried out since 1987, including mortgage originations, foreclosure petitions, foreclosure auctions, and deed transfers, for both foreclosure and non-foreclosure sales. Using the Warren data, we can observe when properties are sold through foreclosure, and we can distinguish properties that are sold at auction to a third party from those that become REO. We can also measure the time REO properties are held by banks before being resold. We also attempted to identify likely short sales, transactions in which the lender has agreed to allow the borrower to pay off a mortgage with the proceeds of a sale in which the price falls short of the loan's unpaid principal balance. The Massachusetts public records data do not identify short sales; in fact, the discharge documents report that the lender "received full payment and satisfaction" of the loan. To get around this constraint, we constructed a rule using a matched sample of loans from the public records and from First American CoreLogic Loan-Performance dataset of securitized subprime loans, which, unlike the public records, reports investor losses on the disposition of a loan and thus allows us to identify short sales. The definition that we developed for a short sale is a transaction in which the seller receives less than 75 percent of the total amount that was borrowed to purchase the property. The matched sample shows low rates of false positives and false negatives using this rule.

The Warren data also include information on property traits, such as the structure's characteristics and assessed valuations. Because only property transactions that have ocurred since 1987 are included in the dataset, we supplement it with information from the City of Chelsea Assessor's Office. We find that over 90 percent of all one- to three-family and condo properties in Chelsea are tracked by the Warren Group.

Mortgage Servicers

The second dataset that we use is a collection of records from large loan-servicing organizations that is maintained by LPS Applied Analytics, Inc.[3] This dataset has fields for key variables set at the time of each loan's origination, including the amount borrowed, the value and location of the property that secures the loan, whether the loan is classified as prime or subprime, and whether the loan is held in the lender's portfolio or has been packaged into a mortgage-backed security (MBS). We can also observe whether the loan is a first lien or a second lien and a host of interest-rate variables (such as whether the loan is fixed-rate or adjustable-rate and the manner in which the interest rate changes in the latter case).

Building Permits

We also obtained records on every building permit filed with the City of Chelsea's Inspectional Services Department between January 1996 and July 2009.[4] For each permit, we know the property address, the issue date, the permit fee paid, and a description and cost estimate of the work to be completed. We cleaned and standardized the addresses, then matched the building permit records to the Warren data for all one- to three-family dwellings. We excluded condominiums because it is often impossible to determine which condo units at a given address received the improvements. We believe that the building permit data in Chelsea are a good approximation of improvements owners made to their properties, since the city patrols neighborhoods seven days a week, issuing stop-work orders to those operating without permits.

Prices

Using sales data for 1987 to 2009, we calculated annual weighted repeat-sales price indices, following the methods developed in Case and Shiller (1987, 1989). Although Case-Shiller house price indices are typically calculated by using only sales of single-family homes, we included single-family, two-family, three-family, and condominium properties for two reasons. First, single-family homes make up only 17 percent of properties in Chelsea. Ignoring other sales would not provide a clear picture of changes in the city's house prices. Second, without including other properties, our sample size would be too small to differentiate between signal and noise in price changes. We also constructed the indices separately by property type to assess the impact of this decision to combine different-sized housing units as well as to gain information on relative rates of price change.

We took care to focus, to the best of our ability, on "non-distressed sales." We excluded all foreclosures, including properties sold at foreclosure auction to third parties and those that became REO.[5] We omitted sales through which properties left REO status, since lenders and servicers may sell properties at deep discounts to avoid managing them. We used our definition of short sales to calculate the price indices with and without these transactions, as some have argued that short sales also essentially represent distressed transactions. For the remaining transactions in our dataset, we omitted sales by owners who held their properties for less than seven days. To reduce the impact of outliers, we removed sales with prices less than $15,000 or over $10 million. We also excluded sales that generated log appreciation in excess of 10.

However, the repeat-sales methodology assumes that no significant changes have been made to an individual property between sales. If properties have been improved, the repeat-sales index will overestimate house price appreciation. To address this problem, we used our information on investments in properties from building permit data and calculated the repeat-sales indices again, controlling for the level of investment made between sales. We included sales by owners of one- to three-family properties who purchased after 1996 and sold by July 2009. Because our building permit data span this period, we were able to measure the full amount of investment (with issued permits) made by these owners.

Finally, we examined price changes using a hedonic model, estimated separately for each property type. We included controls for the number of bedrooms and baths, living area, lot size, and age of the property. We estimated the set of equations a second time, including measures of the owners' investment made in the properties, as evidenced by building permits.

The top panel of Figure 6.1 shows that average prices in Chelsea more than doubled between 2000 and 2005 but fell sharply after 2006; in just two years (between 2007 and 2009), prices fell by about 40 percent. In contrast,

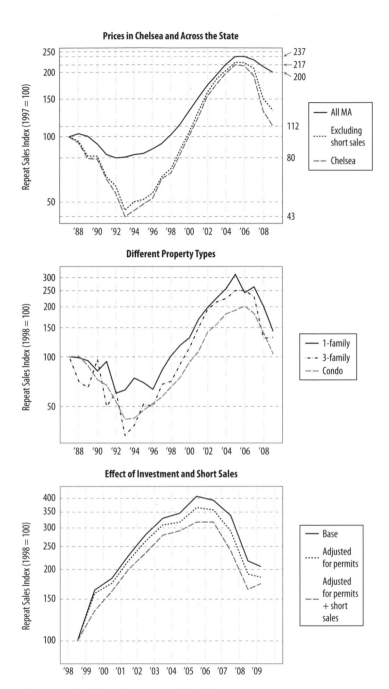

Figure 6.1. House prices in Chelsea, Massachusetts: 1988–2009. Authors' calculations.

prices across Massachusetts rose less dramatically between 2000 and 2005 and fell less than 13 percent between 2007 and 2009. The middle panel of Figure 6.1 shows that while all types of properties have been hard-hit in Chelsea, there has been less volatility in condominium prices, partly because condos did not appreciate as rapidly in 2003–2005 as did single-family, two-family, and three-family properties.

These dramatic price changes were not exclusive to Chelsea. Other Massachusetts communities, including Lawrence, Lowell, Lynn, and New Bedford, were also hard-hit, as Table 6.1 shows. These four communities, like Chelsea, are made up of predominantly low- to moderate-income neighborhoods, as defined by the FFIEC. Like Chelsea, they have older housing stock with more small multi-family properties, higher median home values, greater poverty rates, and more residents who are immigrants than is typical of most other Massachusetts towns.

One possible explanation for the large declines in house prices, as captured by the indices, is the inclusion of short sales. As was previously mentioned, it is difficult to identify these transactions in our data. Short sales have also become more common in recent years, and that trend appears to put a downward bias on estimates of recent house prices. In 2008 and 2009, over 10 percent of all residential real estate transactions in Chelsea were likely short sales, compared to a historical average of only 4 percent of transactions being short sales. Using the argument that these are distressed sales,

Table 6.1. House Prices in Chelsea and Elsewhere in Massachusetts: Mid-1990s

	Chelsea	Lawrence	Lowell	Lynn	New Bedford	Massa-chusetts
Trough Year	1993	1995	1993	1994	1995	1992
Index (1987 = 100)	46	46	57	60	80	84
Percent change	−54	−54	−43	−40	−20	−16
Peak Year	2005	2006	2006	2005	2005	2006
Index (1987 = 100)	223	243	205	240	245	250
Percent change	+385	+431	+257	+304	+207	+199
Trough Year	2009	2008	2009	2009	2009	2009
Index (1987 = 100)	133	131	151	153	181	215
Percent change	−40	−46	−26	−36	−26	−14

Authors' calculations.

like foreclosures, we exclude these transactions from the index calculations. The results, seen in the top panel of Figure 6.1, show 2009 prices falling to 112 percent of 1987 levels, yet 2009 prices fell only to 133 percent when short sales are excluded. The differences in the indices with and without the inclusion of short sales become greater each year since 2007, the same period over which short sales became increasingly common.

Another possible problem is that traditional indices may overestimate changes in house prices by failing to account for the owners' investment in the properties. Adjusting the price index to account for such investments, we find that declines in prices from the 2005 market peak are only slightly overestimated by traditional indices. Recall that this version of the index, shown in the bottom panel of Figure 6.1, includes only sales by owners who purchased after 1995 and sold before July 2009. Recalculating the index by controlling for investment and excluding short sales further reduces estimates of the recent decline in house prices, though the overall change in values remains large regardless of which method is used. The traditional index estimates a 50 percent decline in prices between 2005 and the second quarter (Q2) of 2009, while the index controlling for investment and excluding short sales estimates a 45 percent decline. To verify our findings from the repeat-sales indices, we also calculate a set of hedonic models, using annual fixed effects and a series of property trait covariates to estimate price indices. We find similar patterns in price change using this method.

Foreclosures

In this section, we assess the magnitude of Chelsea's foreclosure problem. We first discuss measurement issues and then turn to a discussion of what factors characterized the failed homeownerships. We conclude the section by quantifying the number of lender-owned properties in the community.

Measuring the Problem

To measure the number of foreclosures in Chelsea, we use two sources. The first is the Warren Group data previously discussed, in which we define a foreclosure as the recording of a foreclosure deed, which, roughly, extinguishes any claim by the mortgagee to the property and allows the lender to sell the property to a new owner. The advantage of public record data is that it is comprehensive because, at least in theory, it includes every transaction for all the residential properties in the state, and it also provides the property's exact location information in the form of a street address.

An alternative to looking at foreclosure deeds is looking at foreclosure starts. In Massachusetts, lenders initiate foreclosure proceedings with a court-filed order of notice in which the lender attempts to find out whether the borrower is in military service and thus protected against some foreclosure activity. The problem with orders of notice is that most do not lead to foreclosure. In some cases, the borrower self-cures; in other cases, the process drags on so long that the lender needs to file a second or third order of notice before actual foreclosure proceedings begin. Finally, the data are problematic, as at least some foreclosures appear to occur without a recorded order of notice.

We then look at the LPS data, which provide much more detailed data on the loan's history. Whereas the public record data accurately record only the final stage of the process, the foreclosure deed, LPS tells us the delinquency status of the loan every month, whether the lender has initiated foreclosure proceedings, and the final disposition of the property. The disadvantage of the LPS dataset is that it covers only the subset of servicers that have a contractual relationship with LPS. This explains why, for example, Table 6.2, which is based on LPS data, shows only 67 foreclosures in 2008, whereas

Table 6.2. Foreclosures in Chelsea: 2007–2010

| | Total | | Originated | | | | | |
| | | | Before 2007* | | In 2007† | | In 2008‡ | |
Year	Petitions	Deeds	Petitions	Deeds	Petitions	Deeds	Petitions	Deeds
2007	71	23	67	23	4	0	—	—
2008	81	67	60	59	20	8	1	0
2009	102	47	85	36	15	10	2	1
2010 (Jan.–Apr.)	30	24	18	20	10	3	2	1
Total	284	161	230	133	49	21	5	2
			13%	8%	15%	6%	2.1%	0.8%

Authors' calculations.

*Number = 1766; †number = 337; ‡number = 240.

Figure 6.2, constructed from Warren data, shows nearly twice as many foreclosures.

Overall Characterization

In the top panel of Figure 6.2, the dashed line shows foreclosure activity in Chelsea since the late 1980s. The current crisis is obviously visible, with foreclosures rising in 2006 after a prolonged period of exceptionally low foreclosure activity. Foreclosure growth accelerated in 2008 and reached an all-time high of 125 foreclosures before falling in 2009. The reasons for this decline are unclear and may involve an increasingly complex legal environment or an unwillingness by servicers to accelerate the foreclosure process in light of the difficulties they faced managing and disposing of distressed properties.

The solid curve in Figure 6.2 shows the total number of distressed transactions, including both foreclosures and short sales. As was previously mentioned, short sales—in which the lender allows the borrower to sell the house for less than the balance on the mortgage—represent an alternative way to end a troubled homeownership, and Figure 6.2 shows that by 2009, short sales were almost as likely to occur as foreclosures. While short sales are generally more attractive for a community because there is no period in which the lender owns the property and therefore the property is less likely to be vacant, short sales still signal mortgage distress, ownership turnover, and potential house price instability in the community.

From 2006 to the end of 2009, lenders had foreclosed on 263 properties in Chelsea. According to assessor's data, there are about 4,500 one- to three-family and condominium dwellings in the city, so this means that since the start of the crisis, lenders have foreclosed on roughly 6 percent of the homes in Chelsea. If we include short sales, the crisis has directly affected 8 percent of the homes, or roughly one in twelve properties in the city. According to the bottom panel of Figure 6.2, the foreclosure problem does not appear to be concentrated in any one part of Chelsea. There have been foreclosures on virtually every residential block, with the exception in the southwest corner of the city, which is largely composed of condominiums.

With the LPS data, we can get a richer portrait of the effects of the crisis on individual borrowers, albeit with the limitation, as mentioned earlier, that it depicts an arbitrary subset of the homes in Chelsea. In particular,

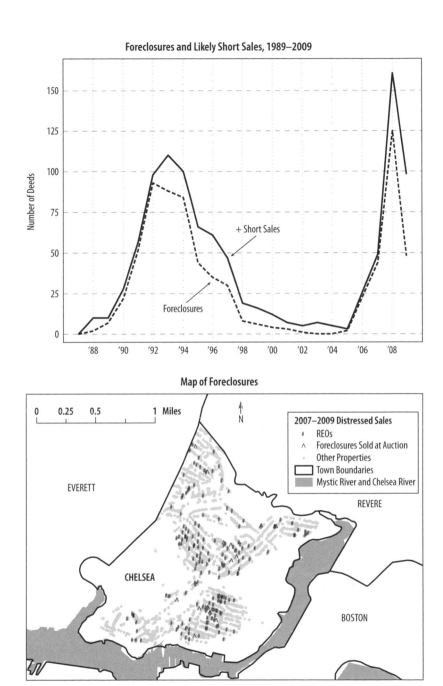

Figure 6.2. Foreclosures in Chelsea, Massachusetts: 1989–2009. Authors' calculations.

we can see that lenders initiated almost twice as many foreclosure proceedings (the 284 petitions in Table 6.2) than they have so far completed (the 161 deeds in Table 6.2), among the sample of 2,343 loans originated before 2009 and active between 2007 and 2009.

Table 6.2 also illustrates the impact of the crisis on households in Chelsea. Of borrowers with loans that were originated prior to 2007 and who were current at the end of 2006, more than 13 percent were the subject of a foreclosure petition and 8 percent lost their homes. Of those who borrowed in 2007, lenders initiated proceeding on an even higher fraction, 15 percent, but completed proceedings on only 6 percent.

The good news is that the 2008 vintage appears to be performing quite well. There are only a handful of serious problem loans, which cannot be attributed to the pool's youth, as the loans from the previous vintage were already in deep trouble at an equivalent point in the cycle. One major reason for this difference is simply that Chelsea's house prices have stabilized somewhat. Another factor is the dramatic improvement in borrowers' creditworthiness. The median borrower in 2006 had a FICO score of 691, but by 2008, the median score had risen to 724. This is not to say that foreclosures have gone away in Chelsea. As of April 2010, there were 1,970 active first-lien mortgages in the LPS dataset. Of these, 98 were identified as "in foreclosure" (many post-petition, pre-deed), and another 152 were more than 90 days delinquent.

The REO Problem

During the mortgage crisis, the buildup of REO, or bank-owned, properties has been a major concern of policymakers. Many have expressed concerns that REO properties are magnets for thieves and vandals and that their very presence on a street makes selling other properties more difficult, reduces prices, and, in turn, generates more foreclosures. Indeed, Figure 6.3 shows that the inventory of REO properties did climb dramatically after the foreclosure crisis started in 2006. The good news is that the stock of REO properties peaked in 2008 and then fell in 2009.

To better understand the evolution of the REO housing stock in Chelsea, it is useful to look at the flows into and out of this category. Figure 6.3 shows that the net additions to REO properties fell in 2009, mostly because the rate at which lenders added to their stock of REO housing fell dramatically. In

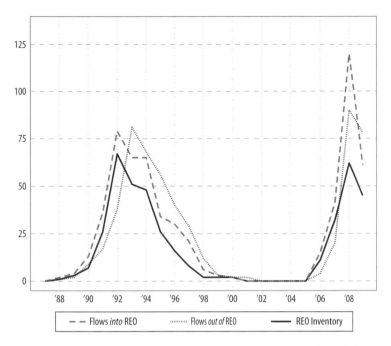

Figure 6.3. Flows and stock of REO properties in Chelsea, Massachusetts: 1987–2009. Authors' calculations.

other words, despite the fact that flows out actually fell, the number of REO properties went down.

To understand why flows into the REO stock fell so much, we look at the disposition of what we call "troubled properties," defined as ones for which the lender concluded in 2007, 2008, and 2009 that the borrower could not afford to service. As was mentioned above, a lender can dispose of a troubled property by allowing a short sale or by foreclosing. If the lender forecloses, it must hold an auction, at which it can choose whether to accept a bid or retain the property as REO in hopes of getting a better price. The LPS data summarized in Table 6.3 indicate that between 2007 and 2009, the share of troubled properties that went into REO status fell from 84 percent to 50 percent. In turn, this decline resulted from a greater willingness of lenders both to sell at auction and to do short sales.

The ability of lenders to sell properties at auction and to allow short sales tells us more, in some ways, about Chelsea than it does about the lenders. The simple fact that they can find buyers, even at depressed prices, means that at least some people believe that Chelsea remains a viable community.

Table 6.3. Disposition of Troubled Property in Chelsea: 2007–2009

	Troubled Properties	Foreclosure		Short Sale	Percent Entering REO
		REO	Auction		
2007	49	41	3	5	84
2008	161	120	5	36	75
2009	121	61	10	50	50

Authors' calculations.

In some depressed U.S. communities, finding buyers who are willing to pay anything more than a token amount for distressed properties has been a challenge (see the discussion in Coulton, Mikelbank, and Schramm 2008).

There is also hopeful news among the REO properties. Of those 181 properties that became REO in 2008 or 2009, 154 (85 percent) have been resold to third-party buyers by the second quarter of 2010 (2010Q2). Community stakeholders are typically concerned with the incidence of REO property flipping; however, we find that only 10 of these 154 REO buyers (6 percent) resold their properties by 2010Q2. This is not to say there are no investors in Chelsea. Among the 2008 and 2009 foreclosures alone, we have identified four unique buyers who have purchased three or four REOs each. However, the concentration of REO purchases among the most active buyers in Chelsea is very small in comparison to that in a city such as Cleveland, where the most active buyers have each purchased between 2 and 6 percent of all REOs sold (Coulton, Schramm, and Hirsch 2008: 7).

Investment

In this section, we look at Chelsea's building permit data as a way to measure how willing owners were to invest in their properties during this period. Since it is forward-looking, owner investment is a particularly useful measure of attitudes toward the community's future, as owners who viewed the community as fatally wounded by the crisis would be unlikely to invest more money in their properties. Furthermore, some have argued that homeowners with negative equity are not really homeowners at all and are less likely to invest (see, for example Haughwout, Peach, and Tracy 2009). But Chelsea tells a different story.

The collapse of the real estate market that began in 2006 does appear to have reduced such owner investment substantially, but some recovery appears under way. The top two curves in Figure 6.4 show the changes in the number and total dollar value of building permits for improving one- to three-family properties, respectively. Our quarterly backward-looking moving average of the number of permits falls by almost half, from a peak of 117 permits per quarter in 2006Q2 to a trough of 65 permits in 2008Q3. The dollar figures tell a similar story, with permits for nearly $1.2 million of work in 2006Q3 dropping to $738,000 in 2008Q3. In the meantime, investment seems to have bounced back, with 92 permits issued in 2009Q2 collectively worth almost $900,000.

Comparing 2009 and 2006 is somewhat misleading, however, because the 2005–2006 period is something of an anomaly. The third quarter of 2005 was the first time Chelsea building inspectors issued more than 100

Figure 6.4. Permit activity in Chelsea, Massachusetts: 1996–2009. Authors' calculations.

permits in a single month for improvements to one- to three-family properties. Thus the number of permits in 2009Q2 is low in relation only to that
exceptional boom period and actually exceeds the total issued for almost
every quarter before 2006.

To add to the interpretive difficulty here, credit supply problems may
account for some of the drop. First, the collapse in house prices and the concomitant reduction in home equity made it difficult for homeowners to get
second mortgages or do cash-out refinances, a traditional source of funding for home improvement. LPS reported 125 cash-out refinances in 2006
and only 24 in 2008. Second, many have argued that the financial market
troubles of 2008, which culminated in the collapse of Lehman Brothers and
AIG, created a credit crunch in which lenders were unwilling to lend to anyone, even if they did have a good business plan or reasonable collateral.

In light of the credit supply issues, which persisted into 2009, the recovery of investment in home improvement during the first half of 2009 is all
the more surprising. Despite house prices falling back to their 2001 level,
which would make cash-out refinances impossible for a large fraction of
homeowners, Chelsea's homeowners were able to make home improvements
at a pace roughly consistent with that of 2005.

To assess the question of whether homeowners with little or no equity
are investing in their properties, we can look at the investment activity of
recent homebuyers. The third line in Figure 6.4 shows the share of permits
accounted for by homeowners who bought in the three previous years. For
example, the 2007 figure shows investments by homeowners who bought in
2005, 2006, or 2007. In general, recent homebuyers account for a dispropor-
tionate share of building permits. Figure 6.4 shows that this share remained
stable through this three-year period, which is remarkable given that in 2008
we are considering owners who bought in 2006, 2007, and 2008 and had seen
their property's value collapse anywhere from 20 to 50 percent. There is no
evidence in our data that we should view homeowners with negative equity
as renters, at least as far as investment in home improvements is concerned.

Sales

In analyzing Chelsea's housing market in the mortgage crisis, we have
focused thus far on prices and foreclosures, as these are the most salient

pieces of evidence. However, the evolution of sales displays equally significant variation and also is important to understanding the crisis. In 2004 and 2005, about forty-five homes, or about 1 percent of the properties in the city, according to 2009 assessor's records, changed hands each month, and with rising prices, almost none of these transactions were distressed sales. This represented a dramatic increase over earlier years, as monthly sales rates were typically under thirty in 2002 and 2003. By 2007, the total number of sales was cut in half, and over one quarter were distressed sales, including sales into foreclosure, sales out of REO, and likely short sales. Total sales increased in 2008 and 2009 to about twenty-eight sales per month, still more than 40 percent below the 2005 peak, and a majority of these were distressed sales.

The first point to make here is that the reduction in sales volume casts doubt on the theory that foreclosures have driven down house prices by increasing the supply of residential real estate on the market. If the effect of foreclosures was to shift the supply curve to the right, we would see a drop in prices and an *increase* in the number of transactions. The drop in both prices and transactions suggests a reduction in demand, not an increase in supply.

But it is possible to go further and argue that the falling sales volume is actually a good sign for Chelsea and reflects the high value that owners place on their properties. Arguably, the entire supply of houses for sale in a market includes *all* properties, not just those currently listed for sale—the idea being that for a sufficiently high price, everyone would eventually sell. The bad news for Chelsea would be if we were to see an enormous number of people selling at low prices, but we find no evidence of that occurring.

The question of why people place high values on their homes, even in a depressed market, is more difficult to answer. One possibility is that they view the current fall in prices as transitory, as indeed the much larger Massachusetts house price fall in the mid-1990s turned out to be. Such logic may have some merit, as the run-up in prices that preceded the 1990s downturn almost exactly parallels the run-up in this cycle.

It is instructive to look at the composition of sales as well. One natural explanation for the low sales volume is that owners suffer from psychological biases and are unwilling to accept that their properties are currently worth less than they paid, a phenomenon that was documented by Genesove and Mayer (2001). In fact, we see the opposite pattern in the Chelsea data.

Table 6.4. Sales by Long-Term Owners* in Chelsea: 2004–2009

Year	Number of Sales	As Percent of All Sales
2004	390	72
2005	398	76
2006	254	67
2007	173	70
2008	126	48
2009	151	59

Authors' calculations.
*More than five years of tenure.

Long-term owners, the ones who are least likely to have witnessed a big price fall since purchase, are *less* likely to sell, as shown in Table 6.4.

The fact that long-term owners in Chelsea are not selling in the currently depressed housing market is potentially positive along another dimension. One concern about a big fall in prices is that homeowners who had built big equity positions would be forced to sell in a down market. The fact that so few are selling suggests that the crisis has had muted equity-destroying effects for long-term owners and that they will be able to take advantage of a recovery if and when it occurs.

Conclusion

The picture of Chelsea that we paint is of a community under enormous economic stress but displaying a fair amount of resilience. Chelsea's location means that, ultimately, its viability depends on that of its big next-door neighbor, Boston. As long as Boston is healthy, there will be demand for real estate in a nearby residential community. Fears that the foreclosure crisis would tip Chelsea into long-term decline do not seem well-founded. Its residents are not running for the exits and selling at any price but rather appear committed and even willing to invest in their community.

But then location is the key issue in comparing Chelsea with other low- and moderate-income communities in the region and in the nation. For similar cities in the industrial Midwest, the collapse of manufacturing has raised questions about their long-term viability. It is likely that a similar analysis of a city adjacent to Cleveland or Detroit or even Springfield, Massachusetts, would not depict such an optimistic scenario.

References

Calem, Paul S., Kevin Gillen, and Susan Wachter. 2004. "The Neighborhood Distribution of Subprime Mortgage Lending." *Journal of Real Estate Finance and Economics* 29, 4: 393–410.

Campbell, John Y., Stefano Giglio, and Parag Pathak. 2009. "Forced Sales and House Prices." Working Paper 14866. Cambridge, Mass.: National Bureau of Economic Research.

Case, Karl E., and Robert J. Shiller. 1987. "Prices of Single-Family Homes Since 1970: New Indexes for Four Cities." Working Paper 2393. Cambridge, Mass.: National Bureau of Economic Research.

———. 1989. "The Efficiency of the Market for Single-Family Homes." *American Economic Review* 79, 1: 125–37.

Coulton, Claudia, Kristen Mikelbank, and Michael Schramm. 2008. "Foreclosure and Beyond: A Report on Ownership and Housing Values Following Sheriff's Sales, Cleveland and Cuyohoga County, 2000–2007." Cleveland: Center on Urban Poverty and Community Development, Case Western Reserve University. http://blog. case.edu/msass/2008/01/13/Foreclosure_and_Beyond_final.pdf.

Coulton, Claudia, Michael Schramm, and April Hirsch. 2008. "Beyond REO: Property Transfers at Extremely Distressed Prices in Cuyahoga County, 2005–2008." Cleveland: Center on Urban Poverty and Community Development, Case Western Reserve University. http://blog.case.edu/msass/2008/12/09/20081209_ beyond_reo_final.pdf.

Fisher, Lynn M., and Lauren Lambie-Hanson. 2010. "Tenure and Foreclosure: Identifying Investor-Owners and Assessing Their Impact: A Case Study of Chelsea, MA." Boston, Mass.: Citizens Housing and Planning Association. http://www.chapa.org/files/ f_1266423752CHAPA_Feb15FisherandLambie-Hanson.pdf.

Foote, Christopher, Kristopher Gerardi, Lorenz Goette, and Paul S. Willen. 2009. "Reducing Foreclosures: No Easy Answers." In *NBER Macroeconomics Annual* 24, ed. Daron Acemoglu, Kenneth Rogoff, and Michael Woodford. Chicago: University of Chicago Press. 89–138.

Foote, Christopher L., Kristopher Gerardi, and Paul S. Willen. 2008. "Negative Equity and Foreclosure: Theory and Evidence." *Journal of Urban Economics* 64, 2: 234–45.

Genesove, David, and Christopher Mayer. 2001. "Loss Aversion and Seller Behavior: Evidence from the Housing Market." *Quarterly Journal of Economics* 116, 4: 1233–1260.

Haughwout, Andrew, Richard Peach, and Joseph Tracy. 2009. "The Homeownership Gap." Staff Report 418. New York: Federal Reserve Bank of New York. http://www. newyorkfed.org/research/staff_reports/sr418.pdf.

Immergluck, Dan. 2008. "The Accumulation of Foreclosed Properties: Trajectories of Metropolitan REO Inventories During the 2007–2008 Mortgage Crisis." Community Affairs Discussion Paper 02-08. Atlanta: Federal Reserve Bank of Atlanta. http://www.atl.frb.org/filelegacydocs/dp_0208.pdf.

Notes

1. A comparable percentage of units were affected by foreclosure. The 357 foreclosures and short sales involved 655 housing units, about 8 percent of the 7,900 total units in Chelsea's one- to three-family and condominium stock.

2. For a discussion of the Warren data, see Foote, Gerardi, and Willen (2008).

3. The dataset was originally created by a company called McDash Analytics; LPS acquired McDash in mid-2008. Among housing researchers, the dataset is still generally called the "McDash data." For more details, see Foote et al. (2009).

4. For a full discussion of this dataset, see Fisher and Lambie-Hanson (2010).

5. For a discussion of issues related to identification of REO in this dataset, see Campbell, Giglio, and Pathak (2009).

Chapter 7

Constructive Credit: Revisiting the Performance of Community Reinvestment Act Lending During the Subprime Crisis

Carolina Reid and Elizabeth Laderman

In 1977, when advocates and legislators were first debating the merits of Senate Bill 406, the Community Reinvestment Act (CRA) of 1977, the key question confronting Congress was whether or not "redlining"—the practice of denying access to credit based on where one lived—was contributing to the decline of inner-city neighborhoods. Advocates argued that banks had a social responsibility to reinvest locally held deposits back into the communities where they had branches; in short, the savings of residents in the inner city should not be directed to promote homeownership in the suburbs. Evidence of geographic discrepancies in areas where local banks were lending, coupled with testimony by Ronald Grzywinski, one of the founders of South Shore National Bank of Chicago that was successfully lending in formerly redlined communities, led Senator William Proxmire to conclude that banks did have an obligation to lend in the same communities in which they were taking deposits and that this could be done in a way that would not require credit allocations or pose undue risks to the institution. In defending an attack on the proposed legislation by the American Bankers Association, Senator Proxmire noted, "What we are trying to do here is not provide for any terrible sanction or require that you make loans that aren't sound. Every loan should be sound. . . . All we are saying is that the job that you do in servicing community needs should be taken into consideration as one element in whether or not branching should be approved. It is a mild proposal, it seems to me" (Proxmire 1977: 323). Indeed, in both its intent and its enforcement mechanism, the CRA sought only to underscore the "long-standing obligation to an institution's local service area implicit in existing law" and provide the regulatory agencies with the authority to enforce this principle.

Three decades later, the subprime crisis has led to a renewed debate about the CRA and whether or not it somehow encouraged banks to make unsound lending decisions. Economist Thomas DiLorenzo, for instance, wrote that the current housing crisis is "the direct result of thirty years of government policy that has forced banks to make bad loans to uncreditworthy borrowers" (DiLorenzo 2007). This "blame the CRA" story has been refuted by industry leaders and researchers. Researchers at the Board of Governors of the Federal Reserve found that the majority of subprime loans were made by independent mortgage lending companies, which are not covered by the CRA and receive less regulatory scrutiny overall (Avery, Brevoort, and Canner 2007). In addition, our previous work found that loans made by CRA-regulated institutions in California performed better on average than loans made by institutions that were not covered under the CRA (Laderman and Reid 2009).

While these research papers have failed to appease CRA's most vocal critics, the intent of this chapter is not to disprove once again the idea that the CRA is to blame for the subprime crisis. Instead, a much more important question is whether or not the CRA succeeded in providing access to credit to residents of historically underserved communities. Did financial institutions covered by the CRA make loans in low- and moderate-income (LMI) communities during the subprime boom? Perhaps more important, did those loans provide constructive credit in the community—in other words, were the loans fairly priced, and did they help borrowers not only achieve but also sustain homeownership? Or did the loans contribute to the current community development crisis, in which neighborhoods are struggling not with suburban flight but rather with the negative spillover effects resulting from subprime lending and subsequent foreclosures? Simply put, during the most recent period when an explosion of private mortgage lending occurred, did the CRA perform as its authors intended? If not, what can we learn from the recent crisis for possibly restructuring the CRA?

To help answer these questions, we analyze mortgage lending patterns and loan performance in three states: California, Ohio, and Pennsylvania. These states represent three distinct housing and mortgage markets. California characterizes the boom-and-bust model of the market, with a period of high price appreciation followed by severe house price declines and a rapid and dramatic rise in foreclosures. Ohio, in contrast, saw minimal house price change between 2000 and 2008; foreclosures began to increase steadily in early 2000, followed by a more rapid rise in foreclosures with the advent of the financial crisis and subsequent recession. Pennsylvania provides an example of a market that sits somewhere between these two extremes in that it experienced moderate house price appreciation between 2004 and 2006 and its foreclosure trends track both the declines in local house prices and the recession.

The Community Reinvestment Act

Passage of the CRA in 1977 followed on the heels of several other pieces of new legislation designed to address discrimination in housing and credit markets. These included the Fair Housing Act (passed as part of the Civil Rights Act of 1968), the Equal Credit Opportunity Act of 1974, and the Home Mortgage Disclosure Act of 1975. The CRA established a "continuing and affirmative obligation" that federally insured banks and thrifts meet the credit needs of the communities that they serve, including LMI areas, consistent with safe and sound banking practices. Regulators consider a bank's CRA record in determining whether to approve that institution's application for mergers with, or acquisitions of, other depository institutions. Since its passage, the CRA has undergone both regulatory and legislative revisions that have affected the way in which a bank is evaluated on its CRA performance. Today, a key component of the CRA is the lending test (accounting for 50 percent of a large bank's CRA rating), which evaluates the bank's home mortgage, small-business, small-farm, and community development lending activity. In assigning the rating for mortgage lending, examiners consider the number and dollar amount of loans to LMI borrowers and LMI areas and whether or not these loans demonstrate "innovative or flexible lending practices."[1]

Researchers who have studied the impact of the CRA find that, on balance, it has reduced information costs and fostered competition among banks that serve low-income areas, thereby generating larger volumes of lending from diverse sources and adding liquidity to the market (Avery et al. 1996; Barr 2005; Belsky, Schill, and Yezer 2001; Evanoff and Siegal 1996; Litan et al. 2001). In a detailed review, William Apgar and Mark Duda of the Joint Center for Housing Studies at Harvard University concluded that the CRA has had a positive impact on LMI communities. In particular, their study notes that "CRA-regulated lenders originate a higher proportion of loans to lower-income people and communities than they would if CRA did not exist" (Apgar and Duda 2003: 176).

Research has also shown that lending by institutions with a CRA obligation is not inherently more risky or less profitable than banks' other lending activities. In 2000, a report issued by the Federal Reserve Board concluded that mortgage loans that satisfy the LMI element of the CRA's Lending Test were at least marginally profitable for most institutions and that CRA lending did not perform differently from other lending (Essene and Apgar 2009). New research on the subprime boom similarly found that the rise in foreclosures was not driven by "unsound" CRA lending. A study by the Center for Community Capital found that prime loans that were originated between 2003 and 2006 through an LMI-targeted community lending program (the Community Advantage Program, or CAP, developed by Self-Help, a community development financial institution) were significantly less likely to be in default than were subprime loans made to borrowers with similar income and risk profiles (Ding et al. 2008). Instead, they found that it is the nature of the loan product and underwriting—for example, whether it had an adjustable interest rate or whether it was originated by a mortgage broker—that predicts default, rather than the characteristics of LMI borrowers. They concluded that the observed higher default risk of subprime loans is attributable not solely to borrower risk profiles but rather to the characteristics of loan products and the origination channel in the subprime market.

While the CRA might not have been the driver of the foreclosure crisis, it is less clear whether it actually succeeded in meeting the credit needs of LMI communities during the subprime boom. Nearly half of all higher-priced loans between 2004 and 2006 were originated by independent mortgage companies (IMCs) rather than by CRA-regulated financial institutions, even though IMCs represented only about one third of the overall mortgage market (Avery, Brevoort, and Canner 2007). More recent analysis by the Federal Reserve Board found that only 6 percent of higher-priced loans were originated by CRA-covered lenders to lower-income borrowers or neighborhoods in their CRA assessment areas—the local geographies that are the primary focus for CRA evaluation purposes (Kroszner 2008). While this does show that the CRA itself did little to cause the subprime boom, it also prompts the question of why LMI communities were predominantly being served by non-CRA-regulated institutions. In her testimony in 1977 in support of the CRA, Carol Greenwald, Commissioner for the Massachusetts State Banking Department, pointed out (1977: 168) that there were home sales in lower-income neighborhoods in Boston but that it wasn't banks that were making the mortgages:

> in a substantial number of Boston neighborhoods, bank mortgages are less than 50 percent of the home sales that take place in that neighborhood. That is very interesting, because bank financing is clearly the easiest and least expensive way of purchasing a home. Using a private mortgage company with its shorter maturity loans and usually higher interest rates is much more expensive. The question then comes: why are individuals choosing to go to private mortgage companies rather than going to banks?

Although this question was posed more than 30 years ago, it is no less salient today.

Banks have increasingly shifted their lending activities away from the neighborhoods in which they have branches—also known as their "assessment areas," the geographic areas in which their loans receive the greatest scrutiny under the CRA (Avery, Courchane, and Zorn 2009). The disappearance of the geographic specificity that once defined mortgage lending has led some to suggest that the whole idea of an "assessment area" has become obsolete. Yet there is growing evidence that locally based lending institutions are an important factor in determining whether or not lower-income borrowers have access to fair credit. For example, researchers at Case Western's Center on Urban Poverty and Community Development used a probabilistic matching technique to link mortgage records from the Home Mortgage Disclosure Act (HMDA) data with locally recorded mortgage documents and foreclosure filings (Coulton et al. 2008). They found that loans that were originated by financial institutions without a local branch had foreclosure rates of 19.08 percent compared to only 2.43 percent for loans that were originated by local banks. Research by Emre Ergungor of the Federal Reserve Bank of Cleveland found that between 1997 and 2004, the foreclosure rate in a county increased significantly with an increasing share of *non*-local and less-regulated bank originations (Ergungor 2007). Similarly, Laderman and Reid (2009) found that in California during the subprime boom, loans that were made within a bank's CRA assessment area performed much better than loans that were made outside of its assessment area.

It is this nexus between local context, mortgage origination channel, and loan performance that is the focus of this chapter. By examining the performance of loans made by CRA-regulated institutions during the subprime boom in three states with distinct housing and mortgage markets, we seek to provide insight into how the CRA might need to be realigned to contemporary mortgage markets (see also Chakrabarti et al. 2009).

Data and Methods

The analysis in this chapter relies on a loan-level dataset that matches data submitted by financial institutions under the HMDA of 1975 with data from a national proprietary dataset on loan performance. From HMDA data, we are able to identify whether or not a lender was subject to the CRA and whether or not the loan was "higher-priced,"[2] which is often used as a proxy for "subprime" (Mayer and Pence 2008). From the loan-performance dataset, we are able to assess the delinquency status of the mortgage as well as the mortgage product features and the borrower's credit (FICO) score. The merged dataset allows us to examine the performance of loans made by CRA-regulated institutions, which is not possible using either the proprietary dataset or HMDA data alone.

However, we are duly cautious about suggesting that our matched set is representative of all loans in California, Ohio, and Pennsylvania. The matched data do not represent a random sample of outstanding mortgage loans. To account for possible bias within the matched dataset, we constructed post-sampling weights to increase our confidence that our findings are more generally applicable (Courchane 2007). To create these weights, twenty-four mutually exclusive cells of data common to the HMDA data and the proprietary data were constructed by interacting race, ethnicity, higher-priced loan, and lender type for both the HMDA data and the matched data, based on the year of origination. The distributions of the HMDA and matched mortgages over each of the mutually exclusive buckets are then calculated and used to create post-sampling weights by dividing the percentage of the HMDA data in each cell by the percentage of the proprietary data in the equivalent cell. These weights are applied to the matched dataset throughout the analysis.

Key to this analysis is the inclusion of mortgage market channel variables that allow us to consider the regulatory framework governing the lending institutions. Specifically, we assess whether or not the loan was financed by a CRA-regulated institution, a CRA-regulated institution within its assessment area, an affiliate or subsidiary of a CRA-regulated institution, or an independent mortgage company. Owing to data limitations, we cannot actually assess whether or not any individual loan was counted as part of a bank's CRA exam. Instead, we use loans made by depository institutions covered by the CRA within their assessment areas as a proxy for CRA-motivated lending. Mortgages made by banks and thrifts in their assessment areas are subject to the most detailed CRA review, including on-site reviews and file checks. The assessment area also correlates with differences in the way mortgages are marketed and sold (Apgar, Bendimerad, and Essene 2007). For example, loans made to borrowers living inside the assessment area are likely to come through the institution's retail channel. In contrast, loans made to borrowers living outside of the organization's CRA-defined assessment area are more likely to be originated by loan correspondents or mortgage brokers. We assume that if a lending institution that is subject to CRA has a branch office in a metropolitan statistical area (MSA), then that MSA is part of the institution's assessment area. Loans that are made in MSAs where the lending institution does not have a branch office are assumed to originate outside of the institution's assessment area.[3]

We also separate lending activity by affiliates and subsidiaries of depository institutions into its own category. Depository institutions have broad discretion as to whether or not to include lending by their affiliates and subsidiaries as part of their CRA evaluation, thus creating a regulatory loophole that complicates attempts at assessing a bank's overall CRA record (Immergluck 2004; Quercia and Ratcliffe 2009). Our final category is IMCs, which fall outside of not only the regulatory reach of the CRA, but also a broader set of federal regulations and guidance designed to protect the "safety and soundness" of the lender (Apgar, Bendimerad, and Essene 2007).

Our merged dataset also includes variables that capture general housing, mortgage market, and economic conditions. These include time-varying Federal Housing Finance Agency (FHFA) house price data measured at the MSA/Metropolitan Division, county unemployment rates from the Bureau of Labor Statistics (BLS), and prevailing contract interest rates on conventional fixed-rate mortgages from Freddie Mac. Static variables include the percentage of college graduates and minority residents at the zip code level from the 2000 U.S. Census and data from the Federal Financial Institutions Examination Council (FFIEC) on whether a census tract qualifies as a low- or moderate-income tract for CRA eligibility.[4] The models also include data on borrower socioeconomic and risk characteristics (race, income, FICO score at origination), loan characteristics (loan–to-value ratio, adjustable or fixed interest rate, higher-priced, prepayment penalty, level of documentation), loan performance (current, in default, or paid off), housing market characteristics (percent change in house values, percent owner-occupied), and neighborhood characteristics (percent minority, percent college-educated, percent unemployment).

For the investigation in this chapter, we limit the analysis to a sample of conventional, first-lien, owner-occupied loans originated in metropolitan areas in California, Pennsylvania, and Ohio between January 2004 and December 2006. Loan performance outcomes are observed through December 2008. Observations with missing data or obvious data-coding errors were excluded from the analysis.

Sample means for the data in each of the three states are presented in Table 7.1 and demonstrate significant market differences among the three states. As expected, incomes and house values in California are higher than those in Ohio and Pennsylvania, as are the proportions of loans with features such as prepayment penalties, no documentation, and adjustable interest rates. California also had a much larger share of mortgage originations among borrowers of color than did Ohio and Pennsylvania. Moreover, interesting differences in the mortgage market channel emerge: while more than 52 percent of loans in California were originated by a CRA-regulated institution within its assessment area, in Ohio this market channel comprised 14 percent of all loans, and in Pennsylvania it made up just 10.5 percent. In comparison, in Ohio and Pennsylvania, nearly one third of all loans were originated by depository institutions outside of their assessment area; these states also saw a greater share of originations by affiliates or subsidiaries. California had a larger share of loans originated by mortgage brokers through the wholesale channel.

We measure two potential impacts that the CRA could have on mortgage lending in LMI neighborhoods. First, using a dichotomous logit model, we assess the relationship between mortgage market channel and the

Table 7.1. Sample Means

	California	Ohio	Pennsylvania
Local Socioeconomic Characteristics			
MSA house price appreciation two years prior to origination	41.30	6.63	20.36
County unemployment rate at origination	5.61	5.70	4.92
Average appraisal amount	590,617	194,976	215,840
Census tract median unit age (2000)	28.66	32.89	37.65
Census tract percent minority residents (2000)	31.72	9.01	9.71
Census tract percent with college education (2000)	60.31	52.75	47.70
Census tract vacancy rate (2000)	5.03	5.64	6.85
FFIEC census tract income designation			
Low-income neighborhood	2.43	1.72	1.96
Moderate-income neighborhood	16.90	10.65	12.63
Middle-income neighborhood	39.93	51.12	53.04
Upper-income neighborhood	40.69	36.49	32.36
Borrower Characteristics			
FICO at origination	709.0	700.9	698.1
Income at origination	124,629	73,612	76,325
Race/ethnicity of borrower			
White	55.70	88.98	89.80
Black	5.95	5.61	7.52
Hispanic	25.70	2.66	1.29
Asian	12.54	2.73	1.37
Loan Characteristics			
Average loan amount	366,392	146,793	156,781
Loan-to-value ratio	84.75	78.11	76.49
Adjustable-rate mortgage	55.87	25.18	20.03
Higher-priced loan	16.82	18.40	21.20
Prepayment penalty	28.05	10.96	11.10
No documentation	31.40	10.60	13.79
Seriously delinquent	7.45	6.99	4.31
Mortgage Market Channel			
Wholesale	40.85	32.04	29.28
CRA-regulated institution	58.42	42.25	36.33
Within assessment area	52.35	14.00	10.50
Outside of assessment area	6.07	28.20	25.80
Affiliate or subsidiary	17.45	31.27	33.19
Independent mortgage company	24.11	26.47	30.47

origination of a higher-priced loan, controlling for borrower and neighborhood risk characteristics. We want to determine whether the CRA was responsible for the growth of subprime lending in LMI communities. Second, we test whether or not loans made by institutions regulated under the CRA are more likely to be in default than those without CRA obligations. Building on the previous literature on mortgage defaults (Quercia and Spader 2008), we use option theory to develop our modeling approach for this question. Option theory posits that borrowers decide each month whether to make a mortgage payment, to exercise the prepayment option (e.g., sell the home or refinance), or to exercise the default option (Foster and Van Order 1984). These options are competing risks; choosing one eliminates the possibility of the other until the next monthly payment is due. Loan performance is observed each month, and we assume that prepayment and default (as opposed to the reference group of making the mortgage payment) are distinct events that are influenced by different underlying mechanisms. We model these competing risks using the multinominal logit (MNL) framework (Clapp et al. 2001). The information for each loan is restructured to include one observation for each time period in which that loan is active (i.e., from origination up to and including the period of termination). Once the data are restructured, the likelihood function is identical, in discrete time, to the continuous-time likelihood function for the Cox model. Estimation of the MNL model identifies the effect of the CRA variable on prepayment and default, after controlling for observed borrower and market risk characteristics.

CRA-Regulated Institutions and the Incidence of Higher-Priced Lending

In Table 7.2 (pages 170–71), we present the results from our dichotomous logit model predicting the likelihood that a borrower received a higher-priced loan. The model shows the strong positive effect of the CRA on the types of loans that were originated. We find that CRA-regulated institutions—both within and outside of their assessment areas—were significantly less likely to originate higher-priced loans than were IMCs, even after controlling for a wide range of borrower, neighborhood, and housing market characteristics. The effects are strong and consistent across all three states. In the context of CRA lending, what is important to note is that the marginal effect of the CRA assessment variable is stronger in LMI neighborhoods than in middle- and upper-income neighborhoods. Running the model independently for these two types of neighborhoods, we find that in LMI neighborhoods—those targeted by the CRA—loans originated by federally regulated lenders within their assessment areas were significantly less likely to be higher-priced (Figure 7.1). Expressed as a marginal effect, the CRA assessment area variable reduces the likelihood that a borrower in an LMI neighborhood received a higher-priced loan by around 30 to 35 percent. In comparison, the marginal effect of the CRA assessment area variable is weaker in middle- and upper-income neighborhoods, though still significant.

The results for the control variables in the model are consistent with expectations. Borrowers with higher FICO scores were less likely to receive a higher-priced loan, whereas borrowers with a higher loan-to-value ratio were significantly more likely to receive a higher-priced loan. In California, loans originated without documentation of income or assets were also more likely to be higher-priced. Race also matters. Even after we controlled for a

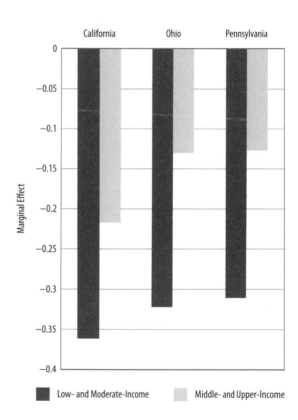

Figure 7.1. Marginal effect of CRA assessment area variable on the likelihood of receiving a subprime loan: California, Ohio, and Pennsylvania. Authors' calculations.

Table 7.2. Logistic Regression Predicting the Likelihood of Receiving a Subprime Loan

	California			Ohio			Pennsylvania		
	Coeffi-cient	Standard Error	Odds Ratio	Coeffi-cient	Standard Error	Odds Ratio	Coeffi-cient	Standard Error	Odds Ratio
Intercept	2.561	0.032‡		5.630	0.078‡		6.921	0.061‡	
Borrower Characteristics									
Black	0.464	0.007‡	1.59	0.743	0.013‡	2.10	0.528	0.013‡	1.70
Hispanic	0.236	0.005‡	1.27	0.520	0.019‡	1.68	-0.104	0.029†	0.90
Asian	-0.073	0.007‡	0.93	-0.216	0.026‡	0.81	-0.940	0.041‡	0.39
Income	0.000	0.000‡	1.00	-0.007	0.000‡	0.99	-0.002	0.000‡	1.00
Risk Characteristics									
Loan-to-value ratio	0.023	0.000‡	1.02	0.027	0.000‡	1.03	0.024	0.000‡	1.02
Borrower FICO score at origination	-0.010	0.000‡	0.99	-0.012	0.000‡	0.99	-0.014	0.000‡	0.99
No documentation	0.848	0.004‡	2.33	0.020	0.012	1.02	0.099	0.011*	1.10
Local Socioeconomic Characteristics									
County unemployment rate at origination	0.011	0.001‡	1.01	-0.009	0.006	0.99	0.033	0.004‡	1.03
MSA house-price appreciation two years prior to origination	0.020	0.000‡	1.02	-0.019	0.003‡	0.98	-0.004	0.000‡	1.00
Census tract percent with college education (2000)	-0.010	0.000‡	0.99	-0.019	0.000‡	0.98	-0.020	0.000‡	0.98
Low-income	0.312	0.013‡	1.37	0.497	0.026‡	1.64	1.015	0.029‡	2.76
Moderate-income	0.284	0.008‡	1.33	0.386	0.016‡	1.47	0.654	0.018‡	1.92
Middle-income	0.232	0.006‡	1.26	0.104	0.011	1.11	0.215	0.013‡	1.24

Table 7.2 (Continued)

	California			Ohio			Pennsylvania		
	Coeffi-cient	Standard Error	Odds Ratio	Coeffi-cient	Standard Error	Odds Ratio	Coeffi-cient	Standard Error	Odds Ratio
Mortgage Market Channel									
Wholesale	0.977	0.004‡	2.66	0.736	0.008‡	2.09	1.104	0.008‡	3.02
CRA-regulated institution within assessment area	−3.511	0.007‡	0.03	−1.547	0.014‡	0.21	−1.610	0.015‡	0.20
CRA-regulated institution outside of assessment area	−1.250	0.008‡	0.29	−1.262	0.011‡	0.28	−1.493	0.011‡	0.23
Affiliate or subsidiary	−1.286	0.005‡	0.28	−1.250	0.010‡	0.29	−1.191	0.009‡	0.30
Year of origination: 2005	1.019	0.006‡	2.77	0.493	0.009‡	1.64	0.439	0.010‡	1.55
Year of origination: 2006	1.905	0.007‡	6.72	0.922	0.014‡	2.51	0.834	0.011‡	2.30
Model Wald chi-square	623,549			118,353			133,699		
N	616,561			65,860			85,442		

$*p < .01$; $†p < .001$; $‡p < .0001$.

wide range of borrower, neighborhood, and mortgage market characteristics, blacks were between 1.6 and 2.1 times more likely to receive a higher-priced loan than were whites. In California and Ohio, Hispanics were also more likely to receive a higher-priced loan. Borrowers in LMI neighborhoods also experienced an increased likelihood of receiving a higher-priced loan; the effect is stronger in Ohio and Pennsylvania than in California, perhaps owing to the high cost of housing in California over this time period, making it more difficult for LMI borrowers to enter the homeownership market. In California, the model reveals the significant influence of house prices on subprime originations. Rapid house price appreciation in the 2 years before origination increased the likelihood of receiving a higher-priced loan, consistent with other research that has shown that the use of subprime mortgages and other "affordability" mortgage products grew substantially in California over this time period (Sanders 2008). This effect is not seen in Ohio and Pennsylvania. Also consistent with previous research (Ernst, Bocia, and Li 2008), we find that borrowers who used a mortgage broker were 2.7 times more likely to get a higher-priced loan in California than were borrowers who were served by the retail arm of a bank; in Ohio, the odds ratio was 2.1, and in Pennsylvania, it was 3.0.

Given the range of control variables in the model, the fact that loans made by lenders covered by the CRA, and especially within their assessment areas, were less likely to be higher-priced is important. It demonstrates a layer of consumer protection that is afforded not only by the CRA but also by more general regulatory oversight and suggests that CRA-regulated institutions may have done a better job within their assessment areas of aligning loan terms to a borrower's risk profile.

Nevertheless, the previous analysis does not provide a ringing endorsement of the implementation of the CRA. Loans made outside of the assessment area and loans made by affiliates were more likely to be higher-priced than those within the assessment area. So while federally regulated depositories were less likely to engage in subprime lending than were IMCs, the subprime lending they provided was generally originated by those parts of the financial institution that did not necessarily receive the same regulatory scrutiny under the CRA. Figure 7.2 provides just one example of how this uneven oversight within federally regulated institutions might have affected disadvantaged communities. African American borrowers with prime credit scores (a FICO over 640) were significantly more likely to get a higher-priced loan from an affiliate or IMC than from a CRA-regulated institution within

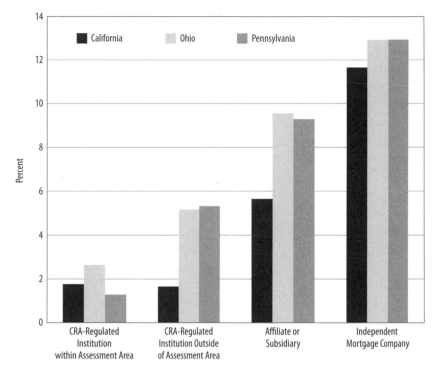

Figure 7.2. Percentage of African American borrowers with a prime credit score who received a higher-priced loan: California, Ohio, and Pennsylvania. Authors' calculations.

its assessment area. If CRA lenders were shifting their high-cost products to their affiliates and subsidiaries (either by increasing their share of subprime lending or by acquiring a mortgage lender as an affiliate), a bank's CRA record could remain strong even if other parts of the institution may have been contributing to the subprime crisis (Quercia and Ratcliffe 2009).

CRA-Regulated Institutions and Loan Performance

In the second stage of the analysis, we examine whether or not loans made by CRA-regulated institutions within their assessment areas performed better than loans made by other mortgage lenders. In Table 7.3, we present the results of our competing risks model of default and prepayment. The effect of CRA is quite different in the three states. In California, loans made by federally regulated depositories performed much better than loans originated by IMCs, even after we controlled for borrower, housing market, and loan characteristics. Indeed, loans originated by CRA-regulated institutions within their assessment areas in California were half as likely to be in default as loans made by IMCs.

In Pennsylvania and Ohio, however, we observe the opposite. In these states, loans originated by CRA lenders within their assessment areas were more likely to be in foreclosure than were those originated by IMCs, all other things being equal. Loans that were originated by affiliates or subsidiaries in Ohio performed worst, increasing the likelihood of foreclosure by nearly 50 percent over IMCs. In Pennsylvania, the performance of loans originated by affiliates or by CRA lenders outside their assessment area was not significantly different from that of loans originated by IMCs.

This finding went against our a priori expectations, since in our previous analyses of lending in California (Laderman and Reid 2009; Reid and Laderman 2009), we found a large and significant positive effect of the CRA on loan performance. To understand the differences among the three markets, we conducted additional analysis on the market composition of loans and their performance across the three states. We find several differences among the three markets. In California, only 2 percent of loans that were originated by CRA-regulated institutions within their assessment areas were higher-priced, compared with 44 percent of loans originated by IMCs. In Ohio and Pennsylvania, around 10 percent of loans that were originated by CRA-regulated institutions were higher-priced, while the share for IMCs was around 32 percent. This suggests that in California, there was much greater product segmentation between CRA-regulated institutions and IMCs.

In addition, serious delinquencies were more evenly distributed across lender types in Ohio and Pennsylvania. In California, only 3.3 percent of loans that were originated by CRA-regulated institutions were in default as of December 2008, compared with 14.7 percent for affiliates and subsidiaries and 11.7 percent for IMCs, more than a threefold difference. In Ohio, default rates for CRA lenders were 4.6 percent, while those for IMCs were 9.3 percent. In Pennsylvania the difference was less pronounced, with default rates ranging from 3.2 percent for CRA lenders to 5.7 percent for IMCs. We attribute these differences to the different drivers of the foreclosure crisis in California versus weaker market areas such as Ohio and Pennsylvania, where unemployment may have played a larger role in the default decision than it did in California. Before 2008, many of the foreclosures in California were

Table 7.3. Competing Risks Model of Default and Payment

	California					
	Default			Prepayment		
	Coefficient	Standard Error	Relative Risk Ratio	Coefficient	Standard Error	Relative Risk Ratio
Intercept	2.202	0.060‡		18.731	0.063‡	
Borrower Characteristics						
Black	0.281	0.011‡	1.33	−0.374	0.016‡	0.69
Hispanic	0.564	0.007‡	1.76	−0.120	0.009‡	0.89
Asian	0.280	0.009‡	1.32	−0.067	0.010‡	0.94
Income	0.000	0.000	1.00	0.000	0.000‡	1.00
FICO score at origination	−0.008	0.000‡	0.99	0.002	0.000‡	1.00
Loan Characteristics						
Higher-priced loan	0.508	0.008‡	1.66	−0.496	0.013‡	0.61
Loan-to-value ratio	0.072	0.000‡	1.07	−0.019	0.000‡	0.98
Adjustable interest rate	0.965	0.008‡	2.63	0.890	0.008‡	2.44
No documentation	0.475	0.006‡	1.61	−0.304	0.008‡	0.74
Prepayment penalty	0.560	0.007‡	1.75	−0.106	0.010‡	0.90
Interest rate	0.086	0.001‡	1.09	0.070	0.001‡	1.07
Loan seasoning	−0.003	0.000‡	1.00	−0.017	0.000‡	0.98
Local Socioeconomic Characteristics						
County unemployment rate at last observation	0.015	0.002‡	1.02	−0.023	0.003‡	0.98
MSA house-price appreciation two years after origination	−0.007	0.000‡	0.99	0.099	0.000‡	1.10
Census tract percent with college education (2000)	−0.005	0.000‡	1.00	0.006	0.000‡	1.01
LMI census tract	−0.006	0.008	0.99	0.095	0.011‡	1.10

(continued on next page)

Table 7.3 (Continued)

	California (Continued)					
	Default			Prepayment		
	Coefficient	Standard Error	Relative Risk Ratio	Coefficient	Standard Error	Relative Risk Ratio
Mortgage Market Channel						
Wholesale	0.273	0.006‡	1.31	−0.084	0.007‡	0.92
CRA-regulated institution within assessment area	−0.824	0.009‡	0.44	−0.101	0.010‡	0.90
CRA-regulated institution outside of assessment area	−0.264	0.014*	0.77	−0.137	0.015‡	0.87
Affiliate or subsidiary	−0.195	0.009‡	0.82	−0.044	0.011‡	0.96
Year of origination: 2005	−0.744	0.012‡	0.48	−3.320	0.011‡	0.04
Year of origination: 2006	−1.008	0.020‡	0.37	−5.856	0.021‡	0.00

	Ohio					
	Default			Prepayment		
	Coefficient	Standard Error	Relative Risk Ratio	Coefficient	Standard Error	Relative Risk Ratio
Intercept	8.418	0.117‡		13.380	0.114‡	
Borrower Characteristics						
Black	0.252	0.017‡	1.29	−0.331	0.026‡	0.72
Hispanic	0.041	0.028	1.04	−0.093	0.033*	1.10
Asian	−0.839	0.050‡	0.43	−0.172	0.029‡	0.84
Income	−0.004	0.000‡	1.00	0.000	0.000	1.00
FICO score at origination	−0.010	0.000‡	0.99	0.002	0.000‡	1.00
Loan Characteristics						
Higher-priced loan	0.407	0.014‡	1.50	−0.028	0.017	0.97
Loan-to-value ratio	0.038	0.001‡	1.04	−0.017	0.000‡	0.98

Table 7.3 (Continued)

	Ohio (Continued)					
	Default			Prepayment		
	Coefficient	Standard Error	Relative Risk Ratio	Coefficient	Standard Error	Relative Risk Ratio
Adjustable interest rate	0.532	0.015‡	1.70	1.063	0.013‡	2.90
No documentation	0.359	0.016‡	1.43	−0.258	0.018‡	0.77
Prepayment penalty	0.705	0.018‡	2.02	−0.035	0.022	0.97
Interest rate	0.063	0.002‡	1.07	0.063	0.002‡	1.06
Loan seasoning	−0.006	0.000‡	0.99	−0.013	0.000‡	0.99
Local Socioeconomic Characteristics						
County unemployment rate at last observation	0.244	0.009‡	1.28	0.320	0.009‡	1.38
MSA house-price appreciation two years after origination	0.138	0.003‡	1.15	0.374	0.003‡	1.45
Census tract percent with college education (2000)	−0.006	0.000‡	0.99	0.005	0.000‡	1.01
LMI census tract	0.252	0.015‡	1.29	−0.421	0.021‡	0.66
Mortgage Market Channel						
Wholesale	0.334	0.013‡	1.40	−0.095	0.013‡	0.91
CRA-regulated institution within assessment area	0.220	0.022‡	1.25	−0.173	0.019‡	0.84
CRA-regulated institution outside of assessment area	0.122	0.016‡	1.13	−0.147	0.016‡	0.86
Affiliate or subsidiary	0.398	0.015‡	1.49	0.050	0.016†	1.05
Year of origination: 2005	−1.639	0.020‡	0.19	−3.155	0.020‡	0.04
Year of origination: 2006	−3.072	0.036‡	0.05	−6.185	0.035‡	0.00

(continued on next page)

Table 7.3 (Continued)

	Pennsylvania					
	Default			Prepayment		
	Coefficient	Standard Error	Relative Risk Ratio	Coefficient	Standard Error	Relative Risk Ratio
Intercept	5.881	0.123‡		9.369	0.085‡	
Borrower Characteristics						
Black	0.190	0.020‡	1.209	−0.097	0.019‡	0.91
Hispanic	−0.257	0.056‡	0.774	−0.229	0.044‡	0.80
Asian	−0.005	0.060	0.995	−0.304	0.038‡	0.74
Income	0.000	0.000	1	0.000	0.000*	1.00
FICO score at origination	−0.011	0.000‡	0.989	0.001	0.000‡	1.00
Loan Characteristics						
Higher-priced loan	0.403	0.018‡	1.497	−0.410	0.015‡	0.66
Loan-to-value ratio	0.033	0.001‡	1.033	−0.001	0.000†	1.00
Adjustable interest rate	0.409	0.020‡	1.505	0.694	0.013‡	2.00
No documentation	0.373	0.017†	1.451	−0.051	0.013‡	0.95
Prepayment penalty	0.279	0.022‡	1.322	−0.881	0.022‡	0.42
Interest rate	0.054	0.002‡	1.055	0.092	0.001‡	1.10
Loan seasoning	−0.003	0.000‡	0.997	−0.010	0.000‡	0.99
Local Socioeconomic Characteristics						
County unemployment rate at last observation	0.070	0.008‡	1.072	0.197	0.005‡	1.22
MSA house-price appreciation two years after origination	0.009	0.001‡	1.009	0.083	0.001‡	1.09
Census tract percent with college education (2000)	−0.009	0.001‡	0.991	0.004	0.000‡	1.00
LMI census tract	0.010	0.020	1.01	−0.111	0.016‡	0.90

Table 7.3 (Continued)

| | Pennsylvania (Continued) | | | | | |
| | Default | | | Prepayment | | |
	Coefficient	Standard Error	Relative Risk Ratio	Coefficient	Standard Error	Relative Risk Ratio
Mortgage Market Channel						
Wholesale	0.495	0.016‡	1.641	0.130	0.011‡	1.14
CRA-regulated institution within assessment area	0.119	0.027‡	1.126	−0.331	0.017‡	0.72
CRA-regulated institution outside of assessment area	−0.050	0.021	0.951	−0.177	0.013‡	0.84
Affiliate or subsidiary	−0.008	0.019	0.992	−0.354	0.013‡	0.70
Year of origination: 2005	−1.171	0.023‡	0.31	−2.813	0.016‡	0.06
Year of origination: 2006	−1.646	0.043†	0.193	−4.446	0.029‡	0.01

Competing risk outcomes are measured against loans still active and not seriously delinquent in December 2008.

$^*p < .01$; $†p < .001$; $‡p < .0001$.

driven by the collapse of the housing bubble (Foote et al. 2009), suggesting that mortgage market segmentation may have played a more important role in shaping default outcomes. Although more research is needed to explore these dynamics, we believe that these findings demonstrate that there are significant geographic differences in how mortgage market channels interact with borrowers and local housing market conditions to shape loan outcomes, with attendant implications for consumer protection.

Conclusion

The findings presented in this chapter provide important insights into the relationships between local conditions, mortgage market channels, and loan performance. First, the chapter demonstrates that the CRA did not contribute to the subprime crisis. We find that institutions regulated under the CRA were significantly less likely to originate subprime loans than were other mortgage lending institutions, and that these protections were more important in lower-income communities. Therefore we believe that loans made by CRA-regulated institutions within their assessment area can be considered constructive credit in LMI communities. The regulatory scrutiny that accompanies CRA assessment area lending provides an important layer of consumer protection in the mortgage market and works to help meet the credit needs of LMI communities in a manner consistent with safe and sound lending practices. This analysis provides additional evidence countering the claim that the CRA caused the subprime crisis and suggests that in some important ways, the CRA was achieving the goals that its founders intended. We also find that in California, loans made by federally regulated depositories within their assessment areas performed significantly better than loans that were not covered by the CRA, even after controlling for borrower, housing market, and loan characteristics.

Yet the analysis also suggests that the CRA needs to be revised as part of an overall framework for consumer protection. We think that there are at least four lessons to be learned from this research that could help to inform the debate about what the CRA should look like going forward. First, we find that there was considerable geographic variation in the coverage of CRA-regulated institutions and their lending activities, variation that becomes even more pronounced when we look at within-assessment-area lending. In Ohio and Pennsylvania in particular, only a small share of the loans that were originated were made by CRA-regulated institutions within their assessment areas, and these loans were actually slightly more likely to be in foreclosure than were loans made by IMCs. In part, this may be due to the economic drivers of foreclosure in these states. For example, lenders cannot necessarily control foreclosures that are driven by unemployment. However, the fact that most of the higher-priced lending in LMI communities was driven by affiliates and IMCs is troubling, suggesting that, just as in 1977, the credit needs of LMI communities are often served not by banks, but by other institutional lenders that were not subject to the same regulatory scrutiny. This dual mortgage market—and the fact that historically disadvantaged communities were predominantly served by the institutions that were the least regulated—has important implications for the future of the CRA. It seems reasonable that consumers should have equal access to the benefits of legally mandated federal oversight regardless of the institutional status of the lender (Essene and Apgar 2009). But our research also raises the question of how federal regulations, whether the CRA or other consumer protection laws, can be written in such a way as to account for the very different mortgage and housing markets that exist across the United States. Adequate consumer protection in California may be different from adequate consumer protection in Ohio, which raises important policy questions around the balance of federal and state laws and preemption (Ding et al. 2010a, b).

Second, our analysis highlights the importance of the assessment area in providing access to constructive credit. Among institutions that were regulated under the CRA, loans that were made within the bank's assessment area were significantly less likely to be subprime than those made outside of its assessment area. More research is needed to understand whether the effect is due to the increased regulatory scrutiny afforded to loans made within the assessment area boundaries or whether there is a separate mechanism embedded within local branch presence and relationship lending that results in more positive outcomes for LMI communities. If it is the former, then expanding the definition of a bank's assessment area to include all the areas in which they do business—even if it is not branch based—could result in better loan outcomes. But emerging research on lending behavior has shown that local social relationships and networks affect who gets capital and at what cost (Moulton 2008; Pittman 2008; Reid 2010; Uzzi 1999), suggesting that there might be a need to create a network of local lenders even as bank consolidation and technological advances push lending in the opposite direction. For example, community development financial institutions (CDFIs) already serve that function in some LMI neighborhoods; among CDFIs that offer mortgage loans, the combination of responsible loan products and financial education has led to very positive outcomes, even among borrowers with subprime credit profiles (Ding et al. 2008). Providing CDFIs with additional capital to play an expanded role in mortgage lending and reach more borrowers could be one way to create a network of local intermediaries that could respond to local conditions and social processes (e.g., developing different interventions in communities composed largely of immigrants than in communities with historically African American residents). Alternatively, it might entail expanding and strengthening the CRA in a way that encourages banks and other financial service institutions to reach out to underserved areas and that emphasizes the community aspect of lending even as assessment areas tied to bank branches become obsolete.

Third, the models reveal significant disparities in housing and mortgage market outcomes for African American and Hispanic borrowers. Minority borrowers were significantly more likely to get a subprime loan, even after we controlled for borrower and neighborhood risk characteristics, and minority borrowers were more likely to be in default. Although some of these disparities are likely due to unobservable differences among racial and ethnic groups (e.g., wealth, intergenerational knowledge, and language barriers), the models nevertheless show that a significant portion of these disparities can be explained by the mortgage market channel. While more research is needed to understand the sorting of consumers among different types of mortgage lending institutions, equal access to fair credit will not become a reality as long as historically underserved borrowers are disproportionately served by subprime lenders. Despite the affirmative obligation to serve all communities under the CRA, prime lenders failed to effectively reach creditworthy minority borrowers. This suggests that there is a need to revisit the CRA within the context of fair lending laws and to explicitly consider the role of race and ethnicity in discussions about policies to promote equal access to credit.

Finally, we believe that there is a need to revisit the emphasis of the CRA on mortgage lending and to pay broader attention to the continuum of financial services that can help families move up the credit path before they climb up the housing ladder. Certainly, the current foreclosure crisis is due at least in part to borrowers receiving loans they could not afford despite evidence of low credit scores, low assets, and unstable income streams. Rather than focusing on making subprime credit widely available through risk-based pricing, we might need to focus instead on improving the borrowers' credit profiles, building relationships between consumers and responsible lenders by providing better access to mainstream financial services, and building a foundation for sustainable homeownership through savings and workforce development. Although these options would entail public costs, the costs seem to be justified when weighed against the very real price we are paying as a result of the existing dual mortgage market.

References

Apgar William, Amal Bendimerad, and Ren Essene. 2007. *Mortgage Market Channels and Fair Lending: An Analysis of HMDA Data.* Cambridge, Mass.: Joint Center for Housing Studies, Harvard University.

Apgar, William, and Mark Duda. 2003. "The Twenty-Fifth Anniversary of the Community Reinvestment Act: Past Accomplishments and Future Regulatory Challenges." *FRBNY Economic Policy Review* (June): 169–91.

Avery, Robert B., Raphael W. Bostic, Paul S. Calem, and Glenn B. Canner. 1996. "Credit Risk, Credit Scoring, and the Performance of Home Mortgages." *Federal Reserve Bulletin* 82: 621–48.

Avery, Robert B., Kenneth P. Brevoort, and Glenn B. Canner. 2007. "The 2006 HMDA Data." *Federal Reserve Bulletin* 94: A73–A109.

Avery, Robert B., Marsha J. Courchane, and Peter M. Zorn. 2009. "The CRA Within a Changing Financial Landscape." In *Revisiting the CRA: Perspectives on the Future of the Community Reinvestment Act*, ed. Chakrabarti et al. 30–46.

Barr, Michael S. 2005. "Credit Where It Counts: The Community Reinvestment Act and Its Critics." *New York University Law Review* 80, 2: 513–652.

Belsky, Eric, Michael Schill, and Anthony Yezer. 2001. *The Effect of the Community Reinvestment Act on Bank and Thrift Home Purchase Mortgage Lending*. Cambridge, Mass.: Joint Center for Housing Studies, Harvard University.

Chakrabarti, Prabal, David Erickson, Ren S. Essene, Ian Galloway, and John Olson, eds. 2009. *Revisiting the CRA: Perspectives on the Future of the Community Reinvestment Act*. Boston: Federal Reserve Banks of Boston and San Francisco.

Clapp, John M., Gerson M. Goldberg, John P. Harding, and Michael LaCour-Little. 2001. "Movers and Shuckers: Interdependent Prepayment Decisions." *Real Estate Economics* 29, 3: 411–50.

Coulton, Claudia, Tsui Chan, Michael Schramm, and Kristen Mikelbank. 2008. "Pathways to Foreclosure: A Longitudinal Study of Mortgage Loans, Cleveland and Cuyahoga County," Cleveland: Center on Urban Poverty and Community Development, Case Western University.

Courchane, Marsha J. 2007. "The Pricing of Home Mortgage Loans for Minority Borrowers: How Much of the APR Differential Can We Explain?" *Journal of Real Estate Research* 29, 4: 399–440.

DiLorenzo, Thomas J. 2007. "The Government-Created Subprime Mortgage Meltdown." http://www.lewrockwell.com/dilorenzo/dilorenzo125.html.

Ding, Lei, Roberto G. Quercia, Janneke Ratcliffe, and Wei Li. 2008. "Risky Borrowers or Risky Mortgages: Disaggregating Effects Using Propensity Score Models." Chapel Hill: Center for Community Capital, University of North Carolina.

Ding, Lei, Roberto G. Quercia, Carolina Reid, and Alan White. 2010a. "The APL Effect: The Impacts of State Anti-Predatory Lending Laws on Foreclosures." Research Report. Chapel Hill: Center for Community Capital, University of North Carolina.

———. 2010b. "The Preemption Effect: The Impacts of Federal Preemption of State Anti-Predatory Lending Laws on the Foreclosure Crisis." Research Report. Chapel Hill: Center for Community Capital, University of North Carolina.

Ergungor, O. Emre. 2007. "Foreclosures in Ohio: Does Lender Type Matter?" Working Paper 07-24. Cleveland: Federal Reserve Bank of Cleveland.

Ernst, Keith, D. Bocia, and Wei Li. 2008. *Steered Wrong: Brokers, Borrowers and Subprime Loans.* Durham, N.C.: Center for Responsible Lending.

Essene, Ren, and William Apgar. 2009. "The 30th Anniversary of the Community Reinvestment Act: Restructuring the CRA to Address the Mortgage Finance Revolution." In *Revisiting the CRA,* ed. Chakrabarti et al. 12–29.

Evanoff, Douglas D., and Lewis M. Siegal. 1996. "CRA and Fair Lending Regulations: Resulting Trends in Mortgage Lending." *Economic Perspectives* 20, 6: 19–46.

Foote, Christopher L., Kristopher S. Gerardi, Lorenz Goette, and Paul S. Willen. 2009. "Reducing Foreclosures." Public Policy Discussion Papers Series, No. 09-2. Boston: Federal Reserve Bank of Boston.

Foster, Chester, and Robert Van Order. 1984. "An Option-Based Model of Mortgage Default." *Housing Finance Review* 3: 351–72.

Greenwald, Carol. 1977. "Testimony: Community Credit Needs." Hearings before the Committee on Banking, Housing and Urban Affairs, U.S. Senate, Ninety-Fifth Congress, First Session on S. 406. Washington, D.C.: U.S. Government Printing Office.

Immergluck, Dan. 2004. *Credit to the Community: Community Reinvestment and Fair Lending Policy in the United States.* Armonk, N.Y.: M.E. Sharpe.

Kroszner, Randall S. 2008. "The Community Reinvestment Act and the Recent Mortgage Crisis." Speech at Confronting Concentrated Poverty Policy Forum, Board of Governors of the Federal Reserve System, Washington, D.C., December 3.

Laderman, Elizabeth, and Carolina Reid (2009). "CRA Lending During the Subprime Meltdown." In *Revisiting the CRA,* ed. Chakrabarti et al. 115–33.

Litan, Robert E. et al. 2001. "The Community Reinvestment Act After Financial Modernization: A Final Report." Washington, D.C.: U.S. Treasury Department.

Mayer, Chris, and Karen Pence. 2008. "Subprime Mortgages: What, Where, and to Whom?" Finance and Economics Discussion Series Working Paper 2008-29. Washington, D.C.: Federal Reserve Board of Governors.

Moulton, S. 2008. "Marketing and Education Strategies of Originating Mortgage Lenders: Borrower Effects & Policy Implications." Paper presented at the Association for Public Policy Analysis and Management 30th Annual Research Conference, Los Angeles, CA, November 6.

Pittman, Cassi L. 2008. "The Use of Social Capital in Borrower Decision-Making." Working Paper. Cambridge, Mass.: Joint Center for Housing Studies, Harvard University.

Proxmire, William. 1977. Community Credit Needs. Hearings Before the Senate Committee on Banking, Housing and Urban Affairs, 95th Cong., 1st Sess., on S. 406.

Quercia, Roberto, and Janneke Ratcliffe. 2009. "The Community Reinvestment Act: Outstanding, and Needs to Improve." In *Revisiting the CRA,* ed. Chakrabarti et al. 47–58.

Quercia, Roberto, and Jonathan Spader. 2008. "Does Homeownership Counseling Affect the Prepayment and Default Behavior of Affordable Mortgage Borrowers." *Journal of Policy Analysis and Management* 27, 2: 304–25.

Reid, Carolina. 2010. "Sought or Sold? Understanding the Linkages Between Origination Channel and Consumer Choice in the Mortgage Market." Paper presented at the Symposium for Financial Security, University of Wisconsin, Madison, April 19.

Reid, Carolina, and Elizabeth Laderman. 2009. "The Untold Costs of Subprime Lending: Examining the Links Among Higher-Priced Lending, Foreclosures and Race in California." Working Paper 2009-09. San Francisco: Federal Reserve Bank of San Francisco.

Sanders, A. 2008. "The Subprime Crisis and Its Role in the Financial Crisis." *Journal of Housing Economics* 17, 4 (December): 254–61.

Uzzi, Brian. 1999. "Embeddedness in the Making of Financial Capital: How Social Relations and Networks Benefit Firms Seeking Financing." *American Sociological Review* 64, 4: 481–505.

Notes

We thank Susan Wachter, Robert Avery, and two anonymous reviewers for helpful comments. The views expressed in this chapter are solely those of the authors and not necessarily those of the Federal Reserve Bank of San Francisco or the Federal Reserve System.

1. As part of their CRA exam, large banks are also evaluated on their investments and services. Under the investment test, which accounts for 25 percent of the bank's CRA grade, the agency evaluates the amount of the bank's investments, its innovation, and its responsiveness to community needs. Under the service test, which makes up the remaining 25 percent of the bank's evaluation, the agency analyzes "the availability and effectiveness of a bank's systems for delivering retail banking services and the extent and innovativeness of its community development services." Different rules apply for "small" and "intermediate small" institutions. For more complete details on the CRA regulations, visit http://www.ffiec.gov/cra/default.htm for text of the regulations and Interagency Q&A.

2. In 2004, information was added to HMDA on the interest-rate spread to the comparable-maturity Treasury for first-lien mortgages with an annual percentage rate (APR) three percentage points over the Treasury benchmark and for junior liens with an APR five percentage points over the benchmark. Mortgages with a reported spread are commonly called "higher-priced" loans. While it is not strictly analogous to "subprime," using the higher-priced designation allows us to avoid the pitfalls of using lenders' own determinations of "B" and "C" rated mortgages.

3. Our methodology is consistent with that of Apgar, Bendimerad, and Essene (2007), who assume that if a lending entity that is subject to CRA has a branch office in a particular county, then that county is part of the entity's assessment area.

4. The FFIEC classifies census codes into "low," "moderate," "middle," and "upper" income tracts to determine CRA eligibility. Census tracts are categorized by the median family income for the tract relative to the median family income for the MSA in which the tract is located. Categories are defined as follows: *Low income* means that median family income for the census tract is less than 50 percent of median family income for the MSA. *Moderate income* means that median family income for the census tract is 50 percent to 79 percent of the MSA median. *Middle income* means that median family income is 80 percent to 119 percent of the MSA median. *Upper income* means that median family income is 120 percent or more of the MSA median.

Chapter 8

Navigating the Housing Downturn and Financial Crisis: Home Appreciation and Equity Accumulation Among Community Reinvestment Homeowners

Sarah F. Riley and Roberto G. Quercia

Homeownership has historically been considered an effective wealth-creation mechanism for low-income households. These households typically hold a very large proportion of their wealth in their homes. In addition, they also historically have greatly benefited from home price appreciation, not only because of overall positive market trends but also because of the high leverage provided by high loan-to-value mortgages. These factors have made homeownership the primary driving factor in wealth creation for many low-income homeowners (Belsky and Calder 2004; Stegman, Quercia, and Davis 2007).

However, as recent economic trends have illustrated on a national scale, such lopsided wealth portfolio allocation has a potentially enormous downside. After doubling between 1995 and 2007, housing prices have experienced an unprecedented national decline, having fallen 14 percent, according to the Federal Housing Finance Agency. The homeownership rate, which peaked at 69.2 percent earlier in 2004, fell to 67.1 percent in the second quarter of 2010. Moreover, First American CoreLogic, a data and analytics consultancy, reports that over 11 million residential properties, or 24 percent of all residential properties with a mortgage, were "underwater" (that is, the property owners owed more than the value of these houses) by the first quarter of 2010.

Of course, the recession has not been limited to the housing market. The Dow Jones Industrial Average (DJIA) fell 53 percent between October 2007 and March 2009. But housing traditionally represents a highly leveraged investment, especially for low-income households, and, if not offset by sufficient investments in assets that have uncorrelated investment returns, can quickly and easily destroy household wealth. In addition to the possibility of direct loss of their initial investments, low-income homeowners potentially face additional costs from negative equity, foreclosure, and reduced access to credit. Moreover, they typically have few resources with which to weather such additional costs. It is natural, then, to ask how low-income homeowners have fared during the decline of the housing market that began in the spring of 2006 and during the financial crisis that ensued in the fall of 2008. In particular, it makes sense to revisit the question of when—or even whether—housing is a viable investment for these borrowers.

Previous research (Ding, Quercia, and Ratcliffe 2008) has addressed how the question of viability can depend in large part on the quality of the loan product. Low mortgage default rates are clearly a prerequisite to successful wealth creation through homeownership, and traditional loan products, such as 30-year prime fixed-rate mortgages, significantly outperform subprime loans for comparable borrowers.

This chapter examines solely the follow-up question of equity gains given the reality that house prices do not always rise. A multivariate model is used to analyze price appreciation among low-income homeowners, since it depends upon the timing of loan origination and local area conditions, such as the percentage of the population in poverty, the unemployment rate, and the median age of nearby houses. Results from this model are presented for five time periods around the peak of the housing bubble, providing an overall picture of how the relationships among the price appreciation rate and these correlates have changed over time and relate to changes in the underlying economy.

Low-Income Homeownership and the Community Advantage Program

In this chapter, we examine the investment experiences of a group of approximately 29,000 low-income homeowners who received Community Reinvestment Act (CRA) mortgages between 1998 and 2004 that later became part of the Community Advantage Program (CAP).

CRA is a law enacted in 1977 that established an affirmative obligation for lenders to serve all neighborhoods in which they have branch offices (i.e., their assessment area). The legislation encouraged lenders to expand access to credit in low- and moderate-income neighborhoods, consistent with safe and sound lending practices.

CAP is a secondary market program initiated in 1998 by the Ford Foundation, Fannie Mae, and the Center for Community Self-Help, a leading Community Development Financial Institution in North Carolina. Under the CAP program, the Center for Community Self-Help purchases existing portfolios of loans for low-income borrowers from originating lenders that are otherwise unable to sell their loans in the secondary market. Over 94 percent of CAP loans are CRA-eligible regardless of assessment area, which means that these loans were made to low- and moderate-income borrowers or in low- and moderate-income areas. These loans feature flexible underwriting and typically include low or no down payment, higher debt-to-income ratios, approval of borrowers with varied credit records or no established credit, and/or a waiver of the usual requirement that a borrower have at least the equivalent of two months of loan payments available as a cash reserve at the time of closing. While the loans feature nontraditional underwriting guidelines, the loans themselves are traditional, as they are prime-priced, 30-year, fixed-rate, lender-originated purchase-money mortgages that are fully underwritten for each borrower's ability to repay.

To be considered for purchase under CAP, loans must meet at least one of the following qualifying requirements: (1) The borrower's income is less than 80 percent of metropolitan statistical area median income (AMI); (2) the borrower is a member of a minority with income less than 120 percent of the AMI; or (3) the borrower's income is below 120 percent of the AMI and the home is located in a high minority (greater than 30 percent) or low-income (less than 80 percent AMI) census tract. Aside from these locational criteria and income restrictions, we are not aware of any systematic differences between CAP properties and properties in other residential markets. The Ford Foundation provided the original underwriting capital for this purchasing arrangement and continues to fund the Community Advantage Panel Survey (CAPS), an ongoing annual survey that collects detailed financial, social, and demographic information from a subset of these borrowers.

Approximately 40 percent of CAP borrowers are members of racial or ethnic minorities, and approximately 50 percent have household incomes that are at most 60 percent of the AMI. The median amount of the loans made to these borrowers was $81,000, or about 2.6 times median household income. The median property value at the time of purchase was $85,200, and the median origination loan-to-value ratio was 97 percent.

The CAP loans were originated during 1998–2004, a period when minority and overall homeownership rates in the United States were steadily increasing. According to data from the U.S. Census Bureau, the homeownership rate for African Americans increased from 45.6 percent in 1998 to 49.1 percent in 2004. Hispanics experienced similar gains, with growth from 44.7 percent to 48.1 percent, while the homeownership rate for other minorities rose from 53 percent to 58.6 percent. In contrast, the overall U.S. homeownership rate increased from 66.3 percent to 69 percent during this period. Thus the growth of the minority homeownership rate ranged between 7 percent and 10 percent, while the homeownership rate for the United States as a whole grew by about 4 percent.

This period was also a time of stable and sustained house-price appreciation. According to data from the Federal Housing Finance Agency, house prices nationally increased at an average rate of 6.2 percent annually during this period. Therefore these CAP loans were originated before the housing market became inflated.

Moreover, CAP loans can generally be viewed as product substitutes for subprime loans, because they serve similar groups of borrowers. In particular, prior research suggests that two thirds of CAP loans substituted for subprime loans between 2004 and 2006 (Spader 2009). Most of the CAP loans that we consider in this chapter were originated before the period of the most rapid growth in the subprime mortgage industry.

As of the end of 2009, the 90-day delinquency rate of CAP borrowers was 8 percent, which is comparable to that for prime adjustable-rate mortgages nationwide and exceeds that for prime fixed-rate mortgages (3 percent), according to data from the Mortgage Bankers Association. The 2009 CAP 90-day delinquency rate of 8 percent represents a one-year increase of three percentage points (or 77 percent) over its 2008 value but nonetheless remains below the 90-day delinquency rates for subprime fixed-rate (13 percent) and adjustable-rate (18 percent) mortgages, which increased at rates of 76 percent and 53 percent, respectively, during the same period. The rate of increase from 2008 to 2009 was greatest for prime fixed-rate mortgages, for which the 90-day delinquency rate more than doubled.

Approximately 12 percent of non-prime loans that were originated nationally between 2000 and 2007 had gone through foreclosure as of the middle of 2009 (GAO 2009). In contrast, cumulative CAP foreclosure sales reached 4.2 percent at the end of 2009, up from 3.7 percent at the end of 2008. Year 2000 CAP originations have experienced the highest cumulative foreclosure sale rate (6 percent), while year 2003 originations have experienced the lowest (3 percent).

The percentage of CAP borrowers with negative equity, or mortgage debt in excess of the value of the house, doubled from 4.5 percent to 9 percent between the end of 2008 and the end of 2009. However, the negative equity rate remains low when compared with the 25 percent or more for subprime loan recipients nationwide (GAO 2009).

It is noteworthy that the CAP population is largely representative of the U.S. low- to moderate-income population with respect to racial and income characteristics but not with respect to geography (Riley and Ru 2009). CAP owners live in more than forty states, but approximately 22 percent of the sample resides in North Carolina, and another 15 percent resides in California. The third and fourth most represented states are Ohio and Oklahoma, which contribute 7 percent and 8 percent of the sample, respectively. Since geography has recently played a critical role in influencing house prices across the nation, it is important to keep these sample characteristics in mind when interpreting the results of the analyses that follow.

Housing as an Asset Class for CAP Borrowers

This section considers how the trend in CAP property values compares to that of the housing market as a whole. It then compares the performance of CAP homes to that of two common alternative asset classes from the perspective of rates-of-return and investigates temporal and geographic variation in appreciation across CAP properties.

Using zip-code-level house-price estimates provided quarterly by Fannie Mae, in conjunction with loan balance information provided by the Center for Community Self-Help, we examine the extent to which CAP properties have appreciated since origination as well as how the appreciation rate on these properties has compared with that of other asset classes, such as stocks and certificates of deposit (CDs). In particular, rates of return are presented for each of five time periods: (1) loan origination to April 2009; (2) loan origination to April 2006 (before the housing downturn); (3) loan origination to October 2008 (before the financial crisis); (4) April 2006 to April 2009 (after the housing market peaked); and (5) October 2008 to April 2009 (since the beginning of the financial crisis). We chose these time periods because April 2006 and October 2008 correspond approximately to key economic turning points. The housing market began to decline in the spring of 2006, while U.S. securities markets declined markedly near the beginning of October 2008, when the Emergency Economic Stabilization Act of 2008 was enacted. We refer to the period following this legislation as the "financial crisis." Thus these comparisons highlight the importance of variation in underlying economic conditions in determining returns to real estate and also emphasize the relative volatilities of the three asset classes (CAP properties, stocks, and CDs) over time. After discussing investment returns, we then discuss how much equity CAP borrowers have accumulated and the rates at which their initial down payments have grown.

House-price index data for the U.S. housing market come from the FHFA, in which the Office of Federal Housing Enterprise Oversight (OFHEO) is now subsumed, while estimates of CAP property values are provided by Fannie Mae. The latter values are derived from a housing-market price index that Fannie Mae uses internally for risk modeling but also reflect additional information about property-specific sales transactions, physical characteristics, and taxes as well as a correction for any refinance bias. Because the Fannie Mae price estimates are derived from a proprietary data process, no further details are available about how these estimates are constructed.

Using these house-price estimates in conjunction with CAP mortgage origination data, we calculate the annualized rate of price appreciation for each property in our sample. Formally, the annualized rate of appreciation r is given by

$$r = (V/O)^{1/t} - 1,$$

where V is the estimated value of the property in a given quarter, O is the original value of the property at the time it was purchased by the CAP borrower, and t is the number of years between the CAP loan origination date and the first day of the quarter of analysis. The annualized return on equity is calculated in a similar fashion using original and accumulated equity values in place of house prices.

Figure 8.1 presents the year-on-year changes in the market value of CAP properties and in the OFHEO national and purchase-only house-price indices. As illustrated in the figure, CAP properties experienced consistent appreciation but did not become inflated during the period of the bubble in the greater housing market. Thereafter, these properties have depreciated largely in line with national trends. During a period when the DJIA declined by 3.4 percent on an annualized basis and six-month CD rates averaged an annual return of 3.4 percent, CAP borrowers experienced median annual appreciation of 2.5 percent between loan origination and April 2009. To better understand the reasons underlying the relative performance of these instruments, it is instructive to consider their rates of return under varied economic conditions.

Between loan origination and the end of the housing-market boom in April 2006, CAP property values rose by a median 5.7 percent annually, compared with 2.7 percent for both the DJIA and six-month CDs. After April 2006, however, CAP property values declined at an annual rate of 2.6 percent, while the DJIA and six-month CDs declined by 11.4 percent and returned 4.7

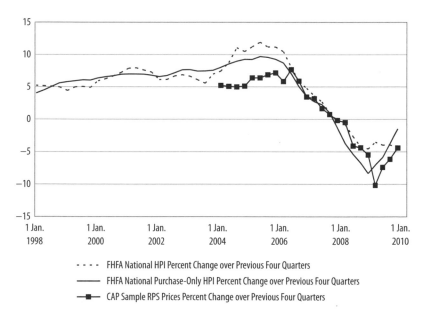

Figure 8.1. Year-on-year change in property value for CAP and FHFA: 1998–2010. Authors' calculations.

percent, respectively. These comparison values represent possible alternative investments that these borrowers could have made if they had purchased the DJIA or a six-month CD on the loan origination date and rolled over the balance at maturity. Thus during a period of housing-market growth, the CAP properties unambiguously outperformed these other two investment options. Moreover, after the housing downturn began in April 2006, CAP properties depreciated slightly but to a much smaller degree than the stock market, even after the financial crisis began. CDs outperformed both of these assets during the downturn, yielding an annual return in excess of 4.4 percent.

Although the appreciation of CAP properties has been positive in the aggregate, some variation naturally exists by the year of loan origination and by state. Submarkets clearly exist within states. However, we focus on state-level variation, because we are primarily interested in broadly highlighting systematic geographic differences in appreciation across the country. In addition, approximately 12 percent of our sample is located outside of metropolitan areas.

Overall, CAP properties increased in value by nearly $16,000 and experienced total appreciation of 21 percent. However, properties that were purchased in 1998 experienced annualized returns of 3.4 percent, while those that were purchased in 2004 appreciated by only .5 percent on an annual basis, yielding a difference in total (i.e., cumulative) appreciation rates between these two groups of nearly 40 percentage points. Moreover, 1 percent of properties purchased in 1998 had declined in value by April 2009, compared with 45 percent of those purchased in 2004.

In addition, properties in Maryland, the most rapidly appreciating state in this sample, had appreciated by 51 percent, or nearly $68,000, overall. At the other end of the spectrum, those in Michigan had declined by 13 percent, or nearly $10,000, since origination. More generally, more than half of the CAP properties in Midwestern states had declined in value, while most CAP properties in the South and West had increased in value.

Housing as a Wealth Builder for CAP Borrowers

As a group, CAP borrowers, since purchasing their homes, experienced a median gain of nearly $23,000 in equity. Put differently, these borrowers benefited from an annualized return on equity of 36 percent. Such large returns resulted partly from price appreciation, as we have seen, but also reflect the very low down payments (median of $2,500) that are typical of the mortgages on these properties. Overall, fewer than 4 percent of CAP borrowers had lost equity since their purchase. Thus if one considers that these borrowers are unlikely to make large leveraged investments in CDs or the stock market, purchasing a home has yielded investment returns for these borrowers far in excess of what they would have made by putting their down payments into either the DJIA or CDs.

Moreover, when considered in the context of household income, the importance of accumulated home equity in wealth gains is especially evident. For these borrowers, equity gains exceeded 50 percent of household income across the board as of April 2009 and exceeded 100 percent of household annual income for those making less than $20,000 a year.

As with overall appreciation gains, equity gains varied with the timing and location of home purchase. Borrowers who purchased in 1998 gained nearly three times the equity of those who purchased in 2004. Similarly, fewer than 1 percent of 1998 borrowers lost equity since loan origination, compared with 8.5 percent of 2004 borrowers. CAP borrowers in most southern states were among the least likely to experience a decline in equity during the period, while those in Michigan and Ohio were among the most likely to lose equity. In particular, borrowers in Maryland gained 15 times as much equity as did those in Michigan.

The Actual Sale Prices and Wealth of CAPS Participants

The previous analyses have considered the capital gains of CAP borrowers under the assumption of continued homeownership. Because the gains are based on house-price estimates, rather than observed property values, the figures in essence provide a picture of the *potential* wealth gains accruing to these borrowers for the period ending in April 2009. But how well does this picture match reality?

To answer this question, we analyzed comparable appreciation information for the group of CAPS participants who sold their homes during the survey period and reported the actual sale prices during their interviews. The total appreciation that this group of approximately 600 borrowers experienced was about 22 percent, which is very close to the preceding projection of 21 percent for all CAP borrowers. Moreover, the percentage of these borrowers who sold their homes at a loss is comparable to the percentage of CAP borrowers in the overall sample whose loans were originated in the same years.

As a further robustness check, we also examined the full set of wealth and assets information provided by all (approximately 2,000) respondents to the 2008 administration of the CAPS. As of the interview date, those owners who retained their CAP homes and original mortgages had accumulated about $21,000 in equity, which again is comparable to what CAP borrowers are projected to have achieved as a group. Those CAPS respondents who had refinanced retained less home equity. However, these borrowers also reported higher levels of housing and total assets, suggesting that their true wealth gains due to housing may exceed those inferred in the previous sections.

Correlates of Price Appreciation

We have seen that CAP homeowners have, as a group, made a reasonable investment decision when deciding to buy their homes with CRA mortgages. We have also seen that these homeowners have generally accumulated considerable equity, the primary component of their wealth, as a result of the appreciation of their houses. However, considerable variation exists in appreciation and equity gains among CAP homeowners.

Understanding the sources of this variation is important for evaluating policies that promote wealth building via homeownership. Therefore, this section presents a statistical analysis that suggests that most variation in house-price appreciation for these homeowners is systematically related to the timing of their home purchases and to local area conditions, such as the unemployment rate and zip-code-level demographics. In particular, this section updates and extends the analysis of Stegman, Quercia, and Davis (2007), who considered similar models of home price appreciation for CAP borrowers for the period from loan origination to the beginning of 2003. Their analyses are reproduced here for the period from loan origination to April 2009.

Estimation Methods

For consistency with the prior analysis and because of a skewed distribution of house-price appreciation, the dependent variable y_i is defined as follows:

$$y_i = ln(1 + r_i)$$

where r_i is the annualized rate of appreciation. A mixture of fixed-effects and random-effects models was estimated in an effort to capture as much local variation in price appreciation as possible. In addition, all of the models use fixed effects to control for differences due to loan origination year (that is, year of purchase and length of tenure).

More formally, the following series of models was estimated for the period from loan origination to the second quarter (Q2) of 2009:

Model 1: $y_{ij} = \alpha_o O_{ij} + e_{ij}$

Model 2: $y_{ij} = \alpha_o O_{ij} + \alpha_z Z_{ij} + e_{ij}$

Model 3: $y_{ij} = \alpha_o O_{ij} + \alpha_z Z_{ij} + \beta_m X_{mij} + e_{ij}$

Model 4: $y_{ij} = \alpha_o O_{ij} + \gamma_k C_{ki} + \beta_m X_{mij} + v_j + e_{iR} R_{ij}$,

where i denotes an individual, for $I = 1$ to N_j, and where j indicates the zip code in which the property is located, for $j = 1$ to J. Moreover, O_{ij} is a set of fixed effects for the origination years (1998–2004); Z_{ij} is a set of fixed effects for zip codes (that is, a dummy variable for each zip code); X_{mij} is a set of independent variables (for $m = 1$ to M and all i, j) with fixed coefficients (in this case, X is a mix of property-level, county-level, and national-level variables and varies from Model 3 to Model 4); C_{ki} is a set of zip-code-level characteristics (C_{ki}, for $k = 1$ to K and $j = 1$ to J) with fixed coefficients that replace the fixed effects for zip code in Model 4; e_{ij} is a random-error term, normally distributed with a mean of 0 and a variance of σ^2; and v_j is a random effect for zip code with a mean of 0 and a variance of τ.

Model 1 serves as a baseline model and controls only for origination year. Model 2 assesses the extent to which price appreciation varies across zip codes. Using fixed effects for zip codes absorbs the maximum amount of variance in price appreciation due to local variations.

In Model 3, variables are added to help explain the variation in price appreciation that is not captured by the zip-code-level differences. The purchase price of the property is included to capture differences among properties when purchased. Appreciation rates may vary by initial property value. The mean of the 10-year Treasury-bill (T-bill) rate between the month of purchase and April is also included as a proxy for macroeconomic conditions and the state of the housing market. In addition, the mean of the county unemployment rate between the month of purchase and April 2009 is added to Model 3 to account for local economic conditions.

Finally, Model 4 provides a substantive assessment of the local variation in price appreciation rates by replacing the fixed effects for zip code with a set of zip-code-specific variables plus a random effect for zip code. Using data from the 2000 census, three broad sets of zip-code-level characteristics for local housing attributes, demographics, and other relevant factors are included. We recognize that Model 4 may explain less of the variation in price appreciation than Model 3, because the array of zip-code-level characteristics will not explain all of the local variation that exists, while the random effect will not absorb as much variation as the fixed effects. Nevertheless, Model 4 provides a greater substantive explanation of local factors that affect price appreciation than any of the preceding models.

For local housing characteristics, we included the zip code's homeownership rate, median house value, and median housing age. Areas with high levels of homeownership and high median house values are generally considered to be among the most desirable neighborhoods in which to live, a factor that should increase property values. Median housing age could have either a negative or positive impact on appreciation, depending on the extent of maintenance and renovations.

Appreciation rates may also vary with the demographic characteristics of the neighborhood. Among the zip-code-level demographic variables that are included in Model 4 are the percentage of the population that is below the poverty level, the percentage of families headed by single parents, the mean unemployment rate during the study period, the percentage of the population that is African American or Hispanic, and population density. All other things being equal, higher local poverty and unemployment rates should be associated with lower price appreciation rates. Population density, which is measured as the number of people per square mile, is included because of its potential impact on the demand for housing. Because common dichotomous classifications of urban and rural markets are defined on the basis of population density, this measure also reflects the contribution of spatial concentration. Because of the large Hispanic immigrant population among CAP buyers, the interaction of percentage Hispanic with percentage foreign-born is included, in addition to standard control variables for race. Finally, the model includes a dummy variable for properties located in California, because of the exceptionally high appreciation rates that CAP homeowners have experienced in that state relative to those in most other states represented in the sample.

Models 1 to 3 are standard linear models that can be estimated by using ordinary least squares. Model 4 can be estimated by using a mixed linear model (to capture the random effect of zip code). Mixed linear models use a maximum-likelihood estimator to estimate models with both fixed and random effects and can estimate the type of heteroskedasticity that is captured in the reliability-specific error terms.

Data for the models are limited to properties located in zip codes that have at least five CAP properties (after observations with missing data have been removed). This created a sample size of about 17,000 properties in 1,500 zip codes. To assess the impact of the five-property cutoff, Model 4 was re-estimated with the data limited to properties in zip codes with at least ten and then at least twenty CAP loans, and substantively similar results were obtained.

Summary statistics for the substantive model variables are presented in Table 8.1. A natural logarithmic transformation was performed on several variables because they had highly skewed distributions. Although it is not the purpose of this chapter to fully describe the neighborhoods in which CAP properties are located, Table 8.1 contains several numbers that are worth highlighting. Sampled CAP properties had an average purchase price of about $93,000 and are in zip codes with about average homeownership and poverty rates and above average minority presence relative to the nation as a whole. CAP communities also have significant levels of foreign-born residents.

Estimation Results

The goodness-of-fit results are summarized in Table 8.2. As was mentioned earlier, Model 1 controls only for the origination year. As the value of R^2 indicates, these control variables account for 8 percent of the local variation in estimated appreciation rates. In addition, two measures of model fit, Akaike's information criterion (AIC) and the Bayesian information criterion (BIC), are presented. These measures are most useful in comparing the fit of two models, the main difference between the two measures being that BIC penalizes more heavily for degrees of freedom. Smaller values (or, in this case, negative values of larger magnitude) are better. Finally, Wald F-tests (not presented) indicate that each set of control fixed effects is statistically significant.

Table 8.1. Descriptive Statistics for 16,722 CAP Properties in 1,500 Zip Codes for Period from Loan Origination to April 2009

	Mean	Standard Deviation	Percent
Dependent variable			
ln(1 + appreciation rate)	0.0258	0.0327	
Property characteristic			
Purchase price*	$92,800	$43,642	
Economic conditions			
Mean of 10-year T-bill rate			
between purchase and April 2009	4.38	0.16	
Mean of county unemployment rate			
between purchase and April 2009	5.36	1.19	
Neighborhood Characteristics			
Housing			
Homeownership rate (%)	64.57	14.00	
Median house value*	$104,663	$46,699	
Median house age	37.12	11.97	
Demographics			
Black (%)*	21.23	22.49	
Hispanic (%)*	13.11	19.13	
Foreign-born (%)*	10.67	12.02	
Single-parent families (%)	11.14	4.46	
Below poverty level (%)	13.49	7.49	
Population density in thousands*	2.60	4.01	
Origination year			
1998			11.3
1999			10.6
2000			18.9
2001			21.2
2002			16.5
2003			10.9
2004			10.5
Geographic identifier			
California			13.4

*Variables are logged in the model.

Table 8.2. Goodness-of-Fit of Models 1–4 for Period from Origination to April 2009

	R^2	AIC	BIC
Model 1	0.08	−69,268	−69,260
Model 2	0.66	−73,959	−73,951
Model 3	0.72	−76,103	−76,096
Model 4	0.72	−82,496	−82,486

The R^2 is approximated as the square of the correlation between the predicted value and the observed value.

Model 2 adds fixed effects for zip codes. This model makes it possible to assess how much local variation remains after the origination year is taken into consideration. The zip-code fixed effects are statistically significant overall and explain an additional 58 percent of the variation in estimated appreciation rates, raising the explanatory power of the price-change model to 66 percent. Both the AIC and BIC indicate an improvement in model fit for Model 2 relative to Model 1. The fixed effects for origination year remain significant.

Model 3 adds the natural log of the purchase price, the mean of the 10-year T-bill rate between loan origination and April 2009, and the mean county-level unemployment rate over the same period. These variables will be discussed in more detail in Model 4, but all three are significant, and these variables explain an additional 6 percent of the variation, raising the model's explanatory power to 72 percent. Both the AIC and the BIC are again improved in Model 3 relative to Model 2.

Model 4 removes the zip-code fixed effects and replaces them with zip-code-level variables for the 2000 Census (which have fixed effects) and a random effect for zip code. Although the explanatory power of this model does not exceed that of Model 3, it provides insight into which local characteristics have driven price appreciation for these low-income borrowers. Detailed results for Model 4 are presented in the first column of Table 8.3.

The natural log of the purchase price has a significantly negative impact, which means that the lowest-priced houses are estimated to be, on average and controlling for other variables in the model, appreciating at a faster rate. The mean of the monthly 10-year T-bill rates between purchase and April

Table 8.3. Model 4 of House Price Appreciation for Five Time Periods with Zip-Code Random Effects and Origination-Year Fixed Effects

Variables	Overall *Before 2009Q2*	Before Downturn *Before 2006Q2*	Before Crisis *Before 2008Q4*	After Downturn *After 2006Q2*	After Crisis *After 2008Q4*
			Time Period		
Property characteristic					
ln(Purchase price)	−3.1‡	−4.1‡	−3.3‡	−0.6‡	1.1‡
Economic conditions					
Mean 10-year T-bill rate	−0,8†	−3.8‡	−2.0†		
Mean county					
unemployment rate	−0.6‡	−1.7‡	−1.0.‡	−0.3‡	−1.0‡
Neighborhood Characteristics					
Housing					
Homeownership rate	−1.8†	9.1‡	0.5	−16.8‡	−31.5‡
ln(Median house value)	4.1‡	2.3‡	4.0‡	5.3‡	5.1‡
Median house age	0.0‡	−0.0‡	−0.0	0.1‡	0.3‡
Demographics					
ln(% Black)	0.2‡	0.1	0.2†	0.8‡	1.5‡
ln(% Hispanic)	0.9‡	1.2†	0.9‡	0.8	0.7
ln(% Foreign born)	0.3	3.3‡	0.8‡	−3.5‡	−6.0‡
ln(% Hispanic) ·					
ln(% Foreign born)	0.2‡	0.4‡	0.2‡	0.1	−0.0
Single-parent families (%)	−7.1‡	1.8	−2.5	−22.0‡	−72.8‡
Below poverty level (%)	8.6‡	19.2‡	11.0‡	−4.2	−27.2‡
ln(Population density)	−0.2‡	0.7‡	0.0	−1.9‡	−4.0‡
Geographic identifier					
California	1.5‡	9.0‡	1.9‡	−10.9‡	−4.4‡
N	16,722	16,655	16,731	16,649	16,716
R^2	0.72	0.85	0.72	0.93	0.75

The R^2 is calculated as the correlation between the observed and predicted dependent variables. All coefficients are multiplied by 100.

‡$p \leq .01$; †$p \leq .05$; *$p \leq .10$.

2009 has a significant negative effect, as expected. Higher interest rates make it more expensive for people to finance home purchases, leading to lower demand and thereby lower appreciation rates. The mean county-level unemployment rate between purchase and April 2009 also has a significant negative effect, as expected.

With regard to the zip-code-level measures, high neighborhood house values have raised appreciation rates; but given that relative price gains have been greater for lower-priced properties, the results confirm the adage that it is better to own the lowest-priced house in the neighborhood than the highest-priced house. In this sample, the age of the neighborhood appears substantively unrelated to appreciation during this time period.

The percentages of Hispanics and African Americans in the neighborhood had a significant positive impact on appreciation rates during the period. The percentage of foreign-born residents had no impact on the appreciation rate unless this percentage reflected a higher percentage of Hispanic immigrants.

Somewhat surprisingly, the poverty rate in the zip code is positively associated with price appreciation and is significant, while population density was a negative contributor to appreciation. These counterintuitive results will be discussed below. Model 4 also includes a control for California properties, which, as expected, is strongly positive and significant.

Overall, Model 4 explains about 72 percent of the variation in the price appreciation of CAP properties and is comparable to Model 3 in this respect. This suggests that the zip-code-level characteristics (and the dummy variable for California) that are included in the model capture nearly all of the local variation, although the significant random effect of zip code means that considerable unexplained local variation remains. With regards to the fit of Model 4 relative to that of Model 3, the AIC and BIC both show a solid improvement, so both tests suggest that this is a more parsimonious model and is preferred to Model 3.

Extended Analysis

Because two major economic developments have taken place since these CAP borrowers purchased their properties, this section discusses the estimation results of Model 4 for four shorter time periods: (1) the period preceding the downturn in the housing market (loan origination to April 2006), (2) the period preceding the financial crisis (loan origination to October 2008), (3) the period following the beginning of the housing downturn (April 2006 to April 2009), and (4) the period following the beginning of the financial crisis (October 2008 to April 2009). As was noted earlier, breaking the analysis down in this fashion provides information about how the relationship of neighborhood characteristics to appreciation may have varied during the period considered and under varied conditions in the economy as a whole.

The second through fifth columns of coefficients in Table 8.3 present the results of these additional analyses. Overall, economic conditions, neighborhood conditions, and the original purchase price all continue to be statistically significant predictors of price appreciation, and the direction of their relationships with price appreciation are unchanged. Each of these four estimations includes fixed effects for loan-origination year and zip-code random effects, all of which are significant as well. Taken together, the included predictors account for over 70 percent of the variation in appreciation. The T-bill rate is omitted for the last two estimations because this variable does not vary across observations in those cases.

Of greater interest is that the relationships of the zip-code-level predictors to the appreciation rate appear to have been markedly different depending on when the appreciation rate was measured. These discrepancies are not due to the omission of the T-bill rate from the post-downturn and post-crisis estimations, as the results for the pre-downturn and pre-crisis periods are unchanged when this variable is also omitted from those estimations.

More specifically, both the homeownership rate and population density are positively and significantly related to appreciation for the period before the housing downturn but have a significant negative relationship thereafter. Ordinarily, an increase in population density or in the homeownership rate would be expected to drive up house prices because of a greater local demand for housing and because of the perceived greater desirability of neighborhoods with a high concentration of homeowners. In this case, it appears that those neighborhoods that are likely to be most affected by changes in the availability of mortgage credit because of population and homeownership clustering experienced greater gains before the crisis and greater losses thereafter, causing an overall inverse relationship between appreciation and these variables for the period between loan origination and the second quarter of 2009.

In addition, the percentage of the population living at or below the poverty level was positively related to appreciation before the financial crisis, while the percentage of single-parent families was unrelated. However, both of these factors are significant and negatively related to appreciation for the period following the beginning of the housing downturn.

Finally, the relationship of the local racial makeup to the appreciation of CAP properties also has varied over time. The appreciation rate has been consistently positive in neighborhoods with a larger percentage of African American residents, and this effect actually increased in significance after the start of the housing downturn. Neighborhoods with a greater percentage of Hispanic residents experienced significantly greater appreciation before the financial crisis, those having a greater percentage of foreign-born Hispanics experiencing the greatest gains but average appreciation thereafter. Communities with a greater percentage of non-Hispanic foreign-born residents also experienced significantly higher appreciation before the crisis, but this trend later reversed.

Evaluating the Findings

The higher appreciation rates in minority and high-poverty areas before the crisis appears counterintuitive. However, the trend is consistent with the concept of a credit-driven housing bubble. Subprime lending increased the availability of mortgage credit most dramatically in areas traditionally underserved. According to tables from the Federal Financial Institutions Examination Council, between 2000 and 2005, the denial rate for a conventional home-purchase mortgage application fell 18 percent nationally but 33 percent for low- and moderate-income borrowers. Mian and Sufi (2009) found evidence of correlations among the decline in mortgage denial rates, an increase in subprime lending, and higher house-price appreciation. Similarly, S&P/Case-Shiller's Tiered House Price Index shows that lower-valued properties experienced the greatest volatility during the housing bubble in almost all of the metropolitan areas for which data are available.

Some readers might take these observations as evidence that credit in general, and that to low-income borrowers in particular, was overextended and unsustainable during the housing bubble. However, a vital distinction must be made in the quality of loan products. A prior study using CAP borrowers suggests that CRA loans and subprime loans are associated with markedly different rates of default for comparable borrowers (Ding, Quercia, and Ratcliffe 2008). Mortgage default has clear wealth repercussions for the borrower, in both direct terms relating to the property and indirect terms relating to the ability of the borrower to borrow in the future.

Moreover, mortgage defaults have neighborhood effects. The recent literature (Harding, Rosenblatt, and Yao 2009; Immergluck and Smith 2006) has found evidence of a significant spillover effect of foreclosure, in which the neglect and abandonment of a foreclosed property create a disamenity that reduces neighboring property values. Because low or negative equity stemming from price declines is an important determinant of foreclosure (Foster and Van Order 1984; Quercia and Stegman 1992; Vandell 1994), a compounding effect exists that can concentrate foreclosures in certain neighborhoods. The implication is that if the quality of the loan product can affect the default rate at the level of the individual borrower, then the dispersion of different types of loan products could also affect the house-price appreciation rate and resulting wealth benefits at the neighborhood level.

The sum of these findings suggests that despite recent house-price volatility, homeownership has been generally a net benefit and strong investment for low-income households. However, loan type may also be an important determinant of whether low-income borrowers sustain homeownership and of how much wealth they are able to accumulate as a result of their investments. The homogeneity of loan products received by borrowers in our investigation and the absence of the neighborhood lending context are important limitations of this analysis.

Conclusion

In summary, CAP property values have largely moved in line with general housing-market trends and have, at the median, appreciated by roughly 20 percent since origination. These properties have generally outperformed the stock market during the period considered. In addition, CAP borrowers have accumulated equity of approximately $23,000 at the median, or more than half of annual income, since purchase and experienced an annualized return on equity of 36 percent. Thus housing has generally been an effective wealth-building strategy for these borrowers, despite recent economic conditions.

Also consistent with national housing trends, considerable variation in appreciation gains exist with regard to the geographic locations of these properties and when they were purchased. Properties that were purchased earlier tended to appreciate to a greater extent. In addition, most of the cross-property variation in appreciation appears to be related systematically to local economic and demographic conditions, including the unemployment rate, the homeownership rate, the percentages of foreign-born and minority residents, the prevalence of single-parent families, the poverty rate, and the population density. Moreover, areas that saw greater appreciation gains during the housing boom generally also experienced larger declines thereafter.

Overall, the current analysis suggests that housing continues to be a viable wealth-building avenue for low-income borrowers with CRA mortgages. Because low-income borrowers do tend to keep such a large percentage of their total wealth in their homes, a home is most likely to be an effective wealth-building avenue for this population when it is purchased as a long-term investment. Finally, as is always the case for real estate investment, careful consideration should be given to neighborhood conditions and economic trends at the time of home purchase.

Future research will endeavor to extend this analysis by considering the role of proximate subprime lending in CAP neighborhoods as well as the user costs associated with CAP homeownership, as compared with renters, and the associated investment risks. While the equity gains from homeownership that result from price appreciation provide one metric of the viability of low-income homeownership, it is important to consider these additional factors in creating an overall picture of the pros and cons of homeownership for this population.

References

Belsky, Eric, and Allegra Calder. 2004. "Credit Matters: Low-Income Asset Building Challenges in a Dual Financial Service System." Report BABC 04-1. Cambridge, Mass.: Joint Center for Housing Studies, Harvard University.

Ding, Lei, Roberto Quercia, and Janneke Ratcliffe. 2008. "Risky Borrowers or Risky Mortgages: Disaggregating Effects Using Propensity Score Models." Working Paper. Chapel Hill: Center for Community Capital, University of North Carolina.

Foster, Chester, and Robert Van Order. 1984. "An Option Based Model of Mortgage Default." *Housing Financial Review* 3, 4: 351–72.

Harding, John, Eric Rosenblatt, and Vincent Yao. 2009. "The Contagion Effect of Foreclosed Properties." *Journal of Urban Economics* 66, 3: 164–78.

Immergluck, Dan, and Geoff Smith. 2006. "The External Costs of Foreclosure: The Impact of Single-Family Mortgage Foreclosures on Property Values." *Housing Policy Debate* 17, 1: 57–79.

Mian, Atif, and Amir Sufi. 2009. "The Consequences of Mortgage Credit Expansion: Evidence from the U.S. Mortgage Default Crisis." *Quarterly Journal of Economics* 124, 4: 1449–96.

Quercia, Roberto G., and Michael A. Stegman. 1992. "Residential Mortgage Default: A Review of the Literature." *Journal of Housing Research* 3, 2: 341–79.

Riley, Sarah, and Hong Yu Ru. 2009. "Community Advantage Panel Survey Technical Sampling Report: Owners, 2003–2008." Chapel Hill: Center for Community Capital, University of North Carolina.

Spader, Jonathan. 2009. "Community Reinvestment Lending in a Changing Context: Evidence of Interaction with FHA and Subprime Originations." Working Paper. Chapel Hill: Center for Community Capital, University of North Carolina.

Stegman, Michael, Roberto Quercia, and Walter Davis. 2007. "The Determinants of Home Price Appreciation Among Community Reinvestment Homeowners." *Housing Studies* 22, 3: 381–408.

U.S. Government Accountability Office. 2009. *Loan Performance and Negative Home Equity in the Nonprime Mortgage Market.* Washington, D.C.: U.S. GAO. http://www.gao.gov/new.items/d10146r.pdf, 03-02-09.

Vandell, Kerry. 1994. "How Ruthless Is Mortgage Default? A Review and Synthesis of the Evidence." *Journal of Housing Economics* 3: 330–56.

Note

We thank our colleagues at the UNC Center for Community Capital for helpful comments and discussion, and we thank Hong Yu Ru for outstanding research assistance. We are grateful to the Ford Foundation for financial support. All opinions and any errors remain our own.

Chapter 9

The Community Reinvestment Act: Evaluating Past Performance and Reviewing Options for Reform

Mark A. Willis

The passage of the Community Reinvestment Act (CRA) in 1977 set in motion a bold experiment that has yet to achieve its full potential. In the language of the legislation, the CRA sought to "encourage" banks to lend ("reinvest") in their "entire community, including low- and moderate-income neighborhoods."[1] While banks had existing statutory responsibilities to serve the convenience and needs of their communities, little or no lending had been taking place in many low- and moderate-income (LMI) neighborhoods. By "encouraging" (but not requiring) increased availability of capital, Congress sought to make banks more proactive in the stabilization and revitalization of their local LMI communities.[2] Banking at that time was mainly a local affair in which local banks collected local deposits and served their local markets through loans to community businesses and individuals.[3]

While the CRA has had numerous successes over the past decades, its effectiveness has diminished over time.[4] Neither the law nor the regulations implementing that law have kept up with structural changes in the banking industry or with community development best practices. More important, perhaps, has been the failure to build continuously on the experiences of what has worked or not worked. The statute has rarely been updated since it was originally enacted, and the last major rewrite of its regulations occurred over 15 years ago, in 1995 (Office of the Federal Register 1995). Slightly more frequent have been updates to the Interagency Questions and Answers— Q&As—which contain informal staff guidance for agency personnel, financial institutions, and the public (see, for example, FFIEC 2010a).

As a result, the CRA is in need of a major overhaul.[5] Fortunately, many of the potential changes can be accomplished simply through regulatory adjustments without requiring congressional action.[6] Maintaining the flexibility to improve the CRA through regulatory changes is also important (at least in theory, it should be easier to adopt updates through regulatory changes than through statutory amendments). Past experience strongly suggests a continuing need to update the CRA on a regular basis to maintain its effectiveness. This chapter analyzes the strengths and weaknesses of implementation of the CRA over the last 33 years and ends with some possible directions for reform. Of course, the CRA's effectiveness is a function not just of the words of the statute and regulations but also of leadership and political will (see Immergluck 2004: 14).

Basic Elements of the CRA

The Community Reinvestment Act imposes on every bank an affirmative obligation to help meet the credit needs of its entire community. The scope of that community is determined by where the bank has deposit facilities, and the statute specifically notes that "entire" includes the LMI neighborhoods within that geography. The statute also requires that the obligation be carried out in a way that is consistent with the safe and sound operation of the banking institution. Implementation of this affirmative obligation is delegated to the four regulatory agencies that oversee the banks: the Office of the Comptroller of the Currency, the Federal Reserve, the Office of Thrift Supervision, and the Federal Deposit Insurance Corporation (FDIC). The statute provides few further details or restrictions except that each bank must be given one of four ratings—"Outstanding," "Satisfactory," "Needs to Improve," or "Substantial Noncompliance"—and that the rating be made public as part of a written document called the Performance Evaluation.[7] The rating is important in its potential impact on a bank's public reputation and on the approval process for banks when they apply for certain additional powers.

The agencies have, in turn, jointly developed regulations that assess compliance with the Act. For retail banks with assets greater than $1 billion,[8] the CRA exams follow the Large Retail Bank Test, which consists of a Lending Test, an Investment Test, and a Service Test, each with a focus on serving lower-income communities and customers.[9] These three tests receive weights of 50 percent, 25 percent, and 25 percent, respectively, toward the determination of a bank's overall score. In addition, any bank that fails to do better on the Lending Test than a "Needs to Improve" is automatically disqualified from receiving an overall rating of "Satisfactory" or better.

Smaller banks, as well as wholesale and special-purpose banks, face different exam protocols.[10] The smallest-sized banks, called "Small Banks," are those that have less than $250 million in assets. They are simply expected to lend back into the community from which they are taking deposits and so are judged only on the amount of local lending compared to their deposit base. No account is taken as to how many, if any, of the loans are to LMI borrowers or made in LMI communities.

Banks that are a size larger (but have less than $1 billion in assets) are called "Intermediate Small Banks" and are also judged on their lending ratio as well as on a community development test that has a clear LMI focus and encompasses loans, investments, and services within the regulation's definition of community development.[11] Examples of community development loans, investments (a category that also includes philanthropic grants), and services include, respectively, loans made to finance the construction of affordable housing and to help finance community development financial institutions (CDFIs),[12] investments in low-income housing tax credits (LIHTCs) and new markets tax credits (NMTCs), and credit and mortgage counseling or other financial education services. The community development test is also at the core of the exams for wholesale and special-purpose banks.[13]

Embodied in the CRA is also a system of carrots and sticks based on the regulators' ability to assign ratings and to decline applications on the basis of a bank's CRA performance. The CRA's most potent tool has been thought to be the power given to the regulators to delay or reject applications by a bank to merge with or acquire another bank on the basis of a finding of inadequate CRA performance.[14] This power proved to be a major motivator during the wave of bank mergers that began in earnest in the 1990s. Regulators were widely believed to move more quickly to approve mergers and acquisitions for banks with a strong CRA record. In addition, no bank wanted to risk having its application rejected, as had happened in 1989 when the Continental Illinois Bank applied to acquire another bank (Knight 1989).

Not only can bank regulators turn down applications, but they can convene, as part of the review process, public meetings to gather oral testimony on the banks' performance in meeting the convenience and needs of their communities. This is an option that the regulators have exercised a number of times, especially for mergers involving the largest banks. Such open forums allow community representatives, advocates, public officials, and others to voice their concerns and criticisms. At these times, bankers particularly like to be able to trumpet an "Outstanding" rating as evidence of their commitment to the entirety of their community.

CRA Successes

Proving that the CRA has made a difference in LMI communities has been a challenge, largely because it is hard to determine how a community would have developed in the absence of the CRA. Many attempts have been made, often using mortgage origination data collected under the Home Mortgage Disclosure Act.[15] Some have found a correlation between the CRA and greater mortgage lending, but they have not been able to prove that the CRA caused the increased investment. A particularly creative approach was used in a recent study by Neil Bhutta. By comparing mortgage lending just above and below the income cutoff for CRA eligibility, he showed that the CRA had a positive but marginal effect in large metropolitan areas (Bhutta 2008: 21–23). Regardless of the difficulties of identifying quantifiable impacts through statistical analysis of mortgage originations, it seems clear that the CRA has encouraged banks to learn more about how to serve the LMI marketplace in a safe and sound way, to recruit and train specialized staff, and to support specialized consortia involving banks, community groups, and government.

By building lines of communication between banks and community groups, the CRA has helped to correct misperceptions about market opportunities and led to the tailoring of products and services that both serve the community and are safe and sound from the point of view of both the bank and the banking system. One notable example was the development in the early to mid-1990s of new underwriting standards for home mortgages, which facilitated a dramatic growth in mortgage lending to lower-income populations and neighborhoods (Barr 2005). Through dialog and testing, banks were able to identify and remove unnecessary barriers to serving this marketplace, resulting in loans that performed (and still perform) relatively well (Ding et al. 2010; Laderman and Reid 2009). The more recent proliferation of toxic loan products in the early 2000s was not a product of the CRA, despite some sensational claims to the contrary in the media and elsewhere (Ludwig 2010: 12–16). In fact, of all the subprime loans that were made in 2005 and 2006 (the peak years of the housing bubble), only 6 percent were extended by CRA-covered lenders to lower-income borrowers or neighborhoods in the communities for which they had a CRA responsibility, that is, where they took deposits (Kroszner 2009). Given these figures, it is hard to argue that the CRA was somehow a driver of the crisis.

A second set of successes surrounded the establishment within many of the larger banks of specialized divisions that became proficient at structuring complex affordable-housing or community economic development deals involving multiple sources of subsidies and players. As these deals proliferated, credit approval officers learned how to think outside the box, recognizing that projects with government-subsidized rents and sale prices actually had, for example, lower exposure to the risk of downturns in the economy. The emergence of these divisions, with their highly skilled staffs, was seen by many bankers and advocates to facilitate the growth of community development lending and investing and also served as important lines of communication and trust between the banks and their communities.

Third, the CRA spurred the growth of new entities and new government programs. Collaborations between banks and community-based organizations helped to spawn the development of many CDFIs with their specialized skills for serving lower-income communities. The banks provide startup funding, technical assistance, loans with interest rates at or below market, and operating support to CDFIs (Pinsky 2002). They collaborated in the development of the LIHTC and NMTC programs and are major investors. Banks have also worked with community groups to set up consortia to provide mortgage counseling or other forms of financial education (e.g., credit counseling).

Learning from Experience

Despite its substantial successes, the CRA has fallen short of its potential and is continuing to lose ground. A core problem is the difficult, if not impossible, one of finding consensus on what the goal or goals are and on finding a single, simple way to measure success.[16] Unlike other laws that lay out a set of prohibited behaviors, the CRA sets forth an aspirational goal—that is, an affirmative obligation to help meet the credit needs of LMI communities and individuals.

The problem lies with what actually gets measured. As the saying goes, what gets measured gets done. Some of the tests that regulators have developed have given too much credit for activities that were not directly linked to revitalizing and strengthening communities while giving too little to other activities that have a significant incremental impact. Some have even been the source of unintended negative consequences.

The 1995 rewrite of the regulations shifted the focus of the exams from evaluating the "process"—such as whether the bank had done a formal assessment of the needs of its communities—to measuring "performance." This change led to the increased use of quantitative measures, giving the impression of rigor and of a system that judged every bank in the same way. While this focus on numbers and output appeared sound, the reality has been a system that rewards production volume and market share regardless of the impact on LMI communities.[17] So smaller loans and investments may simply not happen, even when they could have a disproportionately positive impact on a community.[18] In addition to getting less CRA credit, these types of small loans tend to be less profitable, since they generate lower fees and involve extra effort (e.g., require special knowledge of government programs, special structuring skills, ongoing monitoring, or technical assistance to the borrower who may be unfamiliar with the application or development process).

Another problem is that the test may be requiring banks collectively or individually to do more volume than the market can support on the basis of normal pricing and underwriting standards. As a result, banks have been pushed to undertake activities that are uneconomic and, in some cases, of little or no value to LMI communities. A regulation-imposed production goal that is set too high can lead a bank to seek to increase its market share by reducing its pricing or, worse, lower its credit standards (something that a bank is reluctant to do and is against the statutory requirement for the CRA to be consistent with safety and soundness).

One approach that had seemed to get around this problem was the adoption of parity tests in which a bank's share of the marketplace is compared to its share of the middle- and upper-income segments of that same market. It may, at first, sound reasonable to expect that a bank that is making a reasonable effort to serve the LMI segment for mortgages, for example, would have the same share of that market as it does of the middle- and upper-income segments—for instance, if it has 10 percent of the latter, it should have 10 percent of the former. Unfortunately, the world is much more complicated. In this example, a bank that is looking to ensure that it achieves a 10 percent share will aim higher than 10 percent, especially if seeks an "Outstanding." If all banks do the same, then they will collectively be seeking a total of more than 100 percent—a mathematical impossibility. The situation was made worse by the emergence in the late 1990s of independent mortgage companies that focused on the LMI marketplace. Achieving parity became even more mathematically impossible given the disproportionately large share of the LMI market that was grabbed by these firms. The regulators also apply additional parity tests on mortgages based on non-market, demographic data, such as the number of LMI homeowners, which may be even less related to the market opportunity. Other tests that are built on this concept of parity include measures of small business lending and the location of bank branches.

The result of these imperfect measures has been some unintended negative consequences. Parity and other tests of production volume have led banks to take actions that have not necessarily made good economic sense, thus undermining the credibility of the CRA's core message that serving the LMI marketplace can be good business and potentially discouraging investment by others in these communities. The CRA's increasing focus on production volumes has also led many banks to turn to their mainstream units to meet their CRA obligations and away from the use of specialized units.

Continued reliance on the parity test for mortgages has had at least two effects. The pressure to increase their LMI mortgage market share did not stop even after banks reexamined and modified their mortgage underwriting guidelines in the early to mid-1990s. As a result, banks were prompted to offer more and more subsidy to borrowers.[19] Subsidies grew to $8,000 per loan or more, making these loans clearly unprofitable.[20] As the growth of the independent mortgage companies made it even harder to get to parity, banks had to take even more drastic measures and so increasingly turned to buying LMI-qualified loans from each other, using a provision of the regulations that was designed to encourage the growth of a secondary market. This trading of loans, while often less costly than offering subsidies, failed to provide any additional benefit to the community, since the loans had already been originated. Moreover, the banks, Fannie Mae and Freddie Mac, earned fees and a premium by selling LMI loans, although these had to come out of pocket when the banks found themselves on the other side of the transaction.

Another example of a parity test that led banks to undertake unproductive or uneconomic activities concerns the opening and closing of bank branches. Banks are tested to see whether the geographic distribution of their branch network matches the industry average of branches in LMI census tracts or the LMI's share of the metropolitan population. While local bank branches are clearly one way to serve an LMI community, other ways to serve the same customers include branches near their place of work, web-based technologies, 800 numbers, and automated teller machines (ATMs) in non-bank branches.[21] Unfortunately, some neighborhoods are unable to generate enough banking business to make a local branch economically viable. Yet the test may compel banks to open branches that struggle to make a profit if they can make one at all. Even worse, a new branch may undermine the economics of a pre-existing branch of another bank, hurting banks that have been in the neighborhood for years—a rather perverse and unfortunate result.

Overall, the focus on production has led banks to rely more on their mainstream businesses and less on specialized units to generate the large volumes consistent with the criteria used by the regulators. While mainstream units with their emphasis on scale and mass production have been able to turn out impressive production volumes that meet the criteria for CRA eligibility, they rely on systems that often lack the flexibility to offer one-off products or modify product features to respond to variations in local needs. The managers and staff of these units rarely have the time or expertise to interact and collaborate with the community on a regular basis. Moreover, these units also manage to a bottom line, which makes them reluctant to devote resources that could be deployed more profitably elsewhere and causes them to be constantly looking for the lowest-cost way of meeting their CRA targets. This focus on the bottom line also often means that only products that can be expected to meet internal rate-of-return hurdles will be offered. Thus while many advocates view price as an issue of fairness—especially if it appears that low-income customers seem to be paying more for a comparable product or service than higher-income customers—insistence on such pricing in instances in which costs are higher or revenue is lower can mean that a product will simply not be offered.

The shift away from specialized units has, in at least some cases, moved overall responsibility for the CRA to such non-business units as regulatory compliance and philanthropy. These units are often not well positioned to encourage innovation and engage in active collaboration with communities. They lack the specialized staff to offer one-off, high-impact (but often low-dollar-value) products or services and the ability to vary their products and services across localities depending upon local needs.

The exam protocol for large retail banks also lacks a community development test with its combination of community development lending, investments, and services.[22] Yet this array of activities can be critical for stabilizing and revitalizing neighborhoods.[23] Community development loans, grants, and services are too important to be systematically undervalued as they are at present for large retail banks.[24] At present, the Lending Test focuses on home mortgages and small-business loans, with community development loans serving only as a possible way to enhance a bank's rating on the Lending Test. As for community development grants, their total dollar value is simply added to the dollar volume of community development investments. Since the latter are generally much larger, consisting, for example, of investments in LIHTCs, NMTCs, and mortgage bonds, the grants barely move the needle with regard to the total dollar measurement used for the Investment Test. And community development services receive only minor recognition under the Service Test, which looks mainly at the distribution of bank branches and branch services.

While the exams for large retail banks include a review of local conditions as part of something called the Performance Context, the exams themselves seem to take less and less account of variations in needs across localities.[25] The increased reliance on quantification and set weights for the different components has reduced the incentive for banks to try to tailor products and services to local needs. Yet communities do not all need the same mix of bank products and services. For example, shrinking cities such as Detroit are focusing on demolishing buildings and land banking, while cities with a growing population such as New York continue to face a shortage of affordable housing.

Another factor complicating the CRA exam is that the world of banks has changed dramatically over the last three decades. The share of household financial assets held by banks (and thereby covered by the CRA) fell from 25 percent in 1977 to a low of 11 percent in 1999 and had rebounded somewhat to 15 percent in 2007 (Avery, Courchane, and Zorn 2009). Meanwhile, the industry has witnessed the growth of very large, national banks and of Internet and other banks that serve national markets but take deposits in only a limited number of locations.[26] And the percentage of home purchase loans made by banks and their affiliates not covered by the CRA has increased (Apgar and Essene 2009: 21–3).

The massive increase in size of some banks presents a particular problem for CRA exams. While it might not be difficult for an examiner of a small bank to review all of the loans, investments, and services made by a bank in the communities where it takes deposits, it becomes an overwhelming task in the case of banks that take deposits in many states and across many localities, even when the exam procedures call for only a limited number of geographic locations to be subject to a "full-scope" exam. The exams of these banks can take 18 months or more to complete, tying up both examiner and bank resources for extended periods of time.[27] Moreover, with exams taking such a long time, a bank is not able to incorporate what it learns from an exam into its business plans until it is halfway or more through the period covered by the next exam.

The current system also appears to leave some communities underserved by the CRA, and this particularly concerns the advocates (Taylor and Silver 2009: 151). The emergence of banks with national distribution networks has meant that banks may serve a local community by offering home mortgages, credit cards, student loans, auto loans, and the like but not have a local deposit-taking facility and thus have no direct CRA responsibility. The local banks that do take deposits may consequently be smaller, and some may be subject only to the Small Bank Lending Test that does not even focus directly on serving the LMI community. Even if a large national bank has a local deposit-taking presence, it might not pay much attention to a locality that is too small to have much bearing on the institution's overall rating, since a bank's overall CRA rating is mainly determined by its performance in the communities where it gathers most of its deposits.

Some of these communities could be served by national and regional funds, but the regulations actually discourage banks from investing in such funds. Under current rules, banks receive fractional credit for investments in such funds depending on how much of a fund's proceeds go to locations where the bank takes deposits. Why would a bank invest in a fund where it can get less than 100 percent CRA credit? Yet these funds are excellent vehicles to make credit more available to all communities regardless of their size or the strength of their local banks, and the funds provide a way for banks to diversify their risk geographically. One area in which this has become a particularly acute problem is that of LIHTCs. The financial crisis has created a gap in demand for the tax credits as many of the traditional investors have sharply curtailed their purchases or even exited the market. The need now is to attract new investors, especially to serve projects in geographies that receive less CRA-driven attention. Yet a paucity of geographically diversified funds may prove to be a barrier for investors that would find comfort in investing in such vehicles alongside bankers (Joint Center for Housing Studies 2010).

The current financial crisis has also seriously diminished the CRA's power to influence banks. Expediting the application process for approvals of mergers and acquisitions appears to have been a key motivator for large banks to pursue an "Outstanding" CRA rating (Litan et al. 2001: 3).[28] More recently, however, preserving the safety and soundness of the banking system has become the driving force behind regulators' efforts to combine banks. And the future prospects for mergers and acquisitions do not look bright. It appears that the wave of mega-mergers may be over, thus removing for the very large banks one of the key reasons to seek an "Outstanding" rating. Moreover, the dominance of safety and soundness issues may last for a while in the face of continuing loan losses. Unfortunately, once fewer banks go for or receive an "Outstanding" rating, the tide may turn, and other banks that sought an "Outstanding" rating in part to match their peers may decide it is no longer worth the effort.

While the CRA emerged to a large degree out of concerns for a lack of home mortgage lending in lower-income geographies (often referred to as "redlining"), it is now clear that the process of stabilizing and revitalizing communities requires much more than simply making credit available for homeownership. Vibrant communities are a function of many factors, including access to good jobs, the training of people to fill those jobs, public safety, education, health, and more. Yet, as was noted previously, the Large Retail Bank Test undervalues the importance of community development loans and services and precludes the counting of grants for many of the activities that fit a broader view of what is called comprehensive community development. Finally, the CRA is also out of step with the way in which some affordable housing programs are financed. For example, some

New York programs rely on bond financing, with banks providing letters of credit. However, letters of credit are not given the same value under the CRA as loans are, even though the bank assumes the same credit risk.

Another lesson learned has been the need to address inconsistent treatment across exams. Despite the use of consistent regulatory language across the agencies, differences in interpretation can be significant. Unfortunately, efforts to provide consistency in interpretation across agencies (and even within agencies) have not been as proactive as might be optimal. It makes no sense to allow one bank to get credit for an activity that is denied by another agency. Yet the regulators have been slow to adopt uniform approaches when such disparities appear, impeded at least in part by their inability to rapidly update the regulations, examination procedures, or Q&As.

Efforts to reform the CRA have also suffered from the lack of a naturally occurring consensus among the diverse groups of stakeholders.[29] Differences in perspectives and historical divisions among groups likely play a role, but perhaps more important has been the lack of a forum in which differences could be hashed out and reconciled. Moreover, the weighting system that is embedded in the examination process has created a zero-sum game in which any change that gives more weight to one activity will likely result in reducing the importance of another activity in determining a bank's overall rating. Thus, for example, if community development lending were to get more weight within the Lending Test, then either mortgages or small-business lending would have to get less.

Advocates have also been concerned that, over time, the regulators have become too lax, leading to grade inflation. It is indeed the case that very few banks "fail," and fewer than one fifth receive an "Outstanding" rating, although the percentage is much higher for the twenty-five largest banks, over 70 percent of which receive an "Outstanding" Rating (Avery, Courchane, and Zorn 2009: 44).[30] Bankers have a different perspective and point to the high level of "Satisfactory" or better ratings as reflecting banks' efforts to achieve a "passing" grade on all their regulatory exams regardless of whether they are likely to apply for the types of regulatory approvals covered by the CRA. Other banks feel that a rating of less than "Satisfactory" could hurt their public image. Some even strive for an "Outstanding" rating as a way to validate their commitment to serving their local community.

Also undermining the credibility of the bank CRA rating system may be the requirement that each bank get a single overall rating. Given that an exam, particularly for the larger banks, covers a multiplicity of activities and geographies, it is hard for a single rating to fully reflect the breadth and depth of a bank's CRA performance.[31]

Potential Directions for Reforms

The basic approach to reform needs to be one of continuous improvement. Failure to address issues on a timely basis has been extremely detrimental to maintaining and improving the effectiveness of the CRA. For example, for years, the regulations discouraged the financing of mixed-income housing even as many communities introduced innovative programs such as inclusionary zoning, which seeks to have housing developers include affordable units in their projects, generally in the range of 10 to 30 percent, with the intention of reducing the concentrations of poverty that plague inner cities and, more recently, suburbs. Only in March 2010 were the regulators able to modify their own rules to allow for CRA credit for housing projects in which the units serving an LMI population were less than 50 percent of the total. They now allow credit based on the proportion of LMI units, but it is now long after the issue first arose.

More routine updating of the regulations would allow the system to keep up better with changes in the structure of the banking industry, rectify previous changes that have not yielded the intended results, and resolve issues that lead to inconsistencies among exams. A regular process of amending could yield two additional benefits: (1) It could take the pressure off regulators to update everything at once and so would allow them to take smaller but steadier steps and give more time, where appropriate, to allow the stakeholders to hammer out areas of common ground; and (2) it could increase the willingness of stakeholders in general to try new ideas, given the ability to repeal the change or make midcourse corrections on a timely basis. Past experience has made everyone leery of trying out new ideas that, simply through inertia, might become a permanent burden on the system.

The following discussion examines some of the changes that could help to address failures of the existing regulation. Some of these changes can be made only through statutory adjustment. However, most are within the power of the agencies to make by regulation. As was noted earlier, the enabling statute delegated much of the detail of implementation to regulators. Preserving this flexibility at the regulatory level could be critical to keeping the CRA current over time.

Empower a Lead Agency

Regulatory change is never easy, but the difficulty is more than quadrupled when it is necessary to achieve unanimity among the four banking agencies enumerated in the statute.[32] The Obama administration should designate one agency to take the lead and give the agency a tight timetable, sufficient staffing and analytic resources, and authority to resolve disputes. Congress could add to the sense of urgency by holding hearings that highlight the obvious shortcomings of the current rules and encourage the regulators to undertake the process of reform.

Fix Complementary Laws

While it is tempting to expand the scope of the CRA, the exams already cover so much territory that they are in danger of losing their focus by being spread too thin.[33] The CRA is only one piece of the puzzle for helping LMI individuals and communities. Other legislation that deals with complementary issues—for example, racial and ethnic discrimination—should be fixed and not replicated within the CRA. For example, the enforcement of provisions against unfair or deceptive acts or practices, fair lending laws, and other consumer protection and compliance laws can be critical to helping lower-income communities thrive. It could even make sense to add a CRA-like affirmative obligation to those laws, thereby creating a more level playing field among firms that compete for the same customers and allowing CRA enforcement to focus on other issues. The new consumer financial protection bureau could, for example, make it possible for the regulators to refocus their oversight and enforcement functions under the CRA to other products and services provided by banks.

Measure Impact Through Better Balance of Quantitative and Qualitative, Production and Process

Over the years, the examiners have tried various ways to measure bank compliance with the affirmative obligations imposed by the CRA. None of the tests have been able, by themselves, to measure the incremental impact on the community. Some have even turned out to have unintended negative consequences, and these need to be eliminated or blended with other factors. For example, in addition to measuring the size of a loan or investment, examiners should take into account such other factors as the following: How different are the size and type of loan or investment from those that the bank does as part of its regular course of business? Did the structuring or underwriting of the loan require specialized knowledge of the market or take an extraordinary amount of time because of the complexity of the deal or the number of parties involved in the negotiations (e.g., multiple government agencies, local community participation)? Were lower fees and interest rates charged compared to a standard market rate deal? In this way, the CRA can encourage high-impact loans and investments even though they may be less profitable for a bank to make.

This combination of quantitative and non-quantitative, non-production criteria could also serve to encourage banks to maintain separate, specialized lending units. Process measures, which were a core part of the regulations before the 1995 rewrite, might be especially helpful.[34] Including in an exam a review of whether a bank has conducted valid needs assessments or whether the community truly has access to bank officials with sufficient authority to be responsive to their ideas and concerns would reward banks that maintain an ongoing substantive dialog with the community. An additional criterion for getting an "Outstanding" rating might be evidence not only of innovative products and services but also of the level of expertise and resources available and dedicated to achieving such results.

Implementing such tests would not be easy and would require examiners to be both well trained and empowered to make the necessary judgments in the field and to be able to defend those decisions from attack by one or more of the stakeholders. My experience has been that while some examiners prefer quantitative tests, many find such a system lacking in subtlety.

Create a Community Development Test for Large Retail Banks

A community development test for large retail banks would ensure that community development loans, grants, and services are properly valued as highly as community development investments.[35] Furthermore, by treating all of these activities under one umbrella, the test would allow a bank to choose how best to respond to local needs and opportunities, whether through loans, investments, grants, services, or a melding of all four. The adoption of such a test would add imperative to modifying the parity measures that underlie the Lending Test, the weight of which should also be reduced.[36]

Incorporate a Safety Valve to Guard Against Unintended Consequences

Since the tests are never likely to be able to be perfect measures of the desired outcome, it is important to provide a safety valve to minimize the chances that the regulations will force banks to undertake counterproductive activities, especially ones that are inconsistent with safety and soundness. Before a bank finds itself being asked to oversaturate or oversubsidize a market, it should be allowed to defend its record by showing, for example, that the community is already being well served or that the economics simply cannot work (e.g., subsidies of $8,000 per mortgage loan) and that it has found other ways to have a greater incremental impact on the community. A formal "appeals" process should be established so that banks can make such a case at any time and so be able to avoid a finding of inadequate performance based on volume numbers alone.

Formalize a Process to Recognize Differences Across Localities

Another possibility that is worth exploring is the creation of a more formal process for allowing exams to be adjusted on the basis of variations in local needs, thus allowing banks to offer more tailored programs and products. To get credit for meeting special local needs, a bank can use a document called the "Performance Context" to lay out its assessment of the local needs and how it is addressing them on the basis of the bank's business strategy and on-the-ground capabilities. However, examiners are free to reach different conclusions about what the bank should be doing based on their own review of the data or information learned from the community.

To eliminate this uncertainty, regulators could play a more proactive role and take the lead in compiling an assessment of local needs based on local convenings and data analysis. They could then give banks serving that market the option of shaping their CRA program around either the base

CRA framework or an alternative built on the results of such a special analysis. For the latter to be useful, a local needs assessment would have to be issued sufficiently in advance of the start of the exam period to allow banks to incorporate it into their business plans, which are generally set annually.

An alternative might be to encourage banks to adopt strategic plans that would allow them to set out in advance the criteria by which they want to be judged in each locality.[37] Once the plans have been approved, banks would be able to set their local business plans accordingly. Before adopting this approach, however, it would be necessary to better understand and address banks' historic reluctance to take up the option of creating a strategic plan.

Provide Special Credit for Communities Underserved by the CRA

Even with all of the changes considered in this chapter, many small communities may continue to be unable to garner their fair share of the resources and attention generated by the CRA. Therefore the regulators should identify communities that are being underserved and offer extra credit to any bank that lends, invests, or provides community development services in these communities.[38]

Collect Better Data

One particularly contentious issue that needs to be resolved is the push by advocates and researchers for the collection of more extensive data under the CRA. Regulators need data to conduct their CRA exams and such data should be readily available to them.[39] Regulators also benefit from having well-informed communities that can help them to identify issues to pursue more closely. While it is important that examiners have the data they need to carry out their responsibilities, it does not necessarily follow that all of the data should be made public or with the same degree of loan-level detail. Banks are concerned about cost (which may be particularly burdensome for small banks), customer privacy, providing proprietary information that could be valuable to their competitors, and fueling a proliferation of lawsuits. One reason why the data are both complicated and expensive to compile is that many of the largest banks have multiple systems that are legacies of previous mergers. Moreover, the quality standard for data to be made publicly available may exceed what had been adequate for internal use, as is the case for data that are collected but not used for decision making. Many banks, for example, had to undertake expensive file-by-file reviews of their small-business loan data to achieve quality standards that are expected for public dissemination.

The type and amount of data available to the public help to determine the degree to which public dialog is fact-based and constructive. The challenge is to find a balance between the interest of the banks and that of the public.

Develop Minimum Standards for a "Satisfactory" Rating

Creating some minimum standards for attaining a "Satisfactory" rating might help to address both advocates' concerns about possible grade inflation and bankers' desire for more clarity to build into their CRA business plans. Moreover, the inclusion of minimums in the rating system would help it to break free of the zero-sum syndrome of the current system. Advocates also view a contributing factor in the grade inflation to be the wide range of performances that can qualify for a "Satisfactory" rating. To distinguish more narrowly the ranges of performance that are covered by this category, advocates have proposed breaking "Satisfactory" into two categories—High and Low—with the latter requiring the development of an Improvement Plan (Taylor and Silver 2009: 155). Such a more nuanced grading system would also recognize the efforts of banks that do more than the minimum but fall shy of an "Outstanding" rating. It would require legislation.

The institution of minimums would simply build upon the existing precedent whereby a "passing" grade is required on the Lending Test to be eligible for an overall rating of "Satisfactory" or better.[40] Other products and services or groups of products and services (e.g., a community development test—see earlier discussion) could receive similar treatment, making the passing of each of them of equal importance, at least with regard to being able to achieve a passing grade overall. Failure to achieve these minimums would result in an overall rating below "Satisfactory." (The achievement of a "Satisfactory" rating or better might mean more if the regulations made them prerequisites for approval of any applications for mergers, acquisitions, branch openings, and so forth.[41]) To recognize improvements made by banks in a timely manner, banks could be given the option to request a follow-up exam whenever they apply for an approval that might hinge on having at least a "Satisfactory" CRA rating.

Determining how high to set these "minimums" will not be an easy task. Setting them too low could undermine the effectiveness of the CRA. Setting them too high relative to the value of a "pass" might discourage many banks from even trying. For the bulk of banks that are not likely to need to apply for regulatory approval covered by the CRA, the net benefit of getting a "Satisfactory" rating, let alone an "Outstanding" rating, is limited. And now that mergers and acquisitions are less likely among the largest banks, it might be time to consider enacting additional incentives (see the later discussion).

Maintain Public Participation and Promote Dialog Among Stakeholders to Find Common Ground

Input from the public has played a crucial role in alerting the regulators to community needs and the role a bank plays in a community; it also keeps banks focused on avoiding activities that might jeopardize their public reputations. This input is in danger of being lost, as the decrease in mergers and acquisitions will likely reduce the number of public meetings called by the regulators to receive input on the performance of the subject banks. The regulators should consider working together to hold annual meetings to allow for a public vetting of, for example, the newly released CRA data. Congress could also supplement this process by holding annual hearings. The agenda of these meetings could also be expanded to include a regular dialog among stakeholders on ways to make the CRA work better for all the parties involved.

Consider Additional Incentives

The CRA has worked at least in part because of the incentives it provides banks to serve the LMI marketplace. However, these incentives may be losing their punch. Therefore it might be appropriate to provide other incentives, for example, for a bank to attain an "Outstanding" rating or more directly for it to provide specific products or services that serve the LMI marketplace.[42] Economic theory calls for such government intervention when the benefit to the public exceeds the benefits to individual firms.[43] With regard to the CRA itself, a direction that is worth exploring might be additional positive rewards for firms that make the extra effort to get an "Outstanding" rating. While negative sanctions can also work, they tend to require continual monitoring and enforcement. Positive incentives, by contrast, especially those that turn an unprofitable activity into a profitable one, tend to be more self-enforcing as banks willingly provide the product or service. Some ideas that have been floated to increase the incentive for achieving an "Outstanding" rating include lowering a bank's costs for FDIC insurance and increasing its ability to deduct the interest costs in acquiring qualified tax-exempt obligations.[44] However, regulators have only a limited ability to strengthen incentives and so addressing this issue may require legislation.

Add More Exam Protocols

Not all types of banks fit easily within the existing set of exam protocols. Exams of the very largest banks need to be redesigned so that they can be completed more quickly, or at a minimum, any changes in how different activities are being evaluated need to be communicated on a real-time basis so as to shorten the feedback loop, particularly with regard to guidance for the next exam.[45] Internet banks, industrial loan companies, and other institutions that take deposits in only one or a limited number of communities but serve national retail or business markets should not be made to focus so much of their CRA "resources" in a limited number of cities or states. One idea might be to require these banks to develop a strategic plan that reflects better the bank's broader geographic reach. A revamped strategic plan option could also be applicable for the credit card and other special-purpose banks that are headquartered in the same localities.

Expand Beyond Credit

The CRA statute was passed when redlining was a major concern, so it focused on the unavailability of credit in LMI communities. Over the ensuing three decades, credit has become more universally available (although the recent tightening of underwriting standards may be disproportionately affecting LMI communities). It is now clear that LMI communities and customers also need access to other kinds of bank products and services. The regulators have, to some degree, recognized this fact and so have included within the Service Test not just the location of branches but also the level of services those branches and alternative distribution systems (e.g., Internet-based services) provide to LMI communities as well as a bank's offering of community development services, including various types of financial education. Even within the current statutory language, it is relatively easy to show that the availability of financial education and basic banking products can increase individuals' and businesses' access to credit. Nevertheless, it would make sense to amend explicitly the CRA statute to encompass transaction, savings, and other important types of non-credit banking services to preempt any controversy over how much flexibility can be found within the bounds of the current statutory language to address some of these needs.

Expand Eligibility to Geographies Beyond Where a Bank Takes Deposits

Opposite to the problem of Internet and other banks that take deposits in only limited geographies is that of large national banks that have branches in multiple markets but not necessarily in every market where they provide loans or other banking services. As was noted earlier, advocates are concerned that the growth of these large banks contributed to the fact that some markets seem to be underserved by the CRA; the advocates therefore want to expand the CRA responsibilities of these banks to all the places where they make loans (see, for example, National Community Reinvestment Coalition 2010).

One option is simply to allow banks to get full credit for lending or investing in regional or national funds, regardless of the location of the people, projects, or businesses that are ultimately served by the funds.[46] More money flowing to these funds would help to ensure every community has access to capital at competitive prices. Moreover, the spreading of risk across geographies is consistent with the legislative intent for safety and soundness. In any case, the regulations need to be rewritten to specifically provide full CRA credit, or the current regulations need to be reinterpreted to allow for full credit as long as a bank is adequately meeting credit needs within its deposit-taking footprint.

As for making the CRA responsibility mandatory wherever a bank makes loans, at least two major issues need to be addressed. The first is to determine whether all the CRA tests are applicable in all these geographies or just the tests that are relevant to the types of loans being made. For example, if a bank offers mortgages to residents in a certain location (but neither takes deposits in that location nor has any local staff), is it required to offer products to the LMI part of that local marketplace or is it also required to fulfill other parts of the CRA, such as make investments or provide retail or community development services? If, for example, the requirement goes beyond mortgages, then how will the bank meet those requirements in a place where it might not have any physical presence? Moreover, will these requirements drain resources from other localities, especially with regard to resources that are limited, such as philanthropic dollars, which are budgeted centrally? Similarly rationed and allocated are other bank activities that can negatively affect the bottom line, such as offering long-term capital or below-market-rate loans, particularly at interest rates below a bank's cost of funds.

Second, depending on how low a threshold is set for triggering CRA coverage, banks might find it more sensible to withdraw from serving a local community than to absorb the burden of the CRA obligation.[47] In any case, any broadening of the number of geographic locations that need to be covered in a CRA exam can only increase its length and further attenuate the feedback loop, tying up regulator and bank resources for even longer periods of time.

Expand Beyond Banks

As the share of financial assets held by banks has fallen, advocates have proposed expanding the CRA both to affiliates of banks within the same holding company and to non-bank financial services companies.[48] The CRA statute limits its coverage to deposit-taking institutions only, but the regulations allow banks to include the activities of their affiliates at their option. Making the inclusion of affiliates mandatory could require legislative change, but it might be possible to amend the regulations to take into account the size and nature of the affiliates in determining the appropriate level of CRA activity expected from the institution.

Basically, advocates view as outmoded the basing of coverage on whether the institution takes deposits, particularly as banks' share of the financial services sector has fallen and non-banks have come to compete in many of the same markets as banks.[49] Before expanding the CRA to non-banks such as mortgage and insurance companies, however, a number of issues should be considered on the basis of the experience to date with the CRA, especially with regard to institutions that provide products and services that differ from those provided by banks.[50] For example, what particular products or services should be covered? Is the community underserved with regard to those products or services? Would the benefits to society as a whole exceed the costs? If so, does the CRA statute provide the best regulatory framework for covering all the firms playing in that particular market? Would incentives targeted to the provision of specific products or services provide a more direct and effective way to spur the desired activities? The clearer the answers are to these questions, the more effective the extension of the CRA to these industries will be in helping LMI communities.

Conclusion

The CRA has worked, but it is in need of a major overhaul. The CRA statute grants broad authority to bank regulators, and they need to step forward and play a leading role in making the necessary changes. Historically, the regulators have updated the regulations only sporadically, but the potential exists for them to take action on a more regular and timely basis. Such regular updating is critical to the continued success of the CRA. While reform may also involve legislation, it is important to make sure that it does not become overly prescriptive and so stifle innovation. The banking world will continue to evolve, as will the best ideas on how to revitalize and strengthen communities. Moreover, ongoing experience will continue to inform us as to what is working and what is not. The CRA needs to keep up.

References

Affordable Housing Investors Council et al. to Federal Deposit Insurance Corporation et al. 2009. "Community Reinvestment Act: Towards a sustainable national CRA policy for Low Income Housing Tax Credit (LIHTC) investments." Correspondence, August 31, http://www.enterprisecommunity.org/public_policy/documents/lihtc_cra_comment.pdf.

Affordable Housing Tax Credit Coalition et al. to Sheila C. Bair et al. 2009. Correspondence, December 15, http://www.enterprisecommunity.org/public_policy/documents/cra_letter_to_ffiec.pdf.

Apgar, William C., and Ren S. Essene. 2009. "The 30th Anniversary of the CRA: Restructuring the CRA to Address the Mortgage Finance Revolution." In *Revisiting the CRA: Perspectives on the Future of the Community Reinvestment Act,* ed. Prabal Chakrabarti, David Erikson, Ron S. Essene, Ian Galloway, and John Olson. Boston: Federal Reserve Banks of Boston and San Francisco. 12–29.

Avery, Robert B., Marsha J. Courchane, and Peter M. Zorn. 2009. "The CRA Within a Changing Financial Landscape." In *Revisiting the CRA*, ed. Chakrabarti et al. 30–46.

Barr, Michael S. 2005. "Credit Where It Counts: The Community Reinvestment Act and Its Critics." *New York University Law Review* 80, 2: 513–652.

———. 2009. "Community Reinvestment Emerging from the Housing Crisis." In *Revisiting the CRA*, ed. Chakrabarti et al. 170–77.

Bhutta, Neil. 2008. "Giving Credit Where Credit Is Due? The Community Reinvestment Act and Mortgage Lending in Lower-Income Neighborhoods." Finance and Economics Discussion Series 2008-61. Washington, D.C.: Division of Research and Statistics, Federal Reserve Board.

"Community Reinvestment Modernization Act of 2009, HR 1479, 111th Cong., 2nd sess." *Congressional Record* 156, daily ed., March 12: H3399–3401.

Credit Union National Association. 2009. "Issue Summary: Community Reinvestment Act (CRA)." Washington, D.C.: Credit Union National Association. http://www.cuna.org/gov_affairs/legislative/issues/download/cra.pdf.

Ding, Lei, Roberto G. Quercia, Wei Li, and Janneke Ratcliffe. 2010. "Risky Borrowers or Risky Mortgages: Disaggregating Effects Using Propensity Score Models." Chapel Hill, NC: Center for Community Capital. http://www.ccc.unc.edu/documents/Risky.Disaggreg.5.17.10.pdf.

Federal Deposit Insurance Corporation. 2009. "Summary of Deposits: National Totals by Asset Size (data as of June 30)." Washington, D.C.: FDIC. http://www2.fdic.gov/sod/sodSumReport.asp? barItem=3&sInfoAsOf=2009.

Federal Financial Institutions Examination Council. 2010a. "Community Reinvestment Act: Interagency Questions and Answers Regarding Community Reinvestment; Notice." Washington, D.C.: FFIEC. http://www.ffiec.gov/cra/pdf/2010-4903.pdf.

———. 2010b. "About the FFIEC." http://www.ffiec.gov/about.htm.

Federal Reserve Bank of Dallas. 2005. "A Banker's Quick Reference Guide to CRA, as Amended Effective September 1, 2005." Dallas: Federal Reserve Bank of Dallas. http://www.dallasfed.org/ca/pubs/quickref.pdf.

Gainer, Bridget. 2009. "What Lessons Does the CRA Offer the Insurance Industry?" In *Revisiting the CRA*, ed. Chakrabarti et al. 138–42.

Illinois Division of Banking. 2009. "Illinois Branch Banking History." Springfield, Ill.: Illinois Division of Banking. http://www.obre.state.il.us/cbt/STATS/br-hist.htm.

Immergluck, Dan. 2004. *Credit to the Community: Community Reinvestment and Fair Lending Policy in the United States.* Armonk, N.Y: M.E. Sharpe.

Joint Center for Housing Studies. 2010. "The Disruption of the Low-Income Housing Tax Credit Program: Causes, Consequences, Responses, and Proposed Correctives." Cambridge, Mass.: Joint Center for Housing Studies, Harvard University. http://www.jchs.harvard.edu/publications/governmentprograms/disruption_of_ the_lihtc_program _2009.

Knight, Jerry. 1989. "Fed Rejects Continental Ill. Bid for Bank," *Washington Post,* February 16, A14.

Kroszner, Randall. 2009. "The CRA and the Recent Mortgage Crisis." In *Revisiting the CRA,* ed. Chakrabarti et al. 8–11.

Laderman, Elizabeth, and Carolina Reid. 2009. "CRA Lending During the Subprime Meltdown." In *Revisiting the CRA,* ed. Chakrabarti et al. 115–33.

Lindsey, Lawrence B. 2009. "The CRA as a Means to Provide Public Goods." In *Revisiting the CRA,* ed. Chakrabarti et al. 160–66.

Litan, Robert E., Nicolas P. Retsinas, Eric S. Belsky, Gary Fauth, Maureen Kennedy, and Paul Leonard. 2001. *The Community Reinvestment Act After Financial Modernization: A Final Report.* Washington, D.C.: U.S. Department of the Treasury. http://www.ustreas.gov/press/releases/reports/finalrpt.pdf.

Ludwig, Eugene A., Chief Executive Officer, Promontory Financial Group. 2010. Written Statement before the Subcommittee on Financial Institutions and Consumer Credit, House Committee on Financial Services. 111th Cong., 2nd sess., April 15.

Marsico, Richard D. 2005. *Democratizing Capital: The History, Law, and Reform of the Community Reinvestment Act.* Durham, N.C.: Carolina Academic Press.

National Community Reinvestment Coalition. 2007. "CRA Commitments." Washington, D.C.: National Community Reinvestment Coalition. http://www.ncrc.org/ images/stories/whatWeDo_promote/cra_commitments_07.pdf.

———. 2009. "Credit Unions: True to Their Mission?" Washington, D.C.: National Community Reinvestment Coalition. http://www.ncrc.org/images/stories/mediaCenter_ reports/creditunionreport090309.pdf.

———. 2010. "NCRC Advises Bank Regulators on Community Reinvestment Act." Washington, D.C.: National Community Reinvestment Coalition. http://www.ncrc. org/images/stories/pdf/press_releases/pr%207.19.10%20ensuring%20access% 20to%20credit%20and%20capital.pdf.

Office of Financial Empowerment. (2008). "Neighborhood Financial Services Study: An Analysis of Supply and Demand in Two New York City Neighborhoods." New York: Office of Financial Empowerment, New York City Department of Consumer Affairs. http://www.nyc.gov/html/ofe/downloads/pdf/NFS_Compiled.pdf.

Office of the Federal Register. 1995. "Community Reinvestment Act Regulations." *Federal Register* 60, 86 (May 4): 22156.

Pinsky, Mark. 2002. "Growing Opportunities in Bank/CDFI Partnerships." *Community Developments*. Washington, D.C.: Office of the Comptroller of the Currency. http://www.occ.treas.gov/ cdd/summer-01.pdf.

Seidman Ellen. 2009. "A More Modern CRA for Consumers." In *Revisiting the CRA*, ed. Chakrabarti et al. 105–14.

Taylor, John, and Josh Silver. 2009. "The CRA: 30 Years of Wealth Building and What We Must Do to Finish the Job." In *Revisiting the CRA*, ed. Chakrabarti et al. 148–59.

Traiger, Warren W. 1990. *Federal Community Reinvestment Act Compliance*. New York: Westlaw. http://www.traigerlaw.com/publications/federal_comunity_reinvestment_act_compliance_ westlaw7_9_1990.pdf.

U.S. Comptroller of the Currency. 1999. *Community Reinvestment Act Examination Procedures: Comptroller's Handbook*. Washington, D.C.: Office of the Comptroller of the Currency, U.S. Department of the Treasury. http://www.occ.treas.gov/handbook/craep.pdf.

U.S. Department of the Treasury. *Community Development Financial Institutions Fund*. Washington, D.C.: U.S. Department of the Treasury. http://www.cdfifund.gov.

White, Lawrence. 2009. "The Community Reinvestment Act: Good Goals, Flawed Concept." In *Revisiting the CRA*, ed. Chakrabarti et al. 185–88.

Notes

I would like to thank the Ford Foundation and NYU's Furman Center for Real Estate and Urban Policy for their generous support of my research on CRA. This chapter benefited greatly from the insights and experiences of many bankers, regulators, and advocates, too numerous to list. I would, though, like to thank particularly Vicky Been, Ingrid Gould Ellen, Ellen Seidman, Barry Zigas, Buzz Roberts, and my wife, Carol Willis, for taking the time to review and comment on earlier drafts. I, however, take full and sole responsibility for the opinions expressed in this chapter.

1. Community Reinvestment Act of 1977, P.L. 95-128, §802, U.S. Code 12 (2010), §2901.

2. While the terms "stabilize" and "revitalize" were not used in the statute, they are found in the regulations. In his book *Credit to the Community*, Dan Immergluck (2004: 148) identifies "rebuild[ing] and revitaliz[ation]" as the purpose of the CRA. Interestingly, the CRA statute does not mention race, and race was apparently mentioned only once during the floor debate at the time of its passage (Immergluck 2004: 147). The floor debate did feature extensive discussion of "redlining," which characterized the circling in red of areas on a map where a bank would not lend because of perceived credit risk.

3. Since 1984, the number of banks in the United States has fallen almost by half, from nearly 15,000 to some 8,000, and the three largest banks in the country now hold over 30 percent of total deposits. See the FDIC summary tables for June 30, 2009

at http://www2.fdic.gov/sod/sodSummary.asp?barItem=3. In 1977, some states still restricted banks to only one branch. It was not until 1993 that Illinois, for an example, removed all restrictions on the number and location of branches within the state (Illinois Division of Banking 2009). Additionally, it was not until the passage of the Riegle-Neal bill in 1994 that the federal government provided for interstate banking and branching. See Riegle-Neal Interstate Banking and Branching Efficiency Act of 1994, P.L. 103-328, U.S. Code 12 (2010), §1811.

4. Excellent overviews of the history of CRA can be found in Barr (2005), Immergluck (2004), and Marsico (2005).

5. A number of researchers and policy analysts have also called for major reforms of the CRA. Of particular note are Barr (2009), Seidman (2009), and Apgar and Essene (2009). Others have questioned the need for the CRA at all; see, for example, White (2009).

6. Pursuing the regulatory route has a number of advantages. First, the legislative process is, by design, slow and deliberative. Second, amending the statute may be particularly difficult at this time given the bad press for CRA based on recent, unjustified attacks as the cause of the subprime crisis. For an exploration of the facts regarding CRA and the subprime crisis see the section on CRA Successes and Kroszner (2009) and Ludwig (2010: 12–16).

7. Financial Institutions Reform, Recovery, and Enforcement Act of 1989, P.L. 101-73, §1212, codified at U.S. Code 12 (2010), §2906.

8. These banks account for over 80 percent of total bank deposits in the United States (FDIC 2009).

9. The Lending Test mainly covers home mortgage and small-business loans. The Service Test mainly covers branch locations and banking services. The Service Test also includes a small component for community development services, which, as with the community development investments covered by the Investment Test, are explained more in the text and n.13. For a summary of CRA regulation and examination procedures, see Federal Reserve Bank of Dallas (2005).

10. The regulations also provide for any bank to draft its own strategic plan, but this option has rarely been used, perhaps because of the hurdles that must be met to get the plan approved. For more details, see Federal Reserve Bank of Dallas (2005: 10) and FDIC Regulations, §345.27.

11. See, for example, Federal Deposit Insurance Corporation Regulations, Code of Federal Regulations, title 12 (2010), §345.12(g):

> Community development means: (1) Affordable housing (including multifamily rental housing) for low- or moderate-income individuals; (2) Community services targeted to low- or moderate-income individuals; (3) Activities that promote economic development by financing businesses or farms that meet the size eligibility standards of the Small Business Administration's Development Company or Small Business Investment Company programs (13 CFR 121.301) or have

gross annual revenues of $1 million or less; or (4) Activities that revitalize or stabilize—(i) Low- or moderate-income geographies; (ii) Designated disaster areas; or (iii) Distressed or underserved nonmetropolitan middle-income geographies designated by the Board of Governors of the Federal Reserve System, FDIC, and Office of the Comptroller of the Currency, based on—(A) Rates of poverty, unemployment, and population loss; or (B) Population size, density, and dispersion. Activities revitalize and stabilize geographies designated based on population size, density, and dispersion if they help to meet essential community needs, including needs of low- and moderate-income individuals.

12. CDFIs are generally financial intermediaries that serve LMI communities.

13. Wholesale banks are those that do little or no mass market lending (e.g., serve only a private banking clientele). Special-purpose banks provide a very limited set of products (e.g., credit cards) and do not provide a broad array of retail banking services.

14. Regulators have also been given the ability to reject applications to open and close branches on the basis of a bank's CRA record, but it is unclear to what extent this power has been invoked or quietly threatened.

15. See discussion of some of the analyses in Bhutta (2008: 5–6), Immergluck (2004: 236–46), and Marsico (2005: 144–49). The National Community Reinvestment Coalition (2007) has also pointed to the cumulative total by 2007 of $4.6 trillion of publicly made CRA commitments by banks as indicative of CRA's success.

16. CRA is considered the province of a wide range of "stakeholders" including community residents, community groups, advocates, public officials, banks, regulators, and others, each with their own perspectives on what the CRA should be and with a vested interest in the way in which it is implemented. One particularly difficult dilemma is how to reconcile the views of those who are most concerned about social justice and want CRA to reinforce and expand many of the discrimination and consumer protection laws and those who see CRA as offering a way to build long-term business relationships with banks to their mutual benefit.

17. The current CRA regulations do allow for more credit based on responsiveness, innovativeness, and deal complexity, but these concepts seem to take a back seat to measures of quantity.

18. For example, the $500,000 loan that leverages funding from multiple levels of government may have a more incremental impact on a community's well-being than a more standard $5 million loan for a larger shopping strip located in the same neighborhood (especially if that loan would have been made otherwise in the regular course of business). Yet the latter counts more under a pure dollar volume standard and is likely to be more profitable.

19. While the offering of lower prices also may have made it possible to serve a larger slice of the LMI marketplace, it cannot solve the mathematical problem laid out previously in the text.

20. While lowering credit standards would be another way to gain market share, it does not appear that banks in general pursued that route. The push for market share did, however, make banks particularly susceptible to the demands of some community groups to be able to offer mortgages at below-market rates.

21. A study by New York City's Office of Financial Empowerment (2008) found no correlation between the percentage of unbanked people in a community and the proximity of bank branches.

22. Community development investments are given full recognition under the Investment Test. Were a community development test to be added, a separate Investment Test would no longer be needed, since it would result in double counting.

23. A number of stakeholder groups have signed a letter to regulators urging more credit for community development activities (Affordable Housing Tax Credit Coalition et al. to Sheila C. Bair et al. 2009).

24. The regulators recently proposed to give CRA credit for more of the activities that a bank might undertake consistent with the federal Neighborhood Stabilization Program. Unfortunately, these activities fall within the categories described here that are undervalued in determining a bank's overall CRA rating.

25. For more details on the role of the Performance Context, see FDIC Regulations, §345.21(b).

26. Internet banks and industrial loan companies generally take deposits only in their headquarter cities, which have tended to cluster in a few states, such as Utah and Delaware, that offer favorable regulatory and tax environments. The result has been that a small number of headquarter locations receive a disproportionately large amount of CRA attention at the expense of other areas of the country.

27. For more detail on how the exams are conducted, see U.S. Comptroller of the Currency (1999).

28. While one of the first applications denied under the CRA was to open a branch, CRA protests have seemingly focused much more on mergers and acquisitions (Immergluck 2004: 162–67).

29. See n.16 for a list of some of the different stakeholders in CRA.

30. For a discussion of changes over time in the distribution of CRA ratings across banks, see Immergluck (2004: 177–84).

31. As will be discussed, some proposals for reform contemplate further expanding the activities covered by the CRA, thus making even harder the task of coming up with a single overall rating.

32. The four bank regulators jointly draft regulations and the Q&As through the Federal Financial Institutions Examination Council (FFIEC 2010). The Dodd-Frank Wall Street Reform and Consumer Protection Act eliminates the Office of Thrift Supervision but adds the Consumer Financial Protection Bureau to the FFIEC. See P.L. 111-203, 111th Cong., 2nd. sess. (2010).

33. Care should also be taken in adding provisions that prohibit certain behaviors to a statute built around an affirmative obligation. For example, the detailed and labo-

rious process of reviewing individual loans for illegal activity that is integral to a fair lending exam may not fit well as part of a CRA exam.

34. An example of a process measure was to ascertain how much effort the bank was expending in marketing to the LMI community. This test was one of the twelve assessment factors that governed exams before the 1995 reforms (Traiger 1990).

35. The relative weights within a community development test might also be adjusted to ensure proper reward for philanthropic grants given to support local organizations in line with their strategic importance to the community. Similarly, more credit might be given for long-term investments (sometimes called "patient capital") and below-market financing, especially when it is priced at a loss when compared to a bank's cost of funds. Such long-term and favorably priced money helps to make it possible, for example, for CDFIs to grow and to offer low-cost financing and still earn a small premium to help cover operating costs.

36. One way to implement a community development test within the current framework would be to give banks the option of adding community development loans and services to the existing Investment Test. Banks could also be allowed to increase the weight given to this expanded test up to as high as perhaps 50 percent, with a concomitant reduction in weight given to the Lending Test, which would now cover only home loans and small-business loans.

37. See n.11.

38. Some advocates have proposed to address this problem by expanding a bank's CRA obligation to include communities where they make loans regardless of whether they take deposits. See the discussion later in text under the heading "Expand Eligibility to Geographies Beyond Where a Bank Takes Deposits."

39. The recently passed Dodd-Frank Wall Street Reform and Consumer Protection Act requires banks to collect and make public additional information with regard to small businesses and deposits and amends the Home Mortgage Disclosure Act to require additional data on the characteristics of the loans and the borrowers. See P.L. 111-203, 111th Cong., 2nd sess. (2010).

40. FDIC Regulations, §345.28(b)(3).

41. The Gramm-Leach-Bliley Act of 1999 (P.L. 106-102, 106th Cong. [1999]) effectively barred financial institutions from expanding their activities to include the securities and insurance business unless all the banks within the holding company had received at least a "satisfactory" rating on their most recent CRA exams.

42. An example of a positive incentive based on the provision of specific products is the establishment of the CDFI Fund and tax credits under the LIHTC and NMTC programs. See, for example, U.S. Department of the Treasury. http://www.cdfifund.gov.

43. For a discussion of cases in which the social benefit exceeds that private benefit and therefore calls for government intervention, see Lindsey (2009).

44. The idea of providing incentives through adjustments in FDIC insurance premiums is said to have originated with Ron Gryzwinski, a co-founder of ShoreBank in Chicago.

45. One way to allow for more timely feedback would be to have a formal process for examiners to review a bank's performance on a more regular or even continuous basis. More regular communication with the bank (and also presumably with the community) would also position the examiners to be better able to make more qualitative judgments at the time a rating has to be issued.

46. A narrower approach would be, for purposes of at least the Investment Test, to develop a system with fewer assessment areas, each of which covers a much broader geography. See Affordable Housing Investors Council et al. to Federal Deposit Insurance Corporation et al. (2009).

47. In the proposed Community Reinvestment Modernization Act of 2009, CRA responsibility is triggered if a bank's loans account for 0.5 percent or more of a local market ("Community Reinvestment Modernization Act of 2009").

48. Credit unions are not now covered by CRA even though they take deposits and provide a range of bank services. For the industry's point of view, see Credit Union National Association (2009). For an analysis supporting the inclusion of credit unions, see National Community Reinvestment Coalition (2009).

49. The case for expanding beyond the banks is made, for example, in Ludwig (2010: 99–104) and in Seidman (2009). Moreover, the recent switch by a number of large investment banks to bank holding companies has provided further impetus for expanding CRA to bank and financial holding companies and all of their subsidiaries (see Sorkin and Bajaj 2008).

50. For such a look at expanding CRA to the insurance industry, see Gainer (2009).

PART III

Reforming the Financial Architecture

Information Failure and the U.S. Mortgage Crisis

Adam J. Levitin and Susan M. Wachter

The global financial crisis of 2008 developed out of the failure of mortgage finance markets to adequately price risk. This chapter focuses on the role of securitization in housing finance. It does so both because of the role of securitization in the recent debacle and because of the importance of securitization for ensuring the widespread availability of the long-term fixed-rate mortgage, which has been the bedrock of American homeownership since the Depression and the prevalence of which is critical for rebuilding a sustainable housing finance system.

We argue that markets failed to price risk correctly because of an informational failure, caused by the complexity and heterogeneity of private-label mortgage-backed securities (MBSs) and structured finance products such as collateralized debt obligations (CDOs). Correcting this failure requires not only better disclosure about the collateral supporting MBSs, but also substantive regulation of mortgage forms and MBS and CDO structures in order to make disclosures effective.

When markets work, costs and risks are signaled through prices and rates, which allows for efficient resource allocation based on this information. In markets in which information flows between consumers and producers (such as mortgage borrowers and lenders or investors and sellers of securities) are opaque or blocked, prices do not reflect costs and risks, and resources are allocated inefficiently. Complexity and heterogeneity shroud information. Complex products are more difficult for consumers and investors to analyze. Similarly, heterogeneous products are difficult to analyze because heterogeneity defeats cross-product comparisons.

The housing bubble was marked by the extraordinary growth of two types of complex, heterogeneous products: nontraditional mortgages and private-label securities (PLSs). The growth of these products was inextricably interlinked. Nontraditional mortgages did not qualify for purchase and securitization by the regulated government-sponsored entities (GSEs), Fannie Mae and Freddie Mac, and were far too risky for originators to want to hold them to maturity. The only option, then, was to securitize these mortgages in the unregulated PLS market. The rapid expansion of nontraditional mortgages and the PLS market set the stage for the crisis. The growth of nontraditional mortgages and PLSs was spurred by a set of principal-agent problems inherent to securitization.

Mortgage origination and securitization constitute a volume business, which incentivizes the financial institutions that intermediate between mortgage borrowers and the capital market financiers of mortgages to find products that maximize volume, in terms of both dollar amount and number of mortgages, regardless of the effect on product suitability for borrowers or credit quality for investors. These financial institutions serve as economic (but not legal) agents for the end borrowers and lenders. There are two sets of institutions involved in the intermediation role: mortgage originators and mortgage securitizers. Often, originators and securitizers are affiliated with each other; the origination channel provides product for the securitization operation.

In their intermediation role, these financial institutions do not hold more than a temporary interest in the mortgages they facilitate, so their incentives are very different from and often adverse to those of borrowers and investors, the economic principals in mortgage loans. The financial intermediaries involved in mortgage origination and securitization are incentivized to maximize the volume of mortgages being securitized and the spreads on these mortgages to maximize their own revenue.

Informationally shrouded mortgages and MBSs can serve to disguise risks and costs, thereby inducing greater origination and securitization volume and profits than would have been attained in a deshrouded environment. Therefore, financial intermediaries are incentivized to push these informationally shrouded products, even to the detriment of homeowners and investors. Regulatory standards kept these principal-agent problems in check for GSE securitization, but in the PLS market, there were no such constraints, and the principal-agent problem resulted in a shift in mortgage products to unsustainable nontraditional products that boosted origination and securitization volume—and hence profits—in the short term but with disastrous longer-term effects.

To correct the informational failures in the mortgage finance market, it is insufficient to simply require greater data disclosure about the collateral and borrowers supporting MBSs, as the proposed amendments by the Securities and Exchange Commission to Regulation AB would do (U.S. Securities and Exchange Commission 2010). Instead, investors need to have access to meaningful data that can be analyzed effectively in real time. Disclosure of hundreds of loan-level data elements is useless unless the relationships among those elements are known. While it may be possible to design effective multivariate risk models, excess information and variables reduce the predictability of such models, especially when new terms, for which there is no track record, are introduced. Reducing potential variables through product standardization facilitates mortgage risk modeling and real-time analysis of changes in underwriting standards. This means that whatever the ultimate form of the reconstituted housing finance market, the regulatory response to the crisis should concentrate on ensuring sufficient standardization of MBS products—and, by necessity, standardization of the underlying mortgage products—to make the disclosure of information about credit risk a meaningful basis for pricing.

Ultimately, the expansion of PLS and nontraditional mortgages was its own undoing. These products drove the housing bubble but ultimately priced out too many potential homeowners, making home prices increases unsustainable. Without home price appreciation, homeowners could not refinance their way out of highly leveraged nontraditional mortgages as payment shocks—large increases in monthly mortgage payments upon the expiration of teaser interest rates—occurred. The result was a cycle of foreclosures and declining housing prices. We conclude our discussion with a proposal for restricting securitization to a limited set of proven traditional mortgage products. There are appropriate niches for nontraditional products, but the informational asymmetries and principal-agent problems endemic to the secondary market counsel for restricting these products to banks' books.

Sustainable Homeownership and the Fixed-Rate Mortgage

The United States and many other countries have had a long history of supporting homeownership as a public policy goal. Public policy has favored homeownership because it offers many social benefits. Historically,

> there has been widespread agreement in the U.S. that homeownership is the preferred model for the vast majority of the population, both for reasons of "economic thrift" and "good citizenship," and for reasons of better health, recreation and family life expressed through the physical form of the detached single-family house and garden. (Weiss 1988: 7)

While some of the arguments in favor of homeownership developed in reaction to the condition of renters in urban slums and tenements (Glaeser and Gyourko 2008: 48–49; Stoner 1943: 225) or to fear of urban proletariat unrest (Weiss 1989: 109), there are good modern reasons to support homeownership as the preferred model of residency. For the homeowner, homeownership can act as a hedge against rent increases (Sinai and Souleles 2005) and specifically against being priced out of a neighborhood because of neighborhood improvement, the way renters are priced out by gentrification (although property tax increases can have a similar effect on homeowners). Homeownership is also a major investment that homeowners want to protect. Homeowners thus have an incentive to care for their homes. As the famous Larry Summers adage has it, "In the history of the world, no one has ever washed a rented car." Similarly, no one has ever put a new roof on a rental unit.

These benefits for the individual homeowner have important positive externalities. When homeowners take care of their homes, it improves the value of their neighbors' homes. Homeowners also tend to move less frequently than renters, so homeownership makes for more stable communities, allowing for deeper community ties and civic engagement. Homeowners' incentive to care for their home also extends to caring for their neighborhood; the homeowners' self-interest in protecting their property value extends to protecting the quality of the neighborhood and being concerned with issues such as zoning, schools, traffic, and crime. In a community of homeowners, there is a rich set of positive cross-externalities. Homeownership thus has welfare-enhancing effects for homeowners, communities, and the nation.

Homeownership comes with risks, though. Homes are expensive. Few individuals are able to purchase their homes outright. Most people need to borrow to purchase a home, typically with a mortgage. Mortgage finance has risks, just like any leveraged investment. The homeowner has the upside of the property's appreciation but also the downside of the property's depreciation. Owning a home also typically involves committing a large portion of household wealth into a single, non-diversified asset that cannot be hedged.[1]

There is little point in policies that promote homeownership unless the ownership is sustainable. The public benefits that come from homeownership flow only from long-term, sustainable homeownership. The form of financing matters for sustainable homeownership. Home mortgages divide, on the most generic level, into two types of products—fixed-rate mortgages (FRMs) and adjustable-rate mortgages (ARMs)—depending on whether the interest rate is fixed for the life of the mortgage or adjusts in reference to a public index such as LIBOR (London Interbank Offered Rate) or the federal funds rate.

Globally, ARMs dominate the mortgage world. In almost every country except the United States, Germany, and Denmark, almost all mortgages are ARMs. While the ARM has prevailed in much of the world, it has been able to do so in recent decades because of a very hospitable macroeconomic environment. For the better part of the past three decades, as mortgage markets have developed, global interest rates have been declining. To the extent that rates have gone up in this period, they have gone up by relatively small amounts and slowly. When interest rates are declining, an ARM is a borrower-friendly product; mortgage payments decrease as interest rates decline. If interest rates go up sharply, however, monthly payments on an ARM can shoot up and quickly become unaffordable for the borrower.

Housing finance via ARMs thus always poses the risk of an asset-liability mismatch for homeowners. Homeowners' income tends to be fixed, but their mortgage expense—often their largest single expense—is variable and can exceed income if rates go up. Therefore while the ARM has been a vehicle for increasing homeownership in recent decades, it has the inherent potential to undermine the homeownership goal.

Securitization as a Solution to Asset-Liability Duration Mismatches

The savings and loan (S&L) crisis of the 1980s and early 1990s in the United States shows the danger of asset-liability mismatches due to adjustable-rate obligations. Ever since the Depression, most mortgages in the United States have been long-term, fully amortized FRMs. The Depression showed just how fragile a housing market constructed largely of short-term ARMs (often interest only with a principal "bullet" due at the end) could be, and subsequent federal housing policy strongly encouraged the use of the long-term, fully amortized FRMs as a means of ensuring both affordability and systemic stability.

Most of S&Ls' assets were such FRM loans. This meant that S&Ls had a fixed income stream. The main liabilities of the S&Ls—and their source of operating funds—were deposits, which could be withdrawn with little notice. In the 1970s, S&Ls were restricted in the interest rates they could pay on savings accounts. As interest rates rose in the late 1970s, S&Ls quickly lost deposits to money market mutual funds, which did not have regulated returns. Congress responded to this disintermediation in 1980 by phasing out the savings account interest rate restriction, but this only meant that to compete with money market funds, S&Ls had to offer increasingly high interest rates on deposits. The result was that the cost of funds for S&Ls soared, but their income—from the FRMs—remained constant. The S&Ls were quickly decapitalized, and a drawn-out banking crisis ensued.[2]

The asset-liability mismatch played out on the banks' balance sheets in the S&L crisis, but it could easily recur on the household balance sheet because of ARMs. The lesson from the S&L crisis was that depositaries could not hold long-term FRMs in their portfolios without assuming significant interest-rate risk.

In the United States, in the wake of the S&L crisis, two solutions emerged to the asset-liability mismatch problem. One was increased use of ARMs, which grew in popularity in the 1980s as interest rates fell. Risk-averse consumer tastes, however, generally prefer FRMs, limiting ARM market share when competitive FRMs are available.

FRMs remained widely available even after the S&L crisis because of the second solution: using secondary markets to finance FRMs and shift the interest-rate risk to parties that were better suited to bear it. The secondary market consisted at the time of the GSEs.[3] Fannie and Freddie were regulated entities and would purchase only mortgages that conformed to their underwriting standards, which generally required prime, amortizing mortgages. Moreover, statute limited the GSEs' exposure on any particular loan to the conforming loan limit and restricted the GSEs to purchasing only loans with loan-to-value (LTV) ratios under 80 percent absent private mortgage insurance or seller risk retention (12 U.S.C. §§1454[a][2]), 1717[b][2]). Moreover, the GSEs were expected to operate nationally, creating geographic diversification in their underwriting.

The GSEs would securitize most of the mortgages they purchased, meaning that they would sell the mortgages to legally separate, specially created trusts, which would pay for the mortgages by issuing MBSs. The GSE would guarantee timely payment of principal and interest on the MBSs issued by the securitization trusts. Fannie and Freddie thus linked long-term FRM borrowers with capital market investors, such as insurance and pension funds, that were willing to assume long-term interest rate risk because they did not have the short-term liabilities of depositaries. Securitization thus ensured the continued widespread availability of the FRM in the wake of the S&L crisis as depositaries shied away from holding interest rate risk.

Private-Label Securitization

Growth of the Private-Label MBS Market

By guaranteeing timely payment of interest and principal on their MBSs, Fannie and Freddie assumed the credit risk on the underlying mortgages, while the purchasers of Fannie and Freddie MBSs assumed the interest-rate risk. Investors in GSE MBSs assumed the credit risk of Fannie and Freddie and, only indirectly, the credit risk of mortgages the GSEs purchased. Because Fannie and Freddie were perceived as having an implicit guarantee from the federal government, investors were generally unconcerned about the credit risk on Fannie and Freddie and hence on the MBSs (investors would be concerned only to the extent that defaults affected prepayment speeds). This meant that investors did not need to worry about the quality of the GSE underwriting. Therefore investors did not need good information about the default risk on the mortgages. They did, however, care about prepayment speeds so that they could gauge convexity risk.[4] This was information that was fairly easy to obtain, particularly on standardized mortgage products.

Because the GSEs bore the credit risk on the mortgages, they had every incentive to insist on careful underwriting, and even if they did not, their regulators would.[5] Thus the GSEs, by statute, were limited to purchasing only loans with less than 80 percent LTV ratios unless there was private mortgage insurance on the loan. As long as GSE securitization dominated the mortgage market, credit risk was kept in check through underwriting standards, and there was not much of a market for non-prime, nonconforming, conventional loans.

Beginning in the 1990s, however, a new, unregulated form of securitization began to displace the previously dominant regulated, standardized GSE securitization. This was private-label securitization, which arose in a deregulated market supported by a new class of specialized mortgage lenders and securitization sponsors.

Whereas the GSEs would purchase only loans that conformed to their underwriting guidelines, the investment banks that served as PLS conduits did not have any such underwriting requirements. PLSs thus created a market for non-prime, nonconforming conventional loans.

As with GSE securitization, private-label securitization would involve the pooling of thousands of mortgage loans into trusts. The trusts would then issue MBSs to pay for the mortgage loans. Unlike the GSEs, however, the PLS deal sponsors did not guarantee timely payment of interest and principal on the PLSs. Therefore PLS investors assumed both credit risk and interest-rate risk on the MBSs, in contrast to GSE MBSs, on which investors assumed only interest-rate risk.

Investors in PLSs were familiar with rate risk on mortgages but not with credit risk. As a result, the PLS market initially developed for jumbo mortgages—loans that were larger than the GSEs' conforming loan limit—and for commercial mortgages. Jumbos were essentially prime, conventional mortgages, just for larger amounts than conforming loans. While PLS investors did face credit risk on jumbos, it was low. Loss rates on jumbos had been less than .5 percent since 1992 (Nomura Fixed Income Research 2006: 22).

Credit risk for jumbos was mitigated through high down payments (low LTVs) and private mortgage insurance and through credit enhancements, particularly credit tranching in a senior-subordinate structure. Jumbo PLSs settled on a largely standardized form—the "six pack" structure, in which six subordinated tranches supported a senior, AAA-rated tranche that made up well over 90 percent of the MBSs in a deal by dollar amount (Nomura Fixed Income Research 2006: 22–23). Indeed, jumbo PLSs became sufficiently standardized that jumbo mortgages trade in the "To Be Announced" (TBA) market, meaning that the mortgages are sold even before they are actually originated. This is possible only when there is a liquid secondary market for the mortgages and necessitates mortgage standardization as well.

The success of PLSs depended heavily upon the ability to achieve AAA ratings for most securities. The AAA rating was critical for selling the PLSs.[6] For jumbos, it was relatively easy to achieve AAA ratings because of the solid underlying collateral.[7] As the PLS market moved into non-prime mortgages, however, greater credit enhancements and structural creativity were required to obtain the credit ratings necessary to make the securities sufficiently marketable. For example, the mean number of tranches in non-prime PLSs in 2003 was approximately ten, compared with seven for jumbo six-packs; by 2007, the mean number of tranches had increased to over fourteen (Adelino 2009: 42). Other types of internal and external credit enhancements were also much more common in non-prime PLSs: overcollateralization, excess spread, shifting interest, reserve accounts, and pool and bond insurance. Non-prime PLSs thus involved inevitably more complex and heterogeneous deal structures to compensate for the weaker quality of the underlying assets.

Non-prime PLSs remained a small share of the market through the 1990s. They did not take off until 2004, at which point they grew rapidly until the bursting of the housing bubble. PLSs grew from 22 percent of MBS issuance in 2003 to 56 percent in 2006 and from 9 percent to 21 percent of all mortgages outstanding and 36 percent of all MBSs outstanding (Inside Mortgage Finance 2010). The inflection point came with the introduction and spiraling growth of non-prime mortgages. The non-prime mortgage market (and non-prime PLS market) boomed as the consequence of the tapering off of a preceding prime refinancing boom. The period 2001–2003 was one of historically low interest rates. These low rates brought on an orgy of refinancing (Figure 10.1). The year 2003 in particular was a peak for

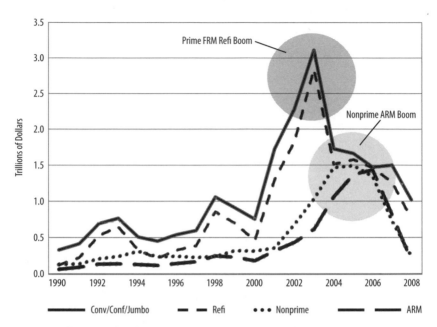

Figure 10.1. Refinancing and purchase money originations: 1990–2008. Inside Mortgage Finance. *2010 Mortgage Market Statistical Annual.*

mortgage originations, and 72 percent of these originations by dollar volume were refinancings (Inside Mortgage Finance 2010). Virtually all of the refinancing activity from 2001 to 2003 was in prime, fixed-rate mortgages. The prime refinancing boom meant that mortgage originators and securitizers had several years of increased earnings.

By 2004, however, rates had started to rise (albeit modestly) and the refinancing boom ended. This meant that the mortgage industry was hard pressed to maintain its earnings levels from 2001 to 2003 (Bratton and Wachter 2010). The solution was to find more "product" to move in order to maintain origination volumes and hence earnings. Because the prime borrowing pool was exhausted, it was necessary to lower underwriting standards and look to more marginal borrowers (Figure 10.2).

Part of the decline in underwriting standards was a shift in product type. Nontraditional mortgage products are generally structured for initial affordability; the costs are back-loaded, either with balloon or bullet payments or with increasing interest rates. As Figure 10.1 shows, ARMs supplanted more expensive (non-option-adjusted) FRMs, even at a time when

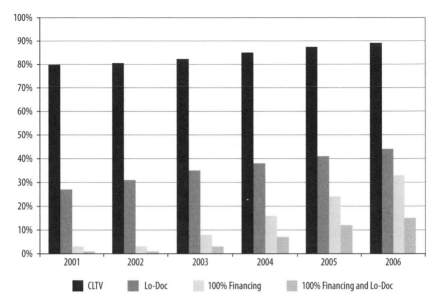

Figure 10.2. Erosion of residential mortgage underwriting standards: 2001–2006.

rates were rising from historical lows, making an ARM a poor financing choice, as rates were likely to adjust only upward in the foreseeable future. Moreover, many of the non-prime mortgages during the housing bubble were nontraditional structures, such as interest-only, pay-option, 40-year balloons or hybrid ARMs (2/28s and 3/27s) (Mayer, Pence, and Sherlund 2009). Interest-only, pay-option, and 40-year balloons expanded from $205 billion in 2004 to $871 billion by 2006 (Inside Mortgage Finance 2010). At the same time as the mortgage product mix was becoming riskier, credit support for AAA tranches was shrinking.

A Supply-Side Explanation of the Housing Bubble

The expansion of these nontraditional products during 2004–2006 can be explained only by their function as short-term affordability products that enabled the mortgage market both to expand to less-creditworthy borrowers and to finance larger mortgages for existing borrowers. Nontraditional mortgage products were also gifts that kept giving to the mortgage industry. Not only did these products help additional borrowers to qualify for mortgages underwritten at the initial teaser rate rather than the fully amortized rate, but the back-loading of costs created an incentive for borrowers to refinance as rates increased, thereby generating future mortgage business. And as housing prices rose during the housing bubble, these sorts of "affordability" products became increasingly attractive to borrowers who saw their purchasing power diminish. Nontraditional mortgage products generated additional mortgage origination business.

This supply-side explanation of the housing bubble is consistent with one of the bubble's most peculiar features: that even as mortgage risk and PLS issuance volume increased, the spread on PLSs over Treasuries *decreased* (Figure 10.3). Declining PLS spreads meant that investors were willing to accept more risk for lower returns. In other words, housing finance was becoming relatively cheaper even as it became riskier.

That PLS spreads fell and PLS volume increased even as risk increased points to a supply-and-demand-side explanation of the housing bubble, rather than demand-side explanations. There was likely a rightward shift in the housing finance demand curve (from D_1 to D_2 in Figure 10.4) as irrationally exuberant consumers sought ever more financing to cope with escalat-

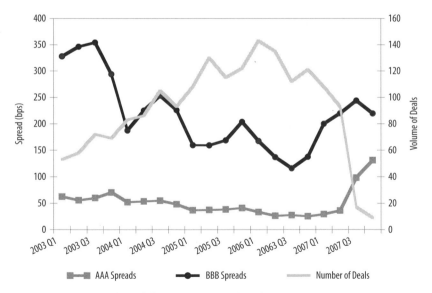

Figure 10.3. PLS issuance and spreads for AAA- and BBB-rated tranches: 2003–2007.

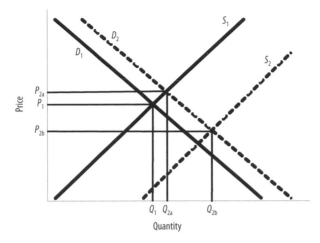

Figure 10.4. Shifts in housing finance supply and demand curves.

ing prices. This would have resulted in both greater supply (Q_{2a}) and higher prices (P_{2a}) and therefore larger PLS spreads. But PLS spreads decreased even as supply increased. This means that the housing finance supply curve must have shifted rightward (from S_1 to S_2) enough to offset any rightward shift of the demand curve in terms of an effect on price ($P_{2b} < P_{2a}$). Put differently, even if there was an increase in housing finance demand, there was a greater increase in housing finance supply. Investors' demand for PLS was outstripping the supply of mortgages.

The dominant explanations of the housing bubble to date have been demand-side explanations. Robert Shiller (2009) has argued that the bubble was driven by consumers' irrational exuberance and belief that real estate prices would continue to appreciate, stoking the demand for housing finance. Edward Glaeser, Joseph Gyourko, and Albert Saiz have argued that the bubble was spurred by population growth encountering a finite frontier of metropolitan-area real estate; real estate supply inelasticity drove up housing prices and thus demand for housing finance (Glaeser, Gyourko, and Saiz 2009).

Our claim of a supply-driven bubble is consistent with these demand-side theories. Consumer demand for housing finance played a critical role in the development of the housing bubble, but the behavior of MBS spreads indicates that the growth in housing finance supply surpassed the growth in housing finance demand.

The growth in housing finance supply required an increase in investment in housing finance. What led to the increase in investor demand for housing finance funding? Or, more precisely, given that most housing finance is done through securitization, and particularly PLSs during the bubble, why was there such demand for PLSs?

Exploiting Information Asymmetries

One factor behind investor demand for PLSs was simply yield. Historically low rates on Treasuries left investors with return hurdles hungry for yield, and PLSs might have been more attractive than other investment options. Yet declining spreads make this explanation unlikely. It was a mortgage bubble, after all. While many factors, including the Basel regulatory capital rules, played a role, we believe that a critical and underappreciated piece of the explanation is that investors as a whole failed to properly price mortgage risk because they lacked adequate information. This failure was driven by the complexity, novelty, and heterogeneity of PLSs, which served to shroud the risks inherent in the product.

There are information failures in mortgage product and mortgage securities markets; both sides of the mortgage finance market are subject to information asymmetries and principal-agent problems. There are lender/broker information advantages over borrowers, and there are borrower information advantages over lenders. Information asymmetries occur between the borrower and lender both because the borrower lacks information on the loan product's risk and because the lender lacks information on the risk posed by the borrower. These asymmetries can feed on each other to result in borrowers receiving unsuitable loans (Ashcraft and Schuermann 2008).

Additionally, both borrowers and lenders have information advantages over securitizers and ultimately investors, because information on mortgage risk is not embedded in the securities' disclosures. These securities are sold without the sellers' having to reveal the full nature of the underlying mortgages. Disclosure for many PLSs took the form of disclosing the *lack* of information on loans bundled in these securities, such as listing the percentage of low- or no-document loans (often not even broken down separately). And there was no verification of the disclosures.[8]

Principal-agent conflicts are rife in these markets. Mortgage brokers, perceived by many borrowers as their legal agents or at least owing them duties, were compensated in part with yield spread premiums, which incentivized brokers to steer borrowers toward more expensive (and ultimately riskier) loans (Jackson and Burlingame 2007). Likewise, because securitization sponsors' income is from fees based on deal volume rather than loan performance, the more and larger the deals, the more they earn, irrespective of long-term performance.[9] This creates a potential "lemons" problem as securitizers are tempted to push ever more questionable product on investors.[10] In doing so, the information asymmetries between securitizers and investors serve the purposes of securitizers' short-run fee maximization.[11]

The combination of information asymmetries on both sides of the housing finance market meant that borrowers were taking out riskier loans than they should, and that investors were funding riskier loans than they should. The result was inevitably the growth of an unsustainable housing price bubble as increased mortgage demand pushed up prices. Directly, this meant that risk could not be tracked or priced. Therefore mortgages were not priced to reflect their risk. If they had been, they would not have been affordable. The immediacy of their risk was hidden as well by higher housing prices, which temporarily prevented defaults. Higher housing prices also had the effect of making PLSs look like safer investments because it inflated the prices of the assets backing the PLSs.

Complexity "pays" for the mortgage product producer. Complexity also "pays" for the securities producer because it allows the securities to be generated without the recognition of risk. Complexity precludes comparison shopping for consumers and risk monitoring for investors. Mortgage finance intermediaries are incentivized to maximize complexity to move more product with higher yields generating higher fees.

The Failure of Normal Market Constraints

Several potential market constraints on the default risk were embedded in the PLS market. These constraints all failed because of the complexity and market structure problems of PLSs.

Credit Ratings

An initial constraint should have been credit ratings. Most investors looked to rating agencies to serve as information proxies regarding default and loss risk. Approximately 90 percent of PLSs bore AAA ratings, and investors in the AAA-rated securities market do not appear to have been informationally sensitive (Adelino 2009: 31). Investors in AAA-rated PLSs did not demand higher yields for what turned out to be riskier deals (Adelino 2009: 22). Thus rating agencies played a critical informational intermediary role for the PLS market.

As it turned out, the rating agencies were inadequate informational proxies; many AAA-rated PLSs were subsequently downgraded (Adelino 2009: 14–15, 43). Many factors contributed to the failure of the rating agencies. Commentators have pointed to the rating agencies' lack of liability for misrating and lack of financial stake in any particular rating beyond the long-term reputational effect. Yet this has long been the case with corporate bond ratings, for which the ratings agencies have generally performed well.

PLS ratings, however, might have been different. The rating agencies became highly dependent on revenue from structured financing ratings, which commanded premium prices; by 2007, structured products accounted for 40 percent of their revenue and 50 percent of their ratings revenue. Because structured products issuers were looking to manufacture as much investment-grade paper as possible, the rating agencies were under pressure to give investment grade ratings, even if it meant making off-model adjustments. As Bolton, Freixas, and Shapiro (2009) have theorized, it is much easier for a rating agency to inflate ratings in a boom market because there is a lower chance of a rating being wrong in the short term, while the benefits of new business generation are larger.

Rating agencies had problems beyond misaligned incentives. Ratings agencies' historical strength has been rating corporate bonds, which are largely homogeneous products for which the ratings agencies have time-tested models going back over a century. Not so with PLSs. The ratings agencies, like everyone else, lacked multi-cycle experience with PLSs. Moreover, PLSs are heterogeneous products; no two deals are alike. The underlying collateral and borrower strength as well as credit enhancements vary across deals. The novelty, heterogeneity, and complexity of structured finance products made ratings much more speculative, and the ratings agencies' models did not account for the possibility of a national housing price decline. The models for structured products proved inadequate.

Furthermore, the ratings agencies, like investors, were not in a position to carefully analyze the underlying collateral of the PLSs to identify the probability of default or price fluctuation (Grant 2008: 183). The assumption that housing prices adequately represented fundamentals, which is implicit in the use of appraised values of collateral, based on comparable properties, made it unnecessary for rating agencies to evaluate the market-specific pricing risk that directly determines default risk.

Moreover, rating agencies had no capacity to undertake such analysis. The ratings agencies received pool-level information rather than loan-level information (Lewis 2010: 170). This meant that the rating agencies, like investors, often lacked sufficient information to adequately assess the default risk on the mortgages. Although PLS prospectuses disclosed information about the underlying collateral—percentage makeups, weighted averages, and ranges for items such as loan balances, LTV ratios, FICO scores, loan interest rates, state-by-state location, fixed-rate versus adjustable-rate structures, property types, loan purpose, amortization type, lien priority, completeness of loan documentation, term to maturity, presence of prepayment penalties, and so on (see, for example, Ace Securities Corp. 2005)—this information was aggregate data, not individual loan data, and it was not verified by an independent source and did not, arguably, include all material information for investors. While a great deal of information was being disclosed, rating agencies and PLS investors invariably knew less about the mortgage loan collateral backing the PLSs than did the financial institutions that originated the mortgages and sponsored the securitizations.

PLS heterogeneity and complexity also enabled issuers to "shop" for ratings. As Skreta and Veldkamp (2009) have argued, increased complexity in products makes ratings more variable among agencies, which encourages issuers to shop for the most favorable rating. The ratings agencies also made their models available to investment banks, which designed their products to game the ratings models (Morgenson and Story 2010: A1).

Subordinated Debt Investors and Collateralized Debt Obligations

While some investors made their purchases entirely on the basis of the ratings given by the rating agencies, other investors did not. Instead, they understood a principle that was widely accepted in securities markets: Ratings are a veil; markets in fact do price securities very differently from ratings (Grant 2008: 181–83). If anything, ratings respond to market conditions rather than revealing market risk. Ratings downgrades are frequently reactive, not predictive.

Indeed, some investors not only did not rely on the ratings, but recognized the risks in PLSs despite (or perhaps because of) PLSs' complexity. Why didn't the risk premium demanded by these investors or short pressure cause a price correction? If the underlying real estate is overpriced, mortgages would be perceived as riskier, and, therefore, their costs would increase in the MBS market. In other words, their return would go up. The interest rate on the MBSs would go up, and that would of course dampen the rise of real estate prices because as interest rates increased, mortgage borrowers would have to pay higher interest, and the mortgage would no longer be affordable.

Subordinated debt buyers often provide a natural limitation on risk. Subordinated debt investors tend to be more circumspect about credit risk precisely because they are the most exposed to it. Even with creative deal structuring, not all tranches received AAA ratings. While the lower-rated, junior tranches had higher yields, they were not always easy for underwriters to place with investors. Adelino (2009: 27) has found that buyers of subordinated PLSs often demanded a premium for investing in riskier deals. Subordinated debt investors' risk tolerance should have thus provided a limit on the expansion of PLSs; if the junior tranches of PLSs became too risky, investors simply would not buy.

The risk limitation on PLSs provided by subordinated debt investors was largely (or at least temporarily) bypassed with the expansion of the CDO market (Adelson and Jacob 2008: 12). CDO is a generic term for securitizations, but deals that are referred to as CDOs typically involve a resecuritization of existing PLSs. Resecuritization (with further tranching) transformed some of the junior (frequently called "mezzanine") tranches of PLSs into senior, investment-grade securities, albeit with a higher degree of implicit leverage. The junior tranches of the CDOs could then be resecuritized as $CDOs^2$, again turning dross into investment-grade gold. By 2005, most subprime PLSs were being resecuritized into CDOs (Barnett-Hart 2009: 10–11). Resecuritization enabled investors to take on additional leverage, which meant that investors in resecuritizations were much more exposed to mortgage defaults than investors in MBSs were (Grant 2008). And because of the high correlation levels between real estate related assets in CDOs, a slight rise in mortgage default rates could have catastrophic results for CDO investors.

The rapid expansion of CDOs occurred in 2006–2007, during the middle and end of the bubble, as the drop in underwriting standards became appar-

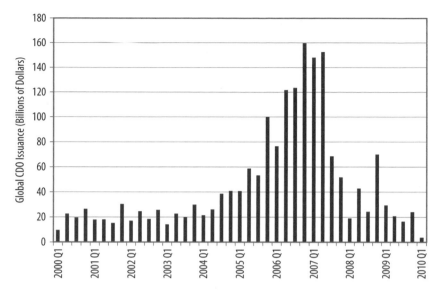

Figure 10.5. Growth of collateralized debt obligations: 2000–2010.

ent (Figure 10.5). This was the period during which subordinated debt investors would have begun to demand larger risk premiums and market appetite for direct investment in junior PLS tranches reached its limit. But as noted in Figure 10.3, spreads were falling on PLSs, and PLS issuance was expanding (Deng, Gabriel, and Saunders 2008: 4, 28). This was possible only because CDOs thus enabled the PLS market to bypass the constraint of subordinated debt investors' limited risk appetite. CDOs thus likely lengthened the housing bubble by at least one-third, making the decline all the more painful.

Short Investors and Credit Default Swaps

Subordinated debt investors were not able to exert market pressure on PLSs that would have controlled against the decline in underwriting standards, but what about short sellers? CDOs did not affect the ability of investors to take out short positions. As it turns out, PLSs were uniquely immune to short pressure as well.

The real estate market presents particular problems for shorts. It is impossible to sell real estate itself short. The product is unique, so the short seller cannot meet its delivery obligation. MBSs can, in theory, be shorted directly, but given how illiquid they are, it is also a risky endeavor and certainly not one that can be undertaken broadly across the market; the risk of being unable to meet delivery obligations at some point would be too great. One illiquid asset, real estate, was augmented with another almost equally illiquid asset: over-the-counter PLSs.

It is possible, however, to short mortgages indirectly by taking out derivative short positions on MBSs using credit default swaps (CDSs). A CDS is a form of credit insurance in which one party (the protection buyer) agrees to pay regular premiums to the other party (the protection seller) until and unless a defined credit event occurs. Upon the occurrence of the credit event, the protection seller pays the protection buyer the agreed-upon level of insurance coverage. A CDS is written on a particular bond, meaning that a single CDS is written on a single MBS tranche, not on an entire MBS deal.

The problem with using a CDS on an individual MBS tranche is that it is difficult to find a counterparty that will take the long position as CDS protection seller. If the counterparty merely wants to be long on the MBS tranche, it is possible to buy the MBS tranche directly. Moreover, the counterparty will necessarily be suspicious that some sort of informational asymmetry exists between it and the short CDS protection buyer. Indeed, it is precisely because of this problem that investors such as John Paulson (the short investor in the Goldman Sachs Abacus CDO scandal) and Magnetar (a hedge fund that executed a major shorting strategy on the housing market) had to use CDOs as their counterparties, rather than direct investors. While there are no data on the percentage of CDS protection sold by CDOs, it appears to have been a significant portion, if only because of the tremendous growth of synthetic and hybrid CDOs during 2006–2007.

The widespread use of CDSs as a means of shorting MBSs led to the development in 2006 of the ABX, a series of indices for tracking CDS pricing on MBSs. While some have argued that the ABX was responsible for the bursting of the mortgage bubble (Geanakoplos 2010), the ABX has two severe limitations as a market discipline tool on mortgage finance. First, the ABX is an index. Indexes are useful only in tracking overall market movements; they do not impose meaningful market discipline on individual assets. For example, the performance of the S&P 500 index does not indicate anything about the particular performance of one of the 500 individual underlying stocks tracked by the index.

The ABX suffers further from being a very narrowly based index. The ABX series track the weighted average price of twenty CDSs on particular MBS tranches of (primarily subprime) PLS. Thus even assuming that CDSs are priced accurately (and given that they are relatively illiquid and traded over the counter, this is doubtful), the ABX does not reflect the risk in most deals or even in all tranches of the deals it tracks. This means that riskier tranches can free-ride off less-risky ones in terms of ABX discipline, and riskier deals can free-ride off of less-risky ones included in the ABX. Given the heterogeneity of MBS deals, the pricing of CDSs on one deal might not mean much relative to the pricing on another deal. The usefulness of the ABX as a market discipline tool is severely limited because it is an index.

The second limitation of the ABX is that it reflects not only the default risk on the particular MBS tranches, but also counterparty risk. For example, the ABX for BBB-rated MBSs that were originated in the first half of 2006 started running up in 2008 and then spiked suddenly in the fall of 2008, right around the time of Lehman Brothers' bankruptcy filing, after which it promptly fell back to historical levels. The risk level of MBSs that were originated in 2006 did not change come 2008; the underwriting of the mortgages was what it had been all along, and housing prices had already peaked at this point. Nor did these mortgages abruptly and temporarily become riskier around the time of Lehman's bankruptcy filing. Instead of displaying mortgage risk, the ABX was displaying counterparty risk. The inability to sort out MBS credit and CDS counterparty risk limits the usefulness of the ABX as a market discipline device.

Smart money shorts were unable to impose market discipline on housing finance markets, as were credit ratings. The expansion of resecuritization via CDOs removed the natural risk appetite limitation on mortgages, and regulation was non-existent in the PLS market and largely absent in the mortgage origination market.[12] The result was that informationally limited investors failed to accurately price for risk and overinvested in MBSs.

Conclusion

When there is a return on heterogeneity and complexity for originators and securitizers, one can, in the absence of effective regulatory oversight, expect heterogeneity and complexity to prevail. This suggests a critical role for regulation as the housing finance system is redesigned and rebuilt. Regulation must concentrate on correcting the informational failures in the housing finance market, and the starting point for this is standardization of MBSs.

GSE securitization functioned well up through the housing bubble. The GSEs' failure stemmed not from poor underwriting on their securitizations but rather from downgrades on PLSs in their investment portfolios that left the GSE undercapitalized and therefore unable to carry on their MBS guaranty business.

Historically, securitization in the United States and Europe has succeeded only when credit risk has been borne implicitly or explicitly by the government (Snowden 1995: 270). Shifting credit risk to the government is but a form of standardization that alleviates the need for investors to analyze credit risk. GSE securitization standardized credit risk by having the GSEs guarantee all of their MBSs, and having the implicit backing of the U.S. government behind that guarantee. A government-backed mortgage finance market poses its own problems, however, such as the socialization of risk and the politicization of underwriting standards. It may well be that lesser forms of standardization—of mortgages and MBSs rather than of credit risk—are sufficient to enable adequate risk pricing without forcing a trade-off between market stability and risk socialization.

To standardize MBSs, it is necessary to standardize not only deal structure features, such as tranching structures and other credit enhancements, but also the underlying mortgages and origination procedures, including documentation requirements. Borrower risk is stochastic, but the risk from particular mortgage products is not.

Standardizing MBS does not mean eliminating consumer choice for mortgages. The U.S. housing market has historically always had niche products, and there will always be borrowers for whom these products are appropriate. But niche products should not be securitized. They involve distinct risks and require more careful underwriting and should remain on banks' books. If securitization were restricted to a limited menu of mortgage forms—the "plain vanilla" 30-year fixed, the "plain chocolate" 15-year fixed, and the "strawberry" 5/1 or 7/1 adjustable-rate mortgages—investors would not be taking on mortgage product risk.

Moreover, by limiting securitization to "Neapolitan" mortgages, certain underwriting standards would be hard-wired into securitization. There is a limit to how weak borrower credit can be with a fully amortized product. Interest-only, pay-option, hybrid ARM, and 30/40 balloon mortgages and other such short-term affordability products present markets with a "Rocky Road" because they enable the weaker or aspirational borrower to get financing that has a high likelihood of failure and that encourages cyclical expansions of credit and housing price increases.

Standardization would restrict investor choices, but we do not believe this to be a critical cost. Investors have far more investment options than homeowners have mortgage product options, and the marginal loss in choice for investors is minimal. And while structured finance has long prided itself on offering securities that are bespoke to particular investors' needs, most PLS deals (unlike CDOs), were not designed for particular investors. Thus standardization of PLS offerings is unlikely to restrict choice for investors in a detrimental way; it is hard to believe that investors want prime jumbos to be largely standardized, but not non-prime PLSs. Indeed, standardization arguably benefits investors by increasing liquidity, which increases the value of securities.

In this chapter, we take no position as to the form of the future secondary housing finance market—whether it should be completely privatized, run through cooperatives, run as a public utility, run through GSEs, or even completely nationalized. Instead, our point is to emphasize that regardless of what form the secondary housing finance market takes, it is necessary that the same regulatory standards apply across the board and that these regulatory standards include product standardization.

Securitization is necessary to guarantee the widespread availability of the 30-year fixed-rate mortgage, which has been the cornerstone of American homeownership since the Depression. The 30-year FRM is a uniquely consumer-friendly product that promotes housing-market stability. Requiring standardization of securitization around well-tested, seasoned products is the only sure method of addressing the principal-agent problem endemic to securitization and ensuring that securitization is a means of enhancing consumer welfare and systemic stability rather than a source of systemic risk.

References

Ace Securities Corp. 2005. Prospectus Supplement dated August 23 (to Prospectus dated June 23), Ace Securities Corp. Home Equity Loan Trust, Series 2005-HE5, S-21-S-33. http://www.secinfo.com/dScj2.z5Tk.htm#1kbi.

Adelino, Manuel. 2009. "Do Investors Rely Only on Ratings? The Case of Mortgage-Backed Securities." Job Market Paper. Cambridge, Mass.: MIT Sloan School of Management and Federal Reserve Bank of Boston. http://web.mit.edu/%7Emadelino/www/research/adelino_jmp.pdf.

Adelson, Mark H., and David P. Jacob. 2008. "The Subprime Problem: Causes and Lessons." *Journal of Structured Finance* 14, 1: 12–7.

Ashcraft, Adam, and Til Schuermann, 2008. "Understanding the Securitization of Subprime Mortgage Credit." Foundations and Trends in Finance 2, 3: 191–309.

Barnett-Hart, Anna Katherine. 2009. "The Story of the CDO Market Meltdown: An Empirical Analysis." Honors Thesis. Cambridge, Mass.: Harvard University.

Blankfein, Lloyd. 2009. "Do Not Destroy the Essential Catalyst of Risk." *Financial Times,* February 9, 7.

Bolton, Patrick, Xavier Freixas, and Jacob Shapiro. 2009. "The Credit Ratings Game." SSRN Working Paper 1342986. EFA 2009 Bergen Meetings Paper.

Bratton, William W., Jr., and Michael, L. Wachter. 2010. "The Case Against Shareholder Empowerment." *University of Pennsylvania Law Review* 158, 3: 653–728.

Deng, Yongheng, Stuart Gabriel, and Anthony B. Sanders. 2008. "CDO Market Implosion and the Pricing of CMBS and Sub-Prime ABS." Working Paper. Real Estate Research Institute. RERI.org.

England, Robert Stowe. 2006. "The Rise of Private Label," *Mortgage Banking*, October 1.

Geanakoplos, John. 2010. "Solving the Present Crisis and Managing the Leverage Cycle." Discussion Paper 1751. New Haven, Conn.: Cowles Foundation for Research in Economics.

Glaeser, Edward L., and Joseph Gyourko. 2008. *Rethinking Federal Housing Policy: How to Make Housing Plentiful and Affordable.* Washington, D.C.: AEI Press.

Glaeser, Edward L., Joseph Gyourko, and Albert Saiz. 2008. "Housing Supply and Housing Bubbles." NBER Working Paper 14193. New York: National Bureau of Economic Research.

Grant, James. 2008. *Mr. Market Miscalculates: The Bubble Years and Beyond.* Mount Jackson, Va.: Axios Press.

Hill, Claire A. 1996. "Securitization: A Low-Cost Sweetener for Lemons." *Washington University Law Quarterly* 74, 4: 1061–26.

Inside Mortgage Finance. 2010. *2010 Mortgage Market Statistical Annual.* Bethesda, Md.: Inside Mortgage Finance Publications.

Jackson, Howell E., and Laurie Burlingame. 2007. "Kickbacks or Compensation: The Case of Yield Spread Premiums." *Stanford Journal of Law, Business, & Finance* 12, 2: 289–361.

Levitin, Adam J. 2009. "Hydraulic Regulation: Regulating Consumer Credit Markets Upstream." *Yale Journal on Regulation* 26, 2: 143–227.

Lewis, Michael. 2010. *The Big Short: Inside the Doomsday Machine.* New York: Norton.

Lockhart, James B., III. 2007. "GSE Challenges: Reform and Regulatory Oversight." Speech at MBA's National Secondary Market Conference and Expo, May 21, http://www.mortgagebankers.org/files/CREF/docs/2007/RegulatoryandLegislativeRoundup-JamesB.LockhartIII.pdf.

Mayer, Christopher, Karen Pence, and Shane Sherlund. 2009. "The Rise in Mortgage Defaults." *Journal of Economic Perspectives* 23, 1: 27–50.

Morgenson, Gretchen, and Louise Story. 2010. "Rating Agency Data Aided Wall Street in Deals." *New York Times*, April 24, A1.

Nomura Fixed Income Research. 2006. "MBS Basics." March 31. Tokyo: Nomura Fixed Income Research.

Shiller, Robert J. 2009. "Derivative Markets for Home Prices." In *Housing Markets and the Economy: Risk, Regulation, and Policy: Essays in Honor of Karl E. Case*, ed. Edward L. Glaeser and John M. Quigley. Cambridge, Mass.: Lincoln Institute of Land Policy. 17–32.

Sinai, Todd, and Nicholas Souleles. 2005. "Owner-Occupied Housing as a Hedge Against Rent Risk." *Quarterly Journal of Economics* 120, 2: 763–89.

Skreta, Vasiliki, and Laura L. Veldkamp. 2009. "Ratings Shopping and Asset Complexity: A Theory of Ratings Inflation." SSRN Working Paper 1295503. NYU Stern School of Business.

Snowden, Kenneth A. 1995. "Mortgage Securitization in the United States: Twentieth Century Developments in Historical Perspective." In *Anglo-American Financial Systems: Institutions and Markets in the Twentieth Century*, ed. Michael D. Bordo and Richard Sylla. Burr Ridge, Ill.: Irwin Professional Publications. 261–298.

Stoner, Paul Matthew. 1943. "The Mortgage Market—Today and After World War I." *Journal of Land & Public Utility Economics* 19, 1: 224–30.

U.S. Securities and Exchange Commission. 2010. "Asset-Backed Securities: Proposed Rule." *Federal Register* 75, 84: 23328–476.

Weiss, Marc A. 1988. "Own Your Own Home: Housing Policy and the Real Estate Industry." Paper presented at the Conference on Robert Moses and the Planned Environment, Hofstra University, New York, June 11.

———. 1989. "Marketing and Financing Home Ownership: Mortgage Lending and Public Policy in the United States, 1918–1989." *Business and Economic History* 2nd ser, 18: 109–18.

Wells Fargo. 2003. Prospectus, February 27, http://www.secinfo.com/dsVsn.2h2.htm.

Notes

The authors would like to thank William Bratton and Sarah Levitin for their comments and encouragement, Manuel Adelino for sharing proprietary data, Grant Mac-Queen for research assistance, and Greg Scruggs for research and editing assistance.

This chapter has benefited from presentations at the Philadelphia Federal Reserve's conference on Reinventing Older Communities and at the Tobin Project's Workshop on Behavioral/Institutional Research and Financial Institutions.

1. Robert J. Shiller (2009: 17) has suggested that housing derivatives could be used to hedge home price fluctuations. He has suggested that housing futures are not used as a hedging device by homeowners either because they do not want to face the fact that they might lose money or because the consumption value of housing is itself a hedge against its market value (Shiller 2009: 27–30). While both of these factors may be at play, we believe that there is a simpler one: housing derivatives are poor hedges against home price decline. Housing derivates exist only for metropolitan statistical areas (MSA), not for particular neighborhoods or blocks. There is only a weak correlation between price changes in an MSA and price changes for a particular house. For example, housing prices in Chevy Chase, Maryland, bear little if any correlation to those in Loudon County, Virginia; Prince George's County, Maryland; Frederick, Maryland; or Southeast Washington, D.C., although all are within the same MSA. In theory, there could be housing futures on an index for a particular neighborhood or block, but trading on such an index would be illiquid, and the index itself would have synthetic volatility because of the sparseness and the heterogeneity in the underlying transaction data. These futures would be a flawed hedge against fundamental movements in house values.

2. The S&L crisis was subsequently exacerbated by regulatory forbearance, as regulators allowed insolvent S&Ls to continue operating by letting them count "regulatory goodwill" toward their capital. Insolvent S&Ls were attracted to high-risk investment strategies because there was no risk capital at stake. Accordingly, S&Ls successfully lobbied to be allowed to invest in commercial real estate. The decapitalized S&Ls moved aggressively into that market. Because the S&Ls' losses were unrecognized, the managers of the decapitalized S&Ls remained agents of the out-of-the-money equity holders, who were happy to have the S&Ls make long-shot gambles with creditors' funds. Thus, the S&Ls made risky, double-down bets on commercial real estate, which exacerbated their losses and deepened their insolvency.

3. In additional to Fannie Mae and Freddie Mac, there were the twelve Federal Home Loan Banks, another smaller GSE system.

4. Admittedly, defaults affect prepayment speed, but in GSE-securitized pools, the GSEs replace defaulted loans with performing ones, so prepayment speed should be largely unaffected.

5. The possibility of a federal bailout by being "too big to fail" did raise potential moral hazard problems for the GSEs, which could have undermined their underwriting quality. It is notable, however, that the GSEs' failure was due not to shoddy underwriting on the mortgages they purchased but to losses in their investment portfolio. The GSEs were major purchasers of PLSs. As Robert Stowe England (2006) pointed out, "In the subprime RMBS category, for example, Fannie Mae and Freddie Mac are

big buyers of AAA-rated floating-rate securities. Indeed, Fannie and Freddie are by far the biggest purchasers of subprime RMBS." At the end of 2006, they held about 11 percent of the outstanding subprime MBSs (Lockhart 2007), but they appear to have increased their market share subsequently. By June 2008, 29 percent of MBSs in the GSEs' investment portfolios were PLSs. While some of these were jumbo loans, there was still a substantial component of Alt-A and subprime PLSs in the portfolios.

Although the GSEs invested only in highly rated tranches of subprime MBSs, these tranches were vulnerable to ratings downgrades. As AAA-subprime MBSs were downgraded, the GSEs were forced to recognize large losses in their trading portfolios. Because the GSEs were highly leveraged, these losses ate heavily into the GSEs' capital, which undermined their MBS guaranty business; the GSEs' guaranty is valuable only to the extent to which the GSEs are solvent.

6. PLS investors are almost entirely institutional investors. Many institutional investors want to purchase AAA-rated securities. Sometimes this is just because these securities are perceived as being very safe investments, albeit with a higher yield than that of Treasuries. Often, though, institutional investors are either restricted to purchasing investment-grade or AAA-rated securities (by contract or regulation) or received favorable regulatory capital treatment for AAA-rated assets. Only a handful of corporate securities issuers have an AAA rating, so structured products were the major source of supply for the AAA-rated securities demand. As Lloyd Blankfein, CEO of Goldman Sachs, noted, "In January 2008, there were 12 triple A–rated companies in the world. At the same time, there were 64,000 structured finance instruments . . . rated triple A" (Blankfein 2009: 7).

7. For example, for Wells Fargo Mortgage-Backed Securities 2003-2 Trust, jumbo deal consisting of mainly prime or near prime (Alt-A) jumbos, 98.7 percent of the securities by dollar amount were rated AAA (see Wells Fargo 2003).

8. Intentional falsification of information in disclosures would violate the securities laws, but the Private Securities Litigation Reform Act of 1996 makes it very difficult for investors to bring suit over such a problem. Investors would have to plead fraud with specific factual allegations, but it would be hard for investors to obtain such facts absent discovery, which they could get only if their pleading were sufficient. PLS trustees could, in theory, bring suit, and they would have greater access to information, but PLS trustees have no incentive to bring suit, and without the ability to plead specific facts, it is unlikely that PLS investors could force the trustee to bring suit. Tort reform has thus created a Catch-22 for PLS investors.

9. The bonus-driven incentives of employees at the entire spectrum of financial intermediaries, from mortgage brokers to securitization sponsors to mono-line insurance companies underwriting credit default swaps (CDSs), all exacerbated this focus on short-term profits.

10. The potential for a "lemons" problem in securitization has long been noted (Hill 1996). The bubble and its aftermath play out Akerlof's lemons problem exactly

as predicted. Once a market becomes a market for lemons, it contracts, which is just what happened starting in the fall of 2007 as the weakness of the mortgage market became apparent.

11. To be sure, the long-term implications of a short-run fee maximization strategy were apparent, but preserving long-term reputation did little to address immediate earnings pressures and was ultimately going to be someone else's problem.

12. Congressional legislation began the deregulation of mortgages in the 1980s with two key federal statutes: the Depository Institutions Deregulation and Monetary Control Act of 1980, Pub. L. No. 96-221, 94 Stat. 161 (codified at 12 U.S.C. §§ 1735f-7[a]–1735f-7a[f] [2006]), and the Alternative Mortgage Transaction Parity Act of 1982, P.L. 97-320, 96 Stat. 1545, 12 U.S.C. §3803[a][3]). These statutes preempted state usury laws for first-lien mortgages and state regulation of nontraditional mortgages. The statutes did not replace the state regulation with alternative federal regulation. Federal regulatory agencies expanded the scope of federal preemption of state regulations, again without substituting federal regulation (Levitin 2009: 124), and the Federal Reserve failed to act on its regulatory authority under the Home Ownership and Equity Protection Act to regulate high-cost mortgages.

Chapter 11

The Expanding Financial Safety Net: The Dodd-Frank Act as an Exercise in Denial and Cover-Up

Edward J. Kane

In 1766, Voltaire famously opined that "Men use thought only to justify their wrongdoings, and speech only to conceal their thoughts." The behavior of many government officials confirms this dictum. Officials routinely misinform the public about the reasons for—or the probable effectiveness of—their economic policies. This behavior violates a duty of accountability that every public servant owes to citizens of his or her country.

Because the integrity of representative democracy turns on this duty, government or media deceptiveness poses a professional and ethical challenge to conscientious news reporters and academic economists to uncover the spin and explain the deception to citizens that might be harmed by it. Ethically, the right to protect high officials from painful criticism that government spokespersons implicitly invoke is overwhelmed by duties of loyalty and care that, as agents, high officials owe to other members of society.

In signing the massive Dodd-Frank Wall Street Reform and Consumer Protection Act, President Barack Obama issued a seemingly straightforward prediction about the effectiveness of the Wall Street reform section of the Act: "The American people will never again be asked to foot the bill for Wall Street's mistakes. There will be no more taxpayer-funded bailouts. Period" (McGrane 2010).

To expose assumptions that might be embedded in the President's prediction, it is sufficient to note that he did not exclude "mistakes made by managers of federal agencies or government-sponsored enterprises (GSEs)" from his first sentence and did not distinguish *implicit* from *explicit* taxpayer funding in the second. This potential logic chopping suggests that we should dismiss the one-word third sentence as a deceitful rhetorical flourish.

The Dodd-Frank Act puts responsibility for avoiding future crises squarely on future regulators, and the insuperable presumption that they can succeed year after year in this task is the wishful element that undermines the President's rosy forecast. As Figure 11.1 shows, at 2,319 pages, the Dodd-Frank Act is orders of magnitude longer than previous financial legislation.

Despite its length, the Act ignores the GSEs (whose appetite for risk fed the housing and securitization bubbles) and offers hundreds of opportunities for the regulatory community to miss its marks. In particular, the Act asks the federal financial regulatory agencies to prepare numerous reports and studies and assigns to these agencies the hard work of specifying and implementing crucial details of the proposed new regulatory structure. Moreover, it authorizes lengthy phase-in periods for most of the changes it mandates. During these periods, lobbyists will seek to undo provisions the industry doesn't like.

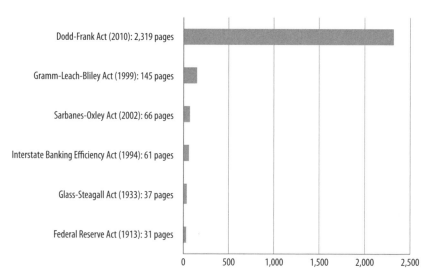

Figure 11.1. Growth in size of legislation.

Our legal system conditions us to accept (and even to admire) the use of clever evasions. Still, even though inviting listeners or readers to misinterpret a shrewdly worded statement is definitely more elegant than lying, most moralists regard such "spinning" of facts as disreputable (Strudler 2010). Producers of artfully spun phrases routinely defend themselves by blaming their victims for swallowing the deception. They can and do argue that listeners ought to realize that they are in a position of caveat emptor and should look for and discount exaggeration and distortion. From this cynical perspective, verbal sleight of hand is okay because it offers its audience an opportunity to reason their way through the deceit. However, the fairer this opportunity becomes, the fewer people the misdirection can ultimately fool.

A Bloomberg National Poll conducted during the week before the signing of the Dodd-Frank Act suggests that that presidential and congressional misdirection failed to sell the U.S. public on the effectiveness of the Act's legislative thrusts. Only 21 percent of respondents believed that the Act "will require big Wall Street banks to make major changes in the way they do business" (Miller 2010).

To explain the divergence in expectations between the political establishment and ordinary citizens, we can make use of Elisabeth Kübler-Ross' model of how people work through the emotional pain generated by personal and societal crises (Kübler-Ross 1969). In recent years, her model has been expanded from five to seven stages: shock, denial, anger, fruitless bargaining for an easy way out, depression (that is, realizing things will never be the same), examining realistic solutions, and settling on a satisfactory way to move forward. The model recognizes that people may easily become trapped in one of the passive early stages of denial, fruitless bargaining, and depression, or cycle back to one of these stages in frustration when realistic solutions seem unreachable.

This chapter advances the hypothesis that federal authorities are cycling between the stages of denial and superficial bargaining, while the public is cycling between anger and depression. Although authorities refuse to admit it, a majority of the citizenry has lost faith in the ability of the financial and regulatory systems to confess and heal their weaknesses.

It is instructive to think of excessive financial-institution risk-taking as a disease and regulators as doctors. During the securitization and housing bubbles, regulatory and supervisory entities misdiagnosed and mishandled the buildup of systemic risk in part to transfer nontransparent subsidies to financial institutions, builders and homeowners (Kane 2009). When the bubble burst, Federal Reserve and Treasury officials passed most of the bill for financial-institution losses to taxpayers through the financial safety net. They did this without assessing the full range of explicit and implicit costs their rescue program entailed and without weighing them carefully against the costs and benefits of alternative programs, such as prepackaged bankruptcies or temporary nationalizations. They also did not report or even acknowledge the distributional effects that financial-sector rescue programs and near-zero interest rates (which also help to recapitalize insolvent institutions) would impose on future taxpayers and on people living on interest incomes (particularly the aged).

The Act's most unforgivable element is its failure to address the culture and techniques of regulatory capture. It is unreasonable to believe that without numerous changes in bureaucratic incentives and reporting responsibilities, the kinds of lobbying pressure that undermined regulatory behavior during the housing and securitization bubbles will play out differently in the future (see Kane 2009). The vastly unequal division of lobbying power across the populace provides good reason to doubt—in line with the results of the Bloomberg poll—that the financial rules and studies that U.S. regulators ultimately produce can come close to meeting the aspirations that the President's signing statement sets for them. During and after the extended post-Act rule-making process, decision makers will be opportunistically lobbied to scale back consumer benefits and to sustain opportunities for extracting safety-net subsidies. Financial-sector lobbyists' ability to influence regulatory decisions remains strong because the legislative framework that regulators have been asked to implement gives a free pass to the dysfunctional ethical culture of lobbying that helped to generate the crisis and to dictate the extravagant cost and diverse ways in which the financial sector was bailed out. Framers of the Act ignored mountains of evidence that, thanks in large part to industry lobbying, incentive-conflicted officials are afraid to attack asset bubbles and regulation-induced innovation. They refused to acknowledge that regulatory capture prevents authorities from treating widespread financial-institution insolvencies in a fair, timely, and efficient fashion.

Elements of Denial

Realistically, the success of any treatment plan depends on the accuracy of the doctors' diagnosis of the particular deficiencies and imbalances that need to be remedied and on the ability of the treatments they propose to remedy the targeted disorder. The diagnosis that guided the treatments the Dodd-Frank Act prescribes is dangerously incomplete. It presumes that the mistakes that mattered were made exclusively by private firms—particularly by those that, because of their size and complexity, were able to spread the consequences of their aggressive risk-taking too widely for the private financial system and the government's formal safety net to handle.

This theory of blame is inadequate in many ways. First, it congratulates rather than censures U.S. and European officials for expanding the safety net during the crisis. Second, it supports a therapy that, without addressing regulatory capture, presumes that the crisis was based on remediable mistakes made in private risk management during the bubble phase. It calls upon the government regulators that failed society during the bubble (the SEC, for example) to devise and enforce a series of tougher rules to avoid future crises. Ostensibly, the agencies' task is to write detailed treatment plans that can compel "systemically important" private firms to monitor and support their risk exposures more effectively in the future. The Act hopes to reduce systemic risk (which officials define subjectively as the likelihood of a cascade of contagious defaults by important *private* institutions) by expanding and reallocating regulatory authority and leaving it to an incentive-conflicted regulatory establishment to figure out both *how* and *how much* they need to revise the system of mortgage finance, to increase capital requirements, and to restrict over-the-counter derivatives trading and executive compensation to protect taxpayers from being billed anew for future financial-institution losses.

The nub of the problem is that government regulators' conception of systemic risk neglects the pivotal role they themselves play in generating the risk. Officials' tolerance of innovative forms of contracting that are designed to be hard to supervise (such as the shadow banking system) and their penchant for rescuing creditors and derivatives counterparties by nationalizing losses in crisis situations cannot be sustained forever. This is why the debt of several European governments currently shows risk premiums that measure in the hundreds of basis points. These attitudes and proclivities encourage opportunistic financial firms simultaneously to foster and to exploit incentive conflicts within the private and governmental enterprises that society asks to identify and police complicated forms of leveraged risk-taking.

Zen Buddhists proclaim that truthfulness eradicates deceit. A complete diagnosis of modern financial crises must acknowledge that lobbyists for systemically important firms (SIFs) help to maintain a loophole-ridden regulatory structure and that risk managers at these firms intend to exploit the loopholes and to invite supervisory blindness and subsidy-generating mistakes by their private and government overseers. Far from paying a fair price for taxpayer credit support, SIFs skillfully extract subsidies from the safety net by devising funding strategies and ownership and guarantee structures that misrepresent and conceal from outside eyes the leverage and interest-rate risk embodied in them (Caprio, Demirgüç-Kunt, and Kane 2010).

The effectiveness of every regulatory system depends on the vigilance and conscientiousness of designated watchdogs (such as accountants, lawyers, and credit-rating firms) and private and public risk managers. The U.S. regulatory system was bound to break down eventually. It broke down in the 2000s because SIFs' incentives to try to shift risks to the taxpayer in clever ways spun out of control. Private and government supervisors did not adapt their surveillance systems conscientiously to curtail their clients' risk-shifting incentives or to recognize burgeoning taxpayer loss exposures in a timely manner.

Elements of Cover-Up

The idea of cover-up embraces any action or strategy that deflects or interferes with efforts to investigate or expose an embarrassing problem situation. By its neglect of political and bureaucratic drivers of systemic risk, the Dodd-Frank package of reforms downplays the practical importance of supervisory incentive conflicts and draws attention away from the need for incentive reform.

Safety-net officials face deeply ingrained conflicts of interest. To understand the gravity of this problem, it is useful to liken the safety net to a government corporation that is owned by taxpayers. The long list of incentive conflicts displayed in Table 11.1 should be alarming. The fiduciary standards that apply to the private sphere would expose managements that tolerated so extensive a conflict with the interests of their enterprise's owners to punitive lawsuits and extensive disclosure requirements.

The size and intricacy of the legislation provide additional misdirection. Table 11.2 lists what one influential reporter regarded as the major differences in the treatment plans that House and Senate conferees had to reconcile. Although the two bills covered a vast amount of ground, neither proposed to resolve—or even to stem—the largest source of taxpayer losses

Table 11.1. Layers of Incentive Conflict Between Regulatory Officials and Taxpayers

1. Asymmetric and uncertain information (supports easy alibis and opportunities for cover-up)
2. Political debts that must be serviced to hold onto their positions (shortens horizons of agency leaders)
3. Reputational and budgetary damage generated by industry criticism (creates dysfunctional accountability)
4. Role of political screening and post-government career opportunities in recruitment (revolving door)
5. Attraction of passively waiting for a cyclical upswing (gambling for resurrection)
6. Budgetary cost of training staff and administrative difficulties of winding down complex firms
7. Political pressure to escape adverse short-run effects that prudential restraints have on the goal of achieving rapid macroeconomic growth

Conclusion: A complete program of reform should mitigate these difficulties by improving public and private compensation structures, performance measurement, training and recruitment procedures and reporting responsibilities.

in the securitization debacle. This is the nearly $200 billion in losses that Fannie Mae, Freddie Mac, and other housing-related government-sponsored enterprises are ringing up to support a flawed system of subsidized (and largely nonrecourse) mortgage finance. Figure 11.2 shows that since the securitization bubble dissolved in 2007, private institutions have lost their appetite for traditional mortgage loans.

Under de facto government ownership, Fannie and Freddie have been purchasing or guaranteeing an increasing percentage of the single-family mortgages being originated in the United States.

Reframing the Policy Problem

Whatever improvements U.S. and European policymakers ultimately make in the administrative framework and toolkit through which regulatory authority is exercised, authorities need to identify and confront the incentive conflicts under which private watchdogs and government safety-net managers operate. The still-to-be-treated part of the policy problem is to incentivize and monitor private watchdogs and private and public managers

Table 11.2. Differences in House and Senate Bills and Conference Reconciliation

Provision	Senate	House	Outcome
Consumer Protection Agency	Creates a Bureau of Consumer Financial Protection, placed inside the Federal Reserve, with an independent director and budget. Its rules could be vetoed by a two-thirds vote of a council of bank regulators.	Creates a new Consumer Financial Protection Agency (CFPA), with an independent director and budget. The CFPA has full rule-writing authority.	The CFPA was renamed the Bureau of Financial Protection and placed within the Federal Reserve.
Derivatives	Mandates exchange trading and clearing for most derivatives, with a limited end-user exemption. Forces federally insured banks to spin off their swaps desks.	Mandates exchange trading and clearing for most derivatives, with wide exemptions for end-users.	Carve-outs and exemptions for bank OTC market making for most quantitatively important derivatives.
Volcker Rule	Gives regulators discretion regarding whether to implement the Volcker rule, which is a ban on proprietary trading.	Does not include a proprietary trading ban.	Outright ban jettisoned, but limits on proprietary trading were imposed.
Auto Dealer Exemption	Did not originally include a provision exempting auto dealers from new consumer protection rules. However, the Senate voted to recommend to the conferees that such an exemption be added.	Includes an exemption for auto dealers from CFPA's rules.	Exemption was included
Resolution Fund	The resolution authority for unwinding systemically risky financial institutions would be funded by an after-the-fact levy on the biggest financial firms. Any money necessary for the unwinding would be fronted by the Treasury Department.	Envisions a $150 billion resolution fund from the biggest financial firms, which would be tapped to unwind a failed institution.	Resolution authority was adopted, but advance funding was abandoned.

Numerous more arcane differences existed between the bills, including the ways in which they address capital requirements, preemption of state consumer protection laws (the Senate allows more preemption leeway), and cracking down on interchange fees (which the Senate bill does but the House does not). In the end, many controversial issues were designated as subjects for further study.

Garofolo, Pat. "Laying Out Some Key Differences Between the House and Senate Financial Reform Bills." http://wonkroom.thingprogress.org/2010/05/21/difference-house-senate-reg/.

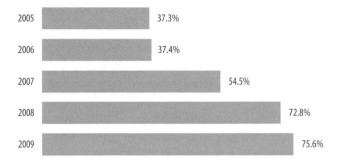

Figure 11.2. Growing guarantees. In 2009, Fannie Mae and Freddie Mac owned or backed three quarters of new single-family mortgages in the United States, double their share from 2005. Federal Housing Finance Agency.

of systemic risk in ways that will lead them to contain the subsidies to risk-taking that financial firms can extract by mixing regulation-induced innovation with well-placed political pressure.

The Act ignores the role that political clout plays in sustaining and expanding safety-net subsidies for major firms. Major institutions become major by deliberately making themselves economically, politically, and administratively difficult to fail and unwind (DFU). Because crisis-management strategies are not worked out and rehearsed in advance, bailout tactics are shaped in circumstances that DFU loss-making institutions make as stressful as they can.

Recruitment and reappointment processes for top regulators typically generate a substantial trail of political debts. Far from emphasizing job skills (such as financial acumen, mental toughness, and loyalty to the taxpaying and voting public), high officials are screened first and foremost for connections and for their anticipated loyalty to the agenda of the President who appoints them. For example, in 2009, Transportation Secretary Ray LaHood attributed his appointment (Leibovich 2009) *not* to being seen as "that great a transportation person," but to credentials that he called "the bipartisan thing" (his roots lay in the Republican party), "the Congressional thing" (his fourteen years in the House of Representatives), and "the friendship thing" (with the President's chief of staff). Missing from his catalog is evidence of the moral fiber and passion for serving the interests of the nation's citizenry that are needed to overcome the nasty political pressures that force unpracticed officials into scary games of chicken that the financial industry seems always to win.

Kane (2010) argues that complete and authentic financial reform must include new and more detailed mission statements and oaths of office for regulatory personnel. These statements and oaths should specify five duties that a conscientious supervisor ought to be willing to agree that its personnel owe to the community that employs them:

1. *Vision.* Supervisors should continually adapt their surveillance systems to discover and neutralize innovative efforts by financial firms to disguise their rule-breaking.
2. *Prompt corrective action.* Supervisors should stand ready to propose new rules and to discipline regulatees whenever a problem is observed.
3. *Efficient operation.* Supervisors should strive to produce their insurance, loss-detection, and loss-resolution services at minimum dollar cost and distributional disruption.
4. *Conscientious representation.* Supervisors should be prepared to put the interests of the citizens they serve ahead of their own.
5. *Accountability.* Implicit in the first four duties is an obligation for safety-net managers to embrace political accountability by bonding themselves to disclose enough information about their decision making to render themselves answerable for mishandling their responsibilities.

In principle, rule-makers and supervisors are recruited from a population of public-spirited individuals who should embrace these fiduciary duties enthusiastically. But Voltaire has also advised us that "from time to time it is necessary to kill one admiral in order to encourage the others." This is his way of saying that accountability is the most important of regulatory duties and that exempting any government program from outside scrutiny is a form of denial and cover-up that encourages other officials to seek carve-outs of their own.

The Federal Reserve has traditionally interpreted its special "independence" as if it were philosophically inconsistent with political accountability. Its leaders have shown little enthusiasm for allowing the U.S. Government Accountability Office to audit its accounts, even if only—as the Act actually envisions—to determine whether any of the creative 2007–2009 tax-transfer schemes Fed officials devised to rescue failing institutions and markets unduly favored particular firms and countries. The agency's resistance to routine third-party scrutiny of these particular policies indicates a reluctance to be held accountable for distributional effects. But if identifiable subpopulations were overburdened by its rescue programs and this result could be traced to elements of the agency's recruitment procedures and corporate culture, taxpayers deserve to know this.

To reinforce the duty of accountability, Kane (2010) calls for a series of informational reforms designed to measure systemic risk on an ongoing and less conflicted basis. Financial institutions could assist in the task of measuring systemic risk by issuing extended-liability stock and other securities that could help inside and outside parties to track the taxpayer's stake in their firm. This information would make the obligations that the safety net passes through to taxpayers more transparent during bubbles and administratively easier to rebalance in times of duress.

As a way to improve accountability, Kane (2010) and others (Levine 2009; Lo 2009) propose to separate the supervisory function of diagnosing systemic risk from that of containing it. Precisely because the emergence of widespread insolvency inevitably embarrasses agency leaders, the Financial Stability Oversight Council (FSOC) and its subsidiary Office of Financial Research (OFR), which were established by the Dodd-Frank Act, do not accomplish this separation because the council is composed of delegates from supervisory agencies. Council members' primary loyalty is toward the bureaucratic interests of the agency that pays their salaries and the political interests of its current leadership. History shows that agencies and their leaders repeatedly succumb to the temptation to understate or cover up surges in financial-sector insolvency and related supervisory problems rather than to treat them when they first occur.

As a practical matter, developing effective statistical metrics for measuring the value of safety-net support at individual institutions requires a prior change in industry ethics. Insolvency detection would have been improved long ago if industry leaders had been willing to acknowledge and fulfill the commonsense fiduciary obligations to taxpayers that safety-net support entails. It is unreasonable for an industry to expect to skin taxpayers forever. Far from treating taxpayers as suckers they can exploit ever more efficiently over time, financial institutions need to show some grace and recognize that the safety-net support they derive from taxpayers creates moral obligations for them.

The first obligation that legislators and safety-net beneficiaries should accept is to help the OFR to develop and use reliable metrics for estimating confidence intervals for the ex ante value of safety-net support and to report these estimates at regular intervals to their various supervisors. To contain the temptation to understate self-reported values of safety-net benefits and overstate the value of associated regulatory burdens, the OFR should have been empowered to challenge the methods used and the calculations reported by private firms and to vet their findings for reasonableness in more or less the same ways that Internal Revenue Service personnel examine personal and corporate tax returns. This implies that OFR and FSOC member agencies must recruit, retain, and advance the careers of risk-management personnel who possess the skills and incentives to keep industry estimates honest.

Data that individual institutions report must next be aggregated across firms and across supervisory agencies. To minimize incentive conflicts that might arise in staffing this aggregation function and in processing such politically sensitive information, the task of aggregating and publicizing the estimates cannot safely be located within the span of existing regulatory agencies. It is important that it be assigned to a new federal entity (Levine 2009; Lo 2009) or to a special division of the U.S. Government Accountability Office that would be charged specifically with measuring and monitoring safety-net costs and benefits. The goal is not just to separate accountability for mismonitoring safety-net subsidies from accountability for underpolicing them. It is also to make someone specifically responsible for identifying on an ongoing basis the ways in which regulation-induced innovation might be exploiting loopholes in the current structure of regulatory authority.

Period-by-period costs of supporting the safety net may be analyzed as the (negative) return generated by what is a portfolio of highly correlated positions in the various firms the safety net protects. As a portfolio value, the capitalized value of taxpayer costs for supporting safety-net benefits would generally be less than the sum of the benefits that accrue to individual firms. But because correlations increase in crises and asset bubbles, it might not be much less. Research on correlations shows that the effects of crisis-generating and other large common industry shocks are more highly correlated than are smaller common shocks that industry capital is expected to absorb (see, for example, Gropp and Moerman 2003). This tendency for institutions protected by the safety net to expose themselves during economic booms to much the same sources of tail risk makes it conservative for safety-net analysts to employ the working hypothesis that correlations across firms are very close to unity.

The layering of blame for the current crisis implies that private and government sources of systemic risk should be monitored and policed jointly. Kane (2010) proposes to divide responsibilities for collecting and processing data on safety-net benefits into at least three pieces. The first segment would task managers of financial firms with estimating and reporting to their primary regulators (on the same quarterly basis on which firms publish other data) interval estimates of the value of the safety-net benefits their firm receives. Especially for large or complicated firms, this task could be streamlined by requiring financial institutions to issue bonds that automatically convert to equity in observable circumstances and/or stock that carries an extended liability. (In fact, the Senate bill contemplated such a requirement.) The second segment would task individual regulators with examining (i.e., conscientiously challenging the accuracy of) these estimates and undertaking correlation studies that would allow them to prepare interval estimates of the aggregate value of taxpayer support accruing to the firms they supervise. The third segment would task the regulators to report and justify their estimates and aggregation procedures to a newly formed Safety Net Forecast Office (SAFO) and task the SAFO with publically reporting interval estimates of the aggregate value of safety-net subsidies for different industry sectors. A fourth segment could eventually task SAFOs in different nations with establishing arrangements for monitoring the quality of one another's work and preparing and publishing interval estimates of the value of bilateral and multilateral cross-country safety-net support.

If the analytical resources of the world's central banks and largest institutions could be given incentives to attack these estimation problems on a massive scale, the assumptions that underlie the estimates emerging from different methods should converge over time. However, each nation's SAFO should also recognize that although the confidence intervals that careful statisticians need to place around the different point estimates might be presumed to narrow with experience, this result will be sabotaged by wave after wave of regulation-induced innovation. For this reason, estimates may be expected to increase sharply in times of financial turmoil.

Adopting these informational reforms would make the jobs and recruitment of top regulators more difficult. For this reason, the United States and other countries would be well advised to make regulatory careers more prestigious by establishing the equivalent of a publicly funded academy (i.e., a nonmilitary West Point) for financial regulators and welcome cadets from anywhere in the world. Reinforced by appropriate changes in regulators' oaths of office and a system of deferred compensation, such an academy would raise the prestige of regulatory service and instill a stronger and broader sense of communal duty in safety-net managers than this generation of officials has shown during the current crisis. In view of the damage financial crises can cause, it is unfortunate that regulators have not been trained and incentivized as carefully as military, police, firefighting, and nuclear-safety personnel.

Summary Implications: The Importance of Addressing Distributional Effects

Ironically, mainstream economic models of the policymaking process are also built on a foundation of truthfulness. Efforts to create a "positive economics" that is independent of any particular ethical position or normative value judgments have produced a generation of economists who prefer to think of society as if it were composed of a collection of identical agents (cf. Solow 2010) and conceive of policymakers as perfectly forward-looking and selfless idealists. Unfortunately, the distributional effects that are generated in managing financial crises invalidate the first assumption and, together with the second assumption, this way of thinking becomes a recipe for helping financial institutions to use the safety net as a way to exploit poorly informed and politically impotent members of society.

To build a robust, reliable, and just system of financial regulation, relationships between regulators and those they regulate must be thought through anew. Financial-institution managers and national regulators must accept joint responsibility for identifying and ameliorating the distributional consequences of regulation-induced innovation.

Most of the profits that the financial industry appeared to have "earned" in 2002–2007 have turned out in retrospect to have been income transfers that were extracted unwillingly and with great pain from the accounts of ordinary taxpayers and of families whose employment and housing opportunities were adversely affected by the crisis. To contain safety-net costs, safety-net beneficiaries and safety-net managers must be made to acknowledge their joint obligations to estimate and contain in timely, proactive, and accountable ways the adverse distributional consequences of innovative financial contracts and institutional structures.

References

Caprio, Gerard, Asli Demirgüç-Kunt, and Edward J. Kane. 2010. "The 2007 Meltdown in Structured Securitization: Searching for Lessons, not Scapegoats." *The World Bank Research Observer* 25, 1: 125–55.

Gropp, Reint, and Gerard Moerman. 2003. "Measurement of Contagion in Banks' Equity Prices." Working Paper No. 297. Frankfurt: European Central Bank.

Kane, Edward J. 2009. "Incentive Roots of the Securitization Crisis and Its Early Mismanagement." *Yale Journal on Regulation* 26 (Summer): 405–16.

———. 2010. "Redefining and Containing Systemic Risk." *Atlantic Economic Journal* 38, 3: 251–64.

Kübler-Ross, Elizabeth, 1969. *On Death and Dying*. New York: Macmillan.

Leibovich, Mark, 2009. "G.O.P. Résumé, Cabinet Post, Knack for Odd Jobs." *New York Times* May 5.

Levine, Ross, 2009. "The Sentinel: An Auxiliary Precaution for Governing Financial Regulations." Presented at the Federal Reserve Bank of Chicago's Twelfth Annual International Conference, September.

Lo, Andrew W., 2009. "The Feasibility of Systemic Risk Measurement." Testimony before House Financial Services Committee, October 19.

McGrane, Victoria, 2010. "Obama Signs Financial-Regulation Bill." *Wall Street Journal*, July 21, http://online.wsj.com.

Miller, Rick, 2010. "Wall Street Fix Seen Ineffectual by Four of Five in U.S." Bloomberg, July 18, http://www.bloomberg.com/news.

Solow, Robert, 2010. Prepared Statement, Hearing on Building a Science of Economics for the Real World, Subcommittee on Investigations and Oversight, House Committee on Science and Technology, July 10.

Strudler, Alan, 2010. "The Distinctive Wrong in Lying." *Ethical Theory and Moral Practice* 13: 171–79.

Note

For valuable criticism of an earlier draft, the author wishes to thank William Bergman, Stephen Buser, Ethan Cohen-Cole, Rex du Pont, Robert Dickler, Larry Wall, Michael Whinihan, and Arthur Wilmarth.

Chapter 12

A Private Lender Cooperative Model
for Residential Mortgage Finance

Toni Dechario, Patricia C. Mosser, Joseph Tracy, James Vickery, and Joshua Wright

For the past several decades, Freddie Mac and Fannie Mae have played a central role in U.S. residential mortgage finance. The design of what replaces Freddie Mac and Fannie Mae, the housing government-sponsored enterprises (GSEs),[1] which are currently in conservatorship, is of enormous consequence to the performance of the U.S. housing market in the future. In our opinion, the goals of the efforts to reorganize Freddie and Fannie should be to promote the availability and stability of mortgage finance for the core of the housing market while minimizing systemic risk and costs to taxpayers. Any new structure should be designed to be resilient over the business cycle so that mortgage financing neither dries up during periods of market stress nor expands excessively during periods of market ebullience.

The recent financial crisis demonstrated how the implicit government guarantee and unique market structure of agency mortgage-backed securities (MBSs) can support the availability of mortgage credit during times of severe market stress. Figures 12.1 and 12.2 show the relative stability of the supply of mortgages that are eligible for securitization through Fannie and Freddie ("conforming mortgages"), compared to jumbo mortgages, which are of credit quality similar to that of conforming loans but are not eligible for agency securitization because of their larger size.[2]

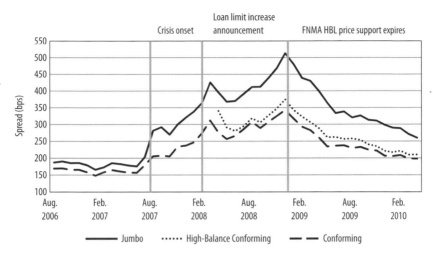

Figure 12.1. Mortgage rates and treasury yield spread: 2006–2010. HSH Associates.

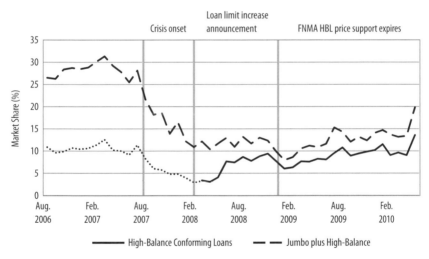

Figure 12.2. Market share of jumbo and high-balance conforming loans: 2006–2010. Lender Processing Services.

Before the onset of the financial crisis, the jumbo segment accounted for around one quarter of the value of mortgage originations (see Figure 12.2), and the interest-rate spread between jumbo and conforming loans was small and declining (see Figure 12.1). However, as the crisis unfolded after August 2007, spreads between jumbo rates and conforming loan rates widened sharply from about 25 basis points to over 100 basis points, and the share of jumbo mortgage originations fell from 30 percent to only 10 percent. This sharp decline in jumbo mortgage supply reflected a collapse in non-agency MBS issuance after mid-2007 and the effect of increasing credit-risk premiums given the lack of a government credit guarantee on jumbo loans.

In response to this trend and to provide additional support for the mortgage market, the conforming loan limit was increased in high-housing-cost areas in February 2008, from \$417,000 to as much as \$729,750.[3] For loans that fell between the old and new conforming loan limits (high-balance conforming loans), which now became eligible for agency securitization, interest rates quickly returned to levels that were very close to those for standard conforming loans, and the quantity of lending expanded significantly. However, the supply of mortgage finance above the new higher conforming loan limits remained low, reflecting the inability of originators to securitize or hedge the credit risk on those loans.

Principles for Reform

We believe that there are five principles that should guide the selection among the options for reorganizing the GSEs.[4] If possible, we should preserve what worked well with the GSEs, in particular the standardization of mortgage underwriting and the "to be announced" (TBA) market. Both are important for providing liquidity to the market.

1. Economies of scale and scope are important design considerations. Scale economies in securitizing mortgages suggest that any mortgage securitizer insurers should be relatively few in number as long as the design can address how this choice affects competition in the market. While the GSEs were active in providing lending to the multi-family sector, these loans proved to be difficult to securitize and generally remained within the GSEs' portfolios as whole loans. This result suggests that there are few economies of scope here and that consideration should be given to separating the support mechanisms for single-family and multi-family lending.
2. Government housing subsidies should be transparent and accounted for on the government's balance sheet. Affordable housing goals will likely be more effective if the mandate is focused in one government

agency, such as the Federal Housing Administration (FHA). In contrast, the new entities that are replacing the GSEs should be given the mandate to focus on the core of the housing market and not be taxed with affordable housing targets.[5]

3. In periods of market stress, it may be necessary to have a liquidity provider or perhaps even a "buyer of last resort" for mortgage securities, but this should not be carried out by the new entities unless they are explicitly a part of the federal government. If a private model is selected, the new entities should not be allowed to have a large portfolio either for investment purposes or to perform a buyer-of-last-resort role, since this creates incentives to emphasize the profitability of the portfolio over policy objectives.

4. A lesson from the recent financial crisis is that the government ineluctably owns the catastrophe or "tail" risk in housing credit, and if the government cannot avoid providing the insurance, then it should make that insurance explicit and fairly priced so that there is no expected long-run cost to the government.

5. The design of any successor to the GSEs must take a stand on whether the 30-year fixed rate amortizing mortgage with no prepayment penalty is going to remain a key mortgage product. We assume that U.S. households and policymakers will continue to have a preference for the fixed-rate mortgage as a staple of housing finance because it insulates homeowners from fluctuations in interest rates. As a result, securitization will remain an attractive alternative for mortgage originators (because they do not wish to hold such assets on the balance sheet against their short-term liabilities or devote capital and liquidity resources to supporting them), so an active secondary market will be needed to support it.

The TBA Market

With respect to the first principle, a great legacy of Freddie and Fannie is that they helped to create a deep and liquid market for residential mortgage finance in the United States. The implicit government credit guarantee and the liquidity of the agency MBS market have lowered and stabilized mortgage rates paid by households. Crucially, this liquidity relies not only on the implicit guarantee and the size of the market, but also on certain technical features of the way in which agency MBSs are traded, a factor whose importance has been underappreciated by most commentators.

The vast majority of agency MBS trading occurs in what is known as the TBA forward market. In a TBA trade, participants agree on a price at which to transact a given volume of agency MBSs at a specified future date (the settlement date). As the name suggests, the defining feature of a TBA trade is that the actual identity of the securities to be delivered at settlement is not specified on the trade date. Instead, participants agree only on six general parameters of the securities to be delivered. A timeline for a typical TBA trade is shown in Figure 12.3, including three key dates. On the day of the trade, the buyer and the seller establish the six general parameters, including the date the corresponding cash and security will actually be exchanged, which may be anywhere from 3 to 90 days later.

This process is enabled by the GSEs' exemptions from the Securities Act of 1933 and by the standardization and automation of the mortgage underwriting process promoted by the GSEs, which have also significantly lowered the transaction costs associated with originating, servicing, and refinancing a mortgage. The TBA market allows mortgage lenders to sell mortgages forward before the mortgages are even originated, reducing the length of time needed to "warehouse" the loans on a balance sheet before issuing an MBS. In addition, the TBA market provides a cheap way for lenders to hedge the interest-rate risk involved in offering borrowers the ability

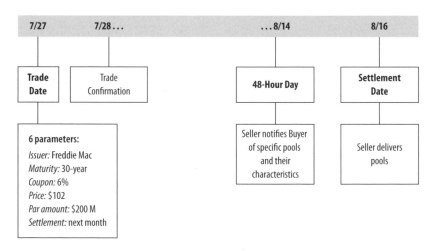

Figure 12.3. A typical TBA timeline. Salomon Smith Barney.

to lock in a rate for 30 days while closing on a mortgage. TBA trading is thus a key link between the primary and secondary mortgage markets and constitutes a major difference from non-agency or private-label MBS, in addition to the credit guarantee of the GSEs.

The delayed disclosure that is inherent in the TBA trading process runs contrary to the underlying philosophy of securities law regarding disclosure and transparency. In fact, TBAs are legal only because the GSEs are exempt from the Securities Act, which requires issuers to file detailed registration documents at the Securities and Exchange Commission (SEC) and to list the specific assets underlying any asset-backed securitization before it is issued. Without this exemption, the GSEs could not issue TBAs, since at the time of issuance, only the limited set of security parameters and the conforming loan underwriting standards are laid out, rather than specific collateral. In a TBA, the underlying mortgage loans have not been identified and might not even have been originated yet (which is essential to the rate-lock hedging function described later); that is, the TBA trade date can precede the origination date of the underlying loans. This contrasts sharply with private-label MBSs, whose loans must be originated before trading because they require many more disclosures with the SEC. Since they are ineligible for TBA trading, non-agency MBSs are much less liquid than agency MBSs are, and although it might be possible to make them eligible, this would require significant amendment of current securities law. More generally, TBA trading can probably be sustained with a variety of organizational structures but fits most easily with institutions that receive some level of government support.

Similar to Treasury futures, TBAs trade on a "cheapest-to-deliver" basis: Traders assume that they will receive the collateral with the most disadvantageous characteristics and trade every TBA at the corresponding price. This convention is much more counterintuitive when applied to mortgages than to Treasuries, since there are so many more features by which mortgage pools can differ from one another. The assumption of homogeneity helps to take what is a fundamentally heterogeneous set of individual underlying mortgages and transform them into a very large set of fungible—and therefore liquid—fixed-income instruments.

This assumption of homogeneity is, of course, also supported by the perceived government backing of the GSEs, which has traditionally assuaged concerns about the underlying mortgage credit risk. However, other factors contribute meaningfully to TBA fungibility as well. At the loan level, the standardization of lending criteria for loans that are eligible for agency MBS (despite some variation over the years) constrains the variation among the borrowers and properties underlying the MBSs. At the security level, homogenizing factors include the geographic diversification incorporated into the pooling process, the limited number of issuers, and the simple structure of pass-through security features.[6] However, Fannie and Freddie did venture into guaranteeing and securitizing some low-quality Alt-A loans in the last decade, but this was arguably due to competitive pressure from the private-label securitizers long after the GSEs had succeeded in establishing the conforming loan standards. Limiting the degree to which competition can result in a "race to the bottom" on quality standards is an important design element to which we will return later in the chapter.

TBA trading thus greatly simplifies the analytical problem that confronts participants in agency MBS markets and restricts its scope to the more tractable set of risks associated with the parameters of the TBA contract. Importantly, this has attracted a number of investors who are unwilling to perform credit analysis—notably foreign central banks and a variety of mutual funds and hedge funds that specialize in interest-rate analysis. That translates into more capital for financing mortgages and therefore lower rates for homeowners. Some economists have proposed formal models for how the temporary restriction of information in TBAs decreases information asymmetries and enhances liquidity (see Glaeser and Kallal 1997).

TBAs also facilitate hedging and funding by allowing lenders to prearrange prices for mortgages that are still in the process of being originated. This effectively allows lenders to hedge their exposure to interest-rate risk after a borrower locks in a rate. This exposure occurs when borrowers exercise an option that lenders frequently give successful mortgage applicants to lock in a mortgage rate (usually the primary mortgage rate prevailing on the date of the application's approval) for a period of 60 to 90 days. Lenders face the risk that interest rates may rise—and mortgage valuations fall—after having promised a rate to borrowers but before the loan closes and they get to sell the loan to the secondary market. Lenders can eliminate this risk by selling a TBA forward and manage their hedges dynamically with options or a hedging mechanism unique to TBAs known as the "dollar roll." (Dollar rolls provide an additional financing vehicle, drawing in market participants whose financing and risk management needs are better suited to the idiosyncrasies of this instrument.[7])

It is important to note that not all agency MBSs are traded as TBAs. Some loans that the GSEs are authorized to purchase are not eligible for delivery as part of a TBA contract, because the criteria for TBA eligibility are set by a private industry trade group—that excludes the GSEs—rather than by any governmental authority. These loans trade at significant discounts relative to TBAs, owing to differences in various prepayment characteristics and, crucially, liquidity.[8] The lack of direct government influence over the TBA trading conventions is all the more notable in light of the repeated failures of private mortgage futures contracts, which in part reflect the challenges of coordinating action among market participants.

A key takeaway point from this discussion is that the TBA market creates significant liquidity, leading to lower and more stable borrowing costs for households. The standardized and relative uniformity of agency MBSs is an important reason why the TBA market works well, and why a similar market structure never developed in the non-agency sector, where there are many more securities issuers, and greater heterogeneity in security design. Correspondingly, policy decisions regarding reform of the housing GSEs should weigh the benefits of maintaining the standardization of agency MBSs and preserving the liquidity of the TBA market. We now turn to a discussion of a model for GSE reform that is designed to retain the benefits of the TBA market.

The Structure of the Cooperative Utility Model

One model for replacing Fannie Mae and Freddie Mac that has so far received frequent mention but little sustained analysis is the lender cooperative utility. Yet while each different model for a successor to the GSEs has its own strengths and weaknesses, a private-lender cooperative utility could provide the best overall solution based on the design principles listed earlier. Under this model, securitization would be carried out by a mortgage securitization cooperative that would be mutually owned by a membership consisting of financial institutions engaged in residential mortgage lending. Cooperative or mutual structures have existed for more than a century in the U.S. financial system, ranging from clearinghouses (e.g., CME until 2000, DTC, CLS, ICE Trust) to banking (e.g., mutual savings banks, credit unions and the Federal Home Loan Bank [FHLB] system) and agricultural finance (e.g., the Farm Credit System). The main goal of a cooperative is to provide services to its members, and because those members are also the cooperative's owners, any excess profits generated by the cooperative are returned to the members. Similarly, losses are shared on a pro rata basis according to each member's equity stake.

Basic Structure and Governance

Only members would be eligible to sell mortgages to the securitization cooperative, and each member would also hold an equity stake in the cooperative entity. Membership should include a broad range of institutions, including large and small lenders as well as both banks and nonbanks. All these members would be able to directly securitize loans through the cooperative and provide correspondent services for non-member access. Such correspondent relationships are a common practice already, owing to larger firms' ability to negotiate more favorable guarantee fees with the GSEs and provide large banks a substantial portion of the mortgages they sell to the GSEs for securitization. Key decision-making authority would be delegated to a board of directors made up primarily of cooperative members but also including independent directors. Since the bulk of mortgage lending tends to be concentrated among a small group of financial institutions (currently, over 60 percent of origination is performed by only four institutions[9]), the cooperative's charter should include provisions to protect small institutions and ensure that they have equal access to the cooperative's services.[10]

Capital and Guarantee Fees

Each member would be required to provide equity capital to the cooperative. The capital structure would include initial ownership shares of paid-in equity and a mutualized loss pool. Members' contributions to the mutualized loss pool would depend on the volume of mortgages securitized (i.e., the intensity of the institution's use of the cooperative, analogous to the approach used within the FHLB system). The mutualized loss pool would, over time, build up to provide the bulk of the capital base and serve as a reserve against credit-related mortgage losses.

As with Freddie and Fannie, the cooperative would receive MBS guarantee fees up front and on a flow basis. These fees would be split among several uses: (1) payments of the required reinsurance fee to the government for tail risk insurance, (2) payments into the general revenue of the cooperative to cover operating and non-credit-related expenses, and (3) payments to the mutualized reserve pool that is used to cover credit losses. An example of a capital waterfall for the cooperative is shown in Figure 12.4.

The lender cooperative would focus on the core of the housing market, letting the FHA take the lead on programs for first-time homebuyers as well as mortgage products to make homeownership more affordable for low-income households. We anticipate that this core market would contain only a few standard mortgage products, such as the 30-year fixed-rate mortgage and "plain vanilla" adjustable-rate mortgages. Innovation in mortgage products would occur on the periphery of the market outside of the cooperative. Products could be considered to be added to the core product set only after sufficient history on these products has been accumulated to be able to estimate the government's tail-risk premium. Since the tail risk is explicitly priced by the government, there is a good argument for the government to avoid "taxing" the lender cooperative to support any specific housing initiatives or assigning it any housing subsidy mandates. The possibility that the tail-risk insurance may be underpriced does not, in our opinion, make a good case for placing affordable housing mandates on the cooperative. A better response would be to adjust the price for the insurance and to focus the mandates in a government entity such as the FHA. However, even a tax

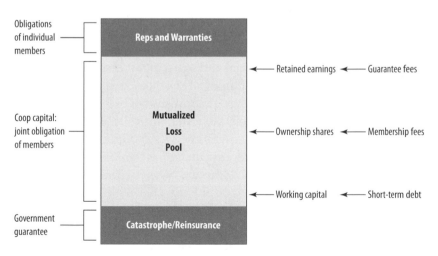

Figure 12.4. Capital waterfall for a private-lender cooperative utility.

is better than quotas or other targets that would distort the cooperative's business decisions.

An important design issue is how to structure the government tail-risk insurance for the lender cooperative. The choice involves a trade-off between increased pooling on the one hand, which implies that the government insurance would pay out infrequently and in response to systemic events, and on the other hand the degree to which the lender cooperative is still a going concern at the time of the payout. At one extreme, the tail-risk insurance could be provided to each specific mortgage (like FHA insurance). At the loan level, the insurance is likely to be triggered by idiosyncratic factors, such as health shocks and divorce, which affect a borrower's ability to pay. Alternatively, the insurance could also be specified at the MBS level (as in Government National Mortgage Association pool insurance). Because insurance would be pooled across mortgages, payouts would be less likely to be triggered by idiosyncratic factors affecting individual borrowers but would still be susceptible to idiosyncratic and more regional shocks, in contrast to macro shocks.[11] This could be addressed by pooling across MBS securities in a specific "vintage," which could be defined by a particular time period in which the securities were created. Finally, the trigger for the insurance could be defined at the level of the cooperative's mutualized insurance fund. That is, the insurance pays out when credit losses have eroded the cooperative's mutualized loss pool below some minimum threshold.

This last triggering mechanism ensures that payouts would occur only in response to systemic events yet may leave the lender cooperative in a weak position to maintain lending even after the government support is provided. A goal of the new entity is to enable the provision of mortgage lending even in periods of stress in credit markets through a robust securitization mechanism that facilitates mortgage liquidity. This goal suggests that the best trade-off for the trigger point in the government tail-risk insurance would be applying it to whole vintages of MBSs. In doing this, the vintage should be defined in such a way that clear information regarding the performance of the vintage is available only after the vintage has been closed for new issuance. This would prevent adverse selection, whereby lenders know that a vintage is performing poorly enough to likely trigger government payouts and therefore lenders with low-quality loans would opt into the vintage and lenders with higher-quality mortgages would opt out.

The other advantage of the vintage-based trigger is that problems with any given vintage or set of vintages will be less likely to inhibit the ability of the lending cooperative to continue to perform its securitization function. As a result, the cooperative remains a going concern even in periods during which the insurance is triggered. This, in combination with lending standards and insurance pricing that are constant over the credit cycle, should help to limit the procyclicality of the provision of residential mortgage credit. The government tail-risk insurance provides a "firebreak" between existing vintages and new lending and helps to ensure that the mutualized insurance fund is never depleted to the point at which market participants question the viability of the cooperative and the market it supports. This concept is illustrated in Figure 12.5.

Limiting moral hazard is always a concern whenever the government is providing tail-risk insurance. Lending standards have to be maintained to ensure that the insurance is paying out only in the case of true tail events. Otherwise, a race to the bottom could occur among lenders, implying that the tail is growing in size over time. Two factors will help to limit moral hazard for the lender cooperative. The first factor is putting borrowers in the first-loss position ahead of the government. Minimum down payment requirements should be enforced for all mortgage products on which the government provides insurance. These down payment requirements should not vary over the cycle.[12] In addition, borrowers should not be able to purchase private mortgage insurance as an alternative to making the required down payment unless they pay a higher mortgage rate to the cooperative and therefore to the government. The second factor is that the cooperative

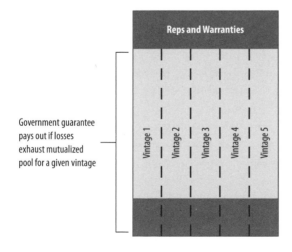

Government guarantee pays out if losses exhaust mutualized pool for a given vintage

Reps and Warranties

Vintage 1 Vintage 2 Vintage 3 Vintage 4 Vintage 5

Figure 12.5. Vintage-level insurance for a private-lender cooperative utility.

would absorb losses on the securities in each vintage ahead of the government. These losses are shared across the members of the cooperative but weighted toward those that participated most heavily in each vintage, which provides incentives for the members to maintain high credit standards and, importantly, to monitor one another.[13] The cooperative may choose to reinsure some of the credit loss exposure to the mutual insurance fund through a private mortgage insurer, subject to regulatory approval.

Regulation and Oversight

While the first-loss positions of the borrower and the cooperative are important safeguards against moral hazard, the government would still need to provide regulatory oversight of the cooperative. The Federal Housing Finance Agency (or a successor agency) would be responsible for regulatory oversight and management of the government's tail-risk insurance fund. The Federal Housing Finance Agency would need enhanced regulatory powers, including (1) approval of all new mortgage products and lines of business that can be conducted by the cooperative; (2) direct oversight of the risk-based pricing framework for guaranteeing principal and interest; (3) oversight of the cooperative's risk management systems, such as stress testing; and (4) the ability to veto any changes in guarantee fees or dividends.

Higher minimum capital standards, as well as more stringent risk-based capital standards, would be required to protect the government's insurance fund. In addition, the regulator should be removed from the annual appropriations process to minimize political influence. The regulator could also determine, establish, and manage the government's tail-risk insurance fund. One option is that tail-risk premiums could be paid into a reserve account that builds up over time, analogous to the reserve funds of the Federal Deposit Insurance Corporation (FDIC) or the FHA. If this reinsurance fund is depleted owing to significant mortgage credit losses, it must be replenished by charging higher tail-risk insurance premiums. An alternative approach is "true" insurance, in which tail-risk premiums are set at some fixed level and any excess losses are simply charged to general government revenue.

A disadvantage of FDIC-style insurance is that it could exacerbate cycles in mortgage lending, because reinsurance premiums would be raised exactly when the mortgage and housing markets are under stress. Conversely, there would be pressure to reduce tail-risk insurance premiums during periods when defaults are low and the reserve account is large, potentially fueling excessive credit booms during such periods. An intermediate solution may be to charge the government reinsurer to recoup losses on tail-risk reinsurance, but only over a longer period (e.g., 10 years). This should reduce the effect on mortgage rates in the short run, since the recoupment is smoothed over a long period of time. Regulation could also stipulate that the fund not seek to recoup past losses during periods of market stress, to further reduce procyclicality.

Advantages and Disadvantages

There are several potential advantages associated with the private lender cooperative model as a successor to the GSEs:

- *Low costs, narrow mission.* Cooperatives have incentives to minimize costs and to maintain a narrow mission to avoid cannibalizing members' other profitable business activities. For instance, DTC provides clearing and settlement for its members but not custodial services, which are provided by several of its members. We envision that several members of the cooperative would also be active participants in lending in the peripheral mortgage market outside of the core products securitized by the cooperative.
- *May help to limit monopoly power.* A mutual organization may have fewer incentives to exercise market power over mortgage originators than a for-profit enterprise. A for-profit firm has incentives to exercise monopoly power to increase profits, as Freddie and Fannie arguably did in the past. Under a cooperative structure, excess profits are simply returned to members (i.e., to the lenders themselves) on a pro rata basis, proportional to securitization activity. Assuming that competition among lenders in the primary market is high, any increase in fees charged by the cooperative would be at least partially competed away in the primary markets, since originators would be aware that they could increase their share of the cooperative's profits by originating more mortgages. An important caveat, however, is

that this argument assumes that mortgage originators do not collude, either implicitly or explicitly. In a range of industries, trade organizations have acted as a coordinating device for enforcing collusive arrangements, particularly when they allow participants to monitor the output and pricing of their competitors and to punish behavior that undermines the market power of the cartel.[14]

- *Low risk-taking.* Mutualization of credit losses should provide incentives for members to monitor the activities of the cooperative and to be conservative when setting criteria for membership, eligible mortgages, and the sensitivity of guarantee fees to mortgage risk. Consistent with this view, research on thrifts and insurance companies has found that mutuals engage in less risk than otherwise similar stock-owned firms.[15]

- *Inside monitors.* Equity holders that are also mortgage bankers could in principle be more effective monitors of the securitizer's activities than could a dispersed group of outside shareholders.

- *Maintains standardization benefits.* The cooperative model could be used to maintain the key standardization benefits of the current system, including the TBA market, and could leverage existing credit guarantee pricing and evaluation platforms established by Freddie and Fannie.

- *Minimizes government involvement.* In this approach, government's role is limited to providing tail-risk insurance and regulating the cooperative. This limits the potential for political pressures to influence the operation of the cooperative, at least relative to a public option.

- *Simplifies pricing.* The lender cooperative simplifies pricing of tail risk compared to the government bond insurer option. Guarantee fees are paid to the cooperative, and the government need only price and charge the tail risk to the cooperative.

There are several potential disadvantages associated with the private lender cooperative model as a successor to the GSEs:

- *Governance may be weaker.* Historically, cooperatives often have weak governance over management, because of their dispersed membership and lack of market discipline or threat of takeover. For example, Cole and Mehran (1998) present evidence that firm performance of mutual thrifts improves after conversion to stock firms, which is also associated with an increase in the share of inside equity. Given the government reinsurance of tail risk, limiting risk-taking and upside returns may be a desirable outcome. In addition, the concentrated nature of mortgage lending may mitigate weak monitoring incentives (e.g., in the first half of 2009, Freddie's top ten sellers provided 71 percent of securitization volume).

- *Limited access to capital markets.* Access to equity capital is limited to members of the cooperative. Greater access to capital markets to fund growth is often cited as a key reason for demutualization by thrifts and insurers (see evidence in Viswanathan and Cummins 2003). However, in a tail-risk event, experience has shown that all financial firms lose access to capital markets, so the advantages of a shareholder structure in this respect may be limited.

- *Broad participation may be difficult.* Relatedly, an initial capital infusion would be required to set up the de novo cooperative. Small or poorly capitalized mortgage lenders may be unwilling to supply this capital. The U.S. Government Accountability Office (2009) cites comments from an unnamed community bank trade group that small institutions may be unwilling to supply sufficient capital to the mutual entity in light of previous losses on preferred stock investments in Fannie and Freddie.

- *Investment and innovation would be more limited.* Focus on cost minimization could result in insufficient resources devoted to necessary activities, such as hiring strong management and technical staff and investing in risk management and operational systems. Lack of a strong profit motive also reduces incentives for the cooperative to innovate.

Conclusion

The U.S. Treasury Department has declared that it intends to foster a broad-based debate on the future of the U.S. housing finance system. Given this mandate and the clear failure of a variety of institutions across the current system, it is important to proceed from an accurate diagnosis of what went wrong. Together, the chapters in this volume by Ellen et al. and Levitin and Wachter lay out many of the key failures and many of the potential solutions. In this chapter, we presented five design principles and explored one model that has so far received frequent mention but little sustained analysis: the lender cooperative utility. We have also discussed the importance of the TBA market and how a cooperative model could accommodate and sustain this product's remarkable success. While cooperative structures face significant challenges, particularly in their governance, we believe that these problems are tractable and are outweighed by the advantages a cooperative has in addressing some of the central incentive problems evident in Fannie Mae and Freddie Mac.

References

Cole, Rebel, and Hamid Mehran. 1998. "The Effect of Changes in Ownership Structure on Performance: Evidence from the Thrift Industry." *Journal of Financial Economics* 50: 291–317.

Ellen, Ingrid Gould, John Napier Tye, and Mark A. Willis. 2010. "Improving U.S. Housing Finance: Assessing Options for the Future of Fannie Mae and Freddie Mac." New York: NYU Furman Center for Real Estate and Urban Policy, April.

Esty, Benjamin. 1997. "Organizational Form and Risk Taking in the Savings and Loan Industry." *Journal of Financial Economics* 44: 25–55.

Flannery, Mark J., and Scott Frame. 2006. "The Federal Home Loan Bank System: The 'Other' Housing GSE." *Federal Reserve Bank of Atlanta Economic Review* 89, 2: 87–102.

Genesove, David, and Wallace Mullin. 2001. "Rules, Communication and Collusion: Narrative Evidence From the Sugar Institute Case." *American Economic Review* 91: 379–88.

Glaeser, Edward L., and Hedi D. Kallal 1997. "Thin Markets, Asymmetric Information, and Mortgage-Backed Securities." *Journal of Financial Intermediation* 6: 64–86.

Lamm-Tennant, Joan, and Laura T. Starks. 1993. "Stock Versus Mutual Ownership Structures: The Risk Implications." *Journal of Business* 66, 1: 29–46.

McAndrews, Jamie, and Rafeal Rob. 1996. "Shared Ownership and Pricing in a Network Switch." *International Journal of Industrial Organization* 14: 727–45.

U.S. Government Accountability Office. 2009. "Fannie Mae and Freddie Mac: Analysis of Options for Revising the Housing Enterprises' Long-Term Structures." Report to Congressional Committees, September. Washington, D.C.: GAO.

Vickery, James, and Joshua Wright. 2010. "TBA Trading and the Agency MBS Market." Staff Report 468. New York: Federal Reserve Bank of New York.

Viswanathan, Krupa, and J. David Cummins. 2003. "Ownership Structure Changes in the Insurance Industry: An Analysis of Demutualization." *Journal of Risk and Insurance* 70, 3: 401–37.

Notes

These views reflect those of the authors and do not necessarily reflect the views of the Federal Reserve Bank of New York or the Federal Reserve System. The authors thank Angela O'Connor, Jeanmarie Davis, Dianne Dobbeck, Lisa Joniaux, Marc Saidenberg, Scott Sherman, and Grace Sone for helpful discussions in the development of this paper.

1. While the Federal Home Loan Bank system also comprises GSEs, we will use this term to refer only to Fannie Mae and Freddie Mac for simplicity's sake.

2. The conforming loan limit is set each year by the GSEs' regulator (the Federal Housing Finance Agency, formerly Office of Federal Housing Enterprise Oversight) based on its home price index. GSEs are forbidden by their charters to purchase loans above that limit.

3. The $729,750 limit was established on a temporary basis and renewed several times, even after a permanent higher limit of $625,500 was set in August 2008. See Vickery and Wright (2010) for a more detailed discussion.

4. The paper by Ellen, Tye, and Willis (2010) and Chapter 13 in this volume provide a good background on U.S. housing finance and the basic options for reorganizing the GSEs.

5. The core of the housing market would exclude the subprime sector. The new entities should be required to meet all fair lending standards and to promote non-discriminatory access to mortgage credit.

6. TBAs are possible only for pass-through securities, whereby the underlying mortgage principal and interest payments are forwarded to security holders on a pro rata basis, with no tranching or structuring of cash flows.

7. The alternative is MBS repo (repurchase transactions), which is a somewhat more expensive means of financing agency MBSs and differs in a variety of features (see Vickery and Wright 2010).

8. Vickery and Wright (2010) provide a detailed comparison of TBAs and one of these ineligible loan types.

9. See http://www.mortgagestats.com/residential_lending/.

10. Consistent with this principle, the FHLB system limits the voting rights of any individual institution and places geographic restrictions on the composition of the Board of Directors in each district, which limits the influence of the largest shareholders. If anything, the FHLB system has been accused of tilting too strongly toward smaller institutions.

11. Even in normal times with rising house prices and a growing economy, the GSEs had to pay out for losses on individual MBSs every year.

12. Maintaining minimum down payment requirements would help to mitigate the procyclicality of leverage over the cycle, which can exacerbate asset price cycles. It may also be helpful to redesign the mortgage contract to prohibit the borrower from taking on subsequent second liens that push the combined loan-to-value ratio above the allowed maximum. This would still allow a borrower to borrow against gains in house prices but would maintain the collateral buffer for the cooperative.

13. The performance of each member's mortgages can also be tracked by the cooperative as a discipline device. If a particular member's mortgages are performing consistently below standard, that member can be prohibited from issuing new mortgages into the cooperative until its underwriting problems have been corrected to the satisfaction of the cooperative.

14. Genesove and Mullin (2001) show how communication through a trade association facilitated collusion in the sugar industry. McAndrews and Rob (1996) theoretically analyze the competitive benefits of a cooperative compared to a for-profit structure in the case of a natural monopoly (e.g., a wholesale switch in an ATM network). Their model structure assumes that the cooperative enables competitors in the downstream market to collude. Under this assumption, a cooperative structure has no clear benefit in terms of promoting competition.

15. Esty (1997) presents evidence from the 1980s that mutual savings banks held less risky portfolios than did otherwise similar stock-owned savings banks. Lamm-Tenant and Starks (1993) present similar evidence for insurance firms. See these papers and Flannery and Frame (2006) for more references. One caveat in applying the lessons of these studies to the current setting is that members of mutual thrifts and insurers hold both debt and equity claims, which limits risk-shifting problems, contributing to the conservative approach taken by mutually owned firms. But in this case, the securitization cooperative would issue outside debt, so risk-shifting incentives would still be present, especially if the cooperative is highly leveraged.

Chapter 13

Improving U.S. Housing Finance Through Reform of Fannie Mae and Freddie Mac: A Framework for Evaluating Alternatives

Ingrid Gould Ellen and Mark A. Willis

As was noted in Chapter 1, the government-sponsored enterprises (GSEs) known as Fannie Mae (the Federal National Mortgage Association) and Freddie Mac (the Federal Home Loan Mortgage Corporation)[1] were, until recently, the largest players in a U.S. housing finance system that provided mortgage financing for millions of Americans. Since early 2008, the firms' insolvency has called their future into question. This chapter lays out criteria for evaluating proposals for reform of the two firms. After we introduce the basic goals of a healthy secondary market for both the single-family and multi-family markets, we offer a framework that will help to describe and understand the different proposals for reform and how variants of Fannie and Freddie might fit into that picture.

Goals of a Secondary Market for Housing Finance

A number of proposals have been put forward to reform the structure of the GSEs since they have been put into conservatorship. In considering these options for reform, policymakers should start with the basic goals of the secondary market as part of the overall housing finance market. For the purposes of this analysis, we assume that the laws against discrimination and unfair and deceptive practices are being enforced and that the risks inherent in different mortgage products are transparent to borrowers and so-called toxic products are generally not available. In this light, the following broad principles seem essential:

- *Access to liquid credit markets nationwide.* The primary goal of a secondary market is to ensure a deep and broad market for mortgage-backed securities that provide financing for both single-family and multi-family borrowers across the country.[2] Higher debt liquidity helps to ensure a reliable and consistent source of capital. It reduces variations across regions in rates and availability for the same mortgage products, and it results in better pricing of securities and ultimately lower mortgage rates for borrowers.
- *Countercyclical stability.* The secondary market should help to ensure consistent access to credit throughout economic cycles.[3] The secondary market should provide credit during downturns to help stabilize the housing finance market and should not expose taxpayers from unnecessary bailouts of the GSEs or their successors. The secondary market should not encourage easy availability of credit or aggressive underwriting during periods of expansion. Finally, a well-functioning secondary market should not exacerbate the impact of an economic downturn by impeding the ability of servicers to modify loans or authorize short sales to help avoid unnecessary foreclosures.
- *Availability of safe products that are reasonably priced and clearly understood by borrowers and investors.* Some mortgage products are less prone to default than others. Given that these products minimize the risk of harm not only to borrowers but also to their children and neighborhoods, government has an interest in ensuring that these products are available and widely used. An example might be the 30-year, self-amortizing, fixed-rate mortgage with the option to prepay. With this product, borrowers have known and fixed monthly payments, and investors can properly assess the risks of investing in the mortgage-backed securities (MBSs) that are backed by these types of mortgages.

- *Provision of credit for the underserved.* The secondary market should help to ensure that appropriate products and resources are available, for both single-family and multi-family mortgages, in markets that would otherwise be underserved because of misconceptions about the degree of credit risk or because of higher origination costs or lower fees (e.g., smaller loans, even if not harder to originate, will generate less revenue from a given amount of up-front points or the same interest-rate margin).

A Framework for Evaluating Reforms

Before evaluating any particular proposals, it is useful to articulate a framework by which to compare and contrast them. We lay out nine characteristics that can be used to distinguish among different approaches for reforming the secondary market, indicating in each case how critical that feature is to meeting the goals laid out previously.

Credit Enhancement

Arguably the most critical feature of any proposal is the existence and nature of any credit enhancement, or guarantee, provided. Since the Great Depression, insurance and guarantees provided by the U.S. government have come to play a large role in the mortgage finance system for both single-family and multi-family properties. These guarantees encourage investment in housing by protecting investors against losses. Guarantees have come in many forms: insurance of individual mortgages through the Federal Housing Administration (FHA), Veterans Administration (VA), and Rural Housing Services (RHS); Federal Deposit Insurance Corporation (FDIC) insurance of bank deposits that are used for mortgage lending; and implicit guarantees of the corporate obligations of the GSEs and of the Federal Home Loan Banks (FHLBs).

It would be extremely difficult to meet all of the preceding goals without some form of federal government credit enhancement. The experience of Fannie and Freddie has shown that government backing (albeit implicit) can help to ensure a deep, liquid market for their mortgage products and provide countercyclical stability.[4] Some observers also credit government guarantees with the ongoing viability of both the 30-year, fixed-rate, no-prepayment-penalty mortgage and the corresponding "to be announced" (TBA) market.[5] Certainly, such backing also helps to ensure that the securities are reasonably priced and therefore can reduce the costs to borrowers of financing the purchase of a home (i.e., as affordable as possible short of the government providing a direct monetary subsidy). The challenge is to design a system that provides liquidity and stability while limiting taxpayer risk.

A single guarantor also has the ability to bring a degree of standardization of products and securities available in the marketplace by limiting the types of mortgages and securities that are eligible for its credit enhancement.[6] Such standards can help borrowers to clarify their choice of products and reduce information costs for investors, thereby creating more liquid markets. Standardization generally reduces an investor's uncertainty about precisely what she or he is buying and thereby leads to higher MBS prices and lower mortgage rates. Further, standardization helps to aggregate markets that, with high trading volume, would tend to be more liquid because buyers are more confident that they can later sell their securities. Thus in addition to reducing investors' exposure to credit and systemic risk, a program of government enhancement can provide liquidity and systemic stability to the secondary mortgage market, especially during downturns and times of crisis.

Of course, like all forms of insurance, any guarantees in the secondary mortgage market carry the possibility of encouraging moral hazard. With a guarantee, neither the buyers of government-backed securities nor the aggregators of the loans will be as motivated to scrutinize the quality of the loans that collateralize the security unless they also have exposure to losses, either because they face a risk of losing capital or their ability to issue more securities in the future. Skeptics question whether any regulatory system can adequately prevent imprudent risk-taking in the presence of government guarantees.[7] Requiring lenders and securitizers to retain some degree of liability in the event of a loss could moderate the moral hazard. This means that the securitizers and the investors in them would need to have significant capital at risk. The liability could come in the form of having to take the first loss up to some percentage of the loan amount.[8] Furthermore, an additional layer of oversight might be helpful to monitor both the type and quality of the loans being securitized as well as counterparty risks (e.g., making sure the providers of loan-level insurance have adequate capital and that the other players in the origination chain are performing their roles properly). Anything short of this level of oversight and monitoring could leave the taxpayers unnecessarily exposed. Policymakers should think carefully about whether the basic regulatory system overseeing the GSEs is sufficient to take on this additional due diligence.

Guaranteeing MBS Versus Corporate Debt

While the implicit credit enhancement for Fannie and Freddie was assumed to apply to their corporate debt and perhaps to equity investors as well, a credit enhancement that applies only to MBSs would likely yield the same liquidity and countercyclical benefits for the mortgage market without taking on any additional risk. Therefore to limit moral hazard and taxpayer risk, the government should only provide a "wrap" for the MBSs, or in other words, it should guarantee MBS holders' timely payment of interest and principal in the case of default rather than guaranteeing the corporate obligations of the issuer or even the underlying mortgage debt. These guarantees would be provided only if underlying loans met pre-specified underwriting standards and the securitizers themselves were sufficiently at risk and sufficiently capitalized. (See the later discussion on limiting the government's role to that of taking catastrophic risk only.) Some research suggests that guarantees of MBS issues, such as the Government National Mortgage Association (Ginnie Mae) provides, can be even more effective in lowering interest rates than guarantees of individual mortgages.[9]

A key benefit of limiting the guarantee to the MBSs only is that it would reduce the incentive that Fannie and Freddie have had to continually increase the size of their portfolios to fuel their profits. Without a guarantee on corporate debt, they would not have benefited from artificially low funding costs, which yielded higher than normal margins in their portfolio investments. (See the later discussion of other possible uses for a portfolio.)

Limits on the Types of Mortgages—Favored Products

While we believe that some credit enhancement is critical to meet the objectives outlined previously, guarantees do not need to be provided for every type of mortgage. Rather, sufficient liquidity and systemic stability can be accomplished through a combination of credit enhancement for a small number of "favored" mortgage products and regulation of the private-label securities (PLS) market (see the later discussion of regulation). A side benefit of having such favored products is that they would gain a price advantage in the market due to their lower funding costs and so would have the salutary effect of encouraging more borrowers to choose these safe products.[10]

Limiting the products that are eligible for enhancement also limits the government's exposure to credit risks and minimizes the areas in which regulation is needed to combat moral hazard. Of course, support for the mortgage market can be easily expanded to a broader set of mortgages during the bad times, if desired, by simply raising the cap for mortgages that are eligible for the government wrap (as was done during the current crisis). Decisions to allow more variation in underwriting should be carefully considered, because such variation would likely expose taxpayers to riskier products.

The decision on which mortgage products to guarantee might be based on some or all of the following criteria:

- Which products should the government make sure are always available, that is, are favored, at as low a spread as possible above Treasuries, making them more affordable?
- What products might not otherwise exist but have a broader social benefit because of their low-risk characteristics (e.g., the 30-year, fixed-rate mortgage with no prepayment penalty or a low down payment loan that requires the borrower to complete a course on budgeting and homeownership)?
- Which products have risk characteristics that are so well understood that the government will be better able to minimize its (and the taxpayers') risk in providing the wrap?
- Which market sectors will be well served by the private market during normal times? What size and type of loans?[11]
- Which market sectors should be served by the FHA, the VA, and Ginnie Mae? Is there a need to have another source of mortgages for people with lower incomes (who presumably will borrow smaller amounts) and with a higher risk profile because of lower credit scores or higher loan-to-value ratios resulting from smaller down payments?
- Which types of multi-family financing products or underwriting standards should be encouraged and supported?

An overarching issue is to think through the potential overlap and the need, if any, to set boundaries between markets to be served by government agencies, GSE successors, and private firms. The debate so far about the future of the GSEs has paid little attention to this topic.

Limits on the Types of Losses

Another approach for limiting the risk undertaken by the government (and hence the taxpayers) is to require sufficient first-loss coverage to minimize the chances that the federal wrap will be called upon. The simplest and most direct way to accomplish this would be to require the securitizer (or the insurer of the MBS) to have sufficient capital to be able to weather the normal ups and downs of the economy and the credit markets. Only when that entity fails, and its shareholders are wiped out, would the government wrap be exercised.

Explicit Versus Implicit Guarantee

Guarantees can be either made explicit or left implicit. Implicit guarantees are by definition ambiguous. This lack of clarity reduces the effectiveness of the guarantee because investors call the guarantee into question during precisely the times when it is most needed to preserve liquidity and reassure investors and because any uncertainty adds to the rate spread over Treasuries. Moving to an explicit guarantee would allow the securities to trade at prices more like the government's direct obligations and so help to make borrowing more affordable.

A commonly voiced worry about explicit guarantees is their implications for the level of U.S. national debt.[12] One of the purposes for spinning off Fannie Mae as a private corporation in 1968 was to keep its liabilities off the federal balance sheet and its annual expenditures out of the federal budget (Congressional Budget Office 2010). But in fact, if an appropriate risk-adjusted fee is charged for each MBS that receives the government wrap, then the impact on the federal budget would be neutral (Fannie and Freddie did in fact charge those who sold mortgages to them a fee for the privilege of getting their guarantee). In theory at least, these fees could be kept in a reserve that would likely be sufficient to cover any future government liabilities. However, making the GSE guarantees explicit with regard to the already existing obligations of the two agencies would cause a one-time increase in federal liabilities based on an assessment of the likely losses inherent in their guarantee business as well as in their portfolios (Congressional Budget Office 2010).

If policymakers decide on moving to an explicit guarantee, they also need to consider whether they should require insured parties to pay actuarially sound fees in exchange for the guarantee. Charging for the government guarantee would raise all mortgage rates, estimated by some to be on the order of 25 to 50 basis points for single-family mortgages.[13] Charging such a fee for both single-family and multi-family MBSs would eliminate any implicit subsidy resulting from the government guarantee, a subsidy that has favored housing over other sectors of the economy. An additional benefit of charging for the insurance would be to reduce the impact on the federal budget of providing such insurance. To the extent that the fee is risk based and covers the expected cost of any losses to the government, the provision of this government wrap would not increase the federal deficit.

As the ultimate source for funding losses, the government has an interest in the solvency, capital adequacy, and operational effectiveness of the securitizers and insurers of the loans as well as an interest in the underwriting standards and the oversight of the originators of the loans. Therefore it will be critical to ascertain whether the agency that is providing the guarantee will set the standards, monitor, and regulate each of these activities or whether other regulators or agencies will perform one or more of these functions. In the case of Ginnie Mae, it is the FHA and the VA that set the standards for the loans they guarantee and that monitor the operations of the entities that originate those loans.

Regulation of All Players in the Mortgage Market

The level and reach of regulation are also critical to the proper functioning of the finance system. As we now understand, the GSEs lowered their underwriting standards and engaged in a race to the bottom as they tried to preserve their market share against competition from the PLS market, which was subject to much lighter regulation. Thus a well-functioning housing system depends on effective regulation not only of the GSEs, but also of other actors in the housing finance system. At least in the case of a housing bubble, even without the existence of a government guarantee and its attendant moral hazard, the private sector took excessive risk despite having its own capital at risk.

The industry needs to be regulated as to its underwriting standards, the quality of the underwriting process, operational risk, the level of capital/reserves, the quality of its servicing of the mortgage loans, and the rating of its securities. The exemption of the GSEs from certain securities laws should also be examined. The ability to regulate these entities could effectively be facilitated by requiring that all securitizers be licensed or chartered and required to report regularly to government about capital reserves and loan performance. Such a regulatory system and environment would help to guard against the proliferation of toxic products, poor quality controls, and unfair and deceptive marketing practices and thereby help to prevent the kind of race to the bottom that we have just witnessed, in which safer products are driven out of the marketplace.

That said, regulation can be excessive. In rethinking the regulatory environment, it will be critical to find the right balance between disciplined oversight and sufficient flexibility to allow for innovation of consumer products; investment vehicles; and operations, systems, technology, and platforms.[14] The GSEs were seen as leaders in the development of automated underwriting systems, which they then made widely available. Too much regulation can arguably inhibit such innovation by reducing competition, increasing costs, or otherwise interfering with the discipline of market forces. Too little regulation or minimal enforcement of regulations can undermine public purposes and effective oversight of systemic risk issues. Maintaining a proper regulatory balance over time is very difficult.

Securitization of Non-Favored Products

Another overarching question is whether to allow non-favored mortgage products to be securitized at all, even if they meet other regulatory restrictions on underwriting standards and transparency to borrowers (Levitin and Wachter 2010). If such securitization is not permitted, then access to capital for these products will be artificially restricted, as portfolio lenders such as banks are constrained in how much of each mortgage product they can hold in their portfolios. Shortages in supply are likely to lead to higher prices paid by borrowers.

However, the decision to allow these products to be securitized means that they will be able to compete more effectively with the favored products and so be able to capture a greater market share. Differences in capital requirements can also tilt the playing field in one direction or the other, as was shown by the competitive advantage of the high leverage allowed for the GSEs. Society as a whole may suffer if too few borrowers have mortgages that are as safe and sustainable as the favored products.[15] This competition could also jeopardize the ability of the securitizers of favored products to cross-subsidize the provision of other socially desirable activities. To redress the balance, government might want to take further action to tip the scales back toward the favored products or at least to ensure that the regulatory system provides a more level playing field across all of the players to avoid mispriced competition from MBSs containing non-favored products.

The next question that is posed by allowing non-favored products to be securitized is whether to allow the same entity to issue both types of securities: those that are backed by favored products (and so can be sold with government backing) and those that are backed by non-favored ones. If a securitizer can offer only one or the other, then the danger exists that the securitizer offering the favored products will be forced out of business by competition from the non-favored products. If a securitizer of the favored products goes out of business, then it will not be there during the downturns to help provide countercyclical support to the housing market. To guard against this possibility, it might be necessary to ensure that the set of favored products is able to hold its own throughout the business cycle and regardless of the steepness of the yield curve. For example, 30- and 15-year fixed-rate products become less attractive in comparison to ARMs as the differential between long- and short-term rates widens. (This situation, in which long-term rates are much higher than short-term rates, is referred to as a steep yield curve.) If a securitizer can issue only MBSs backed by these fixed-rate products, then it could go out of business when the yield curve steepens. Without the ability to compete successfully in all types of markets, the securitizer might also have trouble raising private capital.

On the other hand, if the same securitizers can issue both kinds of MBSs, then regulation becomes more complicated, especially if the government insurer sets higher standards for capital reserves and is unable to ensure that those reserves are walled off from any losses that are incurred on the non-favored MBSs. If the non-favored products start to perform poorly, thus depleting the capital of the securitizer, then the government insurer will become more exposed to loss on the credit-enhanced MBSs. A worse scenario might be for the problems on the non-favored side to lead to failure of the business as a whole. The only way to protect against this might be to require the securitizer to have separate legal entities handling the two types of MBSs, with separate pools of capital.

Market Concentration

Market concentration refers to the degree to which the secondary market is dominated by a few large institutions, as we now have. One question that is posed by the range of proposals for reform of the secondary mortgage market is the right level of concentration. Is the presence of two players too few, just right, or too many? The government can, if it wants, set a maximum number by requiring the firms to be licensed or chartered and limiting the number that it will authorize. Alternatively, the government can hold down the number of players simply by increasing the barriers to entry by, for example, setting high minimum capital requirements.

There are several reasons for considering a limit on the number of firms. The strongest argument for concentration in any market is the existence of economies of scale. In some industries, the cost structure may make the optimal size of a firm quite large and therefore the optimal number of securitizers quite small. In cases like this, in which a natural monopoly or duopoly would evolve on its own, it may be desirable to establish public utilities with the concomitant setting of price and other regulations to limit profitability. Such regulation works best in a market in which demand tends to be relatively stable over time and with slow technological change. When these conditions are not present—as in the cyclical housing and mortgage markets—price regulation could lead to very volatile profits (which would deter private investment) and dampen the rate of innovation.

Another advantage of concentration is that it may make government interventions easier when markets collapse. For instance, the fact that only two firms controlled almost the entire prime mortgage market allowed the government more easily to effectively nationalize the secondary market system for prime mortgages during the financial crisis of September 2008.

Because standardization has arisen in the presence of only two GSEs, it is sometimes assumed that concentration is necessary for standardization. However, even in a world with multiple securitizers, a single government insurance entity could drive standardization by imposing a single set of rules and standards for the products that it insures. Moreover, while concentration may facilitate standardization, the standards that are produced might not be the optimal ones. Regulation or monitoring could be required to ensure that the standards are both sensible and fair to all players in the market.

There are clearly some potential risks in industry concentration. For example, if the securitizers of non-favored products (or even banks that hold loans in portfolio) can raise money at lower costs because they are perceived as being "too big to fail," then the government's credit enhancement may do little to tip the scales toward the favored products. Especially in the wake of the government's recent bailout efforts, it will be very difficult to convince market participants that large financial institutions do not have some kind of implicit guarantee. A number of proposals have been put forth, and this issue will continue to be a challenge (see, for example, the provisions in the recently passed Dodd-Frank Wall Street Reform and Consumer Protection Act).

Another potential downside of market concentrations is the challenge of preventing large and powerful regulated entities from capturing their regulator. That said, a market with many participants may be difficult to oversee, thus making it easier for participants to evade monitoring and game the regulatory system. Moreover, the challenge of having to regulate a large number of entities may also lead the regulators to develop even more extensive and detailed guidelines and standards, which in turn can impede innovation. Thus the ultimate impact of market concentration on regulatory effectiveness is unclear. In truth, effective regulation is difficult, regardless of the level of market concentration.

Separate from the impact of regulation, the rate of innovation can also vary on the basis of market concentration. An environment with too few entities might not create the competitive pressures to develop new products and find ways to reduce costs. Multiple competitors are often thought to be more innovative, although the innovation itself may be subject to high fixed costs and so might need to emanate from third-party vendors that can capture the economies of scale. An example might be the development of software for new origination, production, or servicing platforms.

Provision of Credit to Underserved Markets

One critical aspect of a new housing finance system is the degree to which firms are expected to make loans in underserved communities. Markets can be underserved for a number of reasons, each of which may best be addressed with a different approach. If they are underserved because of discrimination, then the parties involved should be subject to enforcement of existing fair lending laws. If they are underserved because of misinformation or misperception of risk, then an appropriate remedy might be a regulation similar to the Community Reinvestment Act, which encourages lenders to explore serving such markets.[16] However, if a market is underserved because of higher risk or higher origination costs, then more direct government intervention and subsidies might be needed. Higher risk can exist because the population is more vulnerable to job loss during downturns and has fewer savings to bridge the time until they get reemployed. If the required mortgage product is one with a low down payment, then there is the higher risk that the value of the collateral will fall below the amount of the loan and thus be insufficient to make the lender whole. (Interestingly, lower-income borrowers seem to have a high willingness to pay, perhaps even more than a middle-income borrower might have, since the purchase of a home is often considered a crucial first step on the way to the "American Dream.")

As for the appropriate type of intervention when the market is underserved because of higher risk or costs, a key question is whether the government should require private actors to serve these markets themselves or whether it should instead collect a fee from private actors and use it to support affordable housing through other means, the mechanism that was initially proposed for the National Housing Trust Fund and the Capital Magnet Fund as well as for a fund to promote the development and production of innovative mortgage products. In addition, there are a number of options for imposing a tax or fee. For example, it could be imposed on each MBS, on the securitizers of those MBSs, or on a broader set of participants in the market. It could be based on revenues, profits, or the unit or dollar volume of mortgages in the MBS.

On the one hand, many of the skills, areas of expertise, and systems that the GSEs have are the same as those needed to serve these markets. And there have clearly been examples in which the GSEs brought their resources to the table and created very productive partnerships with community development financial institutions and state housing finance agencies. On the other hand, imposing a social mission on a profit-making firm is fundamentally challenging (Willis 2009). Proposals for reforming the housing finance system need to be scrutinized for how they best balance these two approaches to serving the underserved.

Financing Multi-Family Rental Properties

Another critical consideration is the continued availability of credit for multi-family housing. The market for financing multi-family rental properties remains a much more handcrafted business in which each transaction has its own unique characteristics that are best understood and evaluated by specialized lenders.[17] As a result, there is no mass-production approach to underwriting these deals (particularly those that have city, state, or federal dollars to help write down the costs to make the units affordable to low- and moderate-income families). By underwriting and either buying or guaranteeing these types of mortgages, Fannie Mae and Freddie Mac have helped to bring a somewhat larger pool of capital for multi-family housing and have reduced the price of credit in the process.[18] Any proposal for reform of the housing finance system should consider a specific mandate to purchase loans for affordable multi-family rental properties, given that the multi-family market requires more loan-by-loan handcrafting.

As was noted in Chapter 1, the GSEs have at times retained the majority of their multi-family loans in their portfolios rather than securitizing them. It is not clear whether the GSEs have held onto these loans because they find it advantageous, owing to the higher interest rates and thus higher margins of multi-family loans, or because they have found it difficult to securitize them. GSEs might also want to hold these loans in portfolio because it enables them to monitor and address the issues that inevitably arise with these more complicated deals, particularly for deals that have multiple participants. If the GSEs are holding onto these loans because investors are wary (or because there are transactional costs that make holding loans in portfolio desirable), then restrictions on portfolio purchases may significantly reduce the availability of credit for multi-family mortgages (see the later discussion on portfolios).

If instead, the GSEs have held onto the majority of multi-family loans simply because it is more profitable for them, then restrictions on the portfolio will have less impact on the multi-family market (such restrictions may still impose substantial transition costs on the multi-family market in the near term, as new investors have to move into the market). Still, while even complicated multi-family deals may be expected to be securitized once a property is fully rented and has a few years of a consistent income stream, these loans might need to be held in portfolio until they can reach that point of stabilization. Given the uncertainty and the importance of the rental market in serving lower- and moderate-income households, policymakers might want to consider making exceptions for holdings of multi-family loans if portfolios are more strictly limited in the future (which many of the current proposals recommend). Policymakers might also want to consider other strategies to provide funding for multi-family housing. Appendix A outlines one possible idea: supporting the creation of mortgage insurance funds at the state or local level.

It is worth noting that the GSEs have played a particularly important role in what has now become the largest subsidized housing production program, the Low Income Housing Tax Credit (LIHTC) program. Through creating a set of standard products that lenders can offer to tax credit developments, the GSEs have brought a more stable and less expensive supply of loan funds to multi-family projects that rely on the LIHTC for part of their funding (Apgar and Narsimhan 2006). They have also purchased tax credits themselves. Thus in moving to a new model, policymakers should consider the implications for the tax credit program.

Allowing Direct Investments: The Ability to Hold Assets in a Portfolio

Another issue is whether to allow the securitizers to maintain portfolios of mortgages, MBSs, and other investments. For the GSEs, their portfolios were a major source of profit as well as providing a way to maintain liquidity for mortgages in the face of short-term bumps in the MBS market. With low capital requirements and low cost of funds, the opportunity to earn more profit appears to have encouraged them to both grow their portfolios and take on more risk. While the imposition of dollar volume limits on the size of these portfolios might make sense in order to guard against systemic risk, other proposed changes, such as the elimination of any implicit (or explicit) government guarantee of corporate debt and the imposition of higher capital requirements that may be more in line with those of other financial institutions, such as banks, will greatly reduce the profit potential and the ability to grow these portfolios and to take on more risk. It should be noted, however, that the loss of the outsized profits in retained portfolios may limit the ability to cross-subsidize investments in affordable housing and education and training for nonprofit providers.

Limits on the type of investments can also help to reduce risk by restricting firms to holding only investments that are low risk. Allowing them to hold only their own MBSs does not add to their credit risk, although it does add to their interest-rate risk. Yet such capacity would give them the ability to bridge any short-term demand or supply discontinuities in the market, thus making the secondary mortgage market more liquid by smoothing demand for their MBSs' debt market during temporary market interruptions and downturns. (Of course, major disruptions in the marketplace, as happened more recently, were too large to deal with through additions to the portfolio; they required action by the Treasury, and the Federal Reserve directly intervened to purchase agency MBSs.)

Allowing firms even more flexibility as to what they can hold in portfolios could further other public policy objectives. For example, portfolios could be used to focus on sectors of the market that draw fewer private investors and today rely heavily on the GSEs as a source of demand and liquidity.[19] The arguments might be strongest in the case of multi-family projects that draw relatively few private investors and are less likely than subprime investments to generate systemic risk. Other possible markets in which a portfolio capacity might be critical would be loans to borrowers receiving federally approved housing counseling or those with nontraditional forms of credit. Finally, having the ability to hold loans in portfolio might facilitate the testing of new products and programs. In any case, if direct investments continue to be allowed, it is essential that there be full transparency with regard to the contents of the portfolio.

Methods of Ownership

Most of the discussion of the future of the GSEs has focused solely on the question of ownership. Ownership refers to the equity owners of an organization. The spectrum of ownership options runs from full nationalization to full private ownership. There are several alternatives between the extremes of full public ownership and private ownership without even the existence of a government wrap other than the existing one for FHA, VA, and RHS. For example, public utilities are private companies that are granted exclusive rights to operate in a sector in return for accepting rate-of-return regulation. Another ownership alternative is co-operative (co-op) ownership, in which ownership of a property or organization is shared among those who operate and use it, which in the case of secondary housing finance markets would be banks and other mortgage originators, much like now exists with the FHLBs.

As we have learned with the current structure of the GSEs, the form of ownership can have an impact on the way an entity behaves. Therefore this section describes different possible structures and considers their likely advantages and disadvantages in meeting the goals outlined previously (liquidity, countercyclical stability, safe and reasonably priced products, and serving the underserved). An additional criterion for entities that are expected to be privately owned is their ability to raise capital from non-government sources. None of the options for ownership deal directly with the procyclical dangers inherent in the current legal structure of the securities due to the difficulty of doing modifications and short sales, both of which can be critical for mitigating the number of foreclosures. There are also hybrids of these options, including having public-sector or public-interest members on the boards of otherwise private entities.[20]

One option is full nationalization. Nationalization would likely concentrate the prime MBS market in a single, guaranteed, federal agency, which might have a monopoly depending on the ability of other entities to compete in the marketplace for the same borrowers. The new agency's MBSs might receive a "wrap" guarantee similar to that of Ginnie Mae MBSs, backed by the full faith and credit of the U.S. government. Funding for any portfolio operations, beyond those supported by securitization business, would come from selling bonds of the federal government and thus would add to the amount of national debt outstanding.

A key advantage of nationalization is the elimination of the conflict between the GSEs' private interests and public purposes. Government officials would manage portfolio operations not to maximize profits but to attend to the goals of mortgage liquidity, systemic stability, and provision of credit to underserved markets. The problem of regulatory capture would be removed, though it might be replaced by concerns about the corrupting influence of political pressure and the difficulties that government has in regulating itself. Nationalization could also preserve the standardization and consumer protections that are built into current GSE securitization operations and simplify, but not eliminate, the principal-agent problems that are inherent in the web of players now involved in originating

and underwriting of mortgages and then distributing the MBSs to investors. Finally, because nationalization would involve relatively little change
from the conservatorship status quo, it would not likely disrupt the mortgage market.

Nevertheless, most economists believe that public ownership would
likely reduce incentives for technological innovation in processes, such as
improvements in automated underwriting, loan origination, and servicing.
These disadvantages could eventually stifle lower-cost provision and limit
reductions in systemic risk. Nationalization would officially wipe out existing GSE shareholders (though their interests already have no value after the
companies' insolvency), and the GSEs would become a stand-alone government agency or government-owned corporation (like Ginnie Mae).[21] Taxpayers could also be exposed to considerable risk. The government could
mitigate the risk through strict underwriting, monitoring the origination
process, and charging a guarantee fee to build up a capital reserve to protect the taxpayer. An open question would be the extent to which this entity
would look to others (e.g., originators, insurers) to take the first losses and
who would oversee this activity to limit the extent of the government's (and
hence taxpayers') exposure. Some have suggested that rather than creating a
new agency, the government should fold current GSE operations into FHA
and Ginnie Mae. The FHA could extend its guarantee program to the prime
market (or to a specific set of prime mortgages) in exchange for an actuarially sound fee. Ginnie Mae could continue to wrap the securities created from pools of insured mortgages with a guarantee for timely payment
of principal and interest, for which it would also charge a fee. However, the
FHA might not be the best model for government ownership, since it has
suffered from legislative restrictions and chronic underfunding, which has
limited its ability to offer innovative products and adopt the latest technology for processing and underwriting loans.[22]

Nationalization has at least three additional risks. First, creating a new
government agency would be difficult, even as there are serious questions
about whether the FHA has the capacity to handle GSE operations. Second,
moving the existing net liabilities of the GSEs onto the federal government's
balance sheet would increase the nominal value of the national debt. Third,
to state the obvious, the entity would not be expected to pay back the government for its bailout money, though pricing and fees could be set so that it
could earn a surplus over time to help generate government revenues.

Private ownership with a government wrap is another option. Its principal advantages are that it brings private capital to the table to take the first loss risk in advance of the government wrap and that it can bring market discipline and encourage innovation. Under such a system, the entities that take the first loss could be organized as co-operatives or as shareholder-owned corporations. New entities could be started from scratch, or Fannie and Freddie could be transformed into these types of entities. A combination of a number of different types of entities would be possible as long as each had enough capital to limit the government's risk to cases only of catastrophic loss and each could be effectively regulated to ensure proper capitalization and management competence.

Co-operatives (co-ops) are run on a non-profit basis, and each member is required to contribute equity in the new GSE proportional to, for example, the value of mortgage debt that it securitized. In other words, a co-op would be run so as to generate little or no surplus, and any surplus that it did generate would be paid back to member organizations in proportion to how much debt they securitized.

The co-op option would have several advantages. First, it would be likely to maintain high levels of standardization and mortgage debt liquidity. Although member institutions would still have incentives to create innovative, liquid MBS products to distribute their mortgage debt, their at-cost charter and open access to all market participants would prevent the co-op from collecting monopoly rents. The co-op's guarantee structure would encourage liquidity and likely facilitate the continuation of 30-year, fixed-rate, no-prepayment-penalty mortgages as standard. Moreover, the job of the government regulator might be made easier, since the members of the co-op (who have capital at risk) could be more motivated to police themselves (Flannery and Frame 2006).[23] (In fact, the danger may be that the co-ops would be too conservative, particularly in undertaking any mission-related activities.)

The co-op option could have several disadvantages. First, because voting rights would most likely be distributed on the basis of member securitizations and capital contributions, the co-op(s) could be controlled by large private banks whose interests might not coincide with those of smaller originators (including small banks) or of consumer protection.[24] Second, co-operative ownership does not solve the conflict between public and private purposes that currently characterizes the GSEs. Regulatory capture and moral hazard would still be significant risks. If the co-op could securitize riskier, higher-interest loans without increasing the insurance premiums paid to the government, its members and executives might be tempted to take advantage of the opportunity. Third, a secondary mortgage market that was highly concentrated in one or two huge co-ops could be very vulnerable to systemic risk if a co-op became insolvent, as may happen to some of the FHLBs.

Another approach would be to continue to allow private shareholder ownership, as in the pre-conservatorship model, but to limit the government guarantee to the MBSs and to introduce such other changes as higher capital levels, a stronger regulator (and one that would more heavily regulate their PLS competitors), and a limit on their securitization of non-prime mortgage debt, a restriction on—or the complete elimination of—their retained mortgage portfolios.

At the extreme, the entities could be recreated as public utilities. The public utility model would allow for a high level of regulation with regard not just to the types of mortgages that can be bought and the capital requirements, but also to the level of fees that can be charged, the overall level of profitability that can be achieved (presumably based on a return on capital, given the capital requirements), and even the organization structure, including the use of affiliates. The public utility model could have either purely private ownership or a mix of public and private ownership, or mixed representation on board of directors.

The private shareholder model, with a government wrap, offers several advantages. Such a model could provide liquidity and facilitate standardization of consumer and investor products, including a 30-year, fixed-rate, no-prepayment-penalty mortgage. Transition issues would be minimal, as discussed later. The challenge with this approach is to create a vehicle that can attract private capital. Investors might be frightened off, given the history of the GSEs' recent conservatorship, and/or worried about the many restrictions, such as those on portfolio investments. If these entities were subject to regulation as public utilities, investor interest might be further diminished, especially if the lack of stable demand and the potential competition from less regulated companies raise serious concerns about the ability of these entities to earn a steady rate of return. Another challenge in the case of a public utility would be establishing and maintaining an appropriate level of regulation and setting suitable prices and fees.

A third option is full privatization with no government backing. In a fully privatized model, the government would cease to be involved in guaranteeing the market for prime MBSs, and would only guarantee a limited set of mortgages through the FHA, VA, and RHA. The potential advantages of privatization include the greater efficiency that might come from the increased competition in the mortgage market (assuming that there are more than two entities, as exist now with the GSEs). With privatization, there would cease to be any conflict between the GSEs' private and public purposes. Without any government guarantees, firms would have to internalize the risks of their investments. If privatization leads to reduced market concentration, it would decrease systemic risk by purging the market of "too big to fail" institutions. Of course, it is also possible that a few large private financial institutions would dominate the secondary market, even in the·absence of government backing. If so, the dangers inherent in these firms that are too big to fail would now spill over into the secondary mortgage market as well.

However, privatization is likely to have serious disadvantages too. As was noted previously, researchers have shown that GSE-guaranteed MBSs have helped to provide some countercyclical stability to the mortgage market by providing credit even during times of market contraction (Peek and Wilcox 2006; Quigley 2006). The volume of private-label investment is more likely to contract during market downturns. A fragmented market would jeopardize the gains made by standardization. As we saw in the PLS market, multiple versions of the pooling and servicing agreements impeded the ability of servicers to modify loans. Elimination of government guarantees could also make long-term, fixed-rate, no-prepayment-penalty mortgages and the TBA market unviable, and fully private firms might promote riskier mortgage products. It is conceivable that even without the government wrap, investors might be willing to buy securities backed by 30-year, fixed-rate mortgages with no prepayment penalty. However, such securities would require significant structuring into separate tranches with different credit and interest-rate risks. The likely result is that the borrower would have to pay relatively high interest costs for such a mortgage, even compared to the case in which a government wrap is provided and is priced for the risk.

The new, fully private firms might not choose to play such a large role in the multi-family sector, as private investors have generally been more reluctant to buy multi-family mortgages and related securities than single-family MBSs (see, for example, DiPasquale and Cummings 1992). Finally, opponents of privatization argue that the recent experience of private-label MBS issuers demonstrates that a private market with minimal regulation is likely to generate significant systemic risk.

Transition Issues

A final consideration in evaluating any proposal is ease of transition. Any rapid and drastic alteration to the structure of the secondary mortgage market, especially to GSE MBS operations, is likely to cause a costly and unpredictable disruption in the TBA market and the mortgage market more generally, potentially harming homebuyers, investors, and even taxpayers. Another transition issue is how to handle the GSEs' current preferred stock held by the Treasury Department and how to handle the hard-to-value "toxic" assets on the GSEs' current books. Depending on how these issues are resolved, private investors might be hesitant to invest in the GSEs' successor institutions. Given that many of these proposals recommend a reduction in retained portfolios, a third issue is that the rapid sale of portfolio assets would be likely to seriously disrupt the secondary mortgage market. The simplest and least disruptive way to eliminate the retained portfolios would be simply to prohibit the GSEs from making more purchases and to allow their portfolios to mature and shrink over time. Finally, a long or uncertain transition period will accelerate the departure of top talent from the GSEs, which will undermine the capacity of any successor institution. However, the more the successor institutions are able to be run as a privately owned institution, the less likely it is that staff will leave simply because the organizations are not the same type of companies for which they originally signed up.

Each of the different models of ownership presents its own transition challenges. Clearly, continuing to keep the GSEs in conservatorship would represent the easiest short-run option, but it is not a long-run solution. Most nationalization scenarios present a relatively straightforward transition too, given that the two entities are already effectively under government control. The MBS operations would not have to be halted. Policymakers would be confronted with important questions about whether and how to continue GSE portfolio operations, which could be especially important for the multi-family market. The biggest transition risk posed by nationalization is probably the wholesale departure of many top GSE employees, although many have undoubtedly left already.

As for transitioning each of the GSEs into a co-operative or shareholder-owned organization, because these options would allow for the preservation of many of the existing features, they would involve fairly minimal disruption to the secondary mortgage market. To restore the firms to profitability before releasing them from conservatorship, the federal government would have to relieve them of some of the toxic mortgage assets that they still hold (some propose doing this by putting these assets into a "bad" bank, thus creating a viable "good" bank that could compete effectively and provide a return to its investors) as well as the 10 percent dividend they owe the government on the preferred stock it owns. In practice, the viability of this option depends on how quickly the GSEs can regain profitability and repurchase the preferred stock created by the government during conservatorship.

Some of the options, such as the co-op or public utility, might involve a single securitizer and so would require the combination of the two GSEs into one entity. Combining the two could be difficult and might lead to a loss of top talent, but an alternative might be to turn one of them into the "bad" bank and leave it to work through the non-performing assets. The other GSE could then become the "good" bank and be able to recapitalize itself and compete successfully.

Finally, serious disruption to the secondary market could result if Fannie and Freddie were simply fully privatized by removing the benefit of the federal guarantee. A host of issues would need to be dealt with if the TBA market disappears and the markets reprice GSE-guaranteed MBSs (presumably, the government will stand behind previously issued securities). The more abrupt and chaotic the transition, the more likely it is that GSE staff would leave unless given incentives to stay. Portfolio purchases would cease, and the government would likely have to devise a mechanism to take on the GSEs' toxic assets. Securitization could gradually be transferred to private holding companies, for which regulatory and capitalization standards would have to be set. Capital for those firms would have to be raised through equity markets, but it could be difficult to attract shareholders if the successor firms were still liable for the 10 percent dividend due on the preferred stock bought by the government as part of the bailout. Their mortgage databases could be turned over to a separate corporation that would be collectively owned and accessed by all secondary market participants.

Looking Forward

As the debate about the future of the GSEs has intensified, a number of organizations have proposed new models for a housing finance system. Some have suggested the elimination of any government role in the secondary market beyond GNMA, perhaps allowing banks to issue covered bonds to enhance liquidity, as described in Appendix B. Others have proposed nationalizing Fannie and Freddie, while a number of intermediate proposals call for a government wrap for securities backed by mortgages that are considered safe and for which the first-loss is taken by insurers backed by private capital. These intermediate proposals differ in the degree to which a PLS market should be allowed to come back and how it should be regulated as well as what mechanisms should exist to help serve underserved markets. All of these intermediate proposals note the importance of providing a government wrap not just for the single-family market but for the multi-family market as well.

Discussion and debate about these proposals is likely to continue. The secondary market has brought tremendous liquidity to the housing finance system in the United States by drawing capital from all over the world. The two GSEs, Fannie Mae and Freddie Mac, have been key players in this market. As federal government officials contemplate the future of these two entities, we hope that this chapter offers a useful framework to use in evaluating the alternative proposals.

Appendix A: Creating State Mortgage Insurance Funds for Multi-Family Loans

Very few of the existing proposals explicitly address multi-family housing finance. We think one existing program provides an interesting model for how the GSEs (or their successors) might be able to expand the availability of mortgage financing for privately owned affordable housing beyond what they are capable of doing directly themselves.[25] The program is the Mortgage Insurance Fund, which is run by the State of New York Mortgage Agency (SONYMA).

For 35 years, the Fund has provided insurance for the preservation and rehabilitation of both small and large affordable multi-family rental developments across New York State. Losses on insured mortgages have been minimal, and its investment-grade credit rating has helped lower the cost of fixed-rate mortgages and allowed for the financing of mortgages with longer maturities.[26]

State insurance funds have an advantage over large, nationwide organizations like the GSEs because they are better able to tailor mortgage underwriting to local market conditions and to local government programs that support affordable housing. Even with regional offices, the level of nationwide standardization required by the GSEs has made it difficult to accommodate local variations in market conditions and government-aided affordable housing programs. State insurance funds are better positioned to understand the risks inherent in local real estate and local government programs and, where necessary, to ensure that those risks are properly mitigated.

Moreover, state funds are also better able to assess the track record, underwriting skills, and organizational capacity of local lenders and so are able to pre-approve more local lenders, thereby providing them with better financing options for their customers. This local knowledge also allows them to be more open to working with non-bank lenders such as local CDFI loan funds that specialize in lending to not-for-profit developers and to borrowers and deals that are too small for a national insurer to find attractive.

An excellent example of how this has worked in New York is the success of the Community Preservation Corporation (CPC), a nonprofit loan fund that was set up over three decades ago by a consortium of banks and insurance companies to stabilize, strengthen, and sustain low- and mixed-income communities. With access to quality mortgage insurance, CPC has been able to provide reasonably priced construction and long-term, fixed-rate permanent financing for the rehabilitation or new construction of over 135,000 housing units. CPC has been particularly successful in helping small and often less experienced owners access the financing and government programs they need to fix up their buildings.

Yet despite the apparent benefits few, if any, other states have set up such multi-family insurance programs. (New York City itself has its own much smaller rate mortgage insurance program.) One way to encourage more of these funds across the country would be to have the GSEs or their successors offer such funds the opportunity to provide access to funding through government-backed securities. To be eligible funds would, of course, have to meet certain standards. For example, to make sure these local insurance funds have sufficient "skin in the game," they could be required to take the first-loss position in any loan that they wish to be bundled into a government-insured security. They would have to meet minimum capital requirements and demonstrate that they have proper systems in place to review the quality of the underwriting and of the servicing of the loan by the loan originators with whom they work. These loan originators would presumably have to be approved based on their track record in the underwriting, originating, and servicing of mortgage loans. All loans would be subject to some minimal set of underwriting standards covering such items as debt service coverage and the amount of project equity required from the borrower. Other underwriting issues, such as requirements regarding a borrower's net worth—often an issue for small, local building owners—could be left to local discretion. Newly formed lenders might be able to be pre-approved based on the experience of their staffs, the quality of their systems, and their initial capital base. However, they would probably need to start slowly until they can demonstrate a track record of success.

If the NYS Mortgage Insurance Fund is any indication, more state mortgage insurance funds would increase the access to reasonably priced and fixed-rate financing available to developers and landlords, both large and small. Moreover, lower funding cost would also allow for government subsidy dollars to stretch further or to achieve lower rent levels, thus reaching people with lower incomes.

Appendix B: Covered Bonds

The ability of banks to serve the residential mortgage marketplace is limited by both the total amount of funds that they have to loan and their appetite for mortgages as a percentage of their assets. For banks, deposits represent the major source of funds to lend. However, banks may have sufficient capital to lend more but lack the funds. In this case, banks can raise additional money in the capital markets or, as in the case of members of FHLBs, through "advances," which can be collateralized with home mortgages. A number of FHLBs also participate in the Mortgage Partnership Finance

Program, which appears to be dormant but did provide its members with another vehicle with which to tap the secondary market.

Covered bonds are another potential way to expand the funds available for a bank to lend. (FHLB advances are in and of themselves a form of covered bonds.) Covered bonds are issued by depositary institutions and backed by an overcollateralized, actively managed "cover pool" of mortgage loans. Issuing banks make the coupon payments from their general cash flows, and in case of default, the bondholders have exclusive recourse to the cover pool and then to the bank's general assets (i.e., the bank retains 100 percent of the risk). The total amount that the bank can then lend for home mortgages depends on the size of its capital base and the desired diversity of assets. Covered bonds allow a bank to take full advantage of its capital base in those cases in which it otherwise finds itself with insufficient deposits and other sources of funds.

New regulations and legislation have been proposed to facilitate the issuance of these types of instruments. However, to the extent that the legislation gives preferred status to the collateral pledged for these bonds, the collateral that is available for the FDIC to access if the bank should go into receivership will be reduced, increasing the need to raise the fees on all banks for deposit insurance and increasing the possibility that the taxpayer might eventually have to bail out the FDIC. Alternatively, when covered bonds are issued, the FDIC could charge a fee based on the added risk that this senior debt imposes on the FDIC insurance system.

In 2008, the U.S. Treasury issued best-practice recommendations for expanding the use of covered bonds. The FDIC (2008) also issued guidelines on how covered bonds would be treated in the event of a bank's insolvency, and a bill was introduced in Congress in 2008 to expand the use of covered bonds in the United States (Garrett 2008). Although not widely used in the United States—the first covered bond in the United States was issued by Washington Mutual in 2006 (Lucas et al. 2008)—covered bonds are the main vehicle of housing finance in many European countries.

There are two key differences between covered bonds and MBSs. First, in the case of covered bonds, the covered pool of mortgages remains on the bank's balance sheet. Second, regulations typically require that the pool of mortgages be worth more than the value of outstanding bonds, and if the value of the pool falls too low, then the bank must add more collateral to the pool. In that sense, the bonds are overcollateralized by the cover pool. If the bank defaults on the bonds, investors first have an exclusive claim to the mortgage pool and then have recourse to the general assets of the bank.

Covered bonds have three potential advantages over MBSs as a method of mortgage finance. First, they have the potential to reduce principal-agent problems, because the banks themselves would hold the loans' underlying covered bonds, giving them an interest in originating better loans. Second, because the mortgage loans would simply remain on bank balance sheets and not be put into special trusts subject to the incentives of servicers, banks could modify failing loans far more easily than MBS trusts can. This could reduce foreclosures and maximize loan value.

Third, depending on how they are implemented, covered bonds also hold the possibility of improving the options available to homebuyers who find themselves underwater. In Denmark, covered bonds operate according to the balance principle. The balance principle requires a match between each mortgage written and every bond issued. It permits homebuyers two options for paying off their debt: they may either pay off their mortgage at par or repurchase their lender's bonds on the open market, in an amount corresponding to the size of their mortgage, and return those bonds to the lender. This new option could reduce foreclosures.

There is uncertainty, however, about the extent to which covered bonds would deliver the same level of liquidity as GSE MBSs, because in a covered bond system, mortgage loans remain on bank balance sheets. Moreover, it may be difficult for covered bonds to achieve the minimum efficient scale to compete with government-backed GSE MBSs. As in Denmark, an effective covered bond market would require standardized bond forms and a high-volume market that could demonstrate liquidity to potential buyers. If covered bonds were issued by hundreds of banks across the country, each with different underwriting standards and bond structures, the extensive market fragmentation would seriously reduce trading volume and liquidity for any particular covered bond issue. The Danish covered bond system is effective because the market is highly structured and homogenized, with only a few participating banks.[27]

There are also important questions about whether covered bonds could be cost-competitive with existing channels of finance, which benefit from economies of scale, government subsidies, and well-developed regulatory frameworks. Covered bonds might require a phase of incubation and experimentation before they reached a minimum efficient scale and were widely accepted by investors.

It seems unlikely that covered bonds would replace GSE MBSs or any other existing channel of housing finance. Rather, they could provide a new way to increase liquidity for market sectors—like jumbo loans, which the GSEs do not handle. It is also possible that they could directly compete with the GSEs in the prime mortgage market. In a more radical restructuring, the GSEs could be abolished, and the entire system could switch to covered bonds, or the GSEs could be reformed into covered bond issuers. However, these more radical options likely would seriously disrupt the housing finance system.

Many call for an expansion of the covered bond model in the United States, arguing that it may help to make the system more efficient and secure (Soros 2008). At the very least, it might make sense to further explore developing covered bonds, regardless of what other reforms are implemented in the housing finance system.

References

Ambrose, Brent W., and Tao-Hsien Dolly King. 2002. "GSE Debt and the Decline in the Treasury Debt Market." *Journal of Money, Credit, and Banking* 34, 3: 821–39.

Ambrose, Brent W., and Thomas G. Thibodeau. 2004. "Have the GSE Affordable Housing Goals Increased the Supply of Mortgage Credit?" *Regional Science and Urban Economics* 34, 3: 263–73.

Apgar, William, and Shekar Narsimhan. 2007. "Enhancing Access to Capital for Smaller Unsubsidized Multifamily Rental Properties." Prepared for Revisiting Rental Housing: A National Policy Summit, Harvard University, Joint Center for Housing Studies, November 2006.

Center for American Progress. 2009. "Principles to Guide Development and Regulation of a Renewed Mortgage Finance System." Washington, D.C.: Center for American Progress. http://www.americanprogress.org/issues/2009/03/pdf/mortgage_finance_principles.pdf.

Congressional Budget Office. 2010. "CBO's Budgetary Treatment of Fannie Mae and Freddie Mac." Washington, D.C.: Congressional Budget Office. http://www.cbo.gov/ftpdocs/108xx/doc10878/01-13-FannieFreddie.pdf.

Credit Suisse. 2009. "GSEs—Still the Best Answer for Housing Finance," Mortgage Market Comment, October 6. Washington, D.C.: Credit Suisse Group.

DiPasquale, Denise, and Jean L. Cummings. 1992. "Financing Multifamily Rental Housing: The Changing Role of Lenders and Investors." *Housing Policy Debate* 3, 1: 77–115.

Fannie Mae Charter. 1992. 12 U.S.C. 1716 et seq., as amended through October 28, 1992, http://www.fanniemae.com/global/pdf/aboutfm/understanding/charter. pdf.

Federal Deposit Insurance Corporation. 2008. "Covered Bond Policy Statement." 73 Fed. Reg. 21949, April 23. Washington, D.C.: FDIC. http://www.fdic.gov/regulations/ laws/rules/5000-1550.html.

Flannery, Mark J., and W. Scott Frame. 2006. "The Federal Home Loan Bank System: The 'Other' Housing GSE." *Federal Reserve Bank of Atlanta Economic Review* 91, 3: 33–54.

Garrett, Scott. 2008. "Garrett Introduces Equal Treatment for Covered Bonds Act." Press Release, July 30. Office of Congressman Scott Garrett. http://garrett.house. gov/News/DocumentSingle.aspx?DocumentID=99123.

International Monetary Fund. 2006. "Denmark: Financial Sector Assessment Program—Technical Note—The Danish Mortgage Market—A Comparative Analysis." IMF Country Report 07/123. Washington, D.C.: International Monetary Fund. http://www.imf.org/external/pubs/ft/scr/2007/cr07123.pdf.

Joint Center for Housing Studies. 2009. "Meeting Multifamily Housing Finance Needs During and After the Credit Crisis." Cambridge, Mass.: Joint Center for Housing Studies, Harvard University.

Lappin, Michael D. 2001. Statement Before the Millennial Housing Commission. New York City, July 24.

Levitin, Adam, and Susan Wachter. 2010. "Information Failures in the U.S. Housing Market." Presentation at Rethink, Recover, Rebuild: Reinventing Older Communities, Federal Reserve Bank of Philadelphia, May 12–14, http://www.phil. frb.org/community-development/events/reinventing-2010/presentations/levitin- wachter_information-failures-US-mortgage-market.pdf.

Lucas, Douglas J., Frank J. Fabozzi, Laurie S. Goodman, Andrea Montanari, and Armin Peter. 2008. "Covered Bonds: A New Source of U.S. Mortgage Loan Funding?" *Journal of Structured Finance* 14, 3: 44–8.

Millennial Housing Commission. 2002. "Meeting Our Nation's Housing Challenges." Report of Bipartisan Millennial Housing Commission. Washington, D.C.: Millennial Housing Commission. http://govinfo.library.unt.edu/mhc/MHCReport. pdf.

Mortgage Bankers Association. 2009a. "MBA's Recommendations for the Future Government Role in the Core Secondary Mortgage Market." Washington, D.C.: Mortgage Bankers Association. http://www.mbaa.org/files/Advocacy/2009/ RecommendationsfortheFutureGovernmentRole.pdf.

———. 2009b. "Principles for Ensuring Mortgage Liquidity." Washington, D.C.: Mortgage Bankers Association.

Mortgage Finance Working Group. 2009. "A Responsible Market for Housing Finance." Draft White Paper of the Future of the U.S. Secondary Market for Residential Mortgages. Washington, D.C.: Center for American Progress. http://www.americanprogress.org/issues/2009/12/pdf/housing_finance.pdf.

National Association of Realtors. 2009. "Recommendations for Restructuring the GSEs." Chicago: National Association of Realtors. http://www.realtor.org/wps/wcm/connect/430e5f80418e341a9039fda3819af93a/government_affairs_2009_gse_Ref_recomm_121609.pdf?MOD=AJPERES&CACHEID=430e5f80418e341a9039fda3819af93a.

Peek, Joe, and James A. Wilcox. 2006. "Housing, Credit Constraints, and Macro Stability: The Secondary Mortgage Market and Reduced Cyclicality of Residential Investment." Working Paper 298. Berkeley: Fisher Center for Real Estate and Urban Economics, University of California.

Quigley, John M. 2006. "Federal Credit and Insurance Programs: Housing." *Federal Reserve Bank of St. Louis Review* 88, 4: 1–29.

Reed, Anthony T. 2010. Testimony on Behalf of the Housing Policy Council of the Financial Services Roundtable, Before the House Financial Services Committee of the U.S. House of Representatives, April 14.

Reiss, David. 2008. "The Federal Government's Implied Guarantee of Fannie Mae and Freddie Mac's Obligations: Uncle Sam Will Pick up the Tab." *Georgia Law Review* 42: 1019–81.

Schuetz, Jenny, Vicki Been, and Ingrid Gould Ellen. 2009. "Neighborhood Effects of Concentrated Foreclosures." *Journal of Housing Economics* 17, 4: 306–19.

Segal, William, and Edward J. Szymanoski. 1997. "The Multifamily Secondary Mortgage Market: the Role of Government Sponsored Enterprises." Working Paper HF-002. Washington, D.C.: Office of Policy Development and Research, U.S. Department of Housing and Urban Development.

Small, David H., and James A. Clouse. 2004. "The Scope of Monetary Policy Actions Authorized Under the Federal Reserve Act." FEDS Working Paper 2004-40 (July). http://ssrn.com/abstract=622342.

Soros, George. 2008. "A Danish Fix for the U.S. Mortgage Market." *Financial Times*, August 11, http://www.georgesoros.com/articles-essays/entry/a_danish_fix_for_the_us_mortgage_crisis/.

U.S. Department of the Treasury. 2008. "Best Practices for Residential Covered Bonds." Washington, D.C.: U.S. Department of the Treasury. http://www.ustreas.gov/press/releases/reports/USCoveredBondBestPractices.pdf.

U.S. General Accounting Office. 1997. "Potential Effects of Reducing FHA's Insurance Coverage for Home Mortgages." Report to the Chairman, Subcommittee on Housing and Community Opportunity, House Committee on Banking and Financial Services. http://www.gao.gov/archive/1997/rc97093.pdf.

Willis, Mark A. 2009. "It's the Rating Stupid: A Banker's Perspective on the CRA." In *Revisiting the CRA: Perspectives on the Future of the Community Reinvestment Act*, ed. Prabal Chakrabarti, David Erikson, Ron S. Essene, Ian Galloway, and John Olson, Boston: Federal Reserve Banks of Boston and San Francisco. 59–70.

Woodward, Susan, and Robert Hall. 2009. "What to Do About Fannie Mae and Freddie Mac?" Financial Crisis and Recession: Economic Analysis by Susan Woodward and Robert Hall, January 28, http://woodwardhall.wordpress.com/2009/01/28/what-to-do-about-fannie-mae-and-freddie-mac.

Notes

1. The Federal Home Loan Banks are also GSEs, but we use the term "GSEs" to refer only to Fannie Mae and Freddie Mac.

2. Offering financing across the country does not necessarily mean that mortgages should be priced identically across the country. The cost to borrowers also needs to reflect local variations in such factors as the foreclosure process and the ability of the mortgagee to collect personally on the debt. The costs of such variations in risk and servicing costs should be built into the price of a mortgage; otherwise, some borrowers will get somewhat of a free ride by being able to shift these incremental costs onto others.

3. It is possible that the Federal Reserve could provide such liquidity, but its ability to purchase non-government-backed securities appears limited (Small and Clouse 2004). Alternatively, it is possible that the federal government could create a separate entity to buy MBSs and the Federal Reserve could then loan funds to that entity.

4. In retrospect, the temporary explosion of a highly liquid market for non-agency securities was made possible by a failure to understand properly the risk inherent in the products backing those securities. The liquidity available in this market evaporated at the onset of the subprime bust and overall credit crunch.

5. See Chapter 1 for a description of the TBA market.

6. For example, the Government National Mortgage Association, known as Ginnie Mae, helped to standardize the market for its MBSs (backed by standard FHA and VA mortgage products). By contrast, the government left it to Fannie Mae and Freddie Mac to standardize the market for their own securities and their own mortgage products.

7. The situation is somewhat different for Ginnie Mae, since the mortgages in its securities are insured or guaranteed by other government agencies, which oversee the quality of those mortgages. While FHA insurance covers essentially all of the losses from a foreclosure, the VA's guarantee covers only 25–50 percent of the original loan amount (U.S. GAO 1997).

8. Most commentators assume that successors to the GSEs will pool loans, sell securities, and absorb all losses ahead of the government wrap. In fact, these tasks could be performed by separate entities.

9. "Ginnie Mae securitizes already federally insured mortgages made through FHA. The additional guarantee of timely payment of interest and principal from Ginnie Mae was a small extension of the federal backing. But the results were dramatic: the creation of Ginnie Mae lowered FHA borrowing rates by sixty to eighty basis points. With the real, long-term mortgage interest rates in the region of 4 to 5 percent, this was a large, not small, change. This seemingly small transformation of a federally-insured mortgage into a federally-insured liquid security made a big change in the cost of homeownership" (Woodward and Hall 2009).

10. Any pricing advantage will be reduced to the extent to which other large mortgage originators or MBS issuers are judged by the capital markets as being "too big to fail" and so also receive favorable pricing for their debt.

11. Policymakers might choose to vary the cap on loan size by region, depending on the median cost of a home.

12. Of course, implicit guarantees are not free either, even if they are not called upon. Studies suggest that the U.S. government pays higher interest rates on its own debt than it would if the GSEs were fully private, because investors consider the GSEs corporate debt as an implied obligation of the U.S. government (Ambrose and Dolly King 2002).

13. See Quigley (2006) for a summary of studies that provided estimates of the mortgage subsidy to homeowners as well as the yield spreads for the GSEs.

14. One possible option to build into a regulatory scheme to promote product innovation may be to explicitly allow for the testing of new products on a pilot basis to ascertain how they will perform over time. Those that perform well enough could then be approved for more general use. Another option may be to set up a special fund to promote innovation.

15. A number of recent studies have found that foreclosed and abandoned properties also have a number of negative externalities, including depressing the property values of surrounding properties and interfering with the education of the children in the families being displaced (Schuetz, Been, and Ellen 2009).

16. The Community Reinvestment Act places an affirmative obligation (sometimes also referred to as a "duty to serve") on banks to help meet the credit needs of lower-income communities consistent with safety and soundness (see Willis 2009).

17. The loans vary, for example, as to type of collateral, amortization schedule, and subordinated financing layers. There is a lack of generally available information about the historical performance of similar loans (see Segal and Szymanoski 1997).

18. By 2008, Fannie and Freddie accounted for almost one third of outstanding multi-family debt (Joint Center for Housing Studies 2009). While the FHA also accounts for a significant share of the market, the presence of Fannie and Freddie help to ensure that the affordable rental finance market is well served.

19. Ambrose and Thibodeau (2004) show that targeted portfolio purchases of low- and moderate-income mortgages can help to increase the supply of low-income mortgage credit.

20. For example, before conservatorship, five of the eighteen members of the GSE boards were appointed by the President of the United States. See, for example, Fannie Mae Charter 1992: §308(b).

21. Under existing law, the mechanism for folding Fannie and Freddie would be receivership, which would determine a value for the common stock now held by private shareholders.

22. To address the chronic challenges at the FHA, the Millennial Housing Commission (2002) recommended that Congress restructure the FHA to be a wholly owned government corporation within HUD to allow it to make programmatic adjustments without legislative approval.

23. The authors note that the structure of the FHLBs did not necessarily lead to less risk taking than that of the GSEs.

24. The federal home loan banks mitigate the potential problem that its largest members will capture the cooperative by placing limits on the maximum voting rights of any individual member, regardless of its size (see Flannery and Frame 2006).

25. For further elaboration on this idea, see Lappin (2001).

26. The Mortgage Insurance Fund is capitalized by an insurance fee as well as proceeds from the state's mortgage recording tax.

27. "There are eight mortgage credit institutions active in the Danish mortgage market, some affiliated with commercial banks (DLR, LR, Nordea Kredit, RealKredit Danmark, FIH), others operating on a standalone basis, as foundations (BRFKredit, NykreditRealkredit)" (International Monetary Fund 2006: 4).

Chapter 14

Some Thoughts on What to Do
with Fannie Mae and Freddie Mac

Robert Van Order

We have some time to decide on what to with the Federal National Mortgage Association (Fannie Mae) and the Federal Home Loan Mortgage Corporation (Freddie Mac). They, along with the Government National Mortgage Association (Ginnie Mae), are almost all of the market, and no one is going to mess with that any time soon. But something will have to be done. Looking ahead, we need to think about not only what to do with Fannie and Freddie, but also what to do with the whole housing finance system, particularly where the risks will go. Problems of credit risk in mortgage markets would not go away if Fannie and Freddie were gone. Someone else would take on the risks of mortgages, and there is no reason to expect them to do better. Shifting from government-sponsored entities (GSEs) such as Fannie and Freddie to government-guaranteed banks is not an obvious way to diminish costs to taxpayers, and reliance on private-label securitization is not an obviously better way of controlling credit crises.

The two central policy issues are how particular systems affect resource allocation in normal times and system risk when times are bad. These are similar but different issues. The first, micro, issue refers to incentives for pricing and risk-taking as they affect long-term investment in housing versus other investment and allocation of housing among households. For instance, guarantees tend to distort resource allocation by inducing risk-taking and directing too many resources to the benefiting sector (in this case housing) and risking bailout costs. The second, macro, issue refers to spillovers from housing finance markets to the rest of the financial system and the risk of a major recession (or worse).

An important point of comparison is the savings and loan (S&L) failures of the 1980s. It does not appear that, relative to the size of the economy, credit losses by S&Ls or bailout costs were much different from likely costs now. Many of the incentive problems that we see now were apparent then: S&Ls had incentives to take on risk and allocate too much capital to the sectors to which they lent. However, there was nowhere near the systemic collapse that we have been seeing; it was barely a blip on the screen for the economy as a whole. Apparently, the first issue was a bigger deal in the S&L crisis than was the second.

Agency Costs and Dueling Charters

The point of departure is the Modigliani-Miller Irrelevance Theorem (MM) (see Modigliani and Miller 1958). The theorem is that under a set of assumptions, which mainly involve competitive markets, low transaction costs, and widely agreed-upon information, the liability structure of the firm is irrelevant in the sense that changing the way the firm finances its assets will not affect its all-in cost of funds or ultimate resource allocation. This is because different liability strategies are simply different ways of rearranging the same cash flows from the firm's assets, and in a well-informed, competitive market, competition will ensure that all structures will be priced so that none has an overall advantage. The sum of the parts will equal the whole.

The theorem applied to mortgage markets implies that while there are lots of possible institutional structures for funding mortgages and lots of liability structures within the institutional structures, which institutions and structures are chosen does not affect mortgage rates because they are all paid from the same cash flows. For instance, banks that raise funds via deposits and securitizers, such as Fannie and Freddie, that raise money in capital markets have the same all-in costs.[1]

If that is the case, then the way in which we regulate institutions and the incentives with which we provide them are more important than the institutions themselves. However, it is also the case that because there is a plethora of viable institutions, regulation of one type of institution might only shift problems and risks to one of the other institutions. In particular, regulating the risks of GSEs might cause risks to migrate to banks.

MM is one of those ideas that, when you think about it, is obvious but wrong. Markets aren't perfect, though they're often rather good; asymmetric information (and, behind it, moral hazard) is often the rule rather than the exception; transaction costs matter, and subsidies distort relative revenues and costs. But it is not a bad first approximation, and it is a good place to start because it makes us ask the right question: why should we expect one institutional setup to be better than another at financing a particular set of cash flows when they all compete in the same overall financial system? In particular, it suggests that some reasons for particular structures, such as "getting assets off balance sheet," "the high cost of capital relative to debt," or "allowing banks to shed the risk of low down payment loans" are wrong— or at least suspect—pending analysis of what part of MM is violated.

Securitization and Dueling Charters

Broadly speaking, there are two models for funding mortgages: the portfolio lender model, which entails financial institutions (e.g., banks) originating and holding loans in their portfolio and funding them with debt (deposits), and the securitization model, which entails buying loans and putting them into pools and selling (perhaps structured) shares in the pools to capital market investors. Many of the current financial arrangements are combinations of the two. The easiest way of looking at the two models is to think of them as applying to archetypical institutions called "banks" and "securitizers" and to view the rules and benefits that apply to them as their "charters."

There is a trade-off between the advantages and disadvantages of securitization. Securitization provides, relative to bank deposits, a low cost and elastic source of funds from the capital market, but it has agency costs because of information asymmetry between investors (or whoever takes on the credit risk or, like rating agencies, evaluates the risks) and loan originators. Both structures have transactions costs; for instance, banks have costs of running branches and the things necessary to attract depositors, and securitization has costs of setting up and marketing deals as well as costs of monitoring agents' behavior. Competitive balance between the charters depends on the balance of the preceding costs as well as implicit and explicit subsidies, particularly in the form of guarantees. This is further complicated because the neat division between deposit and securities markets no longer holds; banks and "shadow banks" raise money from capital markets too.

Guarantees have been a central aspect of both charters. This began in earnest with the Great Depression and federal deposit insurance. Fannie and Freddie can be best understood within the deposit insurance framework: Their status as GSEs has given them an implicit guarantee that is similar in function to deposit insurance, and they have used this guarantee to compete with banks. This competition has been referred to as "dueling charters" (see Van Order 2000a).

Over the past decade, particularly since 2003, a third (after banks and the agencies) competitor has emerged: "private-label" or "non-agency" securitizers, which are mainly investment and mortgage banks that securitize mortgages that are generally not eligible for agency securitization. That market was not new, but its share increased sharply after 2003, and it has been the major source of problems in the mortgage markets.

As a result, until recently (the private-label market is more or less gone now), there were three charters. All three generated asymmetric information and moral hazard problems because of options to take on risk that was not known to major stakeholders.[2] In the case of Fannie and Freddie and banks, the problems came via guarantees and the inability of guarantors and regulators to assess and control risk quickly. In the private-label market, the problems were due to the option to fool the stakeholders (investors in and insurers of private-label securities) that accept credit risk.

So where does MM fit into this? In the pre-Fannie and Freddie world in the United States, where banks (S&Ls) did most of the mortgage lending, transaction costs and asymmetries were more or less the same for everyone, as were regulations. In that world, MM was violated because holding less capital lowered all-in costs to the banks because it allowed better exploitation of the deposit insurance guarantee. A manifestation of this was the S&L crisis in the 1980s. The violations of MM (low cost guarantees) probably caused too many resources to go to housing (in the absence of positive social externalities for the sector), but they also prevented panics.

The advent of Fannie and Freddie didn't add or subtract much in terms of the existence of guarantees, but it changed the types of guarantees and the possible ways of operating and exploiting the guarantees by allowing institutions to get access to the bond market through mortgage-backed securities (MBSs). These markets have lower transaction costs, a more elastic supply of funds, and a better way of managing interest-rate risk. But Fannie and Freddie were forced, because they were secondary markets, to take on some asymmetric information problems that banks did not have to take on.

So MM was still violated but in different ways, albeit still with a guarantee. The Fannie and Freddie dominance most likely had to do with access to guarantees in long-term debt markets, which made it easier to fund fixed-rate mortgages (Fannie and Freddie never had a big share of adjustable-rate mortgages, or ARMs) than the traditional deposit market for banks (but see note 1). This, too, distorted resource allocation. That Fannie and Freddie had a guarantee helped to control the spread of credit-risk problems to other markets but not as firmly as deposit insurance had; the government had to take over the companies and inject capital to make the implicit guarantee credible and to prevent an incipient panic in September 2008.

The private-label market was largely unburdened by regulation and (perceived) guarantees. It violated MM because of access to capital markets during a time when property-value increases put credit risk into the background and allowed moral hazard and asymmetric information on steroids. This almost certainly distorted resource allocation too,[3] but without a guarantee, it was the main factor in the spread of problems in housing to the rest of the financial system (Gorton 2008).

So why might banks or GSEs matter? First, both get subsidies, in particular in the form of underpriced implicit and explicit guarantees, and having a subsidy matters. Second, GSEs can matter because they get to spend their subsidy in the bond market rather than the deposit market. Third, banks can matter because they tend to have an informational advantage over GSEs.

Recent History

Fannie and Freddie have been losing money for about three years. Major sources of the loss are the following:

- Purchases of Alt-A (and interest-only and option ARM) loans, loans to seemingly "prime" borrowers but without full documentation.
- The sharp decline in house prices, particularly in places such as California, Arizona, Nevada, and Florida, which have left a historically unprecedented share of borrowers with negative equity.

- Defaults on senior pieces of private-label asset-backed securities (ABSs), especially those made up of subprime loans, which were originally rated AAA but have been severely downgraded and fallen in value.

The extent of losses from private-label securities is hard to assess because a large part of the decline in market value of the securities is a liquidity problem as well as a credit problem, and it will take some time to see the extent to which losses have exceeded the securities' subordination. The first two sources of loss are complicated because they are intertwined. The acceleration in Alt-A purchases happened at or around the peak in house prices and tended to be concentrated in the then rapidly growing states. Hence they also had much higher than average levels of negative equity.

The main characteristics of recent history are as follows:

- Foreclosure rates accelerated sharply after 2005 (Figure 14.1).
- All product types have been affected by the recent surge in foreclosures, but subprime loans have been much worse (Figure 14.2).
- Property values, which had already been increasing at an above-average pace, accelerated after 2003 (Figure 14.3).
- The market share of subprime and Alt-A loans rose dramatically after 2003 (Table 14.1), and the market share of the GSEs fell (Table 14.2).
- At the same time, the non-agency (not Fannie, Freddie, or Ginnie, especially subprime and Alt-A) share of securitization grew very rapidly (Figure 14.4).

The year 2003 was pivotal. Around that time, strong markets turned into bubble markets. Then the subprime and Alt-A markets and their subprime securitization grew very rapidly—in retrospect much faster than what was consistent with minimal quality standards. Around 2006, the price bubble burst, and housing production, which had accelerated in response to the increase in prices, fell sharply. In 2007, the subprime and Alt-A markets crashed, which exposed banks and the GSEs to major write-downs and was the major source of the worldwide recession.

In 2003, Fannie Mae and Freddie Mac accounted for 52.3 percent of all residential mortgage loans. Within three years, their share of total outstanding mortgage debt (retained portfolio plus net MBSs outstanding) had fallen to 44 percent. During this period, their retained portfolios declined

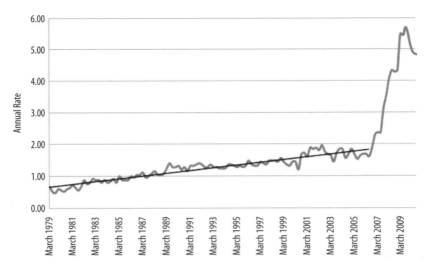

Figure 14.1. All foreclosures started: 1979–2009 quarterly data. Mortgage Bankers Association.

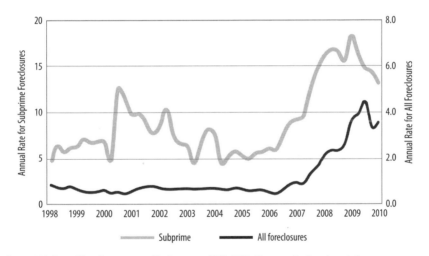

Figure 14.2. Rate of foreclosures started by loan type: 1998–2010. Mortgage Bankers Association.

to 13.6 percent of the total mortgage market from 23 percent in 2003 (see Table 14.1).

As the mortgage market shifted toward non-agency ABSs, Fannie and Freddie became major investors in these securities, particularly in 2003 and 2004. According to some, including their current regulator, Fannie and Freddie were major buyers of ABSs collateralized by subprime mortgages

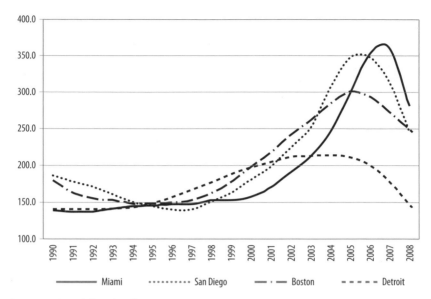

Figure 14.3. Case-Shiller index of house prices in various cities: 1990–2008.

Table 14.1. GSE Share of Mortgage Holdings (billions of dollars)

	Fannie Mae		Freddie Mac		Total Book of Business	Total Mortgage Debt	GSE Share (%)
	Portfolio	Net MBS	Portfolio	Net MBS			
1998	415.2	637.1	255.0	478.4	1,786	4,056	44.0
1999	705.2	858.9	491.7	646.4	2,702	5,325	50.7
2002	790.8	1,029.5	568.2	742.9	3,131	6,034	51.9
2003	898.4	1,300.2	645.5	752.2	3,596	6,882	52.3
2004	904.6	1,402.8	653.6	852.0	3,813	7,838	48.6
2005	727.2	1,598.1	710.0	974.2	4,009	8,866	45.2
2006	724.4	1,780.1	703.6	1,122.8	4,331	9,854	44.0
2007	724.0	2,165.6	720.8	1,381.9	4,992	10,509	47.5

because these securities were "goals rich" (Lockhart 2009). Fannie and Freddie were required to meet affordable housing goals, set by the Department of Housing and Urban Development. The purchase of non-agency ABSs backed by subprime mortgages counted toward meeting these goals to the extent to which the underlying mortgages were made to borrowers who were covered by the goals.

Table 14.2. Market Shares of Single-Family Originations by Loan Type

Year	FHA and VA (%)	Conventional Conforming (%)	Jumbo (%)	Subprime (%)	Alt-A (%)	Home Equity Loans (%)	Total (billions of dollars)
2001	7.4	57.2	19.4	8.6	2.7	4.6	2,215
2002	6.4	59.3	20.0	8.0	2.4	3.9	2,885
2003	5.8	62.4	16.6	8.5	2.2	4.6	3,945
2004	4.6	41.4	17.6	18.5	6.8	11.0	2,920
2005	2.7	35.0	18.3	20.0	12.5	11.5	3,120

Inside Mortgage Finance. *2006 Mortgage Market Annual*, vol. 1.

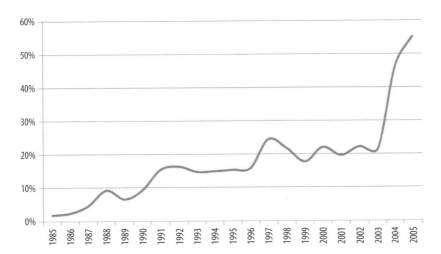

Figure 14.4. Market share of non-agency (not Fannie Mae, Freddie Mac, or Ginnie Mae) securitization: 1985–2005. Inside Mortgage Finance. *2006 Mortgage Market Annual*, vol. 1.

A typical non-agency ABS involves a "waterfall" payment structure. Instead of a traditional pass-through, the ABS note holders are paid according to their seniority, with senior tranches getting paid first and suffering losses from defaults on the underlying collateral, if any, last. The subordination ahead of them functions like capital in a bank holding the same assets. The size of the tranches is chosen to achieve AAA ratings on the senior portion, with the amount of subordinated securities adjusted as necessary to provide the overcollateralization required by rating agencies (see Hu 2007).

Fannie and Freddie were major buyers of the AAA pieces of the ABSs. The subordinated pieces were then generally sold into collateralized debt obligation (CDO) pools. According to Freddie Mac's 2006 annual report, "more than 99.9 percent" of its non-agency ABS were rated AAA. Neither GSE had any exposure to CDOs (Lockhart 2007). The recent Conservator's Report from their regulator (FHFA 2010) suggests that losses on subprime securities overall will be a small part (less than 10 percent) of their overall losses since 2008 and that the first wave of purchases in 2003 and 2004 did not experience significant losses, largely because of subordination and house price growth.[4]

Their market share of risk-taking was not increased by their 2003–2004 purchases. In general, the risk in private-label securities was concentrated in subordinated pieces that were largely funded in the CDO market. In addition to purchasing the AAA pieces of non-agency ABS, Fannie and Freddie began buying nontraditional mortgages in 2005 in an effort to regain market share. Both GSEs' 2005 annual reports lament their declining relevance in the mortgage markets and cite the growth of private-label securities as the biggest threat to their future (Fannie Mae 2005: 25; Freddie Mac 2005: 42). Beginning around 2005, Fannie and Freddie added significant exposure to Alt-A and other nontraditional loans, such as interest-only mortgages and option ARMs.[5] The decision to lower underwriting standards seems to have been driven by a decision to win back market share from the "private-label" issuers, as Fannie and Freddie referred to them in their 2005 and 2006 10-K filings.

The banks and private-label securitizers generally performed worse than Fannie and Freddie. Fannie and Freddie have had default rates that were generally lower than those of the rest of the industry across products and origination years (Table 14.3). From the third quarter of 2007 through the fourth quarter of 2008, Fannie and Freddie had $119 billion in write-offs, compared to $145 billion for insurance companies and $747 billion for commercial and investment banks (see Davidson and Sanders 2009). More recently, the IMF has estimated that overall write-downs from U.S. securities have been well over $2 trillion, about 20 times the write-downs for Fannie and Freddie.[6] Nonetheless, Fannie and Freddie did not have the capital to survive their losses, which is what led to their conservatorship in September 2008.

Unlike the S&L crisis in the 1980s, the current crisis has spread around the world, even though overall mortgage credit losses relative to the size of the economy do not appear to be much bigger. A key difference between now

Table 14.3. Percentage of Loans Seriously Delinquent as of June 30, 2009

	Fannie Mae (%)	Freddie Mac (%)	National Average (%)
Total	3.94	2.89	7.97
Prime	2.47	2.13	5.44
Subprime	21.75	14.21	26.52
Alt-A	11.91	9.44	17.0
< FICO620	13.07	10.74	17.7

LP data and N.Y. Fed.

and then is that the S&Ls were funded almost entirely by insured deposits, so there was little need for the ultimate funders, depositors, to worry and little spillover.

This is in contrast to the complexity of the securitization and resecuritization of non-prime mortgages, which has made it very hard to evaluate the securities and the health of the institutions that hold them (see Gorton 2008). Banks and "shadow banks" today fund their lending with commercial paper, loans from other banks, and repurchase agreements (repos) as well as with deposits, and they set up off-balance-sheet deals that they are sometimes obligated to buy back if things go wrong. Once banks' ability to pay off their obligations and/or the GSE guarantee is called into question, there can be the equivalent of a bank run, albeit not on deposits. As asset values decline and loan loss reserves increase, capital ratios (the ratio of net worth to assets) fall. Even if capital ratios are positive, they can put institutions in a position in which, absent new capital injections, they have to contract lending.

Policy Going Forward

There are five ways that housing finance will get done in the United States:

1. Banks with explicit guarantees on deposits and sometimes implicit guarantees on other liabilities
2. GSEs, such as a revived version of Fannie and Freddie with implicit guarantees but altered parameters, such as stronger capital requirements

3. GSEs with sharply altered charters, such as a public utility or collective model or separating portfolio and guarantee functions into separate institutions
4. Non-agency (not Fannie, Freddie, or Ginnie) securitization by institutions that have turned out to be implicit GSEs with implicit guarantees in emergencies
5. Government-owned institutions like Ginnie Mae with full guarantees

These options all have benefits and costs, and none get taxpayers entirely off the hook. The fourth is the closest thing to private (without guarantee). It runs the risk of fragility—and of bailouts anyway. The first has many similarities to Fannie and Freddie. Both have incentives for risk-taking and risk of bailout. The last presents the problems of government management and inflexibility (e.g., pricing by both the Federal Housing Administration and Ginnie Mae is fixed by statute), and it is not clear that there is less risk. The second and third points address the degree and the manner of restructuring the GSEs. None of the structures is obviously dominant.

The preceding discussion of MM suggests that all of these are probably feasible structures. What is important is regulation and incentives.

Things to Think About for Whatever Institutions Emerge

Overall

Guarantees are likely to distort resource allocation in the long run by providing subsidies to those who get them and directing too much capital into the benefiting industries—in this case, housing. This is not completely certain (see Van Order 2000b) because there are "second best" arguments in favor of extending guarantees. From a more macro perspective, guarantees have important advantages because they mitigate financial panics (see Gorton 2009). This cycle has shown that guarantees are likely to be with us in one form or another.

Fannie and Freddie were not "fatally flawed" or "accidents waiting to happen." Their charters were not all that different from those of banks, and their risk-taking and ultimate cost to the government (adjusted for size of the economy) probably will be no greater than those of the S&Ls in the

1980s. Nor were Fannie and Freddie prone to taking on more risk than the market in general.

The main problems, economy-wide, were a price bubble, which took off while Fannie's and Freddie's market shares were falling, and a panic in the shadow banking system, not in Fannie and Freddie securities (firming up the implicit guarantee took care of that). Fannie and Freddie did not have the capital to survive the decline in property values beginning around 2006, and they ramped up their risk-taking when their market share fell and the franchise was in danger. These are both serious problems, but they are business decisions that are not unique to the GSE structure. The housing goals to which they were subject cannot take much of the blame for their risk-taking, which was mostly in the Alt-A market and which consisted of borrowers with relatively high down payments, loan balances, and credit scores.[7]

So the issue is not as much what to do with Fannie and Freddie as how to regulate and incentivize whatever comes next. There is no reason to believe that Fannie's and Freddie's successors will be automatically immune to the problems that Fannie and Freddie had.

Capital

Whatever we do, we'll need better capital rules. Capital provides a cushion that protects debt holders and guarantors, and it provides incentives to control risk because more investor money is at stake. Before the crisis, Fannie and Freddie had two capital rules applied to them: stress tests that simulated company performance under stressful conditions and required that enough capital be held to survive them and a minimum capital requirement that applied even if they passed the stress tests.

Clearly, the minimum was too low. Fannie and Freddie passed the stress tests, which were stressful by historical standards but less stressful than what actually happened and exacerbated by the low quality of the nonprime, especially Alt-A, loans that they held.[8] Something similar happened with banks and the private-label market. However, simply raising the minimum capital levels is not enough because Fannie and Freddie or banks or private-label issuers can (and probably would) respond by ramping up their risk to match the capital. A solution is to combine stress tests with minimum levels and make the two additive (hold the minimum capital plus the capital required by the stress tests) so that they will have to hold extra capital for any increase in risk. The private-label market may come back only if rating agencies get better at measuring risk.

There are limits to how far we can get by relying on capital ratios and shutting down insolvent institutions. It is very difficult to know whether or not institutions are really insolvent. This is in part because that is a difficult problem but especially because accounting measures of capital are not up to the task. They tend both to overestimate and underestimate net worth, and they tend to be procyclical, requiring institutions to raise capital at exactly the times when this is most difficult. This leaves us with stress tests and manipulating incentives.

Convertible Bonds

A vehicle for manipulating incentives is convertible subordinated debt (sometimes referred to as "conditional convertible" or "Coco bonds") that can be converted into stock if stock price falls below some preset level.[9] These would provide capital at the time when it is most needed without going through bankruptcy or making an insolvency determination, and the automatic conversion would give Coco bond investors a strong interest in risk management (they can't assume a bailout). These bonds would also limit concern about institutions being "too big to fail" because avoiding bankruptcy mitigates concerns about disruptions during bankruptcy.

An important reason for liking Coco bonds is that they address a problem that higher capital ratios cannot easily solve: the problem of banks that are still solvent but with low capital ratios. Suppose that the minimum capital ratio for banks is 5 percent of assets. Banks will keep a cushion above the required level, but not by much because equity is more costly than debt. If a bank's capital ratio falls to, say, 3 percent, it will be solvent but in trouble; it will have to either raise capital or lower assets (lend less) to get back to 5 percent.

In a period in which large numbers of banks are missing their ratios and raising capital is difficult, banks are in the position of having to cut back assets. In the example, getting back to 5 percent by shrinking the balance sheet would mean a 40 percent cut in assets. Otherwise, you need a government program to inject capital. This problem will exist even with higher capital ratios as long as banks keep their ratios just above the minimum. The decline in stock price that accompanies banks' declining asset values will trigger conversion of Coco bonds into stock and move the ratios back up.

Portfolios

Fannie and Freddie, like banks, hold portfolios of mortgages and mortgage-backed securities. These have been widely criticized as too risky, but the criticisms have largely been misdirected. The distinction between what is kept in portfolio and what is sold (securitized as MBS) is an accounting, rather than economic, distinction. Fannie and Freddie take default risk on mortgages whether they are held or sold; their current responsibility for default losses would not have been different if they had securitized everything.

The portfolio issue is interest-rate risk, a problem that arises when assets and liabilities are mismatched, for instance by funding long-term mortgages with short-term debt. Interest-rate risk can be a problem (see Jaffee 2004), but the size of the portfolio is not a good measure of interest-rate risk for two reasons: A very large part of the risk can be hedged, for instance by funding long-term mortgages with long-term debt,[10] and a large amount of risk can be taken in a small portfolio by holding interest-rate derivatives. Furthermore, the issue is becoming moot because current accounting standards seem to require taking MBSs back on the balance sheet anyway. In any event, variations on portfolio lending, from Fannie and Freddie bond issuance to bank portfolios to covered bonds, are all similar and need to be thought of as a whole and not as a separate Fannie and Freddie problem.[11]

Private-Label Markets

Private-label markets are dormant now and probably will not be in the picture anytime soon. But they could come back, and they need to be thought about. They present different problems from those of banks and Fannie and Freddie, but they still present problems. Their guarantees are less direct, occurring only when there is a widespread problem, but that can still be costly. More to the point, the absence of a guarantee makes them more subject to panic (see Gorton 2008) and spread beyond the housing finance system. As a result, as they re-emerge, there will have to be similar rules for equity or equity substitutes, especially for systemically important parts of the system. Note that structuring and subordination provide the same sort of advantage that Coco bonds provide; the question is the level of subordination.

It is likely that we shall not be able to avoid guarantees and bailouts in situations comparable to the recent ones; nor should we want to. While market discipline is generally a good thing and needs to be used as often as possible, it is not always enough in financial markets. When a company produces bad shirts, buyers switch to other brands, and things work themselves out. Financial markets are very information sensitive, and when a company produces a bad financial product, it raises the suspicion that everyone else is producing bad products too, and that can lead to panics, which can have spillovers everywhere else. We are probably best off by trying to set up incentives for all institutions to minimize distortions to resource allocation and to protect both taxpayers and the stability of the financial system and by being prepared to react as well as we possibly can when problems arise.

Policy and Trade-Offs: Let the Charters Duel[12]

The idea from MM is that the institutional structure of mortgage markets (its charters) is less important than its rules and incentives. Good solutions will have to address moral hazard in the market as a whole; otherwise, risk-taking will simply gravitate to wherever it is cheapest to fund. With the demise of the private-label market, Fannie and Freddie (and Ginnie Mae) and the banks are all that is left. Banks have advantages in managing the moral hazard that comes with the "originate to distribute" model of securitization because they do not have to distribute, and they have had the edge on ARMs. Fannie and Freddie, via securitization, have advantages in fixed-rate funding for fixed-rate mortgages through their access to bond markets. Neither advantage is absolute. Banks, for example, can issue covered bonds, which are almost the same as securitization, and they can raise short-term funds in the deposit market and hedge the risk, which is the same as the GSE portfolio. Regarding the originate-to-distribute model, Fannie and Freddie can be allowed to originate loans like banks. More simply, they can require significant recourse from sellers, in the form of reserves set aside until loans have proven themselves, to protect against moral hazard.

A solution is to set regulations that control risk-taking at the banks and GSEs in comparable ways and allow them to duel. This can be done with new institutions or restructured versions of current ones. We don't know which charter is better, and having both is a way of hedging our bets. Fixing one charter and not the other will not decrease moral hazard as much as shift it. So we can try to set subsidies at zero, or at least the same across charters, so that MM is not violated because of policy and then let the economics of the situation prevail.

References

Davidson, Andrew, and Anthony Sanders. 2009. "Securitization After the Fall." Presented at MacArthur Foundation Conference, Laguna Beach, California, February 19–20.

Fannie Mae. 2005. Annual Report. http://www.fanniemae.com/ir/annualreport/index.jhtml.

Federal Housing Finance Agency. 2010. Conservators Report. August 26. http://www.fhfa.gov/webfiles/19585/Conservator's_Report112910.pdf

Freddie Mac. 2005. Annual Report. http://www.freddiemac.com/investors/ar/.

Gerardi, Kristopher, Andreas Lehnert, Shane Sherlund, and Paul Willen. 2008. "Making Sense of the Subprime Crisis." Brookings Papers on Economic Activity. Washington, D.C.: Brookings Institution.

Gorton, Gary. 2008. "The Subprime Panic." Yale ICF Working Paper 08-25. New York: National Bureau of Economic Research.

——.2009. "Slapped in the Face by the Invisible Hand: Banking and the Panic of 2007." Working Paper. New York: National Bureau of Economic Research.

Hu, Jian. "Assessing the Risk of CDOs Backed by Structured Finance Securities: Ratings Agencies Challenges and Solutions." Moody's Investor Service.

International Monetary Fund. 2009. "Executive Summary." Washington, D.C.: International Monetary Fund. http://www.imf.org/external/pubs/ft/gfsr/2009/01/pdf/summary.pdf.

Jaffee, Dwight. 2004. "The Interest Rate Risk of Fannie Mae and Freddie Mac," *Journal of Financial Services Research* 24, 1: 5–29.

Lockhart, James. 2007. "GSE Challenges: Reform and Regulatory Oversight." Presented at MBA's National Secondary Market Conference and Expo 2007, New York, May 21, http://www.mortgagebankers.org/files/CREF/docs/2007/RegulatoryandLegislativeRoundup-JamesB.LockhartIII.pdf.

——. 2009. "FHFA's First Anniversary and Challenges Ahead." Speech at National Press Club, Washington, D.C., July 30. http://www.fhfa.gov/webfiles/14715/FHFA1stAnnSpeechandPPT73009.pdf.

Modigliani, Franco, and Merton H. Miller. 1958. "The Cost of Capital, Corporation Finance, and the Theory of Investment." *American Economic Review* 48, 3: 261–97.

Thomas, Jason. 2010. "An Assessment of Fannie Mae and Freddie Mac's Contribution to the Financial Crisis of 2008." Washington, D.C.: George Washington University

Van Order, Robert. 2000a. "The U.S. Mortgage Market: A Model of Dueling Charters." *Journal of Housing Research* 11, 2: 233–55.

———. 2000b. "The Economics of Fannie Mae and Freddie Mac." *Regulation* 23, 2: 27–33.

Wallison, J. ed., 1999. *Fannie Mae and Freddie Mac: Public Purposes and Private Interests,* Vol. 1. Washington D.C: AEI.

Weicher, John. 2010. "The Affordable Housing Goals, Homeownership and Risk: Some Lessons from Past Efforts to Regulate the GSEs." Paper delivered at Federal Reserve Bank of St. Louis Conference on GSEs, November.

Woodward, Susan, and Robert Hall. 2009. "What to Do About Fannie Mae and Freddie Mac." Financial Crisis and Recession: Economic Analysis by Susan Woodward and Robert Hall, January 28, http://woodwardhall.wordpress.com/2009/01/28/what-to-do-about-fannie-mae-and-freddie-mac.

Notes

1. For example, it might look as though banks have problems making long-term loans because they raise funds in deposit markets at variable short-term rates, creating a maturity mismatch that is avoided by securitization. However, banks can use "swap" transactions to lock in long-term rates and presumably have the same all-in costs as a securitizer and generate the same mortgage rates. If there is a difference (and there probably is), it must have to do with "details" such as transaction costs for swapping, different supply elasticities, and liquidity and regulatory costs.

2. It is important to emphasize that these problems are ubiquitous in financial markets. Information is a scarce resource, and all structures are complicated.

3. How much it was distorted relative to Fannie and Freddie and S&Ls is not clear. For instance, subprime loans were mostly about refinancing existing loans and might have had a smaller effect on resource allocation. But that will require further studies.

4. For instance, Freddie Mac's Form 10-K/A Amendment 1 for 2009 shows stress tests that suggest much lower defaults for loans in private-label securities from 2004 and earlier.

5. On this and for more details on Fannie and Freddie activity, see Thomas (2010).

6. See International Monetary Fund (2009). Note though that write-downs almost certainly overstate likely losses for all investors, including Fannie and Freddie.

7. On the lack of relationship between Alt-A loans and housing goals, see Weicher (2010).

8. A corollary to this is that what happened had little to do with regulations directed at getting Fannie and Freddie to do low-income and minority loans. By and large, Alt-A loans looked like regular prime loans (good credit and high down payments) but with low documentation. This needs further research.

9. An alternative version, currently being tried out in the United Kingdom, is to tie conversion to capital ratios. This can work, but it depends strongly on the accuracy of accounting measures of capital.

10. Special attention does need to be paid to the fact that mortgages have the prepayment option. This can be handled by funding with callable debt, so that the debt can be called when the mortgages are prepaid, or with more complicated hedging instruments.

11. The subprime and Alt-A securities that were a big deal in 2008 were held in portfolio, but the same credit risk exposure could have been had off the balance sheet by resecuritizing the securities. Both companies have done this with their own securities and to some extent with private-label securities.

12. See also Woodward and Hall (2009).

Chapter 15

The Road Not Taken: Our Failure in Redoing the Financial Architecture

Vincent Reinhart

The legislation on financial reform signed by President Barack Obama this year runs over 2,000 pages in length. Its enactment into law changes the scope of permissible activities for financial firms, shifts other activities onto organized exchanges settled in clearinghouses, and limits the scale of bank balance sheets relative to their capital. New responsibilities are given to old agencies, old functions are given to a new agency, and a council of regulators will sit atop it all to identify risks and coordinate responses.

For all the legislation's length, the substantive changes will follow as regulatory agencies write rules to put those sometimes contradictory instructions into practice. When it is done, the nation's financial leadership will not have materially reduced either the odds or the amplitude of the next financial crisis.

This was a missed opportunity as historically significant as the crisis itself.

This failure follows from a misdiagnosis of the root cause of the crisis. Financial institutions and markets amplified the stresses in housing because intermediaries had issued complicated mortgage-related securities and parked residual risk on their own opaque balance sheets. Financial engineering exploited weaknesses in regulation and accounting rules by creating off-balance-sheet entities. And final investors were encouraged to hold mortgage-related products through official suasion.

The most important incentive to the creation of this complexity and size has been the unwillingness of authorities to let institutions that are deemed to be systemically important fail. An opaque balance sheet with uncertain linkages to other firms provides its own protection. At a time of stress, government officials would rather put taxpayer funds at risk than test the resilience of the financial system through the failure of a large, complex entity. Thus managers of the biggest firms were given a strong incentive to stay big, intricate, and opaque.

The net result was that balance sheets became uninformative about the risk-taking of financial firms. This made effective supervision impossible, blunted market discipline, and hindered internal controls within the firms themselves. The rabbit warren that the financial system has become hid many risks from regulators, counterparties, and managers of large firms. It also made the ground less secure when the housing shock hit.

The Dodd-Frank Wall Street Reform and Consumer Protection Act financial reform legislation of 2010 focuses on activities within the existing set-up of the financial system. Some activities formerly done in banks—notably proprietary trading and some derivatives operations—must be moved off the balance sheet. More activities at more institutions will be under the scrutiny of regulators. And financial authorities will have powers to wind down more institutions.

But the incentive to do most of those activities remains intact. In a market economy, this means that those activities will continue to be done. Financial institutions will spin off bits, rename other parts, and make their balance sheets further devoid of meaning. Because the largest of those institutions will remain intricately woven into the fabric of market risk-taking, financial officials will offer them the protection of being "too big to fail," despite the new resolution authority on the books.

Thus the legislative response to this complexity and related failure of regulation has been to make the system more complicated and to rely more on regulation. Indeed, a design principle would seem to be to preserve the status quo of a landscape dominated by large, complex financial intermediaries. More of the same seems a singularly insufficient response to the crisis. This is especially so when compared to the road not taken.

A better result would have been to make it less likely that the government would ever again be put in the position of using public resources to preserve the operations of private entities. This requires eliminating the underlying encouragements to complexity, in terms of both the demand for and supply of complexity. The requirement of simpler and more transparent balance sheets would restore effective supervision, increase market discipline, and tighten internal controls. It would also make officials more confident that an individual firm could fail without bringing down the entire financial system with it.

Such radical simplification might sound, well, radical. But the cost of financial crises is high. This includes the direct outlay of the government, the lingering effect of a sluggish recovery, and the long-term drag associated with a typically inefficient regulatory response. After a crisis, the government invariably raises the costs imposed on financial intermediation. It would be a welcome change to do so in a way that fosters, not inhibits, economic growth. It is also not the road we have taken.

The Demand for and Supply of Complexity

Complexity has been the bane of our financial system for decades and cannot be the solution going forward (see Reinhart 2009). It is a feature both of the largest institutions and of the securities that they have issued and held.

As for institutions, the government provides a powerful incentive for financial firms to be large and interconnected with other firms and markets. This takes the form of having many different depositors or other creditors, having a dominant position in making some market or providing a special service, or having opaque positions in many markets. At a time of stress for the firm, public officials will have serious doubts about letting such an institution fail, fed by fears about a cascade of failures among counterparties expecting repayment, an interruption in some key financial service, or runs on similar institutions. This is the essence of "too big to fail" (as discussed in Stern and Feldman 2004). Creditors and investors of the institution appreciate that the government stands behind them at a time of stress. Thus its equity price is benefited and the terms and availability of credit are more favorable than those for competitors. "Too big to fail" tilts the financial landscape in favor of large firms at the expense of the small and medium-sized institutions that are left to fend for themselves.

As for financial instruments, an elaborate web of economic incentives made some of the securities that were issued over the past decade complicated and opaque. As with any market outcome, it can be thought of as the product of the intersection of the demand for and supply of complexity.

On the demand side, large financial institutions have a footprint in many different jurisdictions, involving overlapping regulations and multiple tax regimes. Gaps in coverage, different definitions of similar activities, and conflicting accounting treatments offer an opportunity to tailor activity to each jurisdiction so as to maximize the scale and scope of services and minimize the tax burden. In particular, the Basel II regulatory framework provides a special incentive to commercial banks to hold highly rated securities. Less capital needs be set aside for such securities commensurate with their lower risk. However, the natural desire of bank managers was to get the highest possible yield within the general category of highly rated securities. The individual attributes of the security—the clarity of the claim, the depth of any secondary market, the responsiveness of its price to a rating change, or the speed to which it could potentially migrate down the ratings ladder—were trumped by the regulatory advantage of its current rating.

But by casting riskiness in terms of a published rating, private firms (the rating agencies) were given a public purpose. It was in the self-interest of financial intermediaries and the rating agencies to construct securities that could provide a higher return while still residing in the broad category of lower risk. These firms were the suppliers of complexity. They burrowed into every nook and cranny of accounting rules and tax codes to construct asset-backed securities that could provide the stamp of the highly rated with a higher yield. This required the effort of legal specialists, accounting experts, and financial engineers. Usually, the solution was to pool a collection of assets together and offer different tranches of claims on their income, from the most likely to be repaid down to a near-equity component. To do so required the balance sheets of large firms to be splintered into a collection of special-purpose vehicles. It also required the cooperation of the ratings agencies, which were paid by the underwriters and often offered consulting services to them. For some complicated asset securitizations, underwriters iterated with raters on details to get the desired outcome, or they went to a competitor rating firm.

As a consequence, securities were issued with no other purpose than extracting as much value as possible from the Basel II Supervisory Accord. The act of creating these highly rated tranches typically left investment banks with the hard-to-sell equity portions. Thus they retained highly levered bets on housing that proved toxic when the full extent of the distress in the housing market became evident.

The Problems of Complexity

The complexity of the financial system introduces three fundamental problems in monitoring behavior.

First, supervisors are at a decided disadvantage in understanding risk-taking and compliance for a firm that might involve dozens of jurisdictions, hundreds of legal entities, and thousands of contractual relationships. Individual instruments offered by such an institution might have been tailored to a small slice of its clientele to take advantage of tax and accounting rules. Its balance sheet might be especially malleable by advances in finance and legal interpretations. And the same risks might be booked in different ways across affiliates, let alone across different institutions, with evident consequences for capital requirements. Indeed, the reliance on self-regulation that is inherent in the Basel II supervisory agreement can be seen as an official admission of defeat: A large complex financial institution cannot be understood from the outside.

But if an institution is so difficult to understand from the outside, how can we expect market discipline to be effective? The second cost of complexity is that the outside discipline of credit counterparties and equity owners is blunted. Creditors are more likely to look to the firm's reputation or to a stamp from a rating agency than at the underlying collateral provided by the financial contract. Equity owners are more likely to defer to senior management, opening the way to compensation abuses and a twisting of incentives to emphasize short-term gains. In this regard, it is probably not an accident that financial firms tend not to be targets for hostile takeovers; their balance sheets are impenetrable from the outside.

Third, the problems in understanding the workings of a complicated firm are not limited to those on the outside. A complicated firm is also difficult to manage. Employers will find it more difficult to monitor employees, especially when staff on the ground have highly specialized expertise in finance, law, and accounting. Simply put, employees who are difficult to monitor cannot be expected to look to the long-term interests of the place where they work. What follows are abuses in matching loans and investments to the appropriate customer and, in some cases, outright fraud.

Note the irony. A firm's effort to take advantage of government-induced distortions by becoming more complicated and by making its instruments more complex lessens the owner's ability to monitor management and management's ability to monitor workers. Market discipline breaks down.

A Potential Solution

Sometimes the answer to a complicated problem is simple, as Alexander found with the Gordian Knot: Cut through the existing tangle of financial regulation. Consolidate federal financial regulators, and assume state responsibilities. Simplify accounting rules and the tax code. Make the components of financial firms modular so that the whole can be split up into basic parts at a time of stress. With simple rules that define lines more sharply, our federal regulators will find enforcement much easier. If firms are more transparent, official supervision will be reinforced by the new-found discipline exercised by shareholders and creditors. And with fewer places of self-interest to hide, employees will be more accountable in their efforts to preserve the longer-term value of their firms.

The consolidation of multiple agencies and the shift of power away from the states to a single federal entity seem daunting. Even harder might be the necessary reduction in the variety of corporate charters and the pruning of the tax code and accounting rules. Indeed, this is an invitation to jurisdictional warfare, with fighting no doubt at the house-to-house level. But a more established set of rules for the resolution of large firms, simplification of regulations generally, and consolidation of supervision specifically should be the aspiration of this Congress.

Considering Consolidation

Among the concerns raised by the specter of consolidation is a practical one: There might be considerable deadweight costs associated with closing existing supervisory agencies and transferring their powers to one winner. Shifting resources could involve waste that might be escalated by bureaucratic infighting. This may be so, but the immediate loss could be mitigated by more intense supervision from the principals (the Congress and the Executive Branch) and has to be weighed against longer-term benefits.

Federal Reserve officials sometimes pose objections to consolidation that are unique to the nation's central bank. In particular, if financial regulatory powers were concentrated, they would not likely be exercised by the Fed. Might such consolidation waste the benefits achieved by having the same officials oversee financial supervision and monetary policy?

Three questions are intertwined in that one. First, should the pooling of responsibilities be examined solely in terms of the complementarities of functions? Second, what are the benefits of knowing about monetary policy when supervising banks? Third, what are the benefits of knowing about supervision when conducting monetary policy?

First, the most useful framework for understanding the role and responsibilities of an independent agency comes from the transactions-cost approach (also known as institutional design) surveyed in Dixit (1998). Essentially, in the United States, the Congress creates an independent agency to write rules and enforce them in areas that require technical competence outside the realm of elected officials or too much detail to be embodied once and for all in legislation. This creates a classic principal-agent problem. In particular, a regulator that is given multiple missions but that is only imperfectly monitored might trade off among the missions in a manner that is not completely conducive to the principals' interest. Giving the central bank dual responsibilities invites potential trading between these missions.

The pooling of responsibilities opens up sources of reputational risk. The public and elected officials view the Federal Reserve in terms of the performance of all its responsibilities. Multiple goals invite multiple opportunities for missteps that damage the Fed's reputation. Compounding the problem are the consequences for the communication of policy as well as its conduct. Public officials have to strike a balance between informing and reassuring the public. This sometimes leads them to shade public statements away from a description of the most likely outcome for events toward a description of the most comfortable one. In talking about the economy, this makes them emphasize fundamentals that are conducive to growth and low inflation rather than near-term risks. Information about industries or firms is even more sensitive. In talking about an industry or firm, this makes them downplay solvency issues. After all, what public official would want to be the trigger for a run? Thus the wider the scope of the responsibilities of an agency, the more likely it is that statements will be emptied of content, to the detriment of its reputation.

Second, the distinction between micro and macro matters. Bank supervision mostly concerns understanding the details of individual balance sheets, the ramifications of law and regulation, and accounting practices. Monetary policy is more about national income determination and inflation pressures. Financial concerns are about the workings of markets and intermediation as a whole. Knowing the details of the national income and product accounts is not obviously transferrable to knowing bank income and balance sheet statements.

Third, any discussion of the benefits to monetary policy from training supervision must place the Fed on the right point along the marginal cost curve of information. True, a central bank that has no expertise in financial markets, institutions, and utilities would work at a disadvantage. But that would not be the Fed if it had been stripped of regulatory powers. As the nation's central bank, the Fed would continue to operate the payments system, shuttling reserves among thousands of institutions to facilitate finance and trade. The Fed would still operate the book-entry system, or the sole registry of ownership of U.S. government securities. As the two panels of Figure 15.1 show, both functions involve recording hundreds of thousands of transactions each day (shown by the bars and measured along the right axis) measured in the trillions of dollars (shown by the line and measured along the left axis).

Moreover, in performing these activities, the Fed often extends credit within the day to financial institutions. These roles give the Fed important insights into institutions, markets, and utilities. The Fed's role as a provider of critical services and essential intra-day credit also gives it a lever to pry information from financial institutions. With that as base, the incremental benefit of retaining supervision appears limited.

Still Too Complex

We have created an intricate, multifaceted terrain of opportunities for financial institutions to lower costs by taking advantage of financial regulations, tax codes, and accounting rules. The result has been the creation of complicated securities held by entities with opaque and complex balance

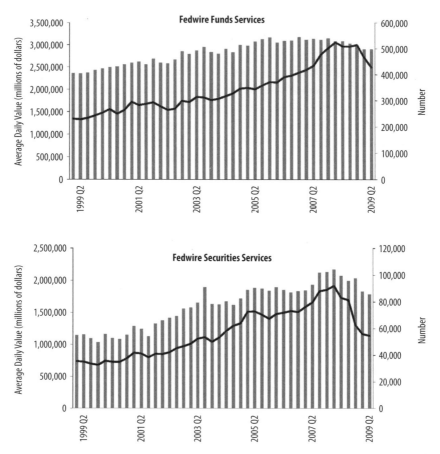

Figure 15.1. Fedwire funds services and Fedwire securities services: 1999–2009. Top panel: http://www.federalreserve.gov/paymentsystems/fedfunds_data.htm; bottom panel: http://www.federalreserve.gov/paymentsystems/fedsecs_data.htm.

sheets. This has made the financial system a transmitter and amplifier of shocks.

The costs are considerable, as is evident from the experience of the past two and a half years. The costs also linger, as is evident from an unemployment rate in the United States that still hovers around 9.5 percent. Less evident are the longer-term costs that will follow in train from the legislated response. The Dodd-Frank Act will not reduce the probability, scale, and scope of the next financial crisis. This is because it does not change incentives for financial institutions to remain complicated. "Too big to fail" will remain a feature of the financial landscape. And a complicated financial system will make supervision difficult, market discipline less effective, and internal controls likely to fail.

References

Bernanke, Ben S. 2010. "The Federal Reserve's Role in Bank Supervision," Testimony Before the House Committee on Financial Services, U.S. House of Representatives, March 17, http://www.federalreserve.gov/newsevents/testimony/bernanke20100317a.htm.

Dixit, Avinash. 1998. *The Making of Economic Policy: A Transaction Cost Politics Perspective*. Cambridge, Mass.: MIT Press.

Reinhart, Vincent. 2009. "For Best Results, Simplify." Testimony Before the Senate Banking Committee, July 23, http://www.aei.org/speech/100069.

Stern, Gary H., and Ron J. Feldman. 2004. *Too Big to Fail: The Hazards of Bank Bailouts*. Washington, D.C.: Brookings Institution Press.

Note

I thank Carmen Reinhart for helpful comments and discussions. Adam Paul and Rohan Poojara provided excellent research assistance. The views in this paper solely represent those of the author and do not necessarily reflect those of the American Enterprise Institute or its staff.

Contributors

Michael S. Barr is a professor at the University of Michigan Law School and co-founded the International Transactions Clinic. He was on leave from 2009–2010, serving as the U.S. Department of the Treasury's Assistant Secretary for Financial Institutions. He has previously served as a senior fellow at the Center for American Progress and at the Brookings Institution; as Treasury Secretary Robert E. Rubin's Special Assistant; as Deputy Assistant Secretary of the Treasury; as Special Advisor to President William J. Clinton; as a special advisor and counselor on the policy planning staff at the State Department; and as a law clerk to U.S. Supreme Court Justice David H. Souter and then-District Court Judge Pierre N. Leval, of the Southern District of New York. Barr received his JD from Yale Law School and an M.Phil in international relations from Magdalen College, Oxford University, as a Rhodes scholar.

Paul S. Calem is a senior economist at the Board of Governors of the Federal Reserve System in the Division of Banking Supervision and Regulation. He provides quantitative support for bank examinations in the areas of mortgage and retail credit risk and regulatory capital, provides policy analysis related to bank capital regulation and banking supervision, and conducts microeconomic research on mortgage markets, retail credit risk, and bank capital regulation. He rejoined the Board after spending several years as an economist in the private sector, including at LoanPerformance from 2005–2006 and at Freddie Mac from 2006–2009. Some of his current research topics include the impact of securitization on the non-agency mortgage market and geographic patterns of mortgage delinquency.

Toni Dechario is a senior financial and economic analyst in the Supervisory and Regulatory Policy Department, part of the Bank Supervision Group at the Federal Reserve Bank of New York. In addition to housing sector topics, Dechario focuses on governance and incentive compensation issues. She also serves on the Secretariat of the

Senior Supervisors Group. Dechario has a master's degree from Columbia University School for International and Public Affairs, where she studied international economic policy.

Jane K. Dokko has been an economist at the Board of Governors of the Federal Reserve System since 2006. Her primary fields of study are public finance and labor. She has written several articles published in the *National Tax Journal, Journal of Empirical Legal Studies*, and *Economic Policy*, and has numerous articles in development. She has lectured at many conferences and has received several honors and fellowships, including the Moore Dissertation Prize from the Department of Economics at the University of Michigan, where she received her PhD degree in economics.

Ingrid Gould Ellen is a professor of public policy and urban planning at New York University Wagner Graduate School of Public Service and Co-Director of the Furman Center for Real Estate and Urban Policy. She joined the Wagner faculty in the fall of 1997. Ellen's research interests center on urban social and economic policy. She is the author of *Sharing America's Neighborhoods: The Prospects for Stable Racial Integration* and has written numerous journal articles and book chapters related to housing policy, neighborhood change, urban growth, and school and neighborhood segregation. Before coming to New York University, Ellen held visiting positions at the Urban Institute and the Brookings Institution.

Kathleen Engel, the Associate Dean for Intellectual Life and a professor of law at Suffolk University Law School, is a national authority on mortgage finance and regulation, subprime and predatory lending, and housing discrimination. Engel's research on financial services markets and the laws that regulate them is frequently cited in the media and she presents her research in academic, banking, and policy forums throughout the United States and around the world.

Lynn Fisher is an associate professor of real estate at the University of North Carolina Kenan-Flagler Business School. She was formerly an associate professor of real estate in the Department of Urban Studies and Planning and the Center for Real Estate (CRE) at the Massachusetts Institute of Technology (MIT), and director of the MIT/CRE Housing Affordability Initiative. She received her PhD in business administration from the Smeal College of Business at Pennsylvania State University, where she concentrated on real estate finance and microeconomics. She also has an MS in business administration from Penn State.

Thomas J. Fitzpatrick, IV is an economist in the Community Development Department at the Federal Reserve Bank of Cleveland. His primary fields of interest are consumer finance and protection, structured finance, and financial regulation, with additional interest in housing policy and community development. Prior to his current position, Fitzpatrick was a research associate and visiting scholar in the Research Department at the Federal Reserve Bank of Cleveland. He has also worked as an investment advisor in the retirement-plan industry. Fitzpatrick received a JD from Cleveland–Marshall College of Law at Cleveland State University.

Christopher L. Foote is a senior economist and policy advisor in the Research Department at the Federal Reserve Bank of Boston. Previously, Foote taught economics at Harvard University, where he also served as Director of Undergraduate Studies. He then accepted a position as a senior staff economist with the Council of Economic Advisers (CEA), becoming Chief Economist at the CEA. From May 2003 to September 2003, he served as an economic advisor to the Coalition Provisional Authority in Baghdad, Iraq, returning briefly to Iraq in January and February of 2004. He joined the Boston Federal Reserve Bank in October 2003 and received a PhD in economics from the University of Michigan in 1996.

Kristopher S. Gerardi is a research economist and an assistant policy adviser in the economics group in the Research Department of the Federal Reserve Bank of Atlanta. His major fields of study are real estate economics and applied microeconomics. Gerardi's work has been published in several journals, including the *Journal of Finance, Journal of Political Economy, Journal of Urban Economics, and Brookings Papers on Economic Activity*. He obtained his PhD in economics from Boston University in 2008.

Edward J. Kane is a professor of finance at Boston College. From 1972–1992, he held the Everett D. Reese Chair of Banking and Monetary Economics at The Ohio State University. Prior to that, he taught at Princeton University and Iowa State University. A founding member of the Shadow Financial Regulatory Committee, Kane rejoined the organization in 2005. He served for 12 years as a trustee and member of the Finance Committee of Teachers Insurance. Currently, he consults for the World Bank and is a senior fellow in the Federal Deposit Insurance Corporation's Center for Financial Research. He is a past president and fellow of the American Finance Association and a former Guggenheim fellow. He also served as president of the International Atlantic Economic Society and the North American Economics and Finance Association. Kane is a longtime research associate of the National Bureau of Economic Research.

Benjamin J. Keys joined the Board of Governors of the Federal Reserve System as an economist in the Division of Research and Statistics in 2009. His primary areas of interest are labor economics, household finance, and applied econometrics, and his recent research has focused on subprime mortgages, personal bankruptcy, student loans, the unbanked, and alternative financial services. Keys holds a PhD in economics from the University of Michigan.

Elizabeth Laderman is an economist in the Research Department of the Federal Reserve Bank of San Francisco. Her research interests include bank market structure, small business lending, and financial market issues related to low-income communities. She has written numerous articles on banking and financial issues for Federal Reserve publications and academic journals. She received a PhD in economics from the University of California at Berkeley.

Lauren Lambie-Hanson is a PhD candidate in urban studies and planning at Massachusetts Institute of Technology (MIT). She has taught and conducted research at MIT and the University of California at Berkeley, as well as conducted research at the City of Boston Department of Neighborhood Development and the Federal Reserve Bank of Boston. She also holds a master's degree in public policy from the University of California at Berkeley.

Adam J. Levitin is an associate professor of law at the Georgetown University Law Center in Washington, D.C., where he teaches courses in bankruptcy, commercial law, contracts, and structured finance. He also serves as Special Counsel to the Congressional Oversight Panel supervising the Troubled Asset Relief Program. In 2009, Levitin was the Robert Zinman Resident Scholar at the American Bankruptcy Institute. Before joining the Georgetown faculty, Levitin practiced in the Business Finance & Restructuring Department of Weil, Gotshal & Manges, LLP, in New York and served as law clerk to the Honorable Jane Richards Roth on the United States Court of Appeals for the Third Circuit. Levitin's research focuses on the role of financial institutions in consumer and business transactions.

Patricia C. Mosser is senior advisor and a senior vice president in the Markets Group at the Federal Reserve Bank of New York. She is responsible for development of Markets Group policy views on financial structure and stability issues arising from the recent financial crisis. She serves as the open market desk's liaison on financial reform inside and outside the Federal Reserve System. During the financial crisis she was senior manager at the open market desk overseeing market analysis and monetary policy operations in domestic and international capital markets. Earlier in her career, she was an economist in the FRBNY Research and Statistics Group. Before joining the FRBNY, Mosser was on the Economics Department faculty of Columbia University. She has a PhD in economics from the Massachusetts Institute of Technology and an MSc with distinction from the London School of Economics and Political Science.

Leonard Nakamura is a vice president and economist in the Federal Reserve Bank of Philadelphia's Economic Research Department and is head of the Regional and Applied Microeconomics section. His primary research interests are information, credit, and innovation. Before joining the Federal Reserve, he was an economist at the Conference Board and Citibank, and taught economics at Rutgers University. He received his MA and PhD from Princeton University.

Roberto G. Quercia directs the Center for Community Capital at the University of North Carolina at Chapel Hill. In addition, he is a professor of city and regional planning and a faculty fellow at the Center for Urban and Regional Studies. Quercia leads major research projects in the areas of low-income homeownership, subprime and predatory lending, and financial services issues. He is the principal researcher on an evaluation of a secondary mortgage market initiative for community reinvestment loans funded by the Ford Foundation. Quercia has conducted extensive research on neighborhood dynamics and poverty for government agencies, municipalities, community organizations, and private entities.

Carolina Reid is the manager of the Research Group in the Federal Reserve Bank of San Francisco's Community Development Department, where she oversees the department's research on trends and issues facing low-income communities in the Federal Reserve's 12th District. Her recent research has focused primarily on understanding the impact of the foreclosure crisis on low-income and minority communities and the role of policy and regulation in consumer protection. Reid earned her PhD in 2004 from the University of Washington at Seattle.

Vincent Reinhart, a former director of the Federal Reserve Board Division of Monetary Affairs, has spent more than two decades working on domestic and international aspects of U.S. monetary policy. He held a number of senior positions in the divisions of Monetary Affairs and International Finance and served for the last six years of his Federal Reserve career as secretary and economist of the Federal Open Market Committee. Reinhart worked on topics as varied as economic bubbles and the conduct of monetary policy, auctions of U.S. Treasury securities, alternative strategies for monetary policy, and the efficient communication of monetary policy decisions.

Sarah F. Riley is a researcher at the Center for Community Capital at the University of North Carolina at Chapel Hill. Her primary research interests concern the ways in which individuals and organizations perceive and respond to risk. Her dissertation examined the role that labor market uncertainty plays in student decisions about whether to double major, and she is currently investigating the causes of house price appreciation and volatility for low-income homeowners. Riley also manages the center's data stores and collaborates on research concerning ways to reduce non-response bias in panel surveys. She received her PhD in economics from the University of North Carolina at Chapel Hill in 2009.

Marvin M. Smith is an economist and Community Development Research Advisor at the Federal Reserve Bank of Philadelphia. Among his many duties, he leads projects and programs that enhance consumer and economic education, including financial literacy. He also heads the Community Development Studies and Education Department's participation in the Bank's Program in Consumer Credit and Payments. In addition, he conducts research in the areas of housing and finance. Smith has authored numerous government and academic publications. He was formerly employed at the Congressional Budget Office and the Brookings Institution, both in Washington, D.C. He received both his master's and doctorate degrees in economics from Cornell University.

Joseph Tracy is a senior advisor to the president at the Federal Reserve Bank of New York, where he focuses on housing and household credit issues. He was head of the Research and Statistics Group from 2004 to 2009. Prior to being named to this position, Tracy was senior vice president. He also served as the senior administrative officer for the group. Tracy joined the Bank as a research officer in August 1996 and was assigned to the Domestic Research Department. He was promoted to assistant vice president in January 1998. In 1999, he was promoted to vice president with responsibility for the domestic research function, and he assumed additional responsibility for the research support function in March 2000.

John Napier Tye has been a non-resident scholar at the Furman Center for Real Estate and Urban Policy at New York University. He was a Skadden Fellow at New Orleans Legal Assistance, and worked at the Southern Poverty Law Center. Tye holds a JD from Yale Law School, and was a Rhodes scholar at Lincoln College, Oxford.

Robert Van Order is a professor of finance and the Oliver T. Carr Professor of Real Estate at George Washington University School of Business. He was a professor of land economics at the University of Aberdeen and has been a visiting professor and lecturer at numerous universities. From 1987 to 2003, he was chief economist/chief international economist for Freddie Mac. Prior to working at Freddie Mac, he served as an economist at the Department of Housing and Urban Development. Van Order has served as a housing finance consultant in Russia and other countries for the World Bank and the U.S. Agency for International Development. He is the author of many papers, reports, and book chapters. His current research interests include the subprime lending crisis and housing price dynamics.

James Vickery is a research economist in the Financial Intermediation Function, where he has worked since 2004. Vickery's research and policy work focuses on topics relating to banking, mortgage finance, and securitization. In a separate line of research, he studies the provision of insurance to households in developing countries. In addition, Vickery teaches an MBA course on real estate capital markets at New York University Leonard N. Stern School of Business, where he was also a visiting assistant professor from 2007 to 2008. Vickery received a PhD in economics from the Massachusetts Institute of Technology in 2004. Prior to graduate school he was an economist at the Reserve Bank of Australia.

Susan M. Wachter is the Richard B. Worley Professor of Financial Management and a professor of real estate and finance at the Wharton School of the University of Pennsylvania. Wachter is also a professor of city and regional planning at the School of Design, as well as the co-founder and co-director of the Penn Institute for Urban Research. Wachter has served as president of the American Real Estate and Urban Economics Association and co-editor of *Real Estate Economics*. Wachter was Assistant Secretary for Policy Development and Research at the Department of Housing and Urban Development, a president-appointed and senate-confirmed position, from 1998 to 2001. Wachter, a nationally recognized expert on real estate markets, is frequently called upon to appear in the national media and testify before the U.S. Congress.

Paul S. Willen is a senior economist and policy advisor in the Research Department at the Federal Reserve Bank in Boston. In his research, Willen studies household financial management and, in recent years, he has spent much of his time focused on mortgage markets. His research on the subprime crisis has garnered wide attention both among researchers and the general public. In particular, his recent paper "Why Don't Lenders Renegotiate More Home Mortgages?" was the subject of front page stories in several major newspapers. Prior to joining the Boston Federal Reserve Bank, Willen was on the faculty at Princeton University and the University of Chicago.

Mark A. Willis is a resident research fellow at New York University Furman Center for Real Estate and Urban Policy. Prior to joining Furman, he enjoyed a year as a visiting scholar at the Ford Foundation, working on issues of community development and housing finance reform. In his 19-year career in community development banking at JPMorgan Chase, Willis developed and oversaw the bank's programs and products to help strengthen low- and moderate-income communities. He has served on the boards of a wide range of banking and community-oriented organizations; he previously chaired the Consumer Bankers Association's Community Reinvestment Committee and currently co-chairs the advocacy group Housing First! in New York. Willis has written and lectured widely and currently teaches housing and community development policy at New York University's Wagner School. He has a PhD in economics from Yale University and a JD from Harvard Law School.

Joshua Wright is an analyst in the Markets Group of the Federal Reserve Bank of New York, where he provides monitoring and analysis of markets in mortgage-backed securities (MBS) for Federal Reserve officials responsible for financial stability, monetary policy, and the Fed's MBS portfolio in particular. In addition to questions of secondary market functioning and institutional ownership structure, he has more recently been researching the role of the private mortgage insurance industry and the prospects for a U.S. covered bond market. Wright holds a master's degree from Harvard University's Kennedy School of Government, where he was a Carnesale Fellow and concentrated on macroeconomics and finance.

Index

Page numbers followed by f or t refer to figures or tables, respectively.

AAA rating, of private-label securities, 251, 258

ABX indices: development of, 262; limitations of, 262–263

Accountability: in financial reform, 280; reinforcement of, 281

Adjustable-rate mortgages (ARMs), 128; global dominance of, 247; housing finance via, 247–248

Advocates, for consumer protection, 128–129

Affordability (AFFORD), vs. homeownership rate (OWN_RATE), 107–108, 107t, 108t

Affordable housing programs, financing of, 219–220

Agency costs, and dueling charters, 340–343

Agnostics: and mortgage crisis, 27–28; in U.S. housing market, 47–52

Akaike's information criterion (AIC), 199

Alt-A loans, 10, 11, 92, 93t; market share of, 344, 347t; rapid growth of, 344

American Bankers Association, social responsibility of, 159–160

Annualized rate of appreciation r, calculation of, 192

Appraisals, biases in, 100

Area medium income (AMI), in community advantage program, 189

Arranger liability, in home mortgage lending, 119–120

"Assessment area": bank-associated, 163; CRA-defined, 165; loans made outside, 172

Asset-backed securities (ABSs): default on, 344; Fannie and Freddie purchase of, 345–346; "waterfall" payment structure of, 347

Asset-liability mismatches: danger of, 248; securitization as solution to, 248–249

Asset markets, real-world, 53–54

Asset-price(s), evaluation of, 54–55

Asset-price bubbles, analysis of, 29–30. See also Housing market bubble

Assignee liability, 117; in home mortgage lending, 117–119; laws in, 118; limited, 117; opposition to, 118–119

Baker's study, of U.S. housing market, 32–34

Balloon payments, racial differences in, 75, 76t–77t

Bank(s): bottom line focus of, 216–217; collaboration between community-based organizations and, 213; communication between community groups and, 212–213; covered bonds available to, 330–333; CRA rating of, 210, 220–221; CRA's affirmative obligation imposed on, 210–212; CRA's diminished influence on, 219; geographic distribution of branch network of, 216; grade inflation of, 220; household financial assets held by, 217–218; regulations discouraging investment by, 218–219;

Bank(s) (*continued*)
  regulatory agencies overseeing, 210–211; safety valve for, 224; satisfactory rating standards of, 226–227; "shadow," 104, 349; specialized divisions within, 213; without direct CRA responsibility, 218
Bank affiliates, expanding financial assets to, 230–231
Bank compliance with CRA: creating community development test for, 223–224; incorporating safety valve for, 224; measurement of, 222–223
Bank mergers, CRA performance and, 211–212
Bank regulators, soft laws issued by, 123–124
Bank services, expanding eligibility to geographies beyond, 229–230
Bayesian information criterion (BIC), 199
Beneficial loans, matching borrowers with, 116
Bills, House and Senate reconciliation of, 276–277, 278t
Black-Scholes formula, 102
Bloomberg National Poll, 273
Bond(s): convertible (Coco bonds), 352–353; covered, 330–333
Bond-backed mortgages, 114
Borrower(s): availability of safe products understood by, 306; CAP (*See* Community advantage program [CAP] borrowers); first-loss position of, 297, 298; intermediaries between loan originators and, 44, 115–116, 212
Borrower characteristics, in California, Ohio, and Pennsylvania, 167t, 170t, 175t, 176t, 178t
Broad standards: argument against, 125; in home mortgage lending, 124–125
Building permits: in Chelsea (Massachusetts), 142; investment and, 152–154, 153f
Building restrictions: in housing pessimism, 36–41, 38f, 39f, 40f
Bureau of Labor Statistics (BLS), 165–166

California: competing risks model of default and payment in, 175t–176t; higher-priced loans within disadvantaged communities in, 172–173, 173f; logistical regression predicting likelihood of receiving sub-

prime loan in, 168–169, 169f, 170t–171t; market data in, 166, 167t
Capital market access: improved rules for, 351–352; in private-lender cooperative utility, 301
Capital market structure and evolution, in home mortgage lending, 113–115
Capital rules, for Fannie and Freddie, 351–352
Capital waterfall, for private-lender cooperative utility, 295, 295f
Case and Shiller index, of house prices, 344, 346f
Case and Shiller study, of U.S. housing market, 34–35
Cash-out refinances, after mortgage crisis, 154
Certificates of deposit (CDs), vs. CAP properties, 192
Chelsea (Massachusetts): building permits in, 142; foreclosures in, 146–148, 147t, 149f, 150; homeowner commitment to, 140; home sales in, 154–156, 156t; house prices in, 142–143, 144f, 145–146, 145t; investment in, 152–154, 153f; location as key issue in, 156–157; low- to moderate-income residents in, 137–138; mortgage crisis in, 137–156; mortgage data from, 140–142; mortgage services in, 142; public records from, 141–142; REO problem in, 150–152, 151f, 152t; repeat-sales indices in, 138
Coco (convertible) bonds, 352–353
Collateral debt obligations (CDOs), 243, 259–260; growth of, 260–261, 261f; subordinated pieces of ABSs sold to, 348
Community(ies): housing crisis damage to, 137 (*See also specific community, e.g.,* Chelsea [Massachusetts]); underserved by CRA, 225
Community Advantage Panel Survey (CAPS), 189; sale prices and wealth of participants in, 196–197
Community advantage program (CAP): LMI homeownership and, 188–191; as secondary market program, 189
Community advantage program (CAP) borrowers: housing as asset for, 191–194, 193f; housing as wealth builder for, 194–195; negative equity or mortgage debt of, 191

Community advantage program (CAP) loans: delinquency rate on, 190–191; evaluation of findings in, 205–206; origination of, 190; qualifying requirements for, 189; to racial and ethnic minorities, 190

Community advantage program (CAP) properties: appreciation of, 191–192, 194; correlates of price appreciation of, 196; decline in values of, 193–194; descriptive statistics for, 199, 200t; estimation of price appreciation of, 196–205; estimation results for, 199, 201–203, 201t, 202t; extended analysis of, 202t, 203–205; goodness-of-fit results for, 199, 201, 201t; year-on-year changes in, 193, 193f; zip-code-level variables in, 201, 202t

Community development test: for large retail banks, 223–224; for wholesale and special-purpose banks, 211

Community Preservation Corporation (CPC), success of, 329

Community Reinvestment Act (CRA), 161–164; basic elements of, 210–212; better data collection under, 225–226; consensus on goals of, 213–215; consider additional incentives under, 227–228; create community development test for bank compliance with, 223–224; create process recognizing differences across localities under, 224–225; critics of, 160; develop minimum standards for satisfactory rating under, 226–227; effectiveness of, 209–210; empower lead agency under, 222; evaluate past performance and review reform options for, 209–231; expand geographic eligibility under, 229–230; expansion beyond banks under, 230–231; expansion beyond credit under, 228–229; fix complementary laws under, 222; impact of, 161–162; incorporate safety valve for bank compliance with, 224; key component of, 161; language of legislation of, 209; learning from experience with, 213–221; maintain public participation and promote dialog among stakeholders under, 227; measure bank compliance with, 222–223; potential changes to, 210; potential directions for reforms under, 221–231; provide more exam protocols under, 228; provide special credit for

communities underserved by, 225; during subprime crisis, 159–182 (*See also* Subprime loans); successes of, 212–213

Community reinvestment homeowners, house appreciation and equity accumulation among, 187–207. *See also* Community advantage program (CAP) *entries*

Complementary laws, fixing of, 222

Complexity of financial system, 360–362; potential solution for, 363; problems concerning, 362–363

Conflicts of interest, facing safety-net officials, 276, 277t

Conscientious representation, in financial reform, 280

Consolidation: Federal Reserve officials objections to, 364; within financial system, 363–365, 366f

Constant-quality new-home price index, accuracy of, 44

Consumer complaints, forum for resolving, 127–128

Consumer Financial Protection Bureau (CFPB), 112

Consumer protection: advocates for, 128–129; in home mortgage lending, 112–131 (*See also* Home mortgage lending); preemption in, 120–122; required disclosure for, 129–130

Convertible (Coco) bonds, 352–353

Co-operative ownership, 323–324

Corporate debt, vs. mortgage-backed securities, 309

Corrective action, in financial reform, 280

Costs, in private-lender cooperate utility, 299

Countercyclical stability, of secondary market, 306

Covered bonds, 330–333; in Danish system, 332; vs. MBSs, 331–332

Cover-up, Dodd-Frank Act as exercise in, 276–277, 277t, 278t, 279f

CRA exam protocols: addition of more, 228; for banks, 211; factors complicating, 217–218; inconsistent treatment across, 220; redesign of, 228

Credit: availability of, 228–229; for communities underserved by CRA, 225; for multi-family housing, 318–319; to underserved markets, 316–318

Credit default swaps (CDSs), 101, 262

Credit enhancement: federal government involvement in, 307–308; in housing finance, 307–312; limiting mortgages and securities eligible for, 308

Credit markets, access to, 306

Credit ratings, constraint failures on, 257–259

Creditworthiness, of homeowners, 67

Cuomo v. Clearing House Association, 121

Database, financial monitoring, 105

Data collection: under Community Reinvestment Act, 225–226; on home mortgage lending, 130–131

Davis, Lehnert, and Martin study, of housing market, 51–52

Debt investors, subordinated, 260

Default rates, in Fannie and Freddie markets, 348, 349t

Defaults, mortgage. *See* Mortgage defaults

Demographic characteristics: of DAHFS study, 63, 64t–65t; home appreciation rates vary with, 198

Demographic trends, in house prices, 33–34

Denial, Dodd-Frank Act as exercise in, 274–276

Denmark, covered bond market in, 332

Depression: fragility of home finance during, 248; launch of secondary market for home finance during, 8

Detroit Area Housing Financial Services (DAHFS) study, 60, 62–64; delaying payment and measuring risk of default in, 67–68, 69t–70t; demographic characteristics in, 63, 64t–65t; homeowner characteristics in, 65–67; homeowner creditworthiness in, 67; homeowner experience in, 62; mortgage characteristics in, 69t–70t; renters in, 66–67; self-reports of payment problems in, 68

Difficult to fail and unwind (DFU) institutions, 279

Disclosures, in home mortgage lending, 129–130

Dodd-Frank Act, 271–285; agencies established by, 281; Consumer Financial Protection Bureau and, 112; effectiveness of, 273; elements of cover-up and, 276–277, 277t, 278t, 279f; elements of denial and, 274–276; financial database included in, 106; focus of, 359; length of, 272, 272f; lobbying pressure undermining, 272, 274; mechanism for data collection under, 131; phase-in periods for changes in, 272; and political establishment, 273; reframing of policy problems and, 277, 279–284; regulatory gaps filled by, 114–115; regulatory preemption restrictions by, 121; signing of, 271–272; unforgivable elements of, 274

Dodd-Frank Wall Street Reform and Consumer Protection Act. *See* Dodd-Frank Act

"Dollar roll," in TBA market, 292

Down payment requirements: in private-lender cooperative utility, 297

Dueling charters: agency costs and, 340–343; securitization and, 341–343

Duties of care, imposed on intermediaries, 116

Economic capital, procyclicality of, 103

Efficient operation, in financial reform, 280

Equal Credit Opportunity Act, 161

Equity, home. *See* Home equity *entries*

Equity capital, required for private-lender cooperative utility, 294

Ethnic minorities, CAP loans to, 190

Explicit guarantee, vs. implicit guarantee, 311–312

Fair Housing Act (FHA), 161

Fair lending laws: enforcement of, 81

Fannie Mae, 339–355; advent of, 342–343; agency costs and dueling charters in, 340–343; asset-backed securities purchased by, 345–348; central policy issues concerning, 339–340; Coco bonds and, 352–353; creation of, 8; credit guarantees of, 101; default rates of, 348, 349t; duopoly power of, 16; foreclosure rates and, 344, 345f; growing guarantees of, 277, 279f; improved capital rules for, 351–352; major losses by, 343–344; model for replacement of, 293–299 (*See also* Lending cooperative utility); mortgage-backed securities packaged by, 9, 249; mortgage holdings of, 344–345, 346t; mortgages eligible for securitization through, 286, 287f; non-fatal flaws of, 350–351; policy and trade-offs affecting, 354–355; portfolio assets of, 353; pre-conservatorship structure of, 13; profits of, 11; property values and, 344, 346f; recent history of, 343–349, 345f, 346f, 346t, 347f, 347t; reform of, 305–333 (*See also* Housing finance system); in residential mortgage finance, 286; securitization and dueling charters in, 341–343; S&L failures and, 340. *See also* Government-sponsored enterprises (GSEs)

Favored mortgage products, 309–311

FDIC-style insurance, in private-lender cooperative utility, 298–299

Federal Deposit Insurance Corporation (FDIC), bank regulation by, 210

Federal Financial Institutions Examination Council (FFIEC), 166

Federal guarantee, of GSEs, 9, 13

Federal Home Loan Banks, 8

Federal Housing Administration (FHA), 8

Federal Housing Finance Agency (FHFA), 165

Federal National Mortgage Association. *See* Fannie Mae

Federal National Mortgage Corporation. *See* Freddie Mac

Federal preemption, in home mortgage lending, 120–121

Federal Reserve: bank regulation by, 210; independence of, 280–281

Federal Trade Commission (FTC), HDC rule abolished by, 118–119

Fedwire funds services, 365, 366f

Fedwire securities services, 365, 366f

Fees: paid by different ethnic groups, 69t–70t, 73, 74t–75t, 75; for private-lender cooperative utility, 294–298, 295f, 297f; upfront, 114

FICO score, 67; borrowing and, 169

Financial crisis: diagnosis of, 275–276; and diminished CRA's influence on banks, 219; government insurance in, 289; jumbo loans before, 287–288; large and interconnected, 360; layering of blame for, 283; mortgage-backed securities in, 286, 287f; regulatory weakness and, 104; theory of blame in, 275; vs. S&L crisis, 340, 348–349. *See also* Mortgage crisis

Financial institutions: complexity of, 360–362; consolidation within, 363–365, 366f;

economic incentives for, 360–361; excessive risk-taking by, 273–274; with footprints in different jurisdictions, 361; future thoughts for, 350–354; as intermediaries between borrowers and mortgage financiers, 44, 212; multifaceted terrain of opportunities for, 365–367; potential solutions for, 363; problems within, 362–363; 2002–2007 profits made by, 284–285; value of safety-net support at, 281–281. *See also specific institution*

Financial monitoring database, 105

Financial reform: authentic, 280; legislation on, 358; missed opportunities in, 358–360

Financial safety net, expansion of, 271–285. *See also* Dodd-Frank Act

Financial Stability Oversight Council (FSOC), establishment of, 281

Fixed-rate mortgages (FRMs), 246–248; fully amortized, 248; secondary market financing of, 249; S&L crisis and, 248

Ford Foundation, GSE partnership with, 15

Foreclosures: in Chelsea (Massachusetts), 146–148, 147t, 149f, 150; collapsing house prices and, 138; in Fannie and Freddie markets, 344, 345f; LPS data on, 147–148; non-local vs. local lending institutions and, 163–164; overall characterization of, 147t, 148, 149f, 150; Warren data on, 146–147

For-profit status: of GSEs, 16

Forum for resolution, in home mortgage lending, 127–128

Freddie Mac, 339–355; advent of, 342–343; agency costs and dueling charters in, 340–343; asset-backed securities purchased by, 345–348; central policy issues concerning, 339–340; Coco bonds and, 352–353; creation of, 8; credit guarantees of, 101; default rates of, 348, 349t; duopoly power of, 16; foreclosure rates and, 344, 345f; growing guarantees of, 277, 279f; improved capital rules for, 351–352; major losses by, 343–344; model for replacement of, 293–299 (*See also* Lending cooperative utility); mortgage-backed securities packaged by, 9, 249; mortgage holdings of, 344–345, 346t; mortgages eligible for securitization through, 286, 287f;

Freddie Mac (*continued*)
non-fatal flaws of, 350–351; policy and trade-offs affecting, 354–355; portfolio assets of, 353; pre-conservatorship structure of, 13; profits of, 11; property values and, 344, 346f; recent history of, 343–349, 345f, 346f, 346t, 347f, 347t; reform of, 305–333 (*See also* Housing finance system); in residential mortgage finance, 286; securitization and dueling charters in, 341–343; and S&L failures, 340. *See also* Government-sponsored enterprises (GSEs)

Fundamental Theorem of Asset Pricing, 28; pure form of, 28–29

Gallin's analysis, of house prices and rents, 50–51

Ginnie Mae, creation of, 8–9

Governance, of private-lender cooperative utility, 294

Government housing subsidies, transparency of, 288–289

Government involvement, in private-lender cooperative utility, 300

Government National Mortgage Association (GNMA), creation of, 8–9

Government-sponsored enterprises (GSEs): critique of, 11; design of successor to, 289; excessive risks taken by, 15–16; and exemption from Securities Act, 290, 291; for-profit status of, 16; future of, 328; implicit federal guarantee of, 9, 13; improved housing finance through reform of, 305–333 (*See also* Housing finance system); investors in, 249–250; lobbying activities of, 16; methods of ownership in, 320–326; mortgage capital provided by, 14; mortgage holdings of, 344, 346t; mortgage standards developed by, 13–14; multi-family loans of, 12–13, 318–319; multi-family market role of, 14–15; net bias created by, 16; non-housing investments of, 11; non-prime investments of, 11–12; options for reorganization of, 288–289; PLS market and, 10; principles for reform of, 288–293; secondary market stability provided by, 14, 249; securitization of mortgages by, 101; state and local partnerships with, 15; strengths and weaknesses of, 13–17; sup-

pressed competition by, 16; TBA market and, 9–10 (*See also* To-be-announced [TBA] market); transition issues in, 326–328; underserved market capital provided by, 15. *See also specific agency*

Guarantee(s): explicit vs. implicit, 311–312; of Fannie Mae and Freddie Mac, 101, 277, 279f; federal, 9, 13; in secondary market, 308–309

Guaranteed fees, for private-lender cooperative utility, 294–298, 295f, 297f

Haines and Rosen study, of housing affordability, 48

Hard vs. soft laws, in home mortgage lending, 123–124

High-balance conforming loans, market share of, 287f

High-cost mortgages, 60–81; broker use in, 78–80, 79t; data and summary statistics in, 62–70 (*See also* Detroit Area Household Financial Services [DAHFS] study); different dimensions of, 60; HOEPA violations by, 118; independent mortgage companies and, 162; loan pricing in, 70–72; racial dispersion and, 72–73, 74t–75t, 76t–77t, 77–78

High-risk mortgages: categories of, 89, 91–94, 91f, 93f, 93t, 94t; factors driving expansion of, 98–105; homeownership and, 94–95, 96f, 97f; meltdown linked to, 97–98

Himmelberg, Mayer, and Sinai study, of housing bubble, 42–43

Holder in due course (HDC) rule, 117; laws abolishing, 118

Home appreciation, among community reinvestment homeowners, 187–207 (*See also* Community advantage program [CAP] *entries*)

Home equity: CAP borrowers and, 191, 194–195; cashing out, 92

Home equity accumulation, among community reinvestment homeowners, 187–207 (*See also* Community advantage program [CAP] *entries*)

Home equity lines of credit (HELOCs), 92

Home equity loans, 93t; closed-end, 92

Home Mortgage Disclosure Act (HMDA), 62, 73, 130, 161

Home mortgage lending: arranger liability in, 119–120; assignee liability in, 117–119; beyond regulatory framework in, 128–131; consumer protection in, 112–131; correlation between CRA and, 212; data on, 130–131; disclosures in, 129–130; evolving landscape of, 54; federal preemption in, 120–121; federal preemption of State laws in, 121–122; forum for resolution in, 127–128; hard vs. soft laws in, 123–124; laws governing, 112–113; market structure and evolution in, 113–115; origination channels in, 115–117; preemption in, 120–122; regulation in, 115–120, 123–127; regulatory preemption in, 121; review of, 128–129; rule enforcement in, 125–127; rules governing, 122–123; rules vs. standards in, 124–125. *See also* Housing finance system; Lending institutions; Mortgage(s)

Homeowners: benefits for, 246–247; creditworthiness of, 67; in DAHFS study, 65–67; housing costs of, 66–67; mortgage payment problems of, 68

Homeownership: blow to sustainable, 87; declining rates of, 88, 89f; high-risk loans and, 94–95, 96f, 97f; impact of bubble and meltdown on, 88–98, 89f, 90f; impact of mortgage meltdown on, 97–98; implications of housing bubble for, 87–108 (*See also* Housing market bubble); in low- and moderate-income neighborhoods (*See* Low- and moderate income [LMI] community; Low- and moderate-income [LMI] households); net present value of, 46; risks associated with, 247; securitized jumbo loans vs. change in, 95, 97f; sustainable, 246–248; vs. affordability in metropolitan areas, 95, 96f; wealth-creation mechanism in, 187

Home Ownership and Equity Protection Act (HOEPA), Truth in Lending Act amended by, 118

Home purchase loans: change in affordability vs. change in share of, 89, 90f; occupancy status of, 89, 90f. *See also* Mortgage(s)

Home sale(s), in Chelsea (Massachusetts), 154–156, 156t

Home sale prices, and wealth of CAPS participants, 196–197

House and Senate reconciliation, of bills, 276–277, 278t

House price(s): Case and Shiller index of, 344, 346f; in Chelsea (Massachusetts), 142–143, 144f, 145–146, 145t; cyclical fluctuations in, 97; deleterious effect of falling, 138–139; demographic trends in, 33–34; interest rates and, 34; rise in, 87 (*See also* Housing market bubble); unsustainable, 245; vs. rents, 33

House-price appreciation: annualized rate of, 192; correlates of, 196; demographics and, 198; estimation methods of, 196–205; and new construction, 37–38, 40f

House-price growth and supply elasticities, in metropolitan areas, 37, 38f, 39f

House price ratios: analysis of, 29; to income per capita, 34

Housing: as asset for CAP borrowers, 191–194, 193f; as wealth builder for CAP borrowers, 194–195

Housing costs, for homeowners vs. renters, 66–67

Housing finance system: ability to hold portfolio assets in, 319–320; adjustable-rate mortgages in, 247–248; affordability in, 219–220; complex process of, 101–101; covered bonds in, 330–333; creation of state mortgage insurance funds in, 328–330; credit enhancement in, 307–312; credit to underserved markets and, 316–318; evaluating reforms in, 307–328; explicit vs. implicit guarantee in, 311–312; guaranteeing MBS vs. corporate debt in, 309; limits on types of losses in, 311; limits on types of mortgage in, 309–311 (*See also* Mortgage[s]); market concentration in, 315–316; methods of ownership in, 320–326; multi-family rental properties and, 318–319; new models for, 328; policy going forward in, 349–350; regulation of players in, 312–313; secondary market in, 7–17, 305–307 (*See also* Secondary market); securitization of non-favored products in, 313–315; shifts in supply and demand in, 254–255, 255f; transition issues in, 326–328. *See also* Home mortgage lending; Lending institutions

Housing market: agnostics in, 47–52; asset-price bubble models in, 30; blocked or opaque information in, 243–244; for CAP properties, 193–194, 193f; before crash, 26–55; early warnings on, 32–36, 33f; failure of normal constraints in, 257–263; house-price index data for, 192; lending decisions and, 31; optimists in, 41–47; pessimists in, 31–41; price forecasts in, 52–55; public policy on, 52–55, 246; during recession, 188

Housing market bubble, 87–108; categories of high-risk loans and, 89, 91–94, 91f, 93f, 93t, 94t; evidence against, 41–42 (*See also* Housing optimism); factors driving, 98–102; homeownership and, 94–95, 96f, 97t; impact of, 88–98, 89f, 90f; indicators of, 35–36 (*See also* Housing pessimism); nontraditional mortgages and, 244; policy discussion and, 102–107; private-label securities and, 244; regression analysis of, 107–108, 107t, 108t; supply-side explanation of, 253–256, 254f, 255f. *See also* Mortgage crisis

Housing market stress, liquidity provider in, 289

Housing optimism: and mortgage crisis, 26–27; in U.S. market, 41–47

Housing pessimism: building restrictions in, 36–41, 38f, 39f, 40f; early warnings and, 32–36, 33f; in U.S. market, 31–41

Housing stock, increased, 88

HUD-Treasury, definition of D class subprime mortgage, 70

Implicit guarantee: federal, 9, 13; vs. explicit guarantee, 311–312

Independent mortgage companies (IMCs), 162

Information failure: correction of, 245; exploiting asymmetries in, 256–257; and mortgage crisis, 243–265

Innovation, in private-lender cooperative utility, 301

Inside monitors, in private-lender cooperative utility, 300

Interest rates: and house prices, 34; racial discrimination in, 73

Intermediaries: between borrowers and loan originators, 44, 115–116, 212; duty of care imposed on, 116; mortgage brokers as, 114

Intermediate small banks, exam protocols for, 211

Internal rates of return (IRRs), 46

Investment: in Chelsea (Massachusetts), 152–154, 153f; in private-lender cooperative utility, 301

Investment banks, securitization deals by, 114

Investment properties, demand for, 88–89, 90f

Investment test: of retail banks, 211

Investors: availability of safe products understood by, 306; in bond-backed mortgages, 114; subordinated debt, 260

Jumbo loans, 10, 92, 93t; credit risk for, 251; before financial crisis, 287–288; market share of, 287f; securitized, 95, 97f. *See also* Private-labeled securities (PLS) market

Jurisdictions, financial institutions with footprints in different, 361

Krainer and Wei pre-crisis study, 49

Krugman's analysis, of U.S. housing market, 30

Krugman's flatland/zoned zone theory, 36–41

Kübler-Ross' model, of pain generated by personal and societal crisis, 273

Large retail bank(s): creation of community development test for, 223–224; exam protocol for, 217

Large Retail Bank Test, 211; community loans and services undervalued by, 219

Lawrence (Massachusetts), house prices in, 145t

Laws: governing home mortgage lending, 112–113; hard vs. soft, 123–124

Lead agency, in CRA reform, 222

Legislators, obligation of, 282

Lending institutions: CRA-regulated, 165; and incidence of higher-priced lending, 168–173, 169f, 170t–171t, 173f; and loan performance, 173–174, 175t–179t, 179; locally based, 163–164. *See also* Home mortgage lending; Housing finance system

Lending test, of retail banks, 211

Limiting moral hazard, in private-lender cooperative utility, 297–298

Liquid credit markets, access to, 306

Loan characteristics, in California, Ohio, and Pennsylvania, 167t, 175t, 176t–177t, 178t, 178t

Loan originators, 115; intermediaries between borrowers and, 44, 115–116, 212

Lobbying activities, of GSEs, 16

Lobbyists: pressure exerted by, 272, 274; for systemically important firms, 275–276

Localities, formalizing process recognizing differences across, 224–225

Local partnerships, with GSEs, 15

Long-term owners, sales by, 156, 156t

Losses: limits on, 311; on securities absorbed by members, 298

Low- and moderate-income (LMI) community: CRA's affirmative obligation serving, 214–217; credit during subprime crisis in, 162–163; lending in, 159, 219; mortgage crisis in, 137–156. *See also specific community, e.g.,* Chelsea (Massachusetts)

Low- and moderate-income (LMI) households: and community advantage program, 188–191; data and summary statistics in, 62–70; delaying payment and measuring risk of default in, 67–68, 69t–70t; demographic characteristics in, 61; in Detroit (*See* Detroit Area Housing Financial Services [DAHFD] study); differential mortgage pricing and, 60; heterogeneity in mortgage pricing and, 72–80; high-cost mortgages in, 60–81; homeowner characteristics in, 65–67; during housing market decline, 188; mortgage pricing and, 70–72. *See also* Community advantage program (CAP) loans

Lowell (Massachusetts), house prices in, 145t

Low Income Housing Tax Credit (LIHTC) program, 15, 319

Low risk-taking: in private-lender cooperative utility, 300

Lynn (Massachusetts): house prices in, 145t

McCarthy and Peach study, of housing market, 43–45

Median price indices, accuracy of, 44

Metropolitan statistical area (MSA), lending institutions in, 165

Minimal government involvement, in private-lender cooperative utility, 300

Mission, of private-lender cooperative utility, 299

Modigliani-Miller (MM) irrelevance theorem, 340–341; of policy and trade-offs, 354–355; in pre-Fannie and Freddie world, 342

Monopoly power, of private-lender cooperative utility, 299–300

Mortgage(s): adjustable-rate (*See* Adjustable-rate mortgages [ARMs]); Alt-A (*See* Alt-A loans); bond-backed, 114; brief history of, 7–13; CAP loans (*See* Community advantage program [CAP] loans); costs of obtaining, 71; deterioration in underwriting standards for, 93–94, 94t, 252–253, 253f; fixed-rate (*See* Fixed-rate mortgages [FRMs]); GSE capital provided for, 14; high-cost (*See* High-cost mortgages); high-risk (*See* High-risk mortgages); jumbo (*See* Jumbo loans); multi-family, 12–13, 328–330; non-agency, 10–11; nontraditional (*See* Nontraditional loans); origination of, 244; parity tests for, 214–216; prepayment penalties with, 71–72; for purchase under CAP, 189; second-lien, 10, 92; securitization of, 101, 244, 249; single-family, 12, 344, 347t; subprime (*See* Subprime loans); "underwater," 187–188. *See also* Home mortgage lending; Housing finance system; Lending institutions

Mortgage-backed securities (MBSs), 9, 243; credit risk of, 100, 244–245; derivative short positions on, 262; in financial crisis, 286, 287f; government wrap for, 309, 312; GSEs issue of, 249; non-favored, 314; optimistic evaluations of credit risk of, 100; standardization of, 245; TBA trading and, 291; vs. corporate debt, 309; vs. covered bonds, 331–332

Mortgage brokers: financial functions of, 70–71; as intermediaries, 114; in matching borrowers with beneficial loans, 116;

Mortgage brokers (*continued*)
   problems associated with, 99; race and, 72; role of, 79t; use of, 78–80, 79t
Mortgage contracts: racial dispersion and, 72–73, 74t–75t, 76t–77t, 77–78
Mortgage crisis: agnostics and, 27–28; information failure and, 243–265; in low- and moderate-income (LMI) community, 137–156 (*See also specific community, e.g.,* Chelsea [Massachusetts]); optimism and, 26–27; performance of CRA lending during, 159–182. *See also* Financial crisis; Housing market bubble
Mortgage debt: CAP borrowers and, 191; as share of gross national product, 91, 91f
Mortgage defaults: associated with CRA and subprime loans, 205–206; in California, Ohio, and Pennsylvania, 175t–178t; DAHFS study of, 67–68, 69t–70t; neighborhood effects of, 206
Mortgage finance, private lender cooperative model for, 286–302. *See also* Private-lender cooperative utility
Mortgage holdings, GSE share of, 344, 346t
Mortgage Insurance Fund, multi-family, 328–329
Mortgage market(s): concentration in, 315–316; information failures in, 256; Modigliani-Miller irrelevance theorem applied to, 340–341; racial discrimination in, 60, 61; regulation of players in, 312–313
Mortgage market channel: in California, Ohio, and Pennsylvania, 167t, 171t, 176t, 177t, 179t; differences in, 166, 168
Mortgage meltdown, and impact on homeownership, 97–98
Mortgage originations by product, 93t
Mortgage pricing, 70–72; differential, 60; heterogeneity in, 72–80
Mortgage products: favored, 309–311; non-favored, 313–315
Mortgage rates, and treasury yield spread, 287f
Mortgage services, in Chelsea (Massachusetts), 142
Mortgage standards, developed by GSEs, 13–14
Multi-family mortgages: creation of state mortgage insurance funds for, 328–330; GSE-sponsored, 12–13

Multi-family rental properties, financing of, 318–319
Multinominal logit (MNL) framework, competing risks using, 168

Nationalization, 321–322
Nationwide credit markets, access to, 306
Neighborhood characteristics, for CAP properties, 199, 200t, 202t
Net present value (NPV), of home ownership, 46
New Bedford (Massachusetts), house prices in, 145t
New-home price index, constant-quality, 44
Non-agency mortgages, 10–11
Non-favored mortgage products, securitization of, 313–315
Non-housing investments, of GSEs, 11
Non-prime investments: of GSEs, 11–12; in PLS market, 251–252, 252f
Nontraditional loans: expansion of, 245–246; growth of, 92–93, 93f, 93t; and housing bubble, 244

Occupancy status, of metropolitan home purchase loans, 89, 90f
Office of Federal Housing Enterprise Oversight (OFHEO) repeat-sales index, 26–27; accuracy of, 44; housing prices measured by, 32
Office of Financial Research (OFR), establishment of, 281
Office of the Comptroller of the Currency: bank regulation by, 210
Office of Thrift Supervision, bank regulation by, 210
Ohio: competing risks model of default and payment in, 176t–177t; higher-priced loans within disadvantaged communities in, 172–173, 173f; logistical regression predicting likelihood of receiving subprime loan in, 168–169, 169f, 170t–171t; market data in, 166, 167t
Optimism. *See* Housing optimism
Origination channels, in home mortgage lending, 115–117
Owner-occupied houses, rental income estimates of, 46–47
Ownership, in GSEs, 320–326

Parity tests, for mortgages, 214–216

Pennsylvania: competing risks model of default and payment in, 178t–179t; higher-priced loans within disadvantaged communities in, 172–173, 173f; logistical regression predicting likelihood of receiving subprime loan in, 168–169, 169f, 170t–171t; market data in, 166, 167t

Period-by-period costs, of safety-net support, 282–283

Personal crisis, pain generated by, 273

Pessimism. *See* Housing pessimism

Points, paid by different ethnic groups, 69t–70t, 73, 75

Policy and trade-offs, affecting Fannie and Freddie, 354–355

Policymaking process, economic models for, 284

Portfolio assets: ability to hold, 319–320; of Fannie and Freddie, 353

Preemption: in home mortgage lending, 120–122; state burdens imposed by, 122

Prepayment penalties, 71–72; racial differences in, 69t–70t, 75, 76t–77t

Price-dividend ratio, for stocks, 49

Price forecasts, in U.S. housing market, 52–55

Price-income ratio: cyclical patterns of, 34–35; drawbacks of, 44; markets evaluation using, 29

Price-rent ratio, 28, 33f; Davis, Lehnert, and Martin study using, 51–52; drawbacks of, 44; equation for, 42–43; Gallin study using, 50–51; Krainer and Wei pre-crisis study using, 49–50; markets evaluation using, 29

Pricing, in private-lender cooperative utility, 300

Private-label markets, 353–354

Private-label securities (PLSs): AAA rating of, 251, 258; declining spreads in, 254, 254f; emergence of, 342; expansion of, 245–246; and housing bubble, 244; investors in, 250; jumbo (*See* Jumbo loans); losses by, 344; success of, 251

Private-label securities (PLS) market, 10; disclosure for, 256; failure of normal constraints in, 257–263; growth of, 100–101, 249–253, 252f, 253f; non-prime, 251–252, 252f; regulation of, 10–11; resecuritization in, 260; trusts in, 250; violation of Modigliani-Miller irrelevance theorem by, 343

Private-lender cooperative utility: advantages of, 299–300; capital waterfall for, 295, 295f; core focus of, 295–296; disadvantages of, 300–301; FDIC-style insurance in, 298–299; first-loss position of borrowers in, 297, 298; goal of, 293–294; governance of, 294; limiting moral hazard in, 297–298; losses on securities absorbed by members in, 298; MBS guaranteed fees for, 294–298, 295f, 297f; member equity capital required for, 294; minimum down payment requirements in, 297; regulation and oversight of, 298–299; for residential mortgage finance, 286–302; structure of, 293–299; tail-risk insurance for, 296; vintage-level insurance for, 296–297, 297f

Private ownership: disadvantages of, 325–326; with government wrap, 323–324; with no government backing, 325

Public ownership, 321–322

Public policy, in U.S. housing market, 52–55, 246

Public records, from Chelsea (Massachusetts), 141–142

Quantitative and qualitative production and process, measuring bank compliance through, 222–223

Quigley's comments, on housing market, 45–46

Race: mortgage broker use and, 72; points paid by different, 69t–70t, 73, 75

Racial discrimination: in interest rates, 73; in mortgage contracts, 72–73, 74t–75t, 76t–77t, 77–78; in mortgage markets, 60, 61

Racial minorities, CAP loans to, 190

Real estate market, recovery of, 153, 153f

"Real estate owned" (REO) properties: in Chelsea (Massachusetts), 150–152, 151f, 152t; hopeful news for, 152; in metropolitan areas, 139

Real-world asset markets, irrational exuberance of, 53–54

Recession, housing market during, 188

Redlined communities, lending in, 159, 219. *See also* Low- and moderate-income (LMI) community

Regulatory law, weakness in, 104–105

Regulatory officials: incentive conflict between taxpayers and, 276, 277t; reappointment processes for, 279; recruitment of, 279, 283–284

Regulatory preemption: in home mortgage lending, 121

Regulatory system: effectiveness of, 276; theory of blame in, 275

Rental costs vs. ownership costs, study of, 42

Rental income estimates, of owner-occupied houses, 46–47

Rental properties, financing of, 318–319

Renters, housing costs of, 66–67

Rents vs. house prices, 33

Repeat-sales indices: annual weighted, 142–143; in low- to moderate-income communities, 138

Residential mortgage finance, private lender cooperative model for, 286–302. *See also* Mortgage *entries*; Private-lender cooperative utility

Risk characteristics, in California, Ohio, and Pennsylvania, 170t

Rule(s), governing home mortgage lending, 122–123

Rule enforcement, in home mortgage lending, 125–127

Rules vs. standards, in home mortgage lending, 124–125

Safety-net beneficiaries, obligation of, 282

Safety Net Forecast Office (SAFO), task of, 283

Safety-net officials, conflicts of interest facing, 276, 277t

Safety-net subsidies, expansion of, 279

Safety-net support: measuring value of, 281; period-by-period costs of, 282–283

Safety valves, in banking regulation, 224

Saiz study, of housing-supply elasticities and price increases, 36–38, 38f, 39f, 40f

Satisfactory rating, developing minimum standards for, 226–227

Savings and loan (S&L) crisis, 248; vs. current financial crisis, 340, 348–349

Scale economies, in securitizing mortgages, 288

Secondary market: alteration in structure of, 326; brief history of, 7–13; community advantage program as, 189; countercyclical stability of, 306; goals of, 305–307; guarantees in, 308–309; for housing finance, 7–17, 305–307; reform of, 315–316; serious disruption to, 327–328; stability of, 14, 249

Second-lien loans, 10, 92

Securitization, 113; and dueling charters, 341–343; mortgage market emerging through, 114; of mortgages, 101, 244, 249; of non-favored mortgage products, 313–315; private-label, 100–101, 249–257 (*See also* Private-label securities [PLS] market); role of, 99; as solution to asset-liability mismatches, 248–249

Service test: of retail banks, 211

"Shadow banking," 104, 349

Short investors, 261–263

Short sales, 141; in low- to moderate-income communities, 138

Single-family mortgages, 12; market share of, 344, 347t

Small banks, exam protocols for, 211

Smith and Smith's study, of owning vs. renting, 46–47

Social responsibility, of American Bankers Association, 159–160

Societal crisis, pain generated by, 273

Socioeconomic characteristics, in California, Ohio, and Pennsylvania, 167t, 175t, 177t, 178t170t

Soft laws, issued by bank regulators, 123–124

Special-purpose banks, exam protocols for, 211

Standardization benefits, in private-lender cooperative utility, 300

State laws, federal preemption of, 121–122

State mortgage insurance funds, for multifamily mortgages, 328–330

State partnerships, with GSEs, 15

Stocks, vs. CAP properties, 192

Subordinated debt investors, 260

Subprime loans, 10, 31; CAP loans as product substitutes for, 190 (*See also* Community advantage program [CAP] loans);

"cherry picking" associated with, 99; in CRA assessment area, 168–169, 169f; D class, 70; in disadvantaged communities, 172–173, 173f; during housing boom, 91–92, 93t; logistic regression predicting likelihood of receiving, 168–169, 170t–171t; market share of, 344, 347t; performance of CRA lending and, 159–182; rapid growth of, 344; securitization of, 99–100

Systemically important firms (SIFs), lobbyists for, 275–276

Tail-risk insurance, for private-lender cooperative utility, 296

Taxpayers, incentive conflict between regulatory officials and, 276, 277t

Theory of blame, in financial crisis, 275

"To be announced" (TBA) market, 9–10, 289–293; defining feature of, 290; delayed closure in, 291; GSEs loans ineligible for, 293; hedging and funding facilitated by, 292; homogenizing factors in, 291–292; jumbo mortgage trade in, 251; liquidity created by, 293; provisions for mortgage lenders in, 290–291; trading process in, 291; typical timeline of, 290, 290f

"Too big to fail" issue, 105–106, 360

Transition issues, in housing finance, 326–328

"Troubled properties," in Chelsea (Massachusetts), 151, 152t

Truth in Lending Act, HOEPA amendment of, 118

Underserved markets, credit to, 225, 307, 316–318

"Underwater" mortgages, 187–188

Underwriting mortgage standards: deterioration in, 93–94, 94t, 252–253, 253f; industry regulation of, 313

User cost of housing: equation defining, 42; estimates of, 43

U.S. gross debt, sectoral contributions to, 91, 91f

U.S. housing market, before crash, 26–55. *See also* Housing market

Vacation properties: demand for, 88–89, 90f

Vibrant communities, 219

Vintage-level insurance, for private-lender cooperative utility, 296–297, 297f

Vision, in financial reform, 280

Wald *F*-tests, 199

Warren data: on foreclosures, 146–147; on property sales, 141–142

"Waterfall" payment structure, of asset-backed securities, 347

Weak governance, in private-lender cooperative utility, 300–301

Wealth-creation mechanism, homeownership as, 187

Wealth portfolio, lopsided allocation of, 187–188

Wholesale banks, exam protocols for, 211

Year-on-year changes, in CAP properties, 193, 193f

Yield spread premiums, ban of, 81

Acknowledgments

Rethink. Recover. Rebuild: Reinventing Older Communities, held on May 12–14, 2010, was the fourth biennial conference of the Federal Reserve Bank of Philadelphia's Community Development Studies and Education Department. The conference occurred on the heels of a steep downturn in housing values, a high level of both subprime and prime mortgage foreclosures, and the disruption of mortgage markets coupled with a national recession. These circumstances posed new challenges not only for reinventing the mortgage system but for the stability of the national economy.

Susan M. Wachter, Co-Director of the Penn Institute of Urban Research, and Marvin M. Smith, Community Development Research Advisor at the Federal Reserve Bank of Philadelphia, as editors of this volume, enlisted leading researchers to present papers at the conference to provide insight on the causes of the crisis and on future reforms. The chapters in this volume are drawn from the papers presented in the conference's research track.

We thank the authors for their dedication and their scholarly work. They aspire, as we do, to rethink, to recover, and to rebuild the American mortgage system.

The research in this volume would not have been possible without the support of the Federal Reserve Bank of Philadelphia, its President and CEO, Charles Plosser, its former Executive Vice President, Rick Lang, its Vice President of Community Development Studies and Education, Dede Myers, and the efforts of all those who participated in the symposium.

We are grateful for the generous support of the many co-sponsors who helped make the conference possible, including the William Penn Foundation, The Brookings Metropolitan Policy Program, the Ford Foundation,

Penn Institute for Urban Research, The Reinvestment Fund, the Federal Home Loan Bank of Pittsburgh, the Pennsylvania Housing Finance Agency, the Local Initiatives Support Corporation, and The Wharton School of the University of Pennsylvania.

We are also indebted to the continued support of Penn IUR's Advisory Board and the Office of the Provost at the University of Pennsylvania, and, in particular, Provost Vince Price and Vice Provost for Research Steven Fluharty. Publications like this one are made possible by their commitment to developing and disseminating the forms of knowledge necessary for sound urban policy and revitalized cities.

In addition, this volume benefitted greatly from the proficient management of the leadership and staff of the University of Pennsylvania Press. Peter Agree, editor-in-chief, and William Finan, development editor, provided excellent advice and guided the volume through the publication process. Sarah Burke, publications manager at the Federal Reserve Bank of Philadelphia, and Hilda Guay, assistant editor, meticulously reviewed the page proofs of the volume. Thank you as well to Greg Scruggs of Penn IUR, who provided excellent editorial assistance and kept the project on track.

The views expressed in this volume are those of the individual authors and not those of their organizations or the conference's sponsors.